Reinventing the Economic
History of Industrialisation

Reinventing the Economic History of Industrialisation

Edited by

KRISTINE BRULAND, ANNE GERRITSEN,
PAT HUDSON, AND GIORGIO RIELLO

McGill-Queen's University Press
Montreal & Kingston • London • Chicago

ISBN 978-0-2280-0090-7 (cloth)
ISBN 978-0-2280-0091-4 (paper)
ISBN 978-0-2280-0206-2 (ePDF)
ISBN 978-0-2280-0207-9 (ePUB)

Legal deposit first quarter 2020
Bibliothèque nationale du Québec

Printed in Canada on acid-free paper that is 100% ancient forest free (100% post-consumer recycled), processed chlorine free

Funded by the Government of Canada   Financé par le gouvernement du Canada   Canada Council for the Arts   Conseil des arts du Canada

We acknowledge the support of the Canada Council for the Arts.

Nous remercions le Conseil des arts du Canada de son soutien.

Library and Archives Canada Cataloguing in Publication

Title: Reinventing the economic history of industrialisation / edited by Kristine Bruland, Anne Gerritsen, Pat Hudson, and Giorgio Riello.

Names: Bruland, Kristine, editor. | Gerritsen, Anne, editor. | Hudson, Pat, 1948- editor. | Riello, Giorgio, editor.

Description: Includes bibliographical references and index.

Identifiers: Canadiana (print) 20190224517 | Canadiana (ebook) 20190224525 | ISBN 9780228000907 (cloth) | ISBN 9780228000914 (paper) | ISBN 9780228002062 (ePDF) | ISBN 9780228002079 (ePUB)

Subjects: LCSH: Industrial revolution. | LCSH: Industrialization—History. | LCSH: Economic history.

Classification: LCC HD2321 .R42 2020 | DDC 338.09–dc23

This book was designed and typeset by Peggy & Co. Design in 10.5/13 Sabon.

Contents

Tables and Figures

Tables

Figures

Reinventing the Economic History of Industrialisation

Reinventing the Economic History of Industrialisation: An Introduction

Kristine Bruland, Anne Gerritsen,
Pat Hudson, and Giorgio Riello

Industrialisation and economic change have been at the core of popular and scholarly historical writing since the 1880s when the idea of an 'Industrial Revolution' entered English academic parlance.[1] Over time, the Industrial Revolution and the concept of industrialisation became foundational topics for the field of economic history.[2] The works of Paul Mantoux, J.H. Clapham, T.S. Ashton, and others successively brought to the fore the classic topics of industrialisation: the commercial expansion of Western Europe, the mechanisation of textile production, the rise of factories, coal and iron production, the steam engine, the proletarianisation of labour, and the birth and diffusion of industrial capitalism.[3] These were the central tenets of the research agenda of economic history in the postwar period, especially in Britain, at a time when the Industrial Revolution was a major topic of study for all students of history. Textbooks by Phyllis Deane, Peter Mathias, Eric Hobsbawm, and later Nick Crafts, Maxine Berg, and Pat Hudson helped in popularising the topic beyond academia and teaching.[4] The 1970s was a decade of altering perspectives. Peter Mathias in the 1983 preface to the second edition of his well-known textbook *The First Industrial Revolution* noted that since the original publication in the late 1960s, the 'the essence of what is known as economic history has been experiencing a sea change'. He attributed this change to the use of computer technologies and the rise of cliometrics, seeing economic history's appeal or sometimes lack of appeal in the embracing of new and varied methodologies.[5] Mathias's viewpoint has been endorsed by succeeding generations. Today the Industrial Revolution – and economic history more generally – cannot claim to have the public interest it commanded in the 1950s and 1960s. The very concept of an Industrial Revolution has been criticised, within the profession, both by economists and postmodern cultural historians whilst much of the increasingly technical and statistical published research became inaccessible to a general readership. Yet, the importance of the Industrial Revolution remains, precisely because of our altered perception of what the process of industrialisation looked like from both national and global perspectives. This book reflects on the major topics of concern for economic historians over the past generation and presents a new view of industrialisation, underpinned by four major claims about the transition in our understanding.

A first major change of approach to the Industrial Revolution is that what was once seen as a geographically bounded phenomenon, is today conceived instead as extending beyond the borders of Britain and even Europe. For a long time economic historians presented a 'diffusionist' story based on the mechanisation of production in Britain in the final decades of the eighteenth century, which then expanded to continental Europe and North America over the next two generations, reaching other parts of the 'developed world' in the nineteenth and twentieth centuries. This older narrative presumed that there were no positive *interactive* linkages between Europe (Britain in particular) and other parts of the world, and that technological and organisational changes in Western Europe were mostly unaffected by changes elsewhere. They grew from talents, skills and insights that were peculiar to the leading nations. Global history in the past two decades has done much to counter this conception, arguing for an interpretation of the Industrial Revolution and, more widely, of long-term economic change that was reliant on global linkages in terms of technological innovation, useful and reliable knowledge and the forces shaping global demand and markets.[6] Even recent work that is Eurocentred in its focus has had to acknowledge that the Industrial Revolution can only be understood in a distinctly global context.

Second, for the past twenty years the Great Divergence debate has posed a serious challenge to the generally accepted chronologies of industrialisation in Britain and Europe by endeavouring to reconceptualise the Industrial Revolution globally and by adopting a comparative framework of analysis. Pomeranz's concept of divergence confirmed a traditional temporal framework confined to the last decades of the eighteenth century.[7] However, much scholarship has questioned this, providing interpretations that see industrialisation in relation to processes such as prior protoindustrialisation, the role of guilds and an 'industrious revolution'.[8] Today the divide between industrial and preindustrial is not just less marked than was thought a generation ago, but continuities over time and the durability of institutions and facets of economic change have become topics of research in themselves.[9]

The Great Divergence debate and its impact upon our understanding of the chronologies of development globally arose as a critical reaction to the first generation of attempts to measure growth and change comparatively via macroeconomic estimations and extrapolations, in particular of the movement of GDP per capita across countries and over time. This is the third methodological strand to have emerged as a key feature of research on industrialisation since the 1960s. It has become central to the work of a number of high profile economic historians working on industrialisation at both country and comparative global levels. They include Jan Luiten Van Zanden, Paulo Malanima, Leandro Prados de la Escosura, R.C. Allen, and Stephen Broadberry.[10] Building upon the published comparative GDP estimates of the late Angus Maddison, emerging from the 1970s, Nick Crafts produced the first new estimates of British economic growth during industrialisation in the mid-1980s (and further refined these in his work with Knick Harley in the following decade).[11] He considerably altered earlier perspectives by emphasising that growth overall was very slow in the classic Industrial Revolution period and thus that change was undramatic until well into the nineteenth century. This new gradualist long run interpretation of Western industrialisation has been followed up by later scholars who argued that significant growth and change had occurred in Britain and the Low Countries in the centuries before the Industrial Revolution such that they had overtaken China and, in the British case at least, had broken the Malthusian ceiling upon population growth before the end of the seventeenth century.[12] The reliability of GDP estimates as well as those of comparative wages and prices is often questioned especially when used for comparative purposes because standard purchasing power parities and silver equivalents (themselves subject to error) need to be engaged. Nevertheless, broad correlations in aggregate measures have been used in much recent causal analysis, in the most prominent example to demonstrate the importance in the British case of high wages as a stimulus to change.[13]

Questionable Western GDP estimates from the Maddison project for China, other parts of Asia, and Africa precipitated much new research and gave rise to divergence debates, but they also provoked a move to other levels and topics of analysis amongst those historians discontent with the estimates and with the conclusions of the aggregators. In relation to Britain, a flurry of work employing regional and local approaches, focusing upon industrialising agglomerations, family work units, child labour, and the intricacies of household incomes followed.[14] Together these helped to create a parallel tradition within the standard Western historiography of industrialisation and provided a critique of conclusions reached by relying upon aggregate macroestimations and their statistical manipulation alone. Starting before and endorsed by her 1992 article 'Rehabilitating the Industrial Revolution', it is within this parallel tradition and critique that Maxine Berg consciously situated her work. [15]

Finally, the past generation has seen a marked change in how the Industrial Revolution and industrialisation are conceptualised within and beyond economic history. Cliometric and quantitative methodologies in economic history are now accompanied by interdisciplinary approaches that integrate economic, cultural, and material histories. Industrialisation is no longer considered as solely the preserve of entrepreneurs, factories, and economic growth, it also includes an engagement with consumers, with demand, and with material goods. This has allowed the field of economic history to expand its coverage and to engage with a variety of other disciplines such as anthropology, sociology, and behavioural economics. [16]

These changes in the ways in which the discipline of economic history works (for instance from a national to a global framework), and in the concepts and tools that it adopts (for instance from supply-led analysis to interpretative models that incorporate demand), and to a focus on useful and applicable knowledge, might appear to be the result of changing historical fashions and of new questions posed by contemporary concerns as argued by David Cannadine more than three decades ago. [17] This book, however, makes a case that specific historians have been influential in reshaping the agenda. It gathers some of them to reflect on how economic history might be written in the twenty-first century and puts them in conversation with contributions by a new generation of historians that are reshaping the field from widely different perspectives. They have rewritten a 'very British story' into one that is relevant at a global level, underlining not just the worldwide consequences of industrialisation but also its global origins. They challenge fellow historians to think 'outside the box' and to consider how luxuries such as Indian cotton textiles or Chinese porcelains were not only essential in the processes of technological change but also in material and 'sensorial' transfer from Asia to Europe, shaping the process of industrial 'catching up' for Europe.

One person's work runs as a prominent influence through all these developments. Maxine Berg's role in reshaping how the Industrial Revolution is conceptualised can be seen far and wide. Since the 1980s Berg has written seminal works including *The Machinery Question* (1980), *The Age of Manufactures* (1985 and 1994), *Luxury and Pleasure* (2005), and a series of equally path-breaking edited collections and articles. As one of very few women in economic history, Berg has achieved recognition in a field dominated by men, as did the subject of her splendid biography, Eileen Power, half a century earlier.[18] The vision that Berg proposed posits the Industrial Revolution as an 'open' process based on profound linkages to the preindustrial economy and to the wider world. Her inspiration and contribution to the wider field of economic history has been profound. Perhaps more than any other economic historian, she has vigorously argued for an understanding of economic change within a cultural matrix. Rather than seeing economic history as a separate field of study (awkwardly positioned between economics and history), Berg has pushed us all to consider it as a field that needs to inform our understanding of the past more generally. As such, she argues, economic history should be part of the vocabulary of any historian and any scholar working in the humanities.

This book is organised around four topics that reflect various phases of Maxine Berg's scholarship. 'The Age of Manufactures' opens with the problem of what Berg called 'the other industrial revolution,' one made by tools, small machines, skilled labour, and the contribution of women and children. 'The Age of Machinery' addresses instead the role of technology in narratives of industrialisation as well as deindustrialisation, highlighting new spatial geographies beyond Europe. 'The Age of Luxury' shifts our attention away from supply-led narratives to consider not just consumption but also its impact on manufacturing and retailing techniques. Finally, 'The Age of Global Trade' take us to a recontextualisation of the Industrial Revolution on a global canvas, connecting recent global history to classic narratives of industrialisation.

The Age of Manufactures

The first part of the book highlights a central and recurring set of concerns prominent in Maxine Berg's scholarship: innovations in the nature of manufacturing that characterised the Industrial Revolution; the role of artisanal skills in economic development; the accumulation and transmission of technical knowledge; the absence of a linear transition from domestic and workshop manufacturing to the factory; and the geopolitical and economic circumstances that generate enduring forms of semiagrarian or 'protoindustrial' manufacturing in different parts of the globe. Such concerns were first raised in her early work on technology and machinery, more fully developed in her seminal text *The Age of Manufactures* (1985), and continued with her detailed research on domestic and workshop manufacturing during the British Industrial Revolution.[19] Berg's more recent exploration of contemporary textile processes carried out by women and families in outworking and small workshop units in the Kutch (India) emphasises the persistence of global alternatives to capital-intensive mass production, which this section of the book addresses.[20]

Berg's early key interventions on the characteristics of British industrialisation, published in the 1980s and 1990s challenged the dominant research that focused solely upon the macroeconomic dimensions of growth in industrial output, productivity, investment levels, and overseas trade, concluding that economic growth was gradual and represented a continuity of earlier trends and traditions of working. By looking closely at changes on the ground and concentrating her empirical analysis on the metal and other trades of Birmingham and Sheffield, Berg – together with a small group of like-minded historians of 'protoindustrialisation' and 'alternatives to mass production' – challenged the view that radical change was restricted largely to one key sector of the economy (cotton textiles) and that change elsewhere was slow and undramatic.[21]

By looking closely at innovations in the regional specialisation and clustering of trades, improvements to products and processes developed in small workshops, and the peculiar skills and adaptiveness of industrial workforces that included women and children, Berg argued for a rehabilitation of the notion that change during the Industrial Revolution had indeed been revolutionary. Emphasising the dynamism of small production units and specialised handicraft skills, alongside machinery, during the process of economic transition led her also to consider the viability and durability of such artisanal forms of labour intensive and skill intensive, rather than capital intensive, forms of manufacturing up to the present time and across the globe where political, economic, and social circumstances affected the supply and relative costs of factors of production and the demand for particular sorts of products both locally and in long distance trade.[22]

Mokyr, Kelly, and Ó Gráda pay tribute to Berg's emphasis upon artisanal skills and knowledge by asking if artisans and the labour of their skilled hands should be regarded as prime movers in British industrial primacy. They consider the conditions (wage levels, nutrition, accumulations of tacit knowledge, and enlightenment culture) that created the multiplication of ingenious mechanics clustered in the industrialising regions of Britain. They argue that the textile industries were exceptional in requiring few inputs from formal science but that across the rest of the economy diminishing returns to artisanal improvements would have set in without infusions of new propositional knowledge. Hilaire-Pérez also tackles the role of artisans as the originators and transmitters of innovative technologies arguing that evaluation of their contribution depends upon resurrecting an older eighteenth-century meaning of the term 'technology' as 'useful knowledge' and 'efficient action', particularly in the processes of subcontracting, coordination of production and design, and in adapting and adjusting consumer goods. Technical activity was organic: artisanal invention was not limited to tacit know-how but could lead to a synthetic understanding of work as a set of operative principles.

In her examination of work practices in the Staffordshire potteries in the eighteenth century, Smith shows the ways in which knowledge circulated in the workplace, promoting product as well as process innovation, quality standardization, tool adaptations, and the development of further skills. The introduction and refinement of the treadle lathe, worked by women and children, is used as an example. Wedgwood, as the leading entrepreneur in novelty product innovation and design, took steps to ensure that such artisanal knowledge was not spread to rivals either by observation or through the movement of skilled workers.

Hudson's chapter provides a case study of the long-term survival of small-scale semirural manufacturing in the face of global competition and change. She highlights the cultural and political context, path dependency, and the durability of rural artisanal forms in the textile industry of Wales. She demonstrates how the conditions promoting persistence of such forms were gradually undermined in the face of globally oriented capitalist enterprise serving entirely different economic and social purposes. Washbrook's chapter also examines the logic of persistence of small-scale manufacturing over two centuries. Indian experience challenges the Western tendency to see modernity as a unilineal or homogenous process. The Indian textile sector should be seen primarily not as a failure to innovate, held back by colonial rule or cultural obstructions, but instead as an adaptive response to contextual conditions, including market segmentation and the incorporation of caste, gender, and kinship as tools for enterprise rather than for its suppression.

The five chapters in Part I, as a whole, illustrate the interaction of the local and the global, the mixed chronologies of industrialisation, innovation, and organisational change, even in the 'core' areas of global transition, and the extent to which an interdisciplinary approach is essential to understanding the nature of manufacturing and the specialised knowledge embodied in the products of industrial regions across global space and centuries of time.

The Age of Machinery

Early histories of industrialisation were bedevilled by a strong reliance on new technologies – mostly developed in Britain – to explain change and growth, without an adequate account of how these technologies came to exist or to have effects. Technologies were often seen purely as artefacts, and organisational change and the factory were consequences of technical change. Moreover, not many technologies counted: industrialisation was a matter of a few key innovations such as steam power and key textile innovations. Internationally, industrialisation was seen in terms of diffusion from Britain, in imitation of the forerunner.

The cobwebs around these ideas began to be blown away in the early 1970s, along several dimensions. Conflict in the workplace came into focus with the publication of Harry Braverman's *Labor and Monopoly Capital* (1974), which concentrated on the labour processes through which technologies are put to work and explored the crises of management, social conflict, and the disorder inherent in technological change.[23] A second shift was a complex transition away from a fixation with big-process technologies towards product innovation and consumption. This led to an exploration of more diffuse technological worlds including agriculture, food processing, small metal manufactures, clothing manufacture, and household equipment. Thirdly, wider organisational forms such as protoindustrialisation, small workshops, and the sweated trades were given more prominent attention. Finally, there was a major transition, owing much to Patrick O'Brien, away from a focus on Britain as an exemplar and leader economy towards a far more sophisticated view of the global economy as an integrated technological and economic complex.[24]

Maxine Berg contributed to reinventing economic history around all four of these intellectual transitions. Her earliest book, *Technology and Toil in Nineteenth Century Britain* (1979), collected original material on labour processes and conflict.[25] Two further works looked at the economics and politics of machinery, and its implications for work across industries.[26] She did not neglect textile technologies but emphasised the extreme diversity of activities and organisational forms within them. She extended this into agriculture and the abundant set of activities in the 'small metal trades'. The extensive world of metals manufactures was seriously neglected prior to her work. Finally, Maxine played an influential role in the reframing of industrialisation into the new global context.

These themes are reflected in the chapters on machinery in this second section of the book. Jan de Vries reexplores the concept of protoindustrialisation. This influential term has been much criticised, but de Vries brings to it an emphasis on what we have learned about the demographic and cultural impact of early manufactures across Europe since the concept of protoindustrialisation was originally proposed, and a theoretical orientation drawing on parallel advances in growth theory. What emerges is a social and organisational context for industrial growth that offers a route towards a deeper and geographically wider understanding of change. O'Brien emphasises the importance of a serious understanding of 'macro' textile inventions, a task hampered by the fact that 'both economists and historians lack a theory of technological progress that might explain this precocious and paradigm case of mechanization.' He dispenses with a number of inadequate explanations for innovation, especially mechanistic models that see innovation as an automatic response to economic or technical pressures. He looks to the inventors themselves, seeking to locate their agency as innovators in specific artisanal and technical environments, and in the context of economic and geopolitical change.

Osamu Saito addresses the 'machinery question' as posed by Ricardo and Hicks, specifically the question of whether the labour-displacing effects of machines were compensated by an increase in employment in machine-building sectors. Looking at labour force data across five countries, he shows that intersectoral shifts of labour are more complex than often imagined. Changes in occupational structure were heavily shaped by population growth, so the primary sector could grow absolutely even as its share of employment fell. Secondary sector growth was negligible over very long periods. Most importantly Saito establishes that the labour force effects of mechanisation can only be understood in terms of gender: it was largely women's occupations that were undermined; the process entailed significant female displacement from the secondary sector. This in turn shaped the growth of sweated trades and tertiary employment. Finally, in this section of the book Bruland and Smith explore a major textile invention, the self-acting mule, which automated spinning and was widely seen (at the time) as an epoch-making invention. However, it diffused slowly. Understanding this involves recognition of the context of conflict and struggle in which the innovation emerged. The skilled spinners, who were being automated away, were also *de facto* production managers who organised and disciplined ancillary workers: that disciplinary function could not easily be replaced. Thus the automatic mule became a deterrent weapon in ongoing struggles between employers and labour, adopted only as industrial conflict and managerial exigencies required.

These chapters follow Maxine Berg in disputing histories of industrialisation that are based on untheorised notions of large-scale technological changes as drivers of industrial growth from the eighteenth century. On the one hand, change was extensive in Europe in the preindustrial period, particularly in terms of new market orientation and changing work organisation. On the other, the genuinely radical innovations that occurred had a strong social history that shaped both innovation and diffusion processes.

The Age of Luxury

In the 1980s economic historians were challenged to rethink their narratives of change beyond existing supply-driven models. New scholarship from social and cultural history posited consumption as central in premodern as it was in contemporary societies. Some argued that a 'consumer revolution' on a par with the political and industrial revolutions of the late eighteenth century came to reshape European societies. Yet, as Maxine Berg has recently observed 'economic historians, apart from a few exceptions, have been reluctant to engage in an analysis of consumption in economic change'.[27] Berg was among a small but important group of economic historians who paid great attention to consumption and its relationship with industrialisation. Rather than conceive industrial production as based on generic categories of supply (of cottons, coal, metalwares, etc.), a new group of scholars – among whom were many female economic historians – became interested in what happened to manufactures once they left the factory. They studied how goods were distributed and retailed and how they came to shape people's tastes and preferences as well as their consumers' identities and habits.[28]

Today a large body of literature exists at the intersection of economic history and the history of consumption that includes both empirical and theoretical studies. Jan de Vries's concept of an 'industrious revolution' was a way to connect production, labour, and consumption. He argued that the rise in consumption levels and the widening of patterns of consumption evident from the late seventeenth century onwards were the result of an increased participation in market exchange on the part of women and, more generally, of households. This was something that Berg had already studied empirically in an article on women's property and the Industrial Revolution published in 1993. De Vries's model became a key interpretation of the connection between protoindustrial and industrial Europe.[29] De Vries's attention was towards staples of consumer need, whilst Berg highlighted the centrality of luxuries in the economic transformation of Europe.

What came to be known as the 'luxury debate' pointed to the fact that luxury was a key category in eighteenth-century society and economy. The difference between Daniel Defoe's *A Plan of the English Commerce* (1731) and Malachy Postlethwayt's *Britain's Commercial Interest Explained and Improved* (1757) published a generation later shows changing attitudes towards consumption and luxury in England. Whilst Defoe was ambiguous if not plainly negative about conspicuous consumption, Postlethwayt considered it a source of economic progress.[30] Berg's research highlighted how contemporaries increasingly saw luxury as a source of innovation and an encouragement towards improving the quality standards and reducing the cost of manufactured commodities. These were the lines of enquiry developed in Berg's 2004 article 'In Pursuit of Luxury' and her 2005 monograph *Luxury and Pleasure in Eighteenth-Century Britain*.[31]

As Berg noted, many of these luxuries were not just produced by skilled metropolitan artisans in Europe but – as in the case of porcelain, silks, and cottons – were imported from Asia. The connection between Europe and Asia through traded commodities and consumption has been one of the distinctive agendas of global history in the past decade. Much work has now been carried out on trade and on global material culture as the final part of this book highlights.[32] Perhaps most importantly, the study of consumption on a global scale has encouraged a new assessment of manufacturing and the ways in which Europeans engaged with techniques and technologies from Asia and elsewhere in the world. As Natalie Zemon Davis points out in her contribution to this volume, such a global dimension of consumption and production was not the prerogative of the eighteenth century. Hassan al-Wazzan, better known as Leo Africanus, was a Moroccan diplomat who had travelled widely in Africa and the Levant. Captured by Christian pirates in 1518 and forced to convert to Christianity, he lived in Italy for several years under his baptismal name Giovanni Leone Africano. Before returning home, he wrote several works in Italian and Latin to tell Europeans about his African world, its religion and culture, one of which, *The Description of Africa*, was later printed and widely read. In this work, he elaborates on the artisans and merchants of North Africa and sub-Saharan Africa, their crafts, and their products, some of which found their way to Europe. His busy world of economic action is in contrast to the negative pictures emerging in Europe at a time of religious war.

Luxury and consumption brought economic historians to expand their analyses to include how people perceived and understood economic and social transformation. Desire has been a key concept for

Berg and all historians interested in the history of consumption, retail, and distribution. As Helen Clifford explains, trade cards – a premodern form of business cards advertising the location of a shop and commodities for sale there – were important tools through which goods were advertised and retailed. Connecting back to chapters in the previous parts of this book, Clifford reminds us that such advertisements were also ways to communicate productive techniques and often depicted artisans at work or machinery. Today's distinction – both historical and historiographical – between production and consumption is thus challenged.

Next to the consideration of advertising and selling techniques, the history of consumption has made use of inventories as a way of quantifying and qualifying changes in consumption patterns through time, especially in the seventeenth and eighteenth centuries.[33] In the 1980s historian Lorna Weatherill was among the first to use computerised systems to study possessions as an indicator of consumption.[34] Johan Poukens and Herman Van der Wee's chapter applies such a methodology and considers 600 probate inventories charting the adoption of crockery, hot drinks, and similar semiluxurious items in the town and hinterland of Lier in present-day Belgium. Their evidence shows that whilst the urban middling sort, as elsewhere in Europe, likely adopted new household goods in a context of private sociability, this was not the case down the social ladder for husbandmen and labourers. Their use of what de Vries has called 'new luxuries' differed considerably from that of the middling sort and retained certain characteristics of 'old luxury'.

Lemire, finally, explores the ways in which objects made by indigenous populations in the colonised spaces of empire circulated through imperial networks and found their way to the metropole. These 'counterflow' objects tell stories that challenge the linear narrative of global goods and British industrialisation. They also point in important new directions where indigeneity and the intensely local, perhaps best studied in microhistorical perspectives, can lead to new global narratives.

The chapters in this third part of the book underline the interdisciplinary nature of much recent research on the process of industrialisation. Rather than seeing the Industrial Revolution as simply a production-led phenomenon, the scholarship that Berg and others have championed has underlined the importance of consumption and retailing but also of cultural factors affecting patterns of consumption of new as well as old things in the premodern period. This scholarship has also done much to rethink manufacturing and industrialisation on a wider geographic canvas, a topic developed in the final part of this book.

The Age of Global Trade

With hindsight, it is clear that the publication of *The Great Divergence* by Kenneth Pomeranz in 2000 marked a watershed moment.[35] Before 2000, economic historians used the European (and especially the British) economy as the benchmark in their research; they wrote, for example, about 'the history of consumption', taking it as given that this was an exclusively European phenomenon; they wrote about 'the history of industrialisation', assuming that any readers would know that this meant industrialisation in Europe. Meanwhile, historians of China and India carried on their scholarly work without seeking to reach an audience beyond the area of their specialism. Pomeranz's book and the network of global economic historians (GEHN) led by Patrick O'Brien at the LSE from 2003 changed things within Western scholarship. The network's aims included 'extending the geographical spaces and lengthening the chronologies'; in practice, this meant bringing historians of the British Industrial Revolution into dialogue with scholars of global trade, with historians of textile production in India, or porcelain manufactures in China. It meant a growing interest in the importance of the influx of global luxuries for the development of manufactures in Britain, in the patterns of consumption beyond the boundaries of Europe, and in the material and intellectual connections between Asia, Africa, the Americas, and Europe. This global approach posed a fundamental challenge to nation-based histories. Pomeranz and others had suggested that Britain and Western Europe did not industrialise and modernise because they were destined to do so but because of a set of serendipitous circumstances in Britain: the location of coal near the centres of textile manufacture and access to human and natural resources acquired by means of colonial expansion and the enslavement of conquered peoples.[36] For scholars like Patrick O'Brien and Maxine Berg, global comparisons and the study of connections appeared as essential for understanding European transformations in the eighteenth century.[37]

In the context of the British Industrial Revolution, the focus on the eighteenth century made sense, but when the geographies changed, chronologies also had to be lengthened. Global history emerged as a field that brought together scholars working not only in wide-ranging parts of the world but with periodisations that were no longer determined exclusively by Europe. Jerry Bentley had attempted to use cross-cultural interactions to produce a new periodisation for world history in 1996, but it was (and remains) difficult to account for all time periods all around the globe.[38] In practice, few historians have an appetite for writing a singular history of the entire globe; most historians who consider themselves participants in the broad field of global history carve out a small chronological and/or geographical space within which they explore comparisons or connections, using the changing patterns in the creation and development of such global connections as their periodisation.

Maxine Berg's work has been extremely important in driving the field of economic history into increasingly global directions. Having largely focused on the British context in her publications before 2000, her inaugural lecture at the University of Warwick in 2001 considered the impact of luxury goods from India and China on British production processes.[39] Without the import of Asian luxuries, she argued, British manufacturers would not have developed the innovative products and processes that led to the Industrial Revolution. In Berg and Eger's 2003 edited collection, *Luxury in the Eighteenth Century*, the global appeared as 'the Exotic' in the final three of sixteen chapters; ten years later, in Berg's 2013 edited volume *Writing the History of the Global*, scholars of India, China, Japan, and Africa had become central participants in the practice of Western history.[40] In her 2015 collection, *Goods from the East, 1600–1800*, Asia featured in each of the twenty-one chapters.[41]

The chapters by Easterby-Smith, Gerritsen, Lemire, and Riello illustrate the multiple ways in which the engagement with global trade has transformed the ways in which history is being written. The starting point of Riello's piece is the global trade that ultimately led to industrialisation, but his focus is on procurement in India. Precisely because the purchase of Indian textiles posed such substantial challenges for the English East India Company (EEIC), as did the ever-increasing demands for quantity and quality, the factories in Britain were transformed into the large-scale production sites that came to characterise industrialisation. Easterby-Smith and Gerritsen are both concerned with broadening the concept of 'useful and reliable knowledge'. Easterby-Smith does so by looking at botany: decorative and 'economic plants' for use in agriculture, industry, and medicine were brought back to Britain from all over the world and systematically integrated into compendia of natural knowledge, showing the importance of the lower officials and middlemen of empire for the success of that project. Gerritsen's piece suggests that the combination of insights from both those who knew things and those who made things, considered by some to be a strictly European occurrence, could also be identified in Chinese pots that depict the manufacture of porcelain. Margot Finn's chapter situates the discussion of property and finance in what she calls a 'transcontinental context' that connects the metropole with the colonies, but she flags up not only the imperial or global circulations of economic goods, persons, and ideas but also the constraints on movement within imperial networks. Finn's emphasis on the frictions and interruptions that limit the 'flow' of capital between India and Britain, as demonstrated by the probate accounts of a surgeon in the East India Company stationed in Bombay (later known as Mumbai, India) during the 1780s, does more than complicate the picture of global trade. It points to new directions in the historiography, where studies of imperial and global trade networks, which have come to form such a central part of economic history since the publication of Pomeranz's book, take fuller account of the financial, human, and ecological costs of developing and maintaining such networks.

Conclusion

This volume reflects the many areas of economic history that have preoccupied Maxine Berg over a career spanning four decades during which she has challenged many long-held assumptions and approaches in her field. Beyond that, it provides new research both by well-established scholars and by those who have directly benefitted from Berg's mentoring. The contributions all use Berg's work as a springboard to extend, qualify, and enhance the historiography of industrialisation as a complex and varied global, as well as a national, regional, and local phenomenon.

Covering the range and implications of Berg's research and career is however impossible in a single volume. The book can only be indicative of that range, not only because it skirts areas of interest and some of her publications that would have taken us beyond the research focus of the present volume but also because an attempt at comprehensiveness would be like capturing a bird that remains in full flight. We have necessarily excluded from our direct frame of reference Maxine's long-term interest in the history of economic history and its varied manifestations as a discipline across time and space, an interest that pervades all of her work often adding a sophisticated element of relativism to her approach and her conclusions. Her detailed examination of the contribution of female scholarship in the early days of the professionalisation of economic history in Britain and reference to her innovative biography of Eileen Power are largely missing. We have also dealt only tangentially with Berg's work on the history of women and gender during the process of industrialisation.[42]

Finally, we have not fully addressed the new areas of economic, social, and cultural history currently benefitting from Maxine Berg's continuing efforts to change the agenda and to expand the boundaries of our field, not least her work in linking global history to innovation in the methodologies of microhistory. Amongst other things, this has generated a superb piece of new research on the trade in sea otter pelts from the Canadian North West to China in the late eighteenth century and a number of innovative conferences and workshops that have encouraged new work by emerging scholars linking micro and macro history and examining the 'space between.'[43]

We have produced a volume that we hope will be seen as both a fitting tribute to Berg's scholarship and a significant addition to research on topics that she has made her own. We also look forward to the new directions in which her work will doubtless travel beyond 2020, and to the continued collegiality and generosity, as well as the intellectual stimulus that characterise her contributions.

Notes

We thank the University of Warwick and the European University Institute for their financial support.

1   Arnold Toynbee, *Lectures on the Industrial Revolution in England* (London: Rivingtons, 1884).

2   For an overview of the historiography of the Industrial Revolution see for instance David S. Landes, 'The Fable of the Dead Horse; or, The Industrial Revolution Revisited', in *The British Industrial Revolution: An Economic Perspective*, ed. Joel Mokyr (Boulder, CO: Westview Press, 2nd ed., 1999), 128–59.

3   Paul Mantoux, *The Industrial Revolution in the Eighteenth Century* (London: Jonathan Cape, 1928); J.H. Clapham, *An Economic History of Modern Britain* (Cambridge: Cambridge University Press, 1926–38); T.S. Ashton, *The Industrial Revolution, 1770–1830* (Oxford: Oxford University Press, 1948).

4   Phyllis Deane, *The Industrial Revolution* (Cambridge: Cambridge University Press, 1965); Eric Hobsbawm, *Industry and Empire: From 1750 to the Present Day* (London: Penguin, 1969); Peter Mathias, *The First Industrial Nation: An Economic History of Britain, 1700–1914* (New York: Charles Scribner's Sons, 1969); N.F.R. Crafts, *British Industrial Revolution in an International Context* (Oxford: Clarendon, 1985); Maxine Berg, *The Age of Manufactures, 1700–1820: Industry, Innovation and Work in Britain* (London: Fontana, 1985); Pat Hudson, *The Industrial Revolution* (London: Edward Arnold, 1992).

5   Peter Mathias, *The First Industrial Nation: An Economic History of Britain, 1700–1914* (London: Routledge, 2nd ed., 1983), preface.

6   See for instance the work of Robert C. Allen, *The British Industrial Revolution in Global Perspective* (Cambridge: Cambridge University Press, 2009); Joel Mokyr, *The Enlightened Economy: Britain and the Industrial Revolution*

1700–1850 (London: Penguin, 2009); and Joel Mokyr, *A Culture of Growth: The Origins of the Modern Economy* (Princeton: Princeton University Press, 2017). See also Laura Cruz and Joel Mokyr, eds., *The Birth of Modern Europe: Culture and Economy, 1400–1800: Essays in Honor of Jan De Vries* (Leiden: Brill, 2010); and Jan Luiten van Zanden and Pim de Zwart, *The Origins of Globalization: World Trade in the Making of the Global Economy, 1500–1800* (Cambridge: Cambridge University Press, 2019).

7 Kenneth Pomeranz, *The Great Divergence: China, Europe, and the Making of the Modern World Economy* (Princeton: Princeton University Press, 2000).

8 Jan de Vries, *The Industrious Revolution: Consumer Behavior and the Household Economy, 1650 to the Present* (New York: Cambridge University Press, 2008); S.R. Epstein and Maarten Prak, eds., *Guilds, Innovation and the European Economy, 1400–1800* (Cambridge: Cambridge University Press, 2009).

9 Giorgio Riello and Tirthankar Roy, 'Introduction: Global Economic History, 1500–2000', in *Global Economic History* eds. Tirthankar Roy and Giorgio Riello (London: Bloomsbury, 2019), 15.

10 Leandro Prados de la Escosura, ed., *Exceptionalism and Industrialism: Britain and Its European Rivals, 1688–1815* (Cambridge: Cambridge University Press 2005); Jan Luiten van Zanden, *The Long Road to the Industrial Revolution. The European economy in a global perspective, 1000–1800* (Leiden: Brill, 2009); Paolo Malanima, 'The Long Decline of a Leading Economy: GDP in Central and Northern Italy, 1300–1913', *European Review of Economic History* 15 (2011): 169–219; Allen, *British Industrial Revolution*; Robert C. Allen, J.P. Bassino, Debin Ma, C. Moll-Murata, and Jan Luiten van Zanden, 'Wages, Prices and Living Standards in China, 1738–1925 Compared with Europe India and Japan', *Economic History Review* 64, Supplement (2011): 8–38; Jan Luiten van Zanden and Bas van Leeuwen, 'Persistent but Not Consistent: The Growth of National Income in Holland 1347–1807', *Explorations in Economic History* 49, no. 2 (2012): 119–30; Carlos Alvarez-Nogal and Leandro Prados de la Escosura, 'The Rise and Fall of Spain (1270–1850)', *Economic History Review* 66, no. 1 (2013): 1–37; Stephen Broadberry, Bruce M.S. Campbell, Alexander Klein, Mark Overton, and Bas van Leeuwen, *British Economic Growth, 1270–1870* (Cambridge: Cambridge University Press, 2015).

11 Angus Maddison, *Contours of the World Economy 1–2030 AD: Essays in Macro-economic History* (Oxford: Oxford University Press, 2007). For myriad updates see The Maddison Project, held at the Groningen Growth and Development Centre at Groningen University: https://www.rug.nl/ggdc/ historicaldevelopment/maddison/; N.F.R. Crafts, *British Economic Growth during the Industrial Revolution* (Oxford: Oxford University Press, 1985); N.F.R. Crafts and C. Knick Harley, 'Output Growth and the Industrial Revolution: A Restatement of the Crafts-Harley View', *Economic History Review* 45, no. 4 (1992), 703–30.

12 Van Zanden and van Leeuwen, 'Persistent but Not Consistent'; Broadberry, Campbell, Klein, Overton, and van Leeuwen, *British Economic Growth*.

13 Allen, *British Industrial Revolution*; Robert C. Allen, 'The High Wage Economy and the Industrial Revolution: A Restatement', *Economic History Review* 68, no. 1 (2015): 1–22.

14 Among these: Pat Hudson, *Regions and Industries: A Perspective on the Industrial Revolution in Britain* (Cambridge, Cambridge University Press, 1989); and Pat Hudson, 'Industrial Organisation and Structure', in *The Cambridge Economic History of Modern Britain*, I: *1700–1870*, eds. Roderick Floud and Paul A. Johnson (Cambridge: Cambridge University Press, 2004), 28–56; Maxine Berg, 'Women's Work and the Industrial Revolution', in *New Directions in Economic and Social History*, eds. Anne Digby, Charles. Feinstein, and David C. Jenkins (London: Palgrave, 1992), 23–36; Jane Humphries, *Childhood and Child Labour in the Industrial Revolution* (Cambridge: Cambridge University Press, 2010); Jane Humphries and Sarah Horrell, 'Women's Labour Force Participation and the Transition to the Male Breadwinner Family 1790–1865', *Economic History Review* 48, no. 1 (1995): 89–117; Jane Humphries and Sarah Horrell, 'Old Questions, New Data and Alternative Perspectives: Families' Living Standards in the Industrial Revolution', *Economic History Review* 52, no. 4 (1992): 849–89.

15 Maxine Berg and Pat Hudson, 'Rehabilitating the Industrial Revolution', *Economic History Review* 45, no. 1 (1992): 24–50.

16 Pat Hudson and Francesco Boldizzoni, eds., *The Routledge Handbook of Global Economic History* (London: Routledge, 2015), esp. Introduction.

17 David Cannadine, 'The Present and Past in the English Industrial Revolution, 1880–1980', *Past & Present* 103 (1984): 131–72.

18 Maxine Berg, *A Woman in History: Eileen Power, 1889–1940* (Cambridge: Cambridge University Press, 1996).

19 Maxine Berg, *The Age of Manufactures, 1700–1820: Industry Innovation and Work in Britain* (London: Routledge, 2nd ed., 1994); Maxine Berg, 'Small Producer Capitalism in Eighteenth-Century England', *Business History* 35, no. 1 (1993): 17–39; Berg and Hudson, 'Rehabilitating the Industrial Revolution'.

20 Maxine Berg, 'Useful Knowledge, Industrial Enlightenment and the Place of India', *Journal of Global History* 8, no. 1 (2013): 117–41; Maxine Berg, 'Craft and Small-Scale Production in the Global Economy', *Itinerario* 37, no. 2 (2013): 23–45; Maxine Berg, 'Skill, Craft and Histories of Industrialization in Europe and Asia', *Transactions of the Royal Historical Society* 24 (2015): 127–48.

21 Michael J. Piore and Charles F. Sabel, *The Second Industrial Divide* (New York: Basic Books, 1984); Charles F. Sabel and Jonathan Zeitlin, 'Historical Alternatives to Mass Production', *Past & Present* 108 (1985): 133–76; Charles F. Sabel and Jonathan Zeitlin, eds., *World of Possibilities: Flexibility and Mass*

Production in Western Industrialization (Cambridge and New York: Cambridge University Press, 1997).

22 Maxine Berg, *The Machinery Question and the Making of Political Economy* (Cambridge: Cambridge University Press, 1980); Maxine Berg, Pat Hudson, and Michael Sonenscher, eds., *Manufacture in Town and Country before the Factory* (Cambridge: Cambridge University Press, 1983); Maxine Berg, ed., *Markets and Manufacture in Early Industrial Europe* (London: Routledge, 1990); Crafts, *British Economic Growth*; Charles Sabel and Jonathan Zeitlin, 'Historical Alternatives to Mass Production: Politics, Markets and Technology in Nineteenth-Century Industrialisation', *Past & Present* 108 (1985): 133–76; Berg, 'Small Producer Capitalism'; Berg, *Age of Manufactures*; Maxine Berg, 'The Genesis of Useful Knowledge', *History of Science* 45, no. 2 (2007), 123–33; Berg and Hudson, 'Rehabilitating the Industrial Revolution'; Maxine Berg and Pat Hudson, 'Growth and Change: A Comment on the Crafts–Harley View of the Industrial Revolution', *Economic History Review* 47, no. 2 (1994), 147–9; Maxine Berg, *Luxury and Pleasure in Eighteenth century Europe* (Oxford: Oxford University Press, 2005); Maxine Berg, 'The British Product Revolution of the Eighteenth Century', in *Reconceptualizing the Industrial Revolution*, eds. Jeff Horn, Leonard Rosenband, and Merritt Roe Smith (Cambridge, MA: MIT Press, 2011), 47–66.

23 Harry Braveman, *Labor and Monopoly Capital: The Degradation of Work in the Twentieth Century* (New York: Monthly Review Press, 1974).

24 Global Economic History Network (GEHN), London School of Economics, http://www.lse.ac.uk/Economic-History/Research/GEHN/Global-Economic-History-Network-GEHN.

25 Maxine Berg, ed., *Technology and toil in nineteenth century Britain: Documents* (London: CSE Books, 1979).

26 Maxine Berg, *The Machinery Question and the Making of Political Economy, 1815–1848* (Cambridge: Cambridge University Press, 1980); and Maxine Berg , *The Age of Manufactures*.

27 Maxine Berg, 'Consumption and Global History in the Early Modern World', in Roy and Riello, *Global Economic History*, 118. A major contribution to the theoretical and historical understanding of consumption is Marina Bianchi, ed., *The Active Consumer: Novelty and Surprise in Consumer Choice* (London: Routledge, 1998).

28 See in particular Joan Thirsk, *Economic Policy and Projects: The Development of a Consumer Society in Early Modern England* (Oxford: Clarendon, 1978); Margaret Spufford, *The Great Reclothing of Rural England: Petty Chapmen and their Wares in the Seventeenth Century* (London: Hambledon, 1984); Beverly Lemire, *Fashion's Favourite: The Cotton Trade and the Consumer in Britain, 1660–1800* (Oxford: Oxford University Press, 1991).

29 de Vries, *Industrious Revolution*.

30 Maxine Berg and Helen Clifford, 'Introduction', in *Consumers and Luxury in Europe, 1650–1850*, eds. Maxine Berg and Helen Clifford (Manchester: Manchester University Press, 1999), 6.

31 Maxine Berg, 'In Pursuit of Luxury: Global History and British Consumer Goods in the Eighteenth Century', *Past & Present* 182 (2004): 85–142; Maxine Berg, *Luxury and Pleasure*. See also Berg and Clifford, eds., *Consumers and Luxury in Europe*; and Maxine Berg and Elizabeth Eger, eds., *Luxury in the Eighteenth Century: Debates, Desires and Delectable Goods* (London: Palgrave, 2002).

32 Maxine Berg, Felicia Gottman, Chris Nierstrasz, and Hannah Hodacs, eds., *Goods from the East, 1600–1800: Trading Eurasia* (London: Palgrave, 2015).

33 Maxine Berg, 'Women's Property and the Industrial Revolution', *Journal of Interdisciplinary History* 24, no. 2 (1993): 233–50.

34 Lorna Weatherill, *Consumer Behaviour and Material Culture in Britain, 1660–1760* (London: Routledge, 1988).

35 Pomeranz, *Great Divergence*.

36 Ibid. Other scholars have been more critical of such a position and emphasize the importance of technologies, human capital, and the role of state policies. See for instance Prasannan Parthasarathi, *Why Europe Grew Rich and Asia Did Not: Global Economic Divergence, 1600–1850* (Cambridge: Cambridge University Press, 2014); Peer Vries, *State, Economy and the Great Divergence: Great Britain and China, 1680s–1850s* (London: Bloomsbury, 2015); William J. Ashworth, *The Industrial Revolution* (London: Bloomsbury, 2017); and Julian Hoppit's *Britain's Political Economies: Parliament and Economic Life, 1660–1800* (Cambridge: Cambridge University Press, 2017).

37 Patrick O'Brien, 'Historiographical Traditions and Modern Imperatives for the Restoration of Global History', *Journal of Global History* 1, no. 1 (2006): 3–39; Berg, 'In Pursuit of Luxury'.

38 Jerry H. Bentley, 'Cross-Cultural Interaction and Periodization in World History', *American Historical Review* 101, no. 3 (1996): 749–70.

39 Berg, 'In Pursuit of Luxury'. This article was based on her inaugural lecture at Warwick.

40 Berg and Eger, *Luxury in the Eighteenth Century*; Maxine Berg, *Writing the History of the Global: Challenges for the 21st Century* (Oxford: Oxford University Press for The British Academy, 2013).

41 Berg et al., *Goods from the East*.

42 Berg, *A Woman in History*; Berg, 'Women's Work'; Berg , 'Women's Property'.

43 Maxine Berg, 'Sea Otters and Iron: A Global Microhistory of Value and Exchange in Nootka Sound, 1774–1792', *Past & Present* Supplement (2019), forthcoming.

PART ONE

The Age of Manufactures: Knowledge, Making, and the Organisation of Production

1

Could Artisans Have Caused the Industrial Revolution?

Morgan Kelly, Joel Mokyr, and Cormac Ó Gráda

Introduction

Maxine Berg's *Age of Manufactures, 1700–1820* (1985; 1994) is one of the finest books ever written about the Industrial Revolution.[1] It combines the best elements of economic and social history with the humanist's instincts for what technological change meant for different groups, including women, children, and a variety of occupations and members of the working class. It rightly criticised the limited view of the Industrial Revolution as confined to a set of glamour industries such as cotton and iron, where expansion was sudden and dramatic. It questioned then-conventional interpretations of the Industrial Revolution which highlighted the roles of resource endowments and agricultural productivity, and located British distinctiveness instead in 'the extraordinary industry and inventiveness of her manufacturing people.'[2] It stressed that progress during the Industrial Revolution took place across a wide array of manufacturing industries, much of it in small workshops in which most of the metal trades industries were located. Berg rightly insisted that the macroeconomic approach to economic change must be supplemented with industry studies on a more regional level.[3]

More than anything else, however, Berg insisted that the credit for progress must be shared between two groups: one group comprises the famous and not so famous engineers, inventors, and highly skilled artisans who did not just turn blueprints into reality and scaled-up models but also introduced myriads of relative minor microinventions and tweaks that cumulatively improved the effectiveness of the equipment, the quality of the product, and the work environment in which labourers toiled.[4] The other, much larger, group, is the large number of women and children who provided an indispensable source of effective, docile, and inexpensive labour deployed in the first generations of factories.

Berg's book was one of the first major works to place appropriate emphasis on the crucial importance of this group to British industrialisation.

Artisans and Economic Progress

In a later essay Berg returned to the issue of artisans and stressed the point already made in her book, namely that 'traditional handicraft' sectors were capable of a great deal more progress than many economic historians of the Industrial Revolution have given them credit for. As she saw it, artisans 'replicated and reconfigured', building an economy of imitation that 'led to a self-sustaining process of improvement'.[5] Perhaps the only doubt we have about this statement is the word 'self-sustaining'. In a purely artisanal world, sequences of microinventions could lead to considerable technological progress.[6] Some of the more interesting 'great inventors' of the age – such as Newcomen and his assistant John Calley, Abraham Darby, John Kay, James Hargreaves, John Harrison, and many others – were artisans by any definition of the term. In both textiles and the metal working trades, early innovations that are traditionally seen as the harbingers of the Industrial Revolution – carding machinery, the flying shuttle, early jennies, as well as stamps, presses, new alloys, and improved machine tools – all came out of artisanal workshops. Artisans, operating in small workshops, were good at making incremental improvements to existing processes, exploiting a finer division of labour, and improving techniques through learning by doing – but rarely revolutionising technology. Without an infusion of new propositional knowledge, diminishing returns to artisanal improvements would have set in.

In some industries, progress was possible without much input from formal knowledge. Most advances in textile machinery required no physical insight that would have surprised Archimedes, as Donald Cardwell once remarked.[7] That said, even the earliest of those cotton-spinning machines required a level of technical sophistication that few artisans possessed. The two emblematic machines of early industrialisation – Arkwright's water frame with its intricate train of gears and rollers, and Watt's steam engine with it elaborate valve gear and sophisticated governors – were unusually complex technologies by the standards of the time. Much of Britain's success in developing these innovations from promising concepts into commercially viable forms rested on the skills and versatility of its uniquely large supply of craftsmen trained to make clocks, watches, and tools for navigation and surveying.[8]

The cotton industry, often seen as the paradigmatic sector of the Industrial Revolution, was the exception here in its reliance on artisanal skills. Coal and steam also required such skilled artisans but in addition depended on insights generated by experimental scientists and well-educated engineer-savants such as John Theophile Desaguliers, René Réaumur, Joseph Black, Joseph Priestley, Charles Augustin Coulomb, Claude Berthollet, and Humphry Davy. Such people moved seemingly effortlessly between what McKendrick has called the various 'gradations of scientific knowledge and expertise' and the spread and adoption of experimental methods, mathematical practice, and the culture of open science.[9] Closely associated with these scientists were a substantial number of individuals who we might call 'mathematical practitioners': applied mathematicians, astronomers, textbook writers, and instrument makers, a large and until recently understudied group of savants who moved back and forth between activities associated with philosophers and those of artisans.[10] As Celina Fox notes, these savants did not need to contemplate the mysteries of the universe in order to create a body of propositional knowledge that was organised, systematic, quantifiable, and empirical, and could be accessed by the best and the brightest of the mechanics. As she put it, Britain was full of philosophical mechanics as well as mechanical philosophers who combined their minds with their hands.[11]

The impact of advances in formal or informal propositional knowledge on technological practices could take many decades. The famous 1786 paper by three French scientists that explained the chemical nature of 'steel and steelmaking', was obviously above the heads of British steelmakers and was 'incomprehensible except to those who already knew how to make steel.'[12] By the 1820s, however, the chemistry of steel was already understood, and while it took another four decades for mass-produced steel to be feasible, its debt to the understanding of steel is not in doubt.[13] The same can be said for one of the more revolutionary if less heralded advances of the Industrial Revolution: gas lighting. Its invention depended on advances in pneumatic chemistry made by some of the giants of eighteenth-century science such as Lavoisier and Volta, yet artisanal skill and accident played important roles. Gas lighting was made possible by a combination of imperfect but experiment-based scientific understanding and artisanal brilliance.[14]

A Culture of Progress

Since the publication of the second edition of Berg's book in 1994, the thinking about the root causes of the Industrial Revolution has undergone some serious revisions. The first is the more precise separation between the "big question" of the Great Divergence between

Western Europe and the rest of the world and the smaller question of "why Britain" as opposed to France or other parts of western Europe. Following Pomeranz's trailblazing book, other works that ask the 'big question' have appeared.[15] The question of Britain's precocity was placed sharply in focus after Gregory Clark's suggestion of a rapidly multiplying bourgeois mentality and Robert Allen's thesis that attributed it to Britain's high wages and enhanced human capital.[16] While a consensus on the 'small question' has predictably failed to emerge, in the past two decades an agreement has formed that cultural and institutional factors played a much larger role than is reflected in Berg's book, even if there are still serious disagreements on the exact nature of these cultural and institutional factors. What exactly it was about British institutions and culture that gave it an advantage has remained a lively topic of conversation.

The somewhat silly notion that in the eighteenth century Britain had an industrial revolution but no Enlightenment whereas France had an Enlightenment but no industrial revolution has long been laid to rest. Both countries had generous amounts of both, but they were different in character. The British Enlightenment mixed the intellectual Enlightenment in Scotland (with its philosophical rationale for economic progress) with the more commercial, pragmatic, and down-to-earth Enlightenment in England but of course Continental ideas made their mark as well.[17] The British Enlightenment was much less focused on political and philosophical issues; instead the somewhat vague concept of 'improvement' became increasingly pervasive in the seventeenth century. As Paul Slack has noted, culture and economies coevolved, but in this case 'culture came first' and the triumph of a culture of improvement set England on a path toward economic progress before anyone else.[18]

An important insight of Berg's *Age of Manufactures* is that we can learn as much or more from looking at the variation *within* England as we can from comparing it to neighbouring countries. Of course, this is not a new argument, but Berg made the point with unusual acumen and insight. The decline of the old cloth industries in the south and west to be overtaken by Lancashire and Yorkshire remains as interesting a challenge as 'why not France? In her analysis of this question, Berg acknowledged Eric Jones's early work on regional comparative advantage. As we argue below, this internal variation in Britain can be exploited to point to the unique advantages that some of Britain's regions had, in addition to being part of the industrial Enlightenment.

British Exceptionalism

What set Britain apart was the confluence of a number of complementary factors that worked together to create the chain reaction of the Industrial Revolution. Like France and much of western Europe, it experienced an industrial Enlightenment, which was the logical continuation of the "spirit of improvement" that Slack describes for the seventeenth century. This spirit extended to the class of high quality craftsmen that the British apprenticeship system was capable of producing. At the most concrete level, an industrial revolution depended on the ability to make mechanical devices actually work. These competences were supplied by myriads of down-to-earth dexterous engineers described by Gillian Cookson, who refers to them as "ingenious mechanics" following James Watt's famous description of his partner Matthew Boulton: 'Mr Boulton was not only an ingenious mechanick, well skilled in all the arts of the Birmingham manufacturers, but he possessed in a high degree the faculty of rendering any new invention of his own or of others useful to the public.'[19]

The Industrial Revolution depended on these ingenious mechanics. The great engineer Marc Isambard Brunel remarked that, 'it was one thing to invent, another thing to make the invention work.' James Watt enquired, 'what is the principal hindrance to erecting engines? It is always the smith work.' The competence and culture of British skilled craftsmen and engineers – despite Watt's frequent impatient complaints on their inadequacy – were decisive. Industrialists on the Continent knew this all too well and hired British mechanics to set up and maintain the machinery embodying the new technology. In the absence of competent mechanics who could turn inventions into reality, French inventors were frustrated, such as the machine-tool maker Senot, who was one of the first to construct a screw-cutting lathe (1795), reputedly superior to that of the American David Wilkinson (1798) and the Englishman Henry Maudslay (1797). Yet it is unknown whether his lathe was ever used, and nothing is known about Senot, not even his first name.[20] Yet not all ingenious mechanics were created equal. France had an artisanal elite that Paola Bertucci has termed *artistes*, a group of learned artisans endowed with *esprit*, wedged between the highly educated *savants* that frequented Parisian salons and the mass of workmen and journeymen.[21] The skills of these eighteenth-century French *artistes* produced the miraculous protorobots and machine tools of Jacques de Vaucanson, the hot air balloons of the Montgolfier brothers, the elaborate clocks of Etienne Lenoir (1699–1778) and his son Pierre-Etienne Lenoir (1724–after 1789), and the well-crafted instruments of Jean-Antoine ('Abbé') Nollet. But these skilled workers were catering to a more upmarket constituency than their British colleagues. Consequently, what was missing in France that Britain had in large quantities was the highly skilled but down-to-earth practical mechanics that Cookson describes in detail, catering to a wider market, asking whether a product was useful and cheap rather than elegant. France thus needed to import them.

Bertucci provides notable examples of such expatriates, especially the clockmaker Henry Sully, the founder of the *Societé des Arts* and his colleague William Blakey, another horologist with deep knowledge of metallurgy, who was a brilliant mechanic and understood steelmaking 'as well as any in Europe'.[22] In Britain, success was largely determined by markets rather than wealthy patrons. In France, the politics of class and status often got in the way of progress. French artisans and savants struggled with each other for patronage, prestige, and status, much of it bestowed by the court and the aristocracy. French *artistes* spent a lot of time and ingenuity manoeuvring in the worlds of politics and power, whereas the artisans in Lancashire and Yorkshire worried first and foremost about rollers and spindles, coke and steam.

The history of technological diffusion between the two nations in the eighteenth century illustrates the difference. John Holker, a Jacobite who fled England in 1746 and rose to the position of 'inspector-general of foreign manufactures' in France in 1756, made his fortune when he moved a number of highly skilled Lancashire workmen to the embryonic cotton industry in Rouen. Less well-known was Michael Alcock, a Birmingham toy and button manufacturer who moved to France and built a large manufactory of ironware in La Charité sur Loire.[23] William Wilkinson (the brother of the more famous Broseley ironmonger, John ['iron-mad'] Wilkinson) travelled frequently between England and France and was instrumental in setting up the French iron works at Le Creuzot and their use of coke in the production of iron used in cannon boring, for which he was paid a huge salary. Major French inventions often found their way to Britain to be turned into economically viable production.[24] Britain may have had a comparative advantage in microinventions and France in macroinventions, even if it is possible that Britain had an *absolute* advantage in both. The test of the hypothesis that Britain had a comparative advantage in microinventions is the flow of skilled mechanics to the Continent, while macroinventions and the knowledge underlying them flowed primarily from the Continent to Britain.

For many generations, artisanal knowledge had been by and large tacit, taught by masters to apprentices without a reliance on written materials. This changed with the Industrial Revolution, when technical books and essays increasingly described technological practices. Here, of course, the *Encyclopédie* and its many imitations and spinoffs, was the paradigmatic document. These books 'exemplified the Baconian faith ... that processes could be changed for the better if their principles were understood and that artisans would improve their skills if they knew the reasons for them.'[25]

The 'Metal Triangle', Coal, and Artisan Skills

The slow but continuous artisanal-driven economic growth already under way in England by the mid-seventeenth century was sustained by innovation across a broad range of industrial sectors ranging from watch-making to pottery, from brewing to papermaking, and from waterpower to the manufacture of machine tools. As in the manufacture of 'middle-class goods' – stressed by Berg – production in these sectors involved a high level of precision manufacturing that embodied sophisticated technological competence.[26] Much of this required artisans who could cast and cut and shape materials, especially metals and wood, skills on which the successful development of cotton and steam technology depended. But it also required more than the simple replication of the same skills from generation to generation: at any point in time a minority of particularly talented and creative artisans were capable of moving the technology frontier slowly outward. A growing body of literature implies that without being able to draw on the proficiency of the most talented of its watch- and clockmakers, toolmakers, millwrights, and foundry men, innovation would have ground to a halt.

As Berg demonstrated, such skills were most plentiful in a region where skilled metalworking had been a feature since the late sixteenth century, what we will call the Liverpool–Birmingham–Sheffield 'metal triangle'. It should therefore not be surprising that the Industrial Revolution began in that region. But what explains metallurgy's concentration in these centres in the first place? Part of the answer is coal.[27] It was the presence of suitable coal, alongside iron ore and fire clay, that stimulated the early growth of iron working in Birmingham and Sheffield. Similarly, the right kind of coal was plentiful in the part of southwestern Lancashire that would become synonymous with watch- and watch-tool making in the eighteenth century.[28] By the same token, the lack of coal in the West Country has been seen by a leading historian of its woollen textile industry as a major reason why that industry failed to mechanise successfully, though others have disagreed.[29]

Coal was a factor in post-1750 British industrial progress, but its role was less as a source of inorganic energy than as a catalyst in generating large clusters of diverse mechanical expertise.[30] Mining both generated skills and required them: practically all the engineers who helped develop the steam engine – George Stephenson, John Blenkinsop, Timothy Hackworth, William Hedley, and Richard Trevithick – were trained and worked in mining. Mining set the most difficult challenges for engineers, and meeting them required a confluence of hydraulics, geology, metallurgy, mechanics, and chemistry.[31] Coal was linked to the gradual accumulation of tacit artisanal expertise as it was adopted in a successively wider range of industrial processes.[32] Starting with simple applications, coal began to be used for more demanding furnace processes like smelting brass and making glass and pottery in the seventeenth century; and subsequently for casting iron and steel in the first half of the eighteenth century.[33]

It was in order to be close to the specialist mechanical skills needed to build his steam engine that James Watt moved from Scotland to Birmingham's Soho in 1769. This need for an entrepreneur or a region to have easy access to large concentrations of diverse mechanical skill in order to industrialise successfully suggests a possible answer to questions raised in the 1970s and 1980s: why did some areas of widespread cottage industry ('protoindustry') like northern and midland England go on to industrialise successfully, whereas others, such as western England, southern Ireland, and northern France, did not? What counted was the supply of mechanical expertise. Abundant labour supply was all good and well, but the rural industrial workers were mostly unskilled; they needed engineers and craftsmen skilled in the more sophisticated techniques that came on line after 1760.

Still, England's large supply of proficient craftsmen depended on more than a fortuitous abundance of coal. On the supply side, England's weaker crafts guilds were much less capable of resisting technological change among skilled artisans.[34] On the demand side, from the mid-seventeenth century on, urban expansion, growing overseas trade, intensified agriculture, and increased market integration were both the symptoms and causes of rising prosperity. England was by international standards a 'high wage economy'. The relative affluence of its working class and the low level of inequality in Britain, as reflected in such things as the quality and variety of their everyday food and clothes, was often noted at the time, whereas its growing middle class sustained a burgeoning market for 'new, semi-luxury, and fashionable consumer goods'.[35] Further evidence for 'the democratization of consumption' in this period is the finding based on criminal records that over time items such as cotton bedspreads were stolen from households progressively further down the socioeconomic scale.[36] Luxury goods, from musical instruments and fancy toys to high-end textiles and footwear, required more precision work, that is, skilled artisans. The English, moreover, were a naval nation, and virtually nonstop naval warfare between 1650 and 1815 created a large and steady market for precisely made metal products ranging from navigational instruments and small arms to the large naval iron cannons constructed with the help of John Wilkinson's boring machine (patented in 1774). Wilkinson's work was inspired and informed by a Dutch iron and brass founder, Jan Verbruggen, who was hired as master founder of the royal brass foundry at Woolwich. Verbruggen was one of the first to apply the technique of horizontal boring for solid-cast guns, first developed by Jean Maritz in Strasbourg in the early eighteenth century, but Wilkinson's machine was a substantial improvement and produced a tolerance low enough to create cylinders for Watt's engines.

Literacy and Human Capital

England's top artisans were far from ignorant, but they learned and plied their skills in workshops, not in schools or from books. They were the products of a system deemed 'altogether unnecessary' by Adam Smith because, in his view, the acquisition of artisanal skills required no 'long course of instruction.'[37] In reality apprenticeship in England, far from being an institutional encumbrance, was an effective vehicle for transmitting artisanal skills before and during the industrial revolution. The system was well designed for the intergenerational transmission of tacit knowledge and added incremental improvements to best-practice technology.[38] On the whole, it worked and worked well – it easily survived the repeal of the Statute of Artificers in 1814. The knowledge was still predominantly tacit: Lancashire watchmakers relied on their sight, not on geometry, to make teeth 'of what is called the bay leaf pattern' for watch wheels, just as Yorkshire metallurgists knew precisely when iron was 'sound', 'strong', or 'tough' without being able to communicate that in any measurable way.[39]

Such artisanal skills were not formal and did not require schooling. Yet when the talented file maker Peter Stubs married on 6 July 1777 at the age of twenty-one he signed the marriage register, and this was typical in his trade at the time. Overall literacy where Stubs grew up was low – even in the 1840s and 1850s one groom in two and nearly three brides in four were unable to sign the marriage register. Yet most watch and file makers – part of the artisanal elite – were able to sign, at least from the 1750s when parish registers first supply the details. In the epicentre of watchmaking around Prescot in Lancashire a relatively high literacy level of watch- and toolmakers is observed. The most plausible reason for this is that the commercial side (as distinct from the craft) of their work – dealing in raw materials, spare parts, and finished clockwork – required literacy.[40] Even in the early eighteenth century early Prescot watchmakers worked for several contacts in London, and the rate at which they supplied the material also suggests that this output was based on the work of others.[41] A closer look at literacy rates in other occupations at the time suggests that, in southwest Lancashire at least, literacy was in demand in occupations linked to self-employment and to trading, among them paradigmatic craftsmen such as shoemakers, wheelwrights, and cabinetmakers. Farmers, too, were likely to be literate – and Thirsk has highlighted the role of print in hastening the diffusion of agricultural techniques.[42]

But here the parish registers yield another surprising result. A comparison of grooms listed as watch- and toolmakers in southwest Lancashire parish records with apprentices from the same parishes recorded in the late Dennis Moore's invaluable compendium implies that only a minority of men employed in the watchmaking trade between the 1750s and the 1800s were formally apprenticed.[43] This suggests that most watchmakers did not go through a fully formal training even when they still were trained by adult masters.[44] While avoiding formal training saved time and money, the trade-off was a lack of mobility and reduced influence with potential trading partners, and so presumably the more ambitious and entrepreneurial and wealthier opted for formal training. Linking apprenticeship and parish register data thus suggests two important points. First, the *formal* apprenticeship system was rather 'weak', in the sense that many apprentices who did not serve their full legal time were not barred from the industry. The weakness of formality underlines the flexibility of the English apprenticeship system and its reliance on trust and reputation that enforced apprenticeship relations. The data also show, rather strikingly, that those who signed formal contracts were more likely to be literate than those who did not.[45]

Although it is true that many of the artisans-made-good of the Industrial Revolution received little formal schooling – Richard Arkwright, Matthew Murray, Henry Maudslay, George Stephenson, and the brothers William and Peter Fairbairn being familiar examples – this does not imply that education and science did not matter to artisans and engineers. Consider watchmaking, the industry that provided Wedgwood and Watt with the high-quality tools and lathes that were so important to them in the 1760s and 1770s. Watchmaking then was a bastion of artisanal culture. Nevertheless, it also benefitted hugely from one of the key breakthroughs of seventeenth-century applied mathematics: the balance spring invented by Robert Hooke and/or Christiaan Huygens. From the early nineteenth century on, the much higher degree of precision required by machine tools – machinery designed to cut and shape metal parts to 'the thousandth part of an inch' in the words of James Nasmyth – required the kind of components that had been developing in astronomy since the sixteenth century.[46] Between then and the early nineteenth century the accuracy of astronomical measurement steadily increased by a factor of 10,000, and exactly cut angular scales and adjustment screws were already being incorporated into mass-produced navigational sextants by the 1790s.[47]

Precision mattered more over time.[48] Many of the advances in industrial technology during the late eighteenth and early nineteenth centuries ultimately came down to adapting the gears, scales, and adjustment screws of mathematical instruments, clocks, and watches (along with the lathes, gear cutters, and other tools used to make them) to iron machinery. When Peter Stubs successfully made the transition from files for watchmakers to much heavier 'Sheffield files' for machinery in the late 1810s, it was still without the help of precise cutting tools: 'whether file A was better than file B [was] largely a matter of opinion and here the mystique of the Stubs mark would have helped sales.'[49] The connection between the worlds of precise scientific instruments and heavy industrial machinery was personified by Joseph Whitworth who would become the world's leading producer of machine tools in the 1830s and 1840s and Britain's foremost evangelist for standardized parts and precision manufacture.[50]

Geography, Living Standards, and the Industrial Revolution

Artisan-led economic growth on the eve of the Industrial Revolution was mostly Smithian growth. It relied on the increased integration and a finer division of labour made possible by improved communications. This was an era of improved shipping, navigation, canals, and turnpikes and the decline in freight rates, both inland and coastal, reduced interregional price deviations. This is reflected below in the reductions in the coefficients of variation (cv) of cereal prices between the mid-seventeenth and mid-eighteenth centuries and in the wedge between Newcastle and London coal prices during the eighteenth century. Better transportation permitted the increasing specialisation of artisanal tasks associated with trades such as watchmaking, calico printing, and cutlery.[51]

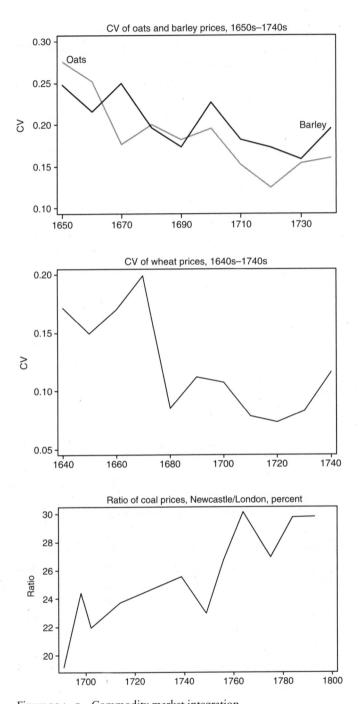

Figure 1.1 A–C   Commodity market integration

Source: Peter Bowden, 'Statistics', in *The Agrarian History of England and Wales*, vol. 5.2, edited by Joan Thirsk (Cambridge: Cambridge University Press, 1985); W. Hausman, 'The English Coastal Coal Trade, 1691–1910: How Rapid was Productivity Growth?', *Economic History Review* 40 (1987): 588–96 (at 592).

Berg's *The Age of Manufactures*, sceptical of 'aggregate and macro-economic analysis' (280), highlighted the regional character of both economic growth and decline before and during the Industrial Revolution. Indeed, the Industrial Revolution turned the economic geography of England upside down, transforming the north and midlands from laggards to leaders, as they overtook the traditionally high-wage agricultural region of the south and east, parts of which for centuries had also been the heartland of England's woollen textile industry. The transformation preceded the Industrial Revolution insofar as outwork and small-scale cottage industry had spawned faster population growth in the north since the seventeenth century, generating those reserve armies of female and child labour needed for the dark satanic mills of the Industrial Revolution. The north also had the advantage of better access to waterpower, which had already given the northern woollen industry the edge over its competitors in the West Country, as well as the coal mines discussed above. And although wages in the north were low, its population was relatively well nourished (as implied by diets and heights). But, above all, the north possessed a large and flexible supply of workers with useful skills – clockmakers, mechanics, toolmakers – who played a key role during the Industrial Revolution and several of whom would become inventors and factory owners in their own right.[52] Moreover, on the eve of the Industrial Revolution these skilful workers, being relatively plentiful, almost certainly cost less than their equivalent in the south in terms of their wages relative to their productivity.[53]

Regional wage dispersion remained constant with a coefficient of variation of 13 per cent in both the 1760s and 1830s. But this hides a dramatic reversal of the north–south divide in wages. At the outset real wages in the north, where industrialisation would be concentrated, were lowest, reflecting the lower productivity of northern agriculture. But the industrialising process, which caused real wages to rise significantly in the north, caused wages to stagnate or even to fall slightly in the south. Keith Snell's particularly rich database of southern wages, based on rural settlement examinations, implies that real wages were falling in southern England between c. 1780 and the 1830s, if not beyond.[54] The contrasting labour demands that drove these wage changes led to very different patterns of population growth. Between 1761 and 1831, the population of the depressed agricultural counties in the south and east grew by less than a third, whereas that of the industrial counties more than doubled, with that of Lancashire more than quadrupling.

What Berg has called 'the richness and variety of early industrial Britain' can be captured by taking a regional approach to modelling the Industrial Revolution.[55] In seeking to test our model, instead of asking 'why was England first?' we focus on why the likes of counties like Lancashire and (west) Yorkshire left Norfolk and Gloucester in their wake. We model the variation in economic growth across England's forty-one counties c. 1750–1830 using variables that capture the features highlighted above, in particular the availability of mechanical skills, cheap labour, and waterpower. In this specification two variables – measures of the supply of artisanal skill and waterpower – account for over four-fifths of the variation in English industrial employment in the 1830s. The explanatory power of this rather simple model turns out to be very strong.[56]

England's top artisans constituted only a small proportion of the total labour force, but they played a crucial role in producing the workshop of the world. This hitherto neglected part of what is known as 'upper tail human capital' may well be the long lost key to understanding why and how the Industrial Revolution took place in Britain.

Conclusion

This paper has focused on one aspect of the Industrial Revolution highlighted by Maxine Berg: the human capital embodied in England's artisans.[57] During the early stages of the Industrial Revolution, human capital resided mainly in the mechanical expertise and occasional genius of craftsmen and artisans-made-good. It accounted for their relatively high wages, and it rested mainly on their superior training, their mechanical dexterity, and on-the-job learning. In those decades, as Cookson has put it, 'most significant technological progress was achieved in a workshop rather than in a laboratory, by machine-makers who apparently had little or no exposure to scientific books or any education in science.'[58] That statement may, however, be a better description of the textile industry than of the rest of industrialising Britain. Elsewhere, the complementarities between natural philosophers and industrialists can be easily discerned by observing the growing dependence of manufacturers on the advice of scientific consultants.[59]

During the Industrial Revolution, England's endowment of science-based knowledge continued to accumulate, but it was only from the early nineteenth century that science fully came into its own in advancing the economy. It was then that the new intellectual horizons opened by Enlightenment science came into their own. Science informed, instructed, and inspired technology, but to be of practical value it needed competent practicioners. In the end, it was the all-powerful complementarity between the people who knew things and those who could make things, between *savants* and *fabricants*, that opened the floodgates of progress. Artisans had a crucial part to play, but by themselves, no matter how ingenious, they could not have brought about the Industrial Revolution that continues until the present day.

Notes

1 Maxine Berg, *The Age of Manufactures, 1700–1820: Industry Innovation and Work in Britain* (London: Fontana Press, 1985 [2nd revised edition, London: Routledge, 1994]).

2 Ibid., 7.

3 Ibid., 6–7, 203–6.

4 An example of this kind of research is Gillian Cookson's recent book, which is clearly inspired by Berg's work, both in title and overall approach. Gillian Cookson, *The Age of Machinery: Engineering the Industrial Revolution, 1770–1850* (Woodbridge: Boydell & Brewer Press, 2018).

5 Maxine Berg, 'The Genesis of "Useful knowledge", *History of Science* 45 (2007): 123–33, quotation on 128.

6 For a recent example, see Morgan Kelly and Cormac Ó Gráda, 'Adam Smith, Watch Prices, and the Industrial Revolution', *Quarterly Journal of Economics* 131, no. 4 (2016): 1727–52.

7 Donald Cardwell, *The Fontana History of Technology* (London: Fontana, 1994), 186.

8 Morgan Kelly and Cormac Ó Gráda, 'From Scientific Revolution to Industrial Revolution: The Role of Mathematical Practitioners', University College Dublin Centre for Economic Research Working Paper no. 15 (2019), 3.

9 Neil McKendrick, 'The Role of Science in the Industrial Revolution', in *Changing Perspectives in the History of Science*, eds. Mikuláš Teich and Robert Young (London: Heinemann 1973), 274–319, quotation on 313. McKendrick uses the example of Wedgwood to illustrate how a literate and learned industrialist could benefit from applied science even if he did not meet A.R. Hall's very strict criteria to being a 'scientist'.

10 Kelly and Ó Gráda, 'From Scientific Revolution'.

11 Celina Fox, *The Arts of Industry in the Age of Enlightenment* (New Haven and London: Yale University Press, 2009), 4, and 41.

12 John R. Harris, *Industrial Espionage and Technology Transfer: Britain and France in the Eighteenth Century* (Aldershot: Ashgate, 1998), 220. The paper was Claude Berthollet, Gaspard Monge, and Alexander Vandermonde, 'Mémoire sur la fer consideré dans ses differens états métalliques' Lu à l'Academie des Sciences, May 1786. Gallica (digital library of the Bibliothèque nationale de France), ID: ark:/12148/bpt6k6359836g.

13 Cyril Stanley Smith, 'The Discovery of Carbon in Steel', *Technology and Culture* 5, no. 2 (1964): 149–75; Theodore A. Wertime, *The Coming of the Age of Steel* (Leiden: Brill, 1961), 188–9.

14 Leslie Tomory, *Progressive Enlightenment: The Origins of the Gaslight Industry, 1780–1820* (Cambridge, MA: MIT Press, 2012).

15 Kenneth Pomeranz, *The Great Divergence: China, Europe, and the Making of the Modern World Economy* (Princeton: Princeton University Press, 2000). The opus classicus on this literature remains Eric L. Jones, *The European Miracle* (Cambridge: Cambridge University Press, 1st ed. 1981). See also, for example, Ian Morris, *Why the West Rules – For Now* (New York: Farrar, Strauss and Giroux, 2010); and Jack A. Goldstone, *Why Europe? The Rise of the West in World History, 1500–1850* (Boston: McGraw-Hill, 2009).

16 Robert C. Allen, *The British Industrial Revolution in Global Perspective* (Cambridge: Cambridge University Press, 2009); Gregory Clark, *A Farewell to Alms* (Princeton: Princeton University Press, 2007).

17 Roy Porter, 'The Enlightenment in England', in *The Enlightenment in National Context*, eds. Roy Porter and Mikuláš Teich (Cambridge: Cambridge University Press, 1981), 1–18; Roy Porter, *The Creation of the Modern World: The Untold Story of the British Enlightenment* (New York: W.W. Norton, 2000).

18 Paul Slack, *The Invention of Improvement: Information and Material Progress in Seventeenth-Century England* (Oxford: Oxford University Press, 2015), 4.

19 Cit. in Samuel Smiles, *Lives of the Engineers*, vol. IV: *The Steam Engine, Boulton and Watt* (New and rev. ed. London: John Murray, 1878), 382.

20 Maurice Daumas, *A History of Technology and Invention* (New York: Crown, 1979), 3: 102, 115. Daumas adds (103) that whereas the first experiments (with new machine tools) were by French engineers, the industrial phase of invention and development was the work of the extraordinary generation of English engineers.

21 Paola Bertucci, *Artisanal Enlightenment: Science and the Mechanical Arts in Old Regime France* (New Haven and London: Yale University Press, 2017).

22 Harris, *Industrial Espionage*, 30.

23 See especially John R. Harris, 'Michael Alcock and the Transfer of Birmingham Technology to France before the Revolution', reprinted in John R. Harris, *Essays in Industry and Technology of the Eighteenth Century* (Croft Road, Hampshire: Ashgate Publishing, 1992), 113–63.

24 For examples, see Joel Mokyr, *The Enlightened Economy* (New Haven and London: Yale University Press, 2009), 114–15.

25 Fox, *The Arts*, 275.

26 Maxine Berg, 'New Commodities, Luxuries, and Their Consumers in Eighteenth-Century England', in *Consumers and Luxury: Consumer Culture in Europe 1650–1850*, eds. Maxine Berg and Helen Clifford (Manchester: Manchester University Press, 1999), 63–87.

27 For empirical support for this proposition, see Morgan Kelly, Joel Mokyr, and Cormac Ó Gráda, 'Perfect Mechanics: Artisan Skills and the Origins of the British Industrial Revolution', University College Dublin Centre for Economic Research Working Paper 14 (2019).

28 F.A. Bailey and T.C. Barker, 'The Seventeenth-Century Origins of Watch-Making in South-West Lancashire', in *Liverpool and Merseyside*, ed. John R. Harris (London: Cass, 1959), 1–15.

29 Jennifer Tann, 'The Textile Millwright in the Early Industrial Revolution', *Textile History* 5, no. 1 (1974): 80–9, states that 'With no large coalfield nearby, no heavy iron or engineering industries, and no other local industry requiring precision engineering, the area lacked a pool of skilled labor to draw upon'. For an opposing view, see Eric L. Jones, *Locating the Industrial Revolution: Inducement and Response* (Singapore: World Scientific Publishing, 2010).

30 Compare Gregory Clark and David Jacks, 'Coal and the Industrial Revolution, 1700–1869', *European Review of Economic History* 11, no. 1 (2007): 39–72; E.A. Wrigley, *Energy and the English Industrial Revolution* (Cambridge: Cambridge University Press, 2010); Mokyr, *Enlightened Economy*, 100–4, 269–70; Alan Fernihough and Kevin H. O'Rourke, 'Coal and the European Industrial Revolution', NBER Working Paper No. 19802 (2014); N.F.R. Crafts and Nikolaus Wolf, 'The Location of the UK Cotton Textiles Industry in 1838: A Quantitative Analysis', *Journal of Economic History* 74, no. 4 (2014): 1103–39.

31 Donald Cardwell, *Turning Points in Western Technology* (New York: Neale Watson, Science History Publications, 1972), 74.

32 John Harris, *Essays on Industry in the Eighteenth-century: England and France* (London: Variorum, 1992), 18–32.

33 John Harris has emphasised that the switch from charcoal to coal-based fuels in the iron industry in the second half of the eighteenth century is often believed to be the first such transition whereas in fact it was 'virtually the last'. Industries such as soap boiling, brewing, and glassmaking had switched to coal centuries earlier. See John Harris, *The British Iron Industry, 1700–1850* (Houndsmill and London: MacMillan Education Ltd., 1988); Eric Kerridge, *Textile Manufactures in Early Modern England* (Manchester: Manchester University Press, 1985), 165.

34 Sheilagh Ogilvie, *The European Guilds: An Economic Analysis* (Princeton: Princeton University Press, 2019).

35 John Styles, *The Dress of the People: Everyday Fashion in Eighteenth-Century England* (New Haven: Yale University Press, 2007), 13; Maxine Berg, *Luxury and Pleasure in Eighteenth-Century Britain* (Oxford: Oxford University Press, 2005).

36 Sara Horrell, Jane Humphries, and Ken Sneath, 'Consumption Conundrums Unravelled', *Economic History Review* 68 no. 4 (2015): 830–57.

37 Adam Smith, *Wealth of Nations*, Part 1, chapter 10, part II.

38 David de la Croix, Matthias Doepke, and Joel Mokyr, 'Clans, Guilds, and
    Markets: Apprenticeship Institutions and Growth in the Pre-Industrial
    Economy', *Quarterly Journal of Economics* 133, no. 1 (2018): 1–70; Joel Mokyr,
    'The Economics of Apprenticeship', in *Apprenticeship in Early Modern Europe*,
    eds. Maarten Prak and Patrick Wallis (Cambridge: Cambridge University
    Press, forthcoming).

39 Joseph Wickham Roe, *English and American Tool Builders* (New York:
    McGraw-Hill, 1916), 65; Berg, *Age of Manufactures*, 257.

40 Ashton noted that many of the workmen who supplied Peter Stubs of
    Warrington also traded with others. T.H. Ashton, *An Eighteenth-century
    Industrialist: Peter Stubs of Warrington, 1756–1806* (Manchester: Manchester
    University Press, 1939).

41 R.A.H. Ward, 'A Watchmaker's Pocket Book', *Transactions of the Historic Society
    of Lancashire and Cheshire* 122 (1970): 153–57.

42 Joan Thirsk, 'Agricultural Innovations and Their Diffusion', in *The Agrarian
    History of England and Wales*, vols. 5, 2, ed. Joan Thirsk (Cambridge:
    Cambridge University Press, 1985), 571–4. The effect of written handbooks
    on agricultural productivity is far from clear, however. The Edinburgh
    physician Francis Home (1719–1813), who wrote one of the first books
    on plant nutrition, argued that the gap between science and practice was
    still huge. See Francis Home, *The Principles of Agriculture and Vegetation*
    (Edinburgh: Sands, Donaldson, Murray and Cochran for A. Kincaid and
    A. Donaldson, 1756), 2–3.

43 Dennis Moore, *British Clockmakers and Watchmakers Apprentice Records,
    1710–1810* (Ashbourne: Mayfield Books, 2003).

44 Compare Berg, *Age of Manufactures*, 218–19.

45 Neil J. Cummins, Morgan Kelly, and Cormac Ó Gráda, 'Artisanal Skills,
    Apprenticeship, and the English Industrial Revolution: Prescot and Beyond'
    (Working Paper, 2018).

46 A.E. Musson, 'Joseph Whitworth and the Growth of Mass-production
    Engineering', *Business History* 17, no. 2 (1975): 109–49, citation on 119. The
    great engineer William Fairbairn, although himself not trained in science,
    fully realised the importance of formal science and in his library he worked
    underneath a picture of Alexander von Humboldt, whom he had met.
    See Richard Byrom, *William Fairbairn: the Experimental Engineer* (Market
    Drayton: Railway and Canal Historical Society 2017), 22, 48.

47 Kelly and Ó Gráda, 'From Scientific Revolution.'

48 For a recent popular survey, see Simon Winchester, *The Perfectionists: How
    Precision Engineers Created the Modern World* (New York: Harper Collins,
    2018).

49 E. Surrey Dane, *Peter Stubs and the Lancashire Hand Tool Industry* (Altrincham:
    Sherratt, 1973), 67.

COULD ARTISANS HAVE CAUSED THE INDUSTRIAL REVOLUTION?   43

50 Musson, 'Joseph Whitworth.'
51 The classic statement is by Rick Szostak, *The Role of Transportation in the Industrial Revolution* (Montreal: McGill-Queen's University Press, 1991). See also Mokyr, *Enlightened Economy*, 202–11; Kelly and Ó Gráda, 'Adam Smith'; Berg, *Age of Manufactures*, 74–5, 255–6, 263.
52 Cookson, *Age of Machinery.*
53 Morgan Kelly, Joel Mokyr, and Cormac Ó Gráda, 'Precocious Albion: A New Interpretation of the British Industrial Revolution,' *Annual Review of Economics* 6 (2014): 363–89.
54 K.M.D. Snell, *Annals of the Labouring Poor* (Cambridge: Cambridge University Press, 1985), 23–66, 411–17.
55 Berg, *Age of Manufacturers*, 280; Kelly, Mokyr, and Ó Gráda, 'Perfect Mechanics.'
56 Kelly, Mokyr, and Ó Gráda, 'Perfect Mechanics.'
57 Maxine Berg and Pat Hudson, 'Rehabilitating the Industrial Revolution,' *Economic History Review* 45 no. 1 (1992): 24–50 (at 31–2); Berg, *Age of Manufactures*, 179–80; Maxine Berg, 'Skill, Craft and Histories of Industrialization in Europe and Asia,' *Transactions of the Royal Historical Society* 24 (2015): 127–48.
58 Cookson, 'The West Yorkshire Textile Engineering Industry,' 51.
59 Among the scientists providing such consultancy services in the early stages of the industrial revolution, the most prominent were the chemists William Cullen and James Keir; the physicists John T. Desaguliers, Joseph Black, and Joseph Priestley; consulting engineers such as Peter Ewart, John Smeaton, and John Rennie; and the clockmaker and geologist John Whitehurst.

2

'What Is Technology?': An Enquiry into the Science of the Arts at the Dawn of Industrialisation

Liliane Hilaire-Pérez

'What Is Technology?' was the title of the inaugural lecture delivered by George Wilson, a Scottish chemist, when he became Regius Professor of Technology of the University of Edinburgh in 1855 and director of the Industrial Museum of Edinburgh.[1] Such a position was new in Great Britain, and Wilson felt he had to explain what was at stake. He began by recalling that 'The Title of the Chair, also, is as novel as its creation, and the term "Technology", by which it is distinguished, is so unfamiliar to English ears, and so inexpressive to English minds, that I must, at the very outset, explain what the branch of knowledge is which I am called upon to profess.' He then argued that the word 'Technology' was better known on the Continent and that it referred to a discipline that was taught in Germany where this notion was associated with the cameralist Johann Beckmann's legacy. Although Wilson did not mention the *Anleitung zur technologie* (1777) or the *Entwurf der algemeinen Technologie* (1806), he did cite the *History of Inventions* (1772), the only book by Beckmann translated in English (1797). Wilson stated that 'The word "Technology" literally signifies the Science of the Art, or a Discourse or Dissertation of these.'[2] Hence, 'Its object is not the Art itself, i.e., the *practice* of Art, but the principles which guide or underlie Art.' Technology was then, the science of the 'Industrial Arts' or the 'Theory of the Arts' and its object was to study the principles by which 'the artist secures his ends.'[3] As such, Wilson was following Beckmann's *Entwurf* in which, for the first time, a classification of trades by their operations, according to the purpose of their action, was proposed.[4]

This meaning of 'Technology' was lost in the second half of the nineteenth century in England and more widely on the Continent and in North America, where the science of the arts had also begun to be adopted.[5] The chair of technology in Edinburgh was withdrawn in 1859 when Wilson died prematurely. The courses of the Industrial Museum were suspended and the acquisitions of artifacts by the museum were directed to the decorative arts, the museum evolving into the Museum of Science and Art – today's National Museum of Scotland. Meanwhile, since the nineteenth century the meaning of the word technology has shifted from the science of the arts to the application of science to industry, and from the study/theory of techniques to the technique itself, at a time when industrial engineering developed as well as the mechanisation and heavy chemical industry. Technology became the science of processes, either mechanic or chemical. It was no longer the science of purposeful action. In 1855, this turn was still to happen. Wilson quoted Friedrich Ludwig Knapp's *Chemical Technology, or Chemistry Applied to the Arts and Manufactures* (1848) for whom 'Technology' had to be understood as 'the systematic definition λόγος (*logos*) of the rational principles upon which all processes employed in the arts τεχηες (*technes*) are based,'[6] which differed from the meaning of the science of the action. As the applied sciences gained ground, both 'useful knowledge' and the idea that the world of industrial arts were based upon efficient action became marginalized.[7]

Nevertheless, since the nineteenth century, an interest in 'Technology' has regularly reemerged, at least in France, either in connection with technical collections[8] or in the ethnographic and anthropological studies of Marcel Mauss, André Leroi-Gourhan, and André-Georges Haudricourt, along with the philosophical approaches such as those of Georges Canguilhem's phenomenology. They all considered technique as 'traditional efficient action' (Mauss), which included not only fabrication ('useful knowledge') but also all sorts of actions including rituals.[9] Mauss's follower, the ethnologist Haudricourt explained that 'if technology is to be a science, it should be as the science of human activities.'[10] Studies that understand 'Technology' to be a codification of techniques have become integral to the conceptualisation of knowledge economies.[11] By avoiding teleological approaches focused on the spread of (European) applied sciences, they contribute in important ways to global history.[12]

Nevertheless, after recovering this meaning of 'Technology', and more widely the importance of codification, a new research trend is emerging. Whereas history of 'Technology' has often focused on theoreticians or academicians, new studies emphasise the part played by practitioners in the making of the science of the arts.[13] This point of view is an inversion of the inherited scholarship, in which artisans have long been considered to rely on local tacit know-how and bound to guilds that prevented the development of a comparative and synthetic understanding of work, hence limiting their invention.

My chapter first considers the research based on the fundamental texts that constituted 'Technology' as a discipline. I will then show how a new trend is enhancing our understanding of the cultural practices that were inherent in the rise of this science. I continue to concentrate on practice to show how, on the shop floor, artisans developed techno-logical reasoning that expressed their capacity to abstract work into operative principles.

Recovering 'Technology' as the Science of Industrial Arts

In 1968 Jacques Guillerme and Jan Sebestik published an article, in the journal *Thales*, entitled 'The Beginnings of Technology', based on research presented in Georges Canguilhem's seminar.[14] As Jan Sebestik recalled, Canguilhem's interest in technique was based on the idea that 'technical operations are irreducible to theoretical knowledge.'[15] Even if the operation of machines belonged to physics, machines were first of all extensions of the human species. The technical activity was organic; for Canguilhem 'Man was in continuity with life through technique.'[16] This irreducibility being set, the challenge was to understand the constitution of the discourse on technical operations as scientific discourse, hence building a theory of technique.

Guillerme and Sebestik collected a corpus of texts ranging from Renaissance technical treatises to eighteenth-century encyclopaedias and nineteenth-century essays on the science of manufactures. Although their work remained largely ignored in the following decades, it formed the basis of what is now a major reference work in the field: Hélène Vérin and Pascal Dubourg-Glatigny, *Réduire en art*.[17] Vérin and Dubourg-Glatigny underlined the importance of the Renaissance learned project in reducing the diversity of techniques to basic principles of action, by observation, comparison, and analogy. This attempt at reducing practices to generic operations was based on the synthesis of concrete actions so as to produce an abstraction. For Vérin and Dubourg-Glatigny, this revealed 'a domain of knowledge. A specific one, that of the "arts", which is distinct both of trades transmitted in workshops and on building sites, and of the scientific knowledge taught in universities.'[18]

Interest in this prescriptive literature has also developed transnation-ally and comparatively. For example, studies on cameralism in Germany made it possible to better identify the emergence of 'technology' as a discipline and to question its relationships with state sciences and bureaucracy.[19] According to Beckmann, 'a very large range of trades – whatever the materials and the manufactured goods, have to carry out various works with the same purpose' adding that 'the work on the plane of a carpenter, the polishing of the glasses, the calendering of fabrics are activities following the same purpose of "surfacing the body"'.[20] The technologist thus intended to construct a general theory of operations across the trades, based upon a language of action. Although interpretations diverge, historians agree that such an endeavour was political because it provided administrators with a better knowledge of natural resources and the technical means for their exploitation. At the same time it improved techniques thanks to transfers across trades that fostered invention.

Joost Mertens, writing on France, stressed the part played by Louis-Sébastien Lenormand, author of the *Dictionnaire technologique* (published between 1822 and 1835 in twenty-two volumes) and a series of other manuals, and an active contributor to the rise of the technological magazine.[21] As a newly established professor of technology, Lenormand thought the mission of 'technology' was to promote the education of the industrious classes: his goal was to encourage workers to compare and transpose processes between trades that fostered their ingenuity. In his *Dictionnaire technologique*, Lenormand provided a double system of references to techniques that allowed comparison and cross-reference across different trades, either through analogy (printing, for instance, could be related to books, wallpapers, printed cotton, or earthenware) or to contiguous trades (for instance, watchmaking was connected to polishing, gilding, making springs, etc.). These classifications of work were very different from the institutional division of trades into guilds (although, as we shall see, cross-skills and interrelatedness produced complex connections, especially through subcontracting networks). They opened what Hélène Vérin has called 'un espace de la technique',[22] meaning the gaining of an autonomy from technical knowledge beyond guilds and trades, as well as academies. This explains why Lenormand claimed the civic virtue of the concept of 'Technology' which he connected to the Tennis Court Oath (*Serment du Jeu de Paume*, made on 20 June 1789, that transformed the Etats généraux into the National Assembly), hence to the birth of the nation and the desire for social harmony, leading to the abolition of old regime society based upon *corporations* and the hierarchy of orders (*la société de corps et d'ordres*).

In England, research has focused on the question of machinery, in the wake of Maxine Berg's work on industrial science and engineering, in what Andrew Ure called 'the philosophy of manufacture' or 'industrial economy.'²³ In a recent study, Joost Mertens compared the Lenormand dictionary to Andrew Ure's *Dictionary of Arts, Manufactures, and Mines* (1839–53): while Lenormand proposed an inclusive view of human activities, with a large emphasis on tooling and actors, Ure listed only processes, his purpose being to describe the transformation of materials by mechanical or chemical means into 'general objects of exchangeable value.'²⁴ 'Technology' thus became the science of the 'operative industry', aimed at lowering the cost of production. It was this 'Technology' that Karl Marx denounced in *The Capital*: this 'new modern science' which has as its principle to dissociate any process of production and discover instead 'the few main fundamental forms of motion, which, despite the diversity of the instruments used, are necessarily taken by every productive action of the human body; just as the science of mechanics sees in the most complicated machinery nothing but the continual repetition of the simple mechanical powers.'²⁵ This approach put an end to the ambition of a general technology of the arts and fostered a radical shift of the meaning of 'Technology.'

More generally speaking, for the whole period from the Renaissance to the nineteenth century, the better understanding of 'Technology', thanks to the gathering by historians of a corpus of fundamental writings, was crucial to the exhumation of the polysemy of the concept. These studies also suggested that the notion of 'Technology' should be analysed in the light of a diversity of contexts and uses, not just as a concept. It is in this direction, taking into account the various practices attached to the promotion of 'Technology', that new contributions have developed.

'Technology' in the Light of Practices

In his *Histoire intellectuelle de l'économie politique*, Jean-Claude Perrot advocated a 'concrete history of abstraction', claiming that 'we must stop seeing texts as the only vehicle of theories and also take into consideration the objects, the material devices' and 'the kinds of social and cultural practices' that are constitutive of abstraction.²⁶ Such an approach has gained favour among historians of culture and ideas in the past generation. This direction is also now followed by historians of 'Technology', encouraging them to expand the range of authors and texts that they consider.

Because 'Technology' was intended to foster communication and interrelatedness across trades, current approaches argue that the social and cultural practices of craftsmen also participated in the process of opening knowledge, quite the opposite of the cliché of artisans' secrecy.

The social basis of technological culture in the eighteenth century appears much wider than the circle of learned elite dealing with the codification of techniques. In many ways it was the artisans who first built a public space for techniques, for example by participating in learned societies like the societies of arts.[27] This European movement started in Paris in 1718, in the wake of an academic commission for a 'Description of Arts and Crafts'. But the Paris Société des Arts was mainly founded by watchmakers, and its rules stated that at least half of its fifty-two members should be practitioners. Each art, such as agriculture, 'works of silk, wool and thread', 'art of measuring time', 'metallic art', was entrusted to a mixed commission. For the arts of working glasses that related to optics, the society called on two geometer-opticians, a physicist, a mechanic, a chemist, a glassmaker, two opticians making glasses, and one enameller. The society inaugurated a contiguous and transverse sort of sociability, to ensure the progress of the 'methods followed in the practice of the arts'.[28] Although the society was unable to continue this innovative project beyond the 1730s (for several reasons and not just due to the pressure of the academicians),[29] it set up an open sociability that went on developing along diverse patterns over the century and encouraged academicians to give more importance to the observation of techniques and to the analysis by practitioners.[30] Especially after 1750, artisans had the opportunity to enter spheres of sociability such as the Société de l'Abbé Baudeau or, during the French Revolution, the clubs of inventors, illustrating artisanal mobilisation around the question of state support for invention when the *brevet* (patent) was created.[31] The model of these societies was the Society of Arts of London, created in 1753, a gathering of a learned elite but open to businessmen, which became a centre for technological knowledge.

The British historiography points to the fact that artisans and other practitioners not only participated in this scholarly movement but also that their cultural practices were integral to this innovative techno-logical culture. An example of this is how in shops and workshops all kinds of new objects and mechanisms were put on show and could be observed, in ways not dissimilar from those exhibited in the Society of Arts' repository. The watchmaker and mechanic Christopher Pinchbeck exhibited at the Society of Arts (of which he was a member) his mech-anical models, previously installed in his curiosity shop (which he also called a repository), alongside musical clocks, moving pictures and accessories, cases, watches, dices, globes, and jewellery.[32] The growth of technological prints such as 'how-to' leaflets published for commer-cial purposes, and other visual media, popularized comparative and analogical reasoning that were the basis of 'Technology'.

A whole range of research has revealed the rise of a diversified prescriptive literature, ranging from travelogues to books of secrets, different types of manuals and instructions for making new objects, which suggest both the participation of artisans in the writing of scholarly technology and the development of specific editorial forms aimed at commercialisation. On the learned side, Valérie Nègre has studied the treatises of artisan-builders who entered the scholarly world, and Dinah Ribard has analysed the treatises of craftsmen that she considers were 'moments of emergence of the intellectual work in the work'.[33] On the commercial side, historians are now encouraged to take account of the advertisement of techniques and of the useful literature such as 'how-to' leaflets and pamphlets which contained a variety of technological classifications and reasoning.[34] These practices intersected with the continual reissuing of Renaissance books of secrets until the nineteenth century, while other forms of technological literature developed as in the case of manuals such as the Roret textbooks.[35] This milieu of 'entrepreneurs in Technology' was driven by a burst of demand for new invented goods. For example, in 1769 the cutler Jean-Jacques Perret (who was involved in the debates on cemented steel and was supported by the Société des Arts of Geneva) published a treatise on handle razors of his invention, with codified drawing of the adequate gestures but the book was actually a catalogue of steels, stones and leathers, designed for the needs of consumers.[36] A few years later, the word 'Technology' appeared in commercial and technical magazines as a classification for advertisements of inventions in the Annales des Arts et Manufactures in 1800 and in the Almanach Sous Verre in 1804.[37] The gap between commercial and learned 'Technology' was blurring, while the latter's connection with markets, consumption, and workshops seemed more and more obvious. The craft economy, which had long been considered the antithesis of 'Technology' by contemporary technologists, and later by historians of technology, was at the forefront of the promotion of the science of the arts and of the process of codification of work into abstract representations.

'Technology' on the Shop Floor

To understand the role of crafts in the spread of technological thought, it is necessary to consider the transformation in the organisation of production created by increased demand in the eighteenth century. The dynamics between markets and techniques explain the rise of an operative knowledge among artisans. Research published in Britain has played a specific part in understanding this phenomenon and that by

Maxine Berg, in particular, has helped in the rethinking of the role of skills, abilities, and useful knowledge in the light of revisions relating to the Industrial Revolution through the demand factor. The eighteenth century gained autonomy in the historiography as a period of Smithian growth, based on a product economy. English historians emphasised the importance of the growing variety of consumer goods and of the continuous renewal of models to answer the need for distinct goods by the urban middle classes. In this context, the resulting technical culture should not to be confused with mechanisation and the search for the lowering of production costs, although this was also part of innovative efforts.[38]

Researchers have created a methodology that enables the interpretation of commercial archives as sources not only for the history of trade and commerce but also for the history of technology and invention. They have shown, for instance, that trade cards and catalogues expressed taste and design skills that were intrinsic to the meaning of invention in the Enlightenment.[39] Patterns displayed in trade catalogues have been shown to reveal the mixed-media composition of commodities and complementarities across entrepreneurs. Such scholarship shows how the transfer-skills and technological convergences reshaped the world of trades, transforming craftwork into commercial enterprises.

It is clear to historians working today that craftsmanship was deeply reshaped by this burst in consumerism. Networks of subcontracting reached a climax as it was impossible to manufacture such a diverse range of articles in a single workshop. This meant managing circuits along extensive operating chains, running a whole externalized process of production – hence coping with the coordination of widely 'distributed' knowledge. In relation to the spread of markets of production, the product economy intensified the inventive capacities (of tools, materials, models, quality improvements) based upon increasing ability to imitate, transpose, adapt shapes, materials, operations – a combining and synthetic activity of the mind. Helen Clifford, working on Huguenot connections in London, underlined the importance of 'the inter-disciplinarity of skills' that allowed great inventivity in the decorative arts: 'It was the universal importance and applicability of drawing, design and modelling that the Huguenots possessed, that enabled them to become indispensable.'[40] Whether through the segmentation of the process of production or inventive transfers, artisans actively participated in the constitution of what Vérin calls 'un espace de la technique.' In this context they developed an understanding of work as an operative, synthetic, and analogous process of tasks. The records of this artisanal 'Technology' that led to an abstraction of work (though not a science or a theory) are the archives of daily practices, for marketing products and managing of subcontractors. Account books of London artisan–entrepreneurs working in assembling trades are illustrative of this technological culture.[41]

London was at the core of product differentiation in Europe, with extreme specialisation of activities, complementarities between districts and coordination of multiple firms and individuals. It specialised in the production of highly composite goods, ranging from watchmaking to furniture making, coach making, goldsmithing, hardware, or toyware that covered all kinds of accessories and curiosities (ornaments, household items, dress, instruments, etc.) made of alloys, of assembled and mixed materials, and of fitted components. The key to this economy was quality in assembling, adjusting and finishing, hence also the importance of repairs. The enlargement of the markets for these complex items involved the production of pieces and fixtures, their resale and storage, and their assembly in finishing workshops. Each supplier and operator had a function in these networks of production that superimposed onto trade identities – like fitting, a skill that was highly praised. In this context, tasks and operations became more visible in artisans' account books – well before the calculation of industrial costs.

The archives of watchmakers Benjamin Gray and Benjamin Vulliamy, at the heart of the economy of the repair and assembly in London, are illustrative of this trend. They mobilised numerous subcontractors and kept detailed accounts of their management over three generations. Their intent was not to produce or transmit any knowledge: they were kept for the purpose of calculating prices – for customers and for subcontractors. In this process the different tasks involved had to be described, noted, and thus revealed in the calculation of prices.

In the 1700s, 80 per cent of the orders listed in Benjamin Gray's ledger concerned repair.[42] Only repairs were associated with tasks, either referring to generic activities such as 'mended' or 'cleaned' or to precise actions – replacement of precise parts, varnishing, polishing, or finishing – associated with the treatment of particular components. An order necessitated the listing of actions in the calculation of costs, and there were several coexisting ways of expressing this. On 2 June 1711 for example, the repair of Colonel Barry's watch ('mended'), required an entry in Benjamin Gray's ledger which bracketed together a series of tasks: tightening of the wheels, cleaning the dial, varnishing the inner case, polishing the case, installing a new glass, and cleaning the watch. This correspondence between verbs and components was even clearer when the recording was done in a tabular fashion: the repair of Collins's watch included six headings that deconstructed the verb 'mended' into a combination of tasks required on individual components and fittings. In

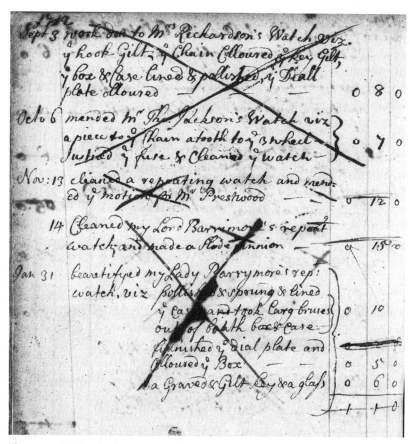

Figure 2.1   Benjamin Gray's account book: 'Beautified my Lady Barrymore's rept. [repeating] watch', 31 January 1712.

some cases, the chain of tasks needed for the mending of one component was detailed. For example for the repair of a watchcase, Benjamin Gray listed polishing, sponging, varnishing (a process of surfacing), then actions of remodelling of the case, with a small bracket for each work process (surfacing and remodelling). Verbal logic took the precedence over that of the product, of its components, hence of its topography (figure 2.1).

Whilst this level of detail was rare in Benjamin Gray's ledger, such an operative formulation structured the sequencing of the account books of his successor, Benjamin Vulliamy from 1798.[43] These 'technographic' practices were widely shared. Beyond their profusion and although they do not follow any established norms, they expressed the rise of a rationalisation of action in trades based upon finishing and assembling, crucial

54 LILIANE HILAIRE-PÉREZ

to the 'world of goods'. The changing patterns of consumption that led artisans to massively produce innovative and fashionable goods neces-sitated they coordinate multiple tasks and to account the interventions of subcontractors. This had an impact on the management of account books where a verbal and codified language developed that expressed an attempt to reduce the diversity of practices to a few generic actions. These accounts were embedded into a merchant economy, the economy of the product; they did not aim to facilitate any cost reduction, as in industry,[44] but to control payments with subcontractors and customers. Although the components of the products were giving coherence to the accounts, this topographical logic was gradually substituted by an operative notation of actions. In that sense, it is possible to consider artisans' account books as archives for the history of 'technology' and as providing forgotten paths into the rationalisation of work practices.

Conclusion

The history of 'Technology' as the science of arts and of purposive actions is most often associated with the learned production of scientists and technologists who codified techniques. However, a technological ration-ality also developed in the artisanal and market-driven environment, via a commercial printed production, and, in a less visible way, in the business records of artisans–entrepreneurs. Because of an increase in the consumption of goods which were varied, composite, and imitative, and which required numerous arrangements of pieces and fixtures and the coordination of a chain of artisans, the artisans–entrepreneurs developed a language of action used in keeping their accounts. The artisanal ledgers provide 'technographies', showing increasing sophisti-cation of the use of verbs and modular locutions. The verbal language, which was central in the emergence of 'Technology' as a science of activity, therefore also belonged to the craft culture. The rise of this language of action in account books raises the question of the bridges and mediations which might have existed between practitioners and learned technologists, since they spoke the same language or better say the same syntax that expressed their sharing a same concept, the operation of which was the basis of the abstraction of work into labour.

Notes

1   George Wilson, *What Is Technology? An Inaugural Lecture Delivered in the University of Edinburgh on November 7, 1855* (Edinburgh: Sutherland & Knox, 1855); Robert G.W. Anderson, "'What Is Technology?'": Education through Museums in the Mid-Nineteenth Century', *British Journal for the History of Science* 35 (1992): 169–84.

2   Wilson, *What Is Technology?*, 4.

3   Ibid.

4   Guillaume Carnino, Jochen Hoock, Liliane Hilaire-Perez, eds., *La technologie générale. Johann Beckmann Entwurf der algemeinen Technologie / Projet de technologie générale (1806)* (Rennes: Presses universitaires de Rennes, 2017).

5   Eric Schatzberg, 'Technik Comes to America: Changing Meanings of Technology before 1930', *Technology & Culture* 47, no. 3 (2006): 486–512.

6   Wilson, *What Is Technology?*, 3–4 quoting Friedrich Ludwig Knapp, *Chemical Technology, or Chemistry Applied to the Arts and Manufactures* (London: H. Baillière, 1848–51), 1:1.

7   Joost Mertens, 'Le déclin de la technologie générale: Léon Lalanne et l'ascendance de la science des machines', *Documents pour l'histoire des techniques* 20 (2011): 107–17.

8   Lionel Dufaux, *L'Amphithéâtre, la galerie et le rail. Le Conservatoire des arts et métiers, ses collections et le chemin de fer au XIXe siècle* (Rennes: Presses universitaires de Rennes, 2017); Géraldine Barron, *Edmond Pâris et l'art naval. Des pirogues aux cuirassés* (Toulouse: Presses universitaires du Midi, 2019); Marie-Sophie Corcy and Liliane Hilaire-Pérez, 'Le premier catalogue des collections du Conservatoire des arts et métiers (1818), jalon d'une pensée technologique', paper presented at the conference Nos Jeunes Années. Les début du conservatoire des arts et métiers, 1794-1830, CNAM, 2 October 2018.

9   Marcel Mauss, 'Les techniques du corps (1934–1936)', *Sociologie et anthropologie (1950)* (Paris: Presses universitaires de France, 1995).

10 André-Georges Haudricourt, *La Technologie, science humaine. Recherches d'histoire et d'ethnologie des techniques* (Paris: MSH, 1988).

11 Joel Mokyr, *Gifts of Athena: Historical Origins of the Knowledge Economy* (Princeton: Princeton University Press, 2004).

12 Dagmar Schäfer and Marcus Popplow, 'Technology and Innovation within Expanding Webs of Exchange', in *The Cambridge World History. Part III: Growing Interactions*, eds. Benjamin Z. Kedar and Merry E. Wiesner-Hanks (Cambridge: Cambridge University Press, 2015), 309–38; Karel Davids, 'Bridging Concepts', *Isis* 106, no. 4 (2015): 835–9.

13 Pamela H. Smith, *The Body of the Artisan: Art and Experience in the Scientific Revolution* (Chicago: University of Chicago Press, 2004); Matteo Valleriani, 'The Epistemology of Practical Knowledge,' in *The Structures of Practical Knowledge*, ed. Matteo Valleriani (Dordrecht: Springer, 2017), 1–19.

14 Jacques Guillerme and Jan Sebestik, 'Les commencements de la technologie,' *Thalès* (1968), republished in *Documents pour l'histoire des techniques* 14 (2007): 49–122.

15 Jan Sebestik, 'Les commencements de la technologie. Postface/préface,' *Documents pour l'histoire des techniques* 14 (2007): 124.

16 Ibid., 126.

17 Pascal Dubourg-Glatigny and Hélène Vérin, eds., *Réduire en art. La technologie de la Renaissance aux Lumières* (Paris: MSH, 2008).

18 Hélène Vérin, 'Rédiger et réduire en art. Un projet de rationalisation des pratique,' in *Réduire en art. La technologie de la Renaissance aux Lumières*, eds. Pascal Dubourg-Glatigny and Hélène Vérin (Paris: MSH, 2008), 22.

19 Guillaume Garner, *État, économie, territoire en Allemagne. L'espace dans le caméralisme et l'économie politique, 1740–1820* (Paris: EHESS, 2005); Thorsten Meyer, Marcus Popplow, and Günter Bayerl, *Technik, Arbeit und Umwelt in der Geschichte: Günter Bayerl zum 60. Geburtstag* (Münster: Waxmann, 2006); Andre Wakefield, *The Disordered Police State. German Cameralism as Science and Practice* (Chicago: University of Chicago Press, 2009).

20 Carnino, Hoock, and Hilaire-Pérez, *La technologie générale*, 21.

21 Joost Mertens, 'Technology as the science of the Industrial Arts: Louis-Sebastien Lenormand (1757–1837) and the Popularization of Technology,' *History and Technology* 18, no. 3 (2002): 203–31.

22 Hélène Vérin, *La gloire des ingénieurs. L'intelligence technique du XVIe au XVIIIe siècle* (Paris: Albin Michel, 1993).

23 Maxine Berg, *The Machinery Question and the Making of Political Economy, 1815–1848* (Cambridge: Cambridge University Press, 1980).

24 Joost Mertens, 'The Mere Handicrafts: Ure's *Dictionary* (1839–1853) Compared with the *Dictionnaire Technologique* (1822–1835),' *Documents pour l'histoire des techniques*, 19 (2010): 277–85.

25 Karl Marx, *The Capital. A Critique of Political Economy*. Volume I. Book One: *The Process of Production of Capital* (1867) (London: Swann Sonnenschein, Lowrey & Co., 1887; Berlin: Dietz Verlag, 1990), 425.

26 Jean-Claude Perrot, 'Quelques préliminaires à l'intelligence des textes économiques,' *Une histoire intellectuelle de l'économie politique (XVIIe-XVIIIe siècle)* (Paris: EHESS, 1992), 7–60.

27 Roger Hahn, 'The Application of Science to Society: The Societies of Arts,' *Studies on Voltaire and the eighteenth century* 35 (1963): 829–36; Liliane Hilaire-Pérez, *L'invention technique au siècle des Lumières* (Paris: Albin Michel, 2000).

28 Hilaire-Pérez, *L'invention technique*, 190–208.

29 Paola Bertucci, *Artisanal Enlightenment. Science and the Mechanical Arts in Old Regime France* (New Haven: Yale University Press, 2017).

30 Arnaud Orain and Sylvain Laubé, 'Scholars versus Practitioners? Anchor Proof Testing and the Birth of a Mixed Culture in Eighteenth-Century France', *Technology and Culture* 58, no. 1 (2017): 1–34.

31 Hilaire-Pérez, *L'invention technique*, 208–23; Valérie Nègre, *L'Art et la matière. Les artisans, les architectes et la technique entre XVIIIᵉ et XIXᵉ siècles* (Paris: Garnier, 2017).

32 Liliane Hilaire-Pérez, *La pièce et le geste. Artisans, marchands et savoir technique à Londres au XVIIIᵉ siècle* (Paris: Albin Michel, 2013).

33 Nègre, *L'Art et la matière*; Dinah Ribard, 'Le travail intellectuel: travail et philosophie, XVIIᵉ-XIXᵉ-siècle', *Annales. Histoire, Sciences Sociales* 3 (2010): 715–42.

34 Maxine Berg and Helen Clifford, 'Commerce and the commodity: Graphic Display and selling new consumer goods in eighteenth-century England', in *Art Markets in Europe, 1400–1800*, eds. Michael North and David Ormrod (Aldershot: Ashgate, 1998), 187–200; Liliane Hilaire-Pérez and Marie Thébaud-Sorger, 'Les techniques dans l'espace public. Publicité des inventions et littérature d'usage au XVIIIᵉ siècle (France, Angleterre)', *Revue de synthèse* 127, no. 2 (2006): 393–442.

35 Joost Mertens, 'Éclairer les arts. Eugène Julia de Fontenelle (1780–1842), ses manuels Roret et la pénétration des sciences appliquées dans les arts et manufactures', *Documents pour l'histoire des techniques* 18 (2009): 95–112.

36 Jean-Jacques Perret, *La pogonotomie ou l'art d'apprendre à se raser soi-même, avec la manière de connoître toutes sortes de pierres propres à affiler tous les outils et instrumens ; et les moyens de préparer les cuirs pour repasser les rasoirs, la manière d'en faire de très bons ; suivi d'une observation importante sur la saignée* (Paris: Dufour, 1769).

37 Liliane Hilaire-Pérez and Marie Thébaud-Sorger, 'Les techniques dans la presse d'annonces au XVIIIᵉ siècle en France et en Angleterre : réseaux d'information et logiques participatives', in *Des techniques dans la presse à la presse technique*, eds. Patrice Bret, Konstantinos Chatzis, and Liliane Hilaire-Pérez (Paris: L'Harmattan, 2008), 7–38.

38 Maxine Berg, *Luxury and Pleasure in Eighteenth-Century Britain* (Oxford: Oxford University Press, 2005); Helen Clifford, *Silver in London: The Parker and Wakelin Partnership, 1760–1776* (New Haven: Yale University Press, 2004); John Styles, 'Product Innovation in Early Modern London', *Past & Present* 168 (2000): 124–69.

39 Berg and Clifford, 'Commerce and the Commodity'.

40 Helen Clifford, 'In Defence of the Toyshop: The Intriguing Case of George Willdey and the Huguenots', *Proceedings of the Huguenot Society* 27, no. 2 (1999): 171–88.

41 Clifford, *Silver in London*; Hilaire-Pérez, *La pièce et le geste*.
42 London Metropolitan Archives, Clockmakers' Company Library: GB
    0074 CLC/B/227–082: Benjamin Gray Collection.
43 The National Archives, Kew, Chancery Masters' Exhibits, C/104/58 II.
44 Neil McKendrick, 'Josiah Wedgwood and Cost Accounting in the
    Industrial Revolution', *Economic History Review* 23, no. 1 (1970): 45–67;
    Richard K. Fleischman, Keith Hoskin, and Richard Macve, 'The Boulton
    & Watt Case: The Crux of Alternative Approaches to Accounting
    History', *Accounting and Business Research* 25 (1995): 162–76.

3

Silence and Secrecy in Britain's Eighteenth-Century Ceramics Industry

Kate Smith

Knowledge, materials, energy, capital, and labour were vital to eighteenth-century manufacturing. In recent years, historians have considered how knowledge circulated between eighteenth-century manufactories, shaping production processes and the creation of new and novel goods during the British Industrial Revolution and the process of European industrialisation.[1] Scholars have also asked how knowledge circulated *within* manufactories and workshops to ensure innovation, standardization, and the development of new skills. Knowledge took multiple forms within eighteenth-century workshops. In response to Joel Mokyr's *The Enlightened Economy*, Maxine Berg and Liliane Hilaire-Pérez reminded historians of the significance of artisans and the tacit knowledge they possessed.[2] Their work prompts us to place greater emphasis on uncovering the nature of tacit knowledge in this period and the ways in which it contributed to economic change.

Questions concerned with the communication of tacit knowledge, its visibility and transferability loom large. When developing manufacturing processes and practices, how did contemporaries understand and circulate knowledge that was learned through practice and proved difficult to articulate? This chapter explores the communication and circulation of tacit knowledge within manufactories. It also examines how manufacturers actively worked to construct silences in the hope of ensuring that knowledge was *not* transmitted and did *not* move beyond their workshops. Eighteenth-century manufacturers understood that the creation and sustaining of silence was crucial and feared the transfer of knowledge from one business to another. Although manufacturers recognised the difficulties in transferring embodied knowledge across time and space, they simultaneously worked to limit its movement. This chapter examines instances of workshop practice, industrial tourism, and the movement of workers related to Josiah Wedgwood's (1730–1795) ceramic manufactory in North Staffordshire, to study tacit knowledge and skilled practice. In doing so, it sheds light on the nature of manufactories, knowledge production, and learning in eighteenth-century Britain.

Collaboration and Communication

Before the nineteenth century potters rarely, if ever, worked as lone artisans.[3] The nature of pottery production processes (particularly material refining) ensured that potters worked with others to create ceramic objects. Working collaboratively meant communicating design ideas and the material and tacit knowledge inherent in processes such as clay beating and throwing with those sharing the shop floor and those working on subcontracted processes elsewhere. Research by sociologists has underlined the importance of exploring the multiple ways in which groups and individuals transfer and negotiate tacit knowledge. Focusing on the workshop practices of car mechanics, sociologist Tim Dant has shown how mechanics interact with each other, tools, and materials to complete specific tasks of repair. Ranging from direct verbal instructions, to barely verbal suggestions, to bodily gestures, Dant's research has revealed the complexity of interhuman and intermaterial communicative strategies.[4] More broadly, theoretical insights on the material world and our relationship to it have prompted scholars to reconsider how each individual worker operated within a series of encounters that shaped their work.[5] Sociologists such as Richard Sennett and anthropologists such as Tim Ingold have explored how bodies carry out skilled work in communication with the material world.[6] In his 2008 book *The Craftsman*, Sennett argued that skill and understanding deepen through a slow process of feedback and communication with the physical world.[7] Materials, objects, and environments constantly change to create frictions, which serve to critique, correct, and develop tacit knowledge through practice.[8] Deepening skill and knowledge of the material world can only occur through interaction with it. Thus, humans need to be recognised as existing and developing within complex social worlds. As Fredrik Fahlander has argued, 'The social world is not simply a matter of differently empowered individuals that interact with things and each other; different kinds of materialities (things, natural features, animals, substances such as rain and snow etc.) often play crucial, although often sublime, roles in social development by just being there.'[9] At the same time Fahlander insists that 'materialities only have a potential in some situations to be social in the sense of stimulating, prompting or determining social action.'[10]

Josiah Wedgwood's correspondence records moments in which he and his workforce used repeated engagements with each other, materials, and tools, to solve production problems and improve production processes. The correspondence reveals that material artifacts played particular roles within workshop practice. By the 1760s, for example, most potteries in North Staffordshire regularly used moulds, casts, wheels, and lathes to reduce the 'risks' of workmanship and ensure that the products of their work would consistently reach set standards.[11] Steven Lubar has argued that designs, instructions, and gauges, 'make it easier to bring technological actions under the control of authority.'[12] By restricting the boundaries of work, greater control and standardization can be enacted. In this reading, tools created firmer boundaries within which potters operated. They were objects with which potters laboured and which defined the potential product of such labour in new, more precise ways. Eighteenth-century potteries saw a proliferation of tools in production processes. Nevertheless, not all tools succeeded. Certain tools failed constantly and all tools failed at least once. It is in their attempts to counter such failure that the voices of Josiah Wedgwood's workforce and their articulations of hard-won knowledge can be heard. In these instances, their communication suggests a desire to work together to solve the problems that tools presented. They employed embodied knowledge dispersed between groups of workers and objects, to create solutions.

In 1774, tablets, plaques, and medallions were an important part of the Wedgwood business. These intricate items featured a diversity of designs, including neoclassical motifs and the portrait silhouettes of famous individuals. A Wedgwood catalogue of the same year listed a total of ninety-three different tablet designs made in black basalt or white biscuit.[13] During this period Wedgwood also worked on creating tablets for his new jasper wares. Jasper ware was materially innovative, particularly in terms of its matt, biscuit finish and the possibilities of producing it in multiple different colours. It became a key component of British design and interior decoration in the late eighteenth century. Writing to his then business partner Thomas Bentley (1731–1780) on 22 August 1774, Wedgwood discussed the difficulties he experienced in adjusting the processes required to make tablets in this innovative material.[14] Wedgwood wanted to standardize the size and depth of tablets by creating evenly-sized balls that would be rolled out on perfectly flat surfaces. Wedgwood sought to do this by implementing the use of 'Balls & Rollers', but he confronted two problems. First, he noted the 'greater difficulty of having perfectly true planes to place them [tablets] upon, has hitherto prevented my attempting to use them [the rollers]'.[15] Clearly, without the seemingly simple addition of 'perfectly true planes', technology such as rollers, which worked with the planes (flat surfaces) to flatten the clay for tablets, was ineffective. Second, he struggled in 'making balls exactly round, & of the same size one with another.'[16] In 1774, he failed to solve these problems and it is uncertain as to whether he achieved it at a later date. Nevertheless, Wedgwood's pursuit of this technology suggests his confidence in the ability of tools to reduce risk and increase standards of execution.

Tools that did succeed often required lengthy periods of negotiation, involving numerous parties. A key piece of ceramic technology in the second half of the eighteenth century was the lathe, a wheel upon which the turner decorated, finished, and buffed each pot. Powered by women or children working foot treadles, the engine-turning lathe allowed vases and wares to be decorated in more intricate ways. Wedgwood used the engine-turning lathe to cut various repetitive patterns such as rosettes and crowns into the surface of the wares. Yet, despite its advantages, the introduction of this new technology proved difficult. Having acquired an engine-turning lathe, possibly as early as 1763, Wedgwood faced the problem of embedding it within his existing manufacturing processes and only used it regularly from 1767 onwards.[17] In trying to implement the engine-turning lathe Wedgwood regularly wrote to Thomas Bentley. In these writings Wedgwood asked Bentley to offer linguistic clarification and advice based on his readings of Charles Plumier's 1701 work *L'Art de Tourner*, a detailed treatise on lathes, which offered new insights both through its text and its seventy engravings.[18] A particular problem in using engine-turning lathes was deciphering the optimal position of various weights and springs in order to offset the 'tremulous shake, or motion.'[19] At the same time as he consulted Bentley and various texts, Wedgwood also entered into a series of negotiations and trials with his workers. It was these negotiations, rather than Bentley's suggestions, that finally allowed them to find the correct position of the weights and springs involved. Wedgwood noted that 'My Workmen have found out by practice, what you say, you are not certain of the reason why it is so.'[20] They had discovered, 'The utility of having the rest as near as possible to the work, & if you consider the tool as a Lever, the rest at its centre, & the work bearing against or rather upon, the end of the tool, as a weight, the reason I think will be very obvious.'[21] Bentley's attempts to correspond at a distance to solve the problem of the lathe proved inadequate. The skilled workmen achieved the 'knack' of the technology through practice and, as J.R. Harris has argued, 'the essence of a "knack" is its difficulty of communication.'[22] Rather than simply removing or reconstituting skilled bodies, the successful use of technology required the creative application of tacit knowledge through trial and error.

Once a certain tool was in use, evolving techniques and environments instigated fresh negotiations. Agate wares were particularly popular in the 1760s and 1770s. Made of coloured clay, or decorated with coloured slip or glazes, these bodies were well suited to ornamental and table wares. Mixing or wedging coloured clays created eye-catching combinations of colour and pattern. Potters mixed the coloured clays to create wares that imitated marble, agate, or stone. Wedgwood used this technique to create solid agate wares after 1768, although possibly before.[23] Mixing was a delicate process. As Wedgwood described to Bentley in 1776, when working with mixed clays, 'if the Workman gives the batts a twist edgeways, instead of keeping them flat when he puts them into the mould, a line of stringiness is produc'd which shews the Pott instead of finely variegated Pebble.'[24] Simply twisting the batt of clay edgeways whilst trying to flatten it into a mould had unattractive ramifications. The accuracy of potters' minor movements was essential to the creation of consistent quality. Once a technology was implemented it required further sensitive (and adaptive) use from skilled operatives to make it work effectively. Embodied knowledge remained vital to ceramic production processes and, as Wedgwood's correspondence reveals, it was central to the continual negotiations involved in manufacture in the eighteenth century.

Lubar has argued that designs, instructions, and gauges make it easier to bring action under control and to implement standardization. Analysing the introduction and use of tools in a specific eighteenth-century workshop, however, reveals the extent to which tools required constant negotiation to ensure effective implementation.[25] Alongside acting as sources of authority, guiding work and shaping practice, tools were simultaneously subject to processes of constant re-appropriation and learning. Making tools work shifted authority to skilled workers who were able to redraw the tools through active communication between each other, their bodies, environments, materials, and tools. At the same time, as workers negotiated and activated innovations, their skills were also reshaped anew. The implementation and maintenance of new technologies was highly dynamic and the constant negotiations required in successful use, enlarged the skills base. Nevertheless, while tacit knowledge and skilled practice were seen, heard, and noted in the historical record in moments of breakthrough and innovation, it is also important to recognise that much embodied knowledge went unnoticed and unrecorded, forming (or being forced to form) a silent backdrop to production processes.

Creating Silence

Broadening our understanding of the multiplicity of communications at work within workshop practices is important in comprehending the complex nature of skilled work and allows for closer tracking of embodied knowledge and skilled practice in the archive. Nevertheless, it continues to be difficult for historians to uncover such complexity. In fact, as the above examples show, it was often only moments of failure and blockage or breakthrough within the production process that came to be noted in the historical record. More broadly, the construction and nature of archives, as well as the concerns of eighteenth-century manufacturers and workers, create limitations in attempting to reveal a fuller picture of manufactory life and the communication of knowledge and collaborative work that was crucial to its development.

After recent wrangling, the Wedgwood Archive is now held (and will remain) at the Wedgwood Museum in Barlaston.[26] Together with the ceramic wares, moulds, models, and firing tests contained in the Wedgwood Museum itself, these documents and objects make up the Etruria Factory archive. Using this vast archive, historians have come to explore diverse topics: from factory discipline and marketing to consumption, science, and the Enlightenment.[27] Nevertheless, shaped by the archive and its extensive cache of correspondence scribed by Josiah Wedgwood, histories of the eighteenth-century Wedgwood manufactory have largely focused on Wedgwood. Through such readings Wedgwood often emerges as chief protagonist rather than engaged collaborator.[28] In contrast, tracking embodied knowledge and skilled practice in the Wedgwood archive reveals the collaborative nature of the manufactory and the problem solving that took place between workers.[29] These insights prompt further questions as to where and how sources for examining skilled work might be enriched and complicated. What other archives might be available for thinking about skill in eighteenth-century pottery manufactories? More particularly, how is it possible to get beyond moments of conflict and innovation to reveal the everyday practices undertaken in manufactories? If we are to understand the quiet accumulation of knowledge that allowed potters to be skilful, as well as the moments in which such knowledge solved problems, where might we look? Historians such as Leora Auslander and Pamela Smith underline the importance of reconstruction as a means of creating alternative archives for exploring the making of the material world.[30] Other scholars support such calls and have suggested the possibilities of operating technology found in museum collections or recreating particular scientific experiments.[31] At the same time close object analysis of large collections of similar, standardized wares might also reveal the slow everyday processes of making and improving. Alternatively, it is equally important to be aware of the silences present in the historical record (as well as in the past) and to interpret the meaning and significance of such pauses.[32]

Alongside critically engaging with the construction and nature of archives, it is also important to remember that due to concerns over industrial espionage, eighteenth-century manufacturers and workers were also keen to create silences around tacit knowledge and skilled practice. Creating and sustaining silence was crucial to eighteenth-century manufactories, which constantly feared the transfer of knowledge from one business to another. Manufacturers believed that industrial espionage was rife and thus actively worked to guard their secrets. As J.R. Harris has demonstrated, the French state, amongst others, sent spies to seek out information. In the 1730s and 1740s, the French state employed the academician Tiquet to travel through England and report on the development of various industries including coal-mining, dyeing, ceramics, and steel manufacture.[33] While manufacturers wished to protect their production processes from such international industrial spies, they also increasingly sought to shield them from local interests and the gaze of tourists. When recalling Josiah Wedgwood's introduction of the engine-turning lathe for example, Enoch Wood (1759–1840) described how once they had got the lathe to work, other potters such as John Shrigley and Thomas Wedgwood (1716–1773) had ventured to see it in action.[34] Yet, having attempted to make this viewing 'without asking leave of Josiah Wedgwood to see it' they were denied access and 'he [Wedgwood] ordered Cox, to shut the door against them.' Moreover, 'next time they came so Mr Cox refused to let them see the Lathes at work.'[35]

Alongside fears around the implementation of new technologies, manufacturers were also nervous about the transfer of design information to competitors. Writing in the nineteenth century, the potter Enoch Wood recalled how, when working for Thomas Whieldon (1719–1795) in the middle of eighteenth century, his father Aaron Wood (1717–1785) was 'always lock'd up, while he made the models & moulds for Whieldon which consisted of knife shafts, cabbage & other leaves for desert sets, crabtree handles & cabbage leaf spouts for Teapots, Coffee pots, Chocolate cups, Candlesticks etc.'[36] The design of objects was as important as the technologies that made them. In response to such threats, manufacturers used different strategies to secure their premises. Just as Whieldon insisted that Wood work behind locked doors, Josiah Wedgwood regularly asserted his right to prohibit the admission of certain individuals. Manufacturers needed to be on the alert in the

second half of the eighteenth century as advances in road and communication infrastructure allowed genteel Britons to tour the country more
extensively.[37] Significantly, industrial tourism emerged as an important
part of such tours. In her classic study of domestic tourism, Esther
Moir argued that visiting industrial sites allowed people to appreciate
the technological progress at work in England.[38] As industrial tourism
increased in the second half of the eighteenth century, visitors to ceramic
manufactories became a frequent occurrence. In 1771, Wedgwood noted
to Bentley how 'We have company at the works almost every day.'[39]
With an eye on industrial espionage, manufacturers scrutinized the
'company' that presented themselves and dismissed visitors they did
not wish to welcome.

During his travels in 1791 for example, the natural scientist Edward
Daniel Clarke expressed his initial anxiety about approaching the
Wedgwood factory. He remembered how he 'was fearful of being denied
admittance to the works, as I know that it is customary in these places
to introduce [a] stranger to what is called the store room, and then
dismiss them without any further trouble.'[40] Nevertheless, after sending
in their names to Wedgwood, Clarke received 'full permission from him
to see the whole of the manufactory, except the rooms where the black
and the new discovered blue ware is made, and these they never shew
to any one.'[41] The jasper wares described here had only been developed
by Wedgwood in the mid-1780s and clearly remained protected from
the threat of spies from other manufactories. Although visitors such as
Clarke, were welcomed (albeit partially) into these commercial concerns,
in visiting in the later decades of the eighteenth century, he was right to
feel apprehensive about his visit. In this period manufacturers became
increasingly aware of the need to manage numbers and exercise caution.
For instance, William Duesbury (1725–1786), manager of the Derby
Porcelain Factory until 1786, even went so far as to consider establishing
a visitor policy.[42] A draft of the policy asserted that 'W Duesbury respectfully requests the favour of any Company to honour him with inspecting
the Manufactory.'[43] Yet it went on to stipulate, more specifically, that
any company 'desiring to honour W Duesbury with this inspection
are respectfully requested to signify this instruction previous to their
coming down.'[44] Their reasoning for this procedure was simple: they
believed that a visit would 'be most interesting to strangers' when of
least inconvenience to the manager. The distinction highlighted by
both Clarke and Duesbury is that of 'stranger'. Gaining entrance was
an increasingly tentative procedure, if individuals were unknown to
the manufactory.

In seeking to prohibit visual access to certain objects and the processes that created them, manufacturers demonstrated their heightened awareness of the need to protect the 'novel' nature of the goods they manufactured. As Maxine Berg has argued, in the growing world of marketing and retailing, achieving 'novelty' and newness was key.[45] Producing wares that exhibited new materials or forms allowed manufacturers to distinguish themselves in the competitive (global) market for ceramics.[46] Manufacturers sought to conceal rather than communicate knowledge in order to ensure that their businesses remained solvent and successful by keeping their materials and wares new. Their desire to prohibit access must also be understood as part of a larger project embarked on by manufacturers who were canny enough to understand the importance of controlling how consumers perceived the production of their wares.[47] The valency of these motivations, rather than the threat of industrial espionage, is further strengthened when we consider that despite their fears it was rare that processes were 'stolen.' The complex mixtures of knowledge involved meant that transfer was difficult even when explicitly embarked upon. As Wedgwood wrote to Bentley in 1772, 'There may be no harm in knowing what value he sets upon the secret & then we can consider what is best to be done but I apprehend it wo'd be the same thing to our selling the secret of Throwing, Turning, or handling, which after all the instructions we could give the purchaser, it wo'd require several years actual practice before he could do anything to the purpose.'[48] Hence, simply viewing processes of production or machines at work rarely made the knowledge they contained legible or communicable to others. Tacit knowledge, honed through repeated bodily practices over years, proved difficult to transfer on sight.

Due to the difficulties inherent in communicating tacit knowledge and transferring it to others, one of the greatest fears in the ceramics industry was the movement of potters themselves. Wedgwood was constantly concerned with the possibilities of the whole-scale movement of skilled workers from the Potteries region in North Staffordshire to new potteries elsewhere (for example, in North America). He regularly became agitated by such perceived threats and in 1783 published *An Address to the Workmen in the Pottery, on the Subject of Entering into the Service of Foreign Manufacturers*. In this twenty-five-page pamphlet, Wedgwood warned 'If I was able to give you an account of all these emigrations of our workmen into foreign parts, with the severe distresses they have fallen into, it would look more like romance than real history.'[49] Parliamentary acts and various threats from Wedgwood encouraged potters to stay in Britain. At the same time, as Miranda Goodby argues,

until the early nineteenth century the prospect of migrating to North
America was not wholly alluring for potters in North Staffordshire
who enjoyed secure work opportunities and strong social ties. The
first substantial period of migration did not take place until the 1840s
when the market in North America expanded and the infrastructures
needed for manufacturing supplies (fuel, clay etc.) began to emerge.[50]
Nevertheless, by voicing fears around the migration of skilled workers,
Wedgwood reveals the importance of those he worked and negotiated
problems with on a daily basis. He valued their very bodies and the
archives of somatic memories of everyday working held there.

Conclusion

Focusing on Wedgwood's attempts to restrict the communication of
processes and skills through controlling industrial tours and ensuring his
workers remained, underlines the valuable nature of tacit knowledge to
eighteenth-century manufactories. Earned through long days of making
in workshops, learning materials, processes, and the gestures that ensured
their successful completion, potters' skills remain difficult to see in
the historical record. The moments of communication and articula-
tion that are present often relate to problem solving, innovations, and
breakthroughs rather than the everyday work of manufacture. Yet such
ordinary knowledge was vital to the continuation of such manufacturing
and its improvement, as Wedgwood's efforts to ensure his workers
remained in Staffordshire demonstrate. Potters' everyday work and the
knowledge they accrued from such experience often formed the basis
from which problems could be solved and new materials and tools
could be successfully embedded in manufacturing processes. While it
is difficult to find such evidence in extant historical archives, it emerges
in the importance given to keeping Staffordshire potters in Staffordshire
and in the silencing that such acts suggest.

Notes

1   Helen Clifford, 'Concepts of Invention, Identity and Imitation in the
    London and Provincial Metal-Working Trades 1750–1800', *Journal of Design
    History* 12, no. 3 (1999): 241–55; Helen Clifford, 'Innovation or Emulation?
    Silverware and Its Imitations in Britain 1750–1800: The Consumers Point of
    View', *History of Technology* 23 (2001): 59–80; Maxine Berg, 'From Imitation to
    Invention: Creating Commodities in Eighteenth-Century Britain', *Economic
    History Review* 55, no. 1 (2002): 1–30.

2 Joel Mokyr, *The Enlightened Economy: An Economic History of Britain 1700 to 1850* (New Haven and London: Yale University Press, 2009); Maxine Berg, 'The Genesis of Useful Knowledge', *History of Science* 45 (2007): 123–33; Liliane Hilaire-Pérez, 'Technology as Public Culture in the Eighteenth Century: The Artisans' Legacy', *History of Science* 45 (2007): 135–53.

3 Sarah Richards, *Eighteenth-Century Ceramics: Products for a Civilised Society* (Manchester and New York: Manchester University Press, 1999), 50.

4 Tim Dant, 'The Work of Repair: Gesture, Emotion and Sensual Knowledge', *Sociological Research Online* 15, 3, 7 (2010), n.p.

5 Bruno Latour, *Reassembling the Social: An Introduction to Actor-Network Theory* (Oxford: Oxford University Press, 2005); Manuel De Landa, *A New Philosophy of Society: Assemblage Theory and Social Complexity* (London: Continuum, 2006).

6 Richard Sennett, *The Craftsman* (London: Penguin, 2008); Tim Ingold, *Making: Anthropology, Archaeology, Art and Architecture* (Abingdon: Routledge, 2013).

7 Sennett, *The Craftsman*, 44.

8 Also see Glenn Adamson on the importance of frictions and resistance: Glenn Adamson, *Thinking Through Craft* (Oxford and New York: Berg, 2007).

9 Frederik Fahlander, 'Differences That Matter: Materialities, Material Culture and Social Practice', in Håkon Glørstad and Lotte Hedeager, eds., *On the Materiality of Society and Culture* (Lindome: Bricoleur Press, 2008), 131.

10 Fahlander, 'Differences that Matter', 134.

11 David Pye, *The Nature and Art of Workmanship* (London: Studio Vista, 1971), 7.

12 Steven Lubar, 'Representation and Power', *Technology and Culture* 36 (1995), S55.

13 Robin Reilly, *Wedgwood* (London: Stockton Press, 1989), 1: 576.

14 Josiah Wedgwood and Thomas Bentley went into partnership in 1768.

15 Wedgwood Museum Trust (WMT hereafter), MS E25-18554, 'Letter from Josiah Wedgwood to Thomas Bentley', 22 August 1774.

16 Ibid.

17 Reilly, *Wedgwood*, 1: 306.

18 Ibid., 691.

19 WMT, MS E25-18136, 'Letter from Josiah Wedgwood to Thomas Bentley', 16 February 1767.

20 Ibid.

21 Ibid.

22 John R. Harris, 'Skills, Coal and British Industry in the Eighteenth Century', *History* 61 (1976): 182.

23 Reilly, *Wedgwood*, 1: 343.

24 WMT, MS E25-18647, 'Letter from Josiah Wedgwood to Thomas Bentley', 27 January 1776.

25 Lubar, 'Representation and Power', S55.

26 Caroline Davis, 'Wedgwood Collection Saved for the Nation by £2.74m of Public Donations', *The Guardian*, 3 October 2014. The archive for Josiah Wedgwood's Etruria factory contains four key collections: the 'Etruria Collection', primarily made up of Josiah Wedgwood's personal correspondence; the 'Liverpool Collection', containing papers from the company up until Josiah II's death in 1843; the 'Mosely Collection', which includes Wedgwood family correspondence from the eighteenth and nineteenth century; and finally the 'Barlaston Collection', made up of factory records from the 1930s to the 1950s.

27 Neil McKendrick, John Brewer, and J.H. Plumb, *The Birth of a Consumer Society: The Commercialization of Eighteenth-Century England* (London: Europa Publications, 1982); Maxine Berg, *Luxury and Pleasure in Eighteenth-Century Britain* (Oxford: Oxford University Press, 2005); Mokyr, *The Enlightened Economy*; Robert C. Allen, *The British Industrial Revolution in Global Perspective* (Cambridge: Cambridge University Press, 2009).

28 See particularly, Neil McKendrick, 'Josiah Wedgwood: An Eighteenth-Century Entrepreneur in Salesmanship and Marketing Techniques', *Economic History Review* 12, no. 3 (1960): 408–33; Neil McKendrick, 'Josiah Wedgwood and Factory Discipline', *Historical Journal* 4, no. 1 (1961): 30–55; Neil McKendrick, 'Josiah Wedgwood and Cost Accounting in the Industrial Revolution', *Economic History Review* 23, no. 1 (1970): 45–67. More recently, see Allen, *The British Industrial Revolution in Global Perspective*, 238–71.

29 These arguments are explored in greater depth in Kate Smith, *Material Goods, Moving Hands: Perceiving Production in England, 1700–1830* (Manchester: Manchester University Press, 2014), 83–120.

30 Pamela H. Smith, 'In the Workshop of History: Making, Writing and Meaning', *West 86th* 19, no. 1 (2012): 4–31; Leora Auslander, Amy Bentley, Leor Halevi, H. Otto Sibum, and Christopher Witmore, 'AHR Conversation: Historians and the Study of Material Culture', *American Historical Review* 114, no. 5 (2009): 1354–1404.

31 See Klaus Staubermann, 'What Machine Tools Can Tell Us about Historic Skills and Knowledge', *International Journal for the History of Engineering and Technology* 80, no. 1 (2010): 119–32; Peter Heering and Roland Wittje, eds., *Learning by Doing: Experiments and Instruments in History of Science Teaching* (Stuttgart: Franz Steiner Verlag, 2011).

32 See William Pooley on the importance of giving attention to phenomenological, cultural, coded, and indifferent silences: William Pooley, 'Silences of the People', The Many-Headed Monster Blog: https://manyheadedmonster.wordpress.com/2015/07/10/silences-of-the-people/.

33 J.R. Harris, *Industrial Espionage and Technology Transfer: Britain and France in the Eighteenth Century* (Aldershot and Brookfield: Ashgate, 1998), 36.

34 Potteries Museum and Art Gallery (PMAG hereafter), Enoch Wood Papers, PM 1/1/2, 'Compendium Volume of Enoch Wood's Evidence and Recollections', 1834–40; 53.

35 Ibid.

36 Ibid., 16.

37 Ian Ousby, ed., *James Plumptre's Britain: The Journals of a Tourist in the 1790s* (London: Hutchinson, 1992), 10.

38 Esther Moir, *The Discovery of Britain: The English Tourists, 154–1840* (London: Routledge & K. Paul, 1964), 97.

39 WMT, LH W/M 1441, 'Letter from Josiah Wedgwood to Thomas Bentley', 7 September 1771.

40 Edward Daniel Clarke, *A Tour through the South of England, Wales, and Part of Ireland, Made during the Summer of 1791* (London: R. Edwards, 1793), 362.

41 Ibid.

42 Although a draft note on this policy survives in the Derby Local Studies Library (hereafter DLSL), it is not dated. DLSL, DL82 6/31, 'Draft of Memorandum from William Duesbury'.

43 Ibid.

44 Ibid.

45 Maxine Berg, 'Cargoes: The Trade in Luxuries from Asia to Europe', in *Empire, The Sea and Global History: Britain's Maritime World, c. 1763–c. 1840*, ed. David Cannadine (New York and Hampshire: Palgrave Macmillan, 2007), 60.

46 Robert Batchelor, 'On the Movement of Porcelains: Rethinking the Birth of Consumer Society as Interactions of Exchange Networks, 1600–1750', in *Consuming Cultures, Global Perspectives: Historical Trajectories, Transnational Exchanges*, eds. Frank Trentmann and John Brewer (Oxford and New York: Berg, 2006), 95–122; Robert Finlay, *The Pilgrim Art: Cultures of Porcelain in World History* (Berkeley, Los Angeles and London: University of California Press, 2010); Anne Gerritsen and Stephen McDowall, 'Global China: Material Culture and Connections in World History', *Journal of World History* 23, no. 1 (2012): 3–8.

47 Smith, *Material Goods, Moving Hands*, 60.

48 WMT, MS E25-18357, 'Letter from Josiah Wedgwood to Thomas Bentley', March 1772.

49 Josiah Wedgwood, *An Address to the Workmen in the Pottery, On the Subject of Entering into the Service of Foreign Manufacturers* (Newcastle, 1783).

50 Miranda Goodby, '"Our Home in the West": Staffordshire Potters and Their Emigration to America in the 1840s', *Ceramics in America* (2003): http://www.chipstone.org/article.php/75/Ceramics-in-America-2003/.

4

Is Small Beautiful? Workshop Organisation, Technology, and Production in South India, 1700–1960

David Washbrook

Maxine Berg's contributions to economic history have been many and varied. Beginning with inquiries into technology in the British Industrial Revolution, she has considered both the broader nature of that 'revolution' and its origins. The latter question took her into the commercial revolution that preceded it and, inevitably, to the global trade in 'luxury' goods that put Indian textiles at the centre of the world economy before the late eighteenth century.[1] Her most recent work has carried her into the history of Indian textiles themselves where she has sought also to bring their remarkable history forward into the present day with special focus on Kutch where premodern technologies of production have become married to modern methodologies of marketing: selling 'medievally-manufactured' goods to twenty-first century global consumers often through 'digital' systems of communication and payment.[2] For western historians, honed to think of modernity as unilineal and homogenous, the ways of the Indian economy rarely appear less than paradoxical.

The Importance of Being Small

This chapter is focused on one such paradox – and one which brings together several of the different strands of Maxine's rich researches. It concerns the persistence of 'smallness' in Indian organisations of production with special reference to the textile industry and even more special reference to southern India. This 'smallness', most obviously expressed in the scale of manufacturing units, has had significant effects on the adoption (and, indeed, invention) of appropriate technologies. Even Kay's celebrated flying-shuttle made demands for scale that were too large for most south Indian weaving households to meet until the dawn of the twentieth century.[3] By contrast, light wooden-framed looms were adapted for centuries to support production of the most sophisticated, multithread fabric designs known to man.[4]

The persistence of 'smallness' in Indian manufacturing frequently defied what many would see as the logic of modern history. While household methods of production may have been near-universal in the world before the first Industrial Revolution, they were steadily challenged and overtaken in the principal centres participating in the global economy from the middle decades of the nineteenth century: when 'work' and 'home' became increasingly separated. However, the shift was largely 'resisted' in India until well into the twentieth century although it did appear to be catching up with the country by its middle decades when, from the 1930s to the 1960s, India experienced its own 'factory age' of large-scale and heavy-industrial development.[5] But, then, the motor started to go into reverse and to shed factory workers and 'formal' (i.e. contractual and regulated) relations of wage labour. From over 40 per cent in the 1970s, the proportion of non-agricultural workers in the 'formal' economic sector has fallen to around 20 per cent today (which, in turn, represents only 10 per cent of the total labour force). Eighty-plus per cent of India's registered manufacturing enterprises employ ten workers or less.[6] In Tamilnadu in 2010, more than 700,000 families were sustained by household hand- or power-looms alone.[7] The textile industry has been in the vanguard of the return to 'smallness' where, as Jan Breman has seen, outsourcing to home- and/or small workshop-based power-looms has become the dominant mode of production (again).[8]

The latest revisionist historiography of the textile industry suggests that 'smallness' never really went away. Doug Haynes and Tirthankar Roy have argued that, while the eyes of economic historians have been drawn towards the icons of India's modern economic development – steel factories, power plants and hydroelectric dams – they have overlooked other and no less significant processes and dynamics. In particular (and par excellence in the textile industry), household and extended household (i.e. small workshop) forms of production did not merely survive the onslaught of the factory: they revived and thrived as a result of it. From the late nineteenth century, Indian hand-loomed cloth started to find new markets overseas, as well as at home, and to relaunch a process of expansion which has been near continuous ever since.[9] Today the small workshop economy is responsible for the overwhelming bulk of industrial employment – and hence earnings and hence consumption.

Without it, there would be very little economy at all. Roy, in particular, has related the Indian case to Kaoru Sugihara's wider thesis of an
alternative 'labour-intensive' pathway to industrialisation, which is
characteristic of Asian experience in contrast to that of 'the West'.[10]

So why, exactly, has 'smallness' persisted and/or returned? In looking
at the historiography of the issue, it is hard not to be struck by how
far the assumptions of the historians exploring it have come to shift
over the last thirty years and, along with that shift, how far perceptions
of the *problematique* which it represents have come to change – not
least as those historians themselves have been moved from location in
industrial to postindustrial societies.

Smallness as Failure

Until the 1980s, the 'problem' was largely seen in terms of how Indian
methods of production had 'failed' to innovate technologically or adapt
to changing market conditions: which assumed that – for whatever
reasons – they should have done, in effect should have 'modernised'
along the lines first seen in the British Industrial Revolution.[11] The issue
was first put to the Indian textile industry at the point of that revolution:
why, given the predominant role that India then played in preindustrial
(cotton) textile manufacture, had it not led mechanisation but allowed
itself to be overtaken by a competitor from a place which did not even
produce the raw material and was extremely clumsy at handling it?[12]

The issue then developed towards the second question of why, once
the new technologies of production had been invented elsewhere, India
should have remained so passive across the nineteenth century and not
adopted them but allowed its erstwhile markets at home and, especially,
abroad to be taken over with little competitive response. Even the industrial spinning of yarn did not get under way in India until the 1860s
or become widespread until the 1880s. Before the First World War, the
quantity of Indian industrially woven cloth remained much less than
that imported or produced on handlooms.[13]

Explanations offered for India's 'missed opportunity' to lead the world
have been many and varied, and unsurprisingly so. The question of why
Britain itself had an industrial revolution (and, even, if it did) has always
been controversial with different historians offering different readings of
the evidence. How much more difficult, then, to specify why somewhere
else did not undergo the same ultimately indeterminate experience?
However, asking questions in this way does presuppose that the event
under consideration should have happened unless something prevented
it. But why should it be presupposed that because India excelled at

preindustrial textile manufacture, it should necessarily lead the world in industrial manufacture too? This is even more the case because, as David Landes argued in his *Unbound Prometheus* (1969), technological innovation has almost always involved shifts in geographical location: since it is cheaper to invest in green- than in brown-field sites that need to be cleared of obsolescent technologies first.[14] Connectedly, what incentives did eighteenth-century Indian textile manufacturers have to invest in new technologies when they were already dominant in the world market of their time?

The question gains greater coherence when applied to the later context of the nineteenth century after the Industrial Revolution had happened in Britain – or, at least, after the first industrial textile machinery had been invented and, notionally, become available to the world. Why did Indian manufacturers limit and delay its adoption? Here, the historical literature has been divided between analyses critiquing colonialism and those laying blame on Indian society itself for 'backwardness' and/or obstruction. Famously from Karl Marx (quoting Governor General William Bentinck), a combination of Britain's colonial rule and industrial revolution was seen to have devastated textile manufacturing and '[left] the bones of the cotton weavers ... bleaching the plains of India.'[15] Moreover, from the perspective of Indian nationalists (if not Marx), colonial rule also prevented the rise of a modern textile industry it in order to keep Indian markets captive to British producers.[16]

On the other side, and informed more by neoclassical or 'liberal' economics, a countercase has also long been made that, if not very supportive of Indian industrial enterprise, British rule was not entirely inimical to it and provided, if inadvertently, sets of conditions – free markets, improved transportation, a rule of law – notionally conducive to its development. If little 'big' industry did actually develop, this was due to the inherited 'backwardness' of the Indian economy – its poverty and lack of endowment – and/or the 'obstructions' posed to economic rationality by 'traditional' forms of society, especially those manifested in the relations of caste, religion, and gender.[17]

The debate between these positions raged strongly across the post-independence generation (1950–70s) but has noticeably died down in recent years. In part, this may be because – while damaging the Indian economy in various ways and, certainly, always seeking to put British interests first – it has never been clear why colonialism should have wanted to impoverish India entirely nor that, with specific reference to textiles, it actually did.[18] Rich colonies are more lucrative to exploit than poor ones and, at least after the 1813 Charter Act freed British enterprise from East India Company monopoly, British capitalists were not confined to investing only in British production but could set up factories in India too. And so they did in the second half of the nineteenth century when a large part of the world jute industry was transferred from Dundee to Calcutta.[19] Admittedly, until the 1840s, Britain attempted to control the spread of textile machinery, whose export was formally illegal. But this prohibition never prevented it from leaking out to other parts of the world – even within the empire. As early as the 1770s, an attempt was made to set up silk-thread factories in Calcutta, and between 1818 and 1829 at least three further attempts were made (by private Anglo-Indian investors) to set up cotton-spinning factories in Broach, Pondicherry, and Calcutta.[20] However, and for reasons seemingly unconnected to prohibitions on the import of machinery, all three attempts failed.[21] Moreover, when industrial methods of cotton textile production did start to be adopted on a greater scale in the last third of the nineteenth century nothing the British did could prevent it from expanding.

Also, the arguments supposing economic 'backwardness' and social obstruction hardly stand up these days. As our knowledge of premodern India has grown, so our appreciation of the sophistication of its 'traditional' endowment and infrastructure has risen. India may not have had good roads but a combination of (*banjara*) pack caravans, seaborne traffic around the peninsular coastline, and inland shipping along waterways did not mean that it lacked all transport facilities. At the height of handloom manufacturing in the seventeenth and eighteenth centuries, large quantities of cotton grown in western India (especially Broach) found their way to weavers in the east, especially in Bengal, which grew very little of the crop itself. The roads that the East India Company eventually built shifted the direction of trade more than automatically increasing its volume or reducing its costs.[22]

The arguments that 'big' industry was precluded by social obstructions of one kind or another are no less difficult to sustain. This is not to say, of course, that economic activity was not inflected by sociocultural conventions such as caste, religion, and gender (as we shall take up later). A common objection heard in South India by officials of the Department of Industry, who tried to disseminate the flying shuttle at the end of the nineteenth century, was what would a weaver's wife and children do if they were not standing by his loom to hand-throw the shuttle back to him?[23] Equally, a gendered labour force similar to that working in Britain's first factories was never likely to appear in India: families and castes did not regularly abandon their daughters and small children to be drafted into dark satanic mills or other public workplaces outside patriarchal control.

However, this scarcely meant that, when other incentives were strong enough, Indian workers were not prepared to modify or even abandon some of their social conventions. The flying shuttle did become widely adopted by the early twentieth century when conditions changed to make it more marketable, and women and girls did come to work outside the home and, even, to take up factory employment (if never on a wide scale) when alternative employments failed. Social conventions are rarely unbending in the face of hard economic necessity.

The central difficulty with all these formulations, as noted earlier, is their assumption that 'modernity' – in this case represented by the shift to large-scale factory industrialisation – is normal, universal, and bound to happen unless something, be it colonialism or tradition, intervenes to prevent it. But, again, why should this be assumed? In a brilliant satirical essay on the Bombay textile industry, Raj Chandavarkar showed how the reasoning behind modernisation theory is teleological, proceeding from known ends to predestined means. In particular, it overlooks the need to specify the mechanisms through which historical change actually takes place, and it fails to address issues of context, which may alter reasoning and take the logic of development towards conclusions other than the universal replication of the British/western industrial experience.[24]

Smallness as Success

Perhaps for this reason, approaches to the question of 'smallness' have moved in a different direction in recent years. Rather than being seen as the result of a 'failure', smallness now has started to be viewed in a more positive light as a response to specific contextual conditions. Also, rather than a manifestation of rigid and unchanging 'tradition', it has started to be considered in terms of different kinds of adaptation and innovation. The position is put especially strongly in the work of Doug Haynes and Tirthankar Roy on artisanal and small-scale manufacture. Noting not only the survival but also the success of such manufacture in India, at least from the later nineteenth century, they seek to show both how it was favoured by prevailing economic conditions and how it was supported more than threatened by the arrival of 'big' industry.[25]

The market for Indian textiles, for example, has always been highly segmented with consumers favouring innumerable 'niches' reflective of elaborate caste, status, and religious preferences and needs. This gives rise to a high degree of specialisation in the production of cloth, which in turn favours small-scale and specialist methods of production. Indeed, it is not clear that some such goods – for example, the Kanchipuram silk marriage sari adopted in elite circles in the south – could be produced by methods of mass manufacture or would retain much value if they could. The Kanchipuram sari's prestige comes from the golden thread hand-embroidered around its edge.

Also, a certain conjuncture with 'modernity' has helped. Industrially spun yarn, once it became plentiful in the Indian market from the later nineteenth century, reduced the cost of handwoven goods and created conditions for the expansion of their manufacture. As Roy has argued, one reason for the reluctance of weavers to adopt the flying shuttle may have been the scarcity of yarn, which limited the possibilities of increased production. Improved steam shipping also enabled reconnection to foreign markets (especially in the diaspora). Eventually, the availability of household electricity made it possible to utilise dispersed power sources and operate power looms even in the home.[26]

Roy's account especially emphasises the adaptability of small-scale textile manufacture, which again raises questions about its supposed 'traditionality.' When thread became more plentiful and market demand started to expand in the later nineteenth century, weavers in the south and elsewhere showed much less reluctance in adopting the flying shuttle – which, in turn, necessitated the introduction of the pit-loom and changes in family and gender relations of work. As manufacturing developed, also some of it, moved out of the home, marking a species of separation from place of work. However, it moved much less into the classic large-scale factory than into the small workshop, employing rarely more than ten people.[27] Caste and family relations need not be broken and could even be extended: where 'hired' workers were very likely to be caste- and family-kin and where women could work in the company of their 'uncles.' In south India especially, most of society possessed bilateral kinship systems connecting them to their mother's as much as their father's kindred. Caste, gender, and kinship were used here as tools of enterprise, not instruments for its suppression.[28]

Indeed, in broader terms, recognition of the positive features of 'small' manufacturing has forced a reappraisal of the supposed economic dysfunctionality of Indian sociocultural convention. Caste, for example, as it was actually lived, by no means lacked material purpose and consequence. It created the multiple niche-markets which artisanal industry then served. It also provided the banks of skills, knowledge, and capital on which manufacturers could draw. Craft was usually learned within (and protected by) the caste and the family – and to a remarkable degree still is. By the most recent estimate, only 4 per cent of Indian workers receive any 'public' form of training for their work.[29] Also, long-term exposure gave particular castes and families special knowledge of specific niche-markets, reducing the transaction costs of commerce. Caste *panchayats* and councils also could reinforce the authority of employers over their workers, as patriarchs over their children. Viewed this way, the 'small' in India has started to appear 'beautiful' again – as it was in preindustrial days when Indian textile manufacture was the wonder of the early modern world.[30] Indeed, Roy has sought to connect it to the broader argument made by Sugihara that Asia promoted its own variant of industrialisation based on labour-intensive forms of production. Like Sugihara's early modern Japan, India possessed abundant labour but scarce capital: its logic of development necessarily took a different path to that of the labour-scarce/capital-rich West.[31]

Moreover, here, economic history may also have started to catch up with a social commentary which has long held that, whatever its material outcome, 'small' manufacturing – which keeps home and work closer together – offers a more humanly satisfying way of life than the modern industrial complex. Famously, Mahatma Gandhi claimed the superiority in human terms of life inside the village community where artisans of different kinds could handmake and exchange their goods and services.[32] However, even he never suggested that 'small' might be more successful in material terms too. But that point was essayed by other Indian economic thinkers, such as Radhakamal Mukherjee in his *Foundations of Indian Economics* (1916), who posited its superior efficiency – even though he was never quite able to demonstrate it.[33] Now the 'revisionist' historiography of India's enduring artisan offers to do precisely that. The 'small' in Indian manufacturing has persisted because it not only offers a desirable alternative way of life but, also, makes the most of the economic opportunities available.

The Price of Smallness

But perhaps the argument goes too far, especially if viewed from the angle of the relationship between capital and labour? For example, if worker productivity is made the yardstick, then Indian manufacturing has a problem. While 80 per cent of India's industrial labour force today may be employed in enterprises containing less than ten workers, they are responsible for barely 20 per cent of total industrial output.[34] Productivity in the economy of 'smallness' is very low and, reciprocally, wage levels and earnings are too.[35] In effect, 'smallness' equates to poverty and, in the Indian case, perhaps always did. Descriptions of the pitiful condition of weavers and artisans litter the pages of European accounts of Indian textile manufacturing in the early modern era.[36] In a bold bid to reverse the image, Prasannan Parthasarathi attempted to show that, by comparative standards, preindustrial Indian textile workers could achieve high earnings.[37] But the adequacy of his data has been questioned and their meaning, in terms of sustained living standards, must be deflated by the recurrence of famine, which regularly struck the south Indian region that he principally studied. When chronic dearth arrived, wage-dependent weavers suffered first.[38]

By all accounts, too, the middle decades of the nineteenth century were difficult times for handloom weavers feeling the first impact of the British Industrial Revolution, which took their most lucrative export markets. If they survived, it was by serving local markets for the cheapest sorts of cloth.[39] Admittedly, as Haynes and Roy argue, the later nineteenth century saw a recovery of manufacture and a steady expansion of the workforce. However, the returns to workers themselves, and even small-scale capitalists, can hardly have been lavish. Between the 1860s and the First World War, food prices rose faster than those for manufactured goods, squeezing the market for industrial products and the real wages of those producing them.[40] Indeed, that weakness of Indian consumption was an underlying cause of late-colonial India's slow rate of economic growth is one of the few things agreed upon by both anticolonial and neoclassical economic historians (if not for the same reasons). Ironically, the Great Depression in the 1930s reversed the agricultural–industrial goods price ratio and did lead to a brief boom in manufacturing – but noticeably more in the 'big' sector, which started to take off in these years.[41]

After Independence, both politico-legal and fiscal conditions in India changed so drastically that comparisons with earlier periods are difficult. However, the continued growth of 'small' manufacturing, especially the use of household power looms, cannot always be associated with rising prosperity. Jan Breman has shown how the shift from 'big' to 'small' in the Gujarat textile industry from the 1980s was precipitated by factory owners 'out-sourcing' production to home workers in order to evade rigorous labour laws and strong trade unions so as to cut their wage bills. The earnings of workers participating in the shift frequently fell by half or more.[42] In an even more recent study of Tamilnadu, Janet Beckwith has noted the steady 'decline' in the social status of the industry where workers from the once craft-protected and prestigious weaving castes have increasingly been replaced by women and members of the lowest castes at knock-down wages.[43] Here, caste and gender 'traditions' have certainly proved useful tools of capitalism but in reducing labour share of the social product rather than facilitating technological adaptation and innovation.

Indeed, in welfare terms, many of those engaged in 'small' manufacturing today would hardly be viable without heavy subvention from the Indian state. Indian government strongly subsidises the 'craft and handloom' sector and directs other economic sectors to protect it for social and political rather than purely economic reasons. Banks, for example, are compelled to devote a significant amount of their lending to 'small and medium enterprises'. With legal penalties and restrictions falling heavily on enterprises hiring more than twenty workers, and cheap credit and fixed subsidies available to those who hire less than ten, there is a case that Indian government policy today artificially helps small businesses to stay small.

These small businesses also have not played a very prominent part in the recent 'rise' of the Indian economy, which has grown by an average 6-plus per cent per year since the onset of economic liberalization and intensified globalisation after 1991. In the 1990s, Roy anticipated that textiles would become (or be restored as) a leading sector of India's 'new' economy.[44] However, twenty years on, this clearly has not happened. The share of textiles in India's exports has fallen sharply from 24.3 per cent in 2000–01 to 9.3 per cent in 2010–11.[45] By contrast, India's recent growth has been led by its services sector (notably IT) and by capital-intensive manufacturing (such as automobiles). The employment elasticity of output ratio fell from 0.27 in 1990–2000 to 0.05 in 2000–10 as the economy hit peak growth rates.[46] In India at least, Sugihara's alternative Asian path of labour-intensive manufacture has not carried the country very far. Indeed, manufacturing as a share of GDP has remained remarkably static at around 15 per cent over the last fifty years and as a share of the workforce at around 11–12 per cent for the last century.

In his classic study of the first, 'modern' big industry that India generated – Bombay textiles from the late nineteenth century – Raj Chandavarkar raised questions about how functionally 'modern' it ever was and, relatedly, how 'big'. He noted that profitability depended above all on beating down workers' wages (in a context of regular strikes); that employers made use of every division of caste, gender, and religion to control the workforce; that technology choices were guided not only by what was cheapest but also what could be negotiated in the face of worker resistance. The logic of investment was essentially speculative, favouring the low-cost and the disposable. Individual factories rose and fell and changed ownership, with great rapidity and, by the 1930s (within fifty years of starting up), even began leaving Bombay.[47]

Chandavarkar's explanations turned, in part, on the extremely hostile market conditions facing the industry: where the domestic economy was a proverbial 'gamble on the monsoon' with wildly fluctuating consumer demand from year to year, and overseas markets were unsecured against foreign competition. In part, too, he emphasised the lack of 'public' goods and infrastructure provided under colonial rule: where workers and their skills came as socially constituted, public order and the rule-of-law were nominal, and neither labour nor capital markets were strongly institutionalised. In these circumstances, investment in fixed capital and the development of long-term relations of employment and skilling were discouraged because they involved the escalation of risk.

In many ways, hostile economic conditions – if for very varying reasons – can be seen to have provided the context for Indian textile manufacture from the early modern period down to today and to have informed decision making which consistently favoured 'smallness', especially in units of production. Elsewhere, I have argued that chronic instabilities of climate in the premodern period deterred fixed invest-ment and promoted alternative survival strategies based on mobility and exchange. Labour and capital moved location to find better conditions and value was added more by transporting goods than manufacturing them in the first place. India was *par excellence* the land of merchant capital. Textile manufacturing reflected this in various phases: from contracting in advance for goods to designing light-framed looms that could be uprooted and carried easily.[48] Virtually by definition, India in this era (as the rest of the world) also lacked much in the way of public goods and infrastructure.

However, it is not clear that these problems changed very dramatic-ally under colonial rule. Certainly the threat of famine did not recede; it became more acute in the later nineteenth century. Moreover, public goods such as accessible law courts, schools, training programs, health facilities, 'modern' banking systems, organised labour markets, etc., also remained desperately sparse – and this continued deep into the postcolonial twentieth century. It was not until 1991, for example, that even half the population was literate. Also, the legal system today groans under a paralyzing backlog of 33 million cases.[49] As a result, 'impersonal' forms of authority and trust are extremely difficult to secure: risk is institutionally unmediated.

To combat such hostile conditions, entrepreneurs necessarily relied (and rely) on networks of social relations which provided extrapublic means of gaining trust, skill, capital, and labour discipline: in effect, they rely on relations of caste, religion, and gender. The particular forms which these relations take were (and are) not necessarily fixed. The household can be expanded into the wider kinship group, which can also be expanded further through the addition of 'fictive' kin relations. As Roy has shown, textile production has moved out of the household and into the workshop, accommodating a certain amount of technological innovation (such as the power-loom).[50] However, there are obvious physical limits to expansion of this kind and the tendency must always remain for units of production/control to be 'small'.

This logic is further reinforced by the continuing segmentation of the market into specialist niches and by violent oscillations in annual patterns of demand. Both factors accentuate the risks of heavy fixed capital investment and put a premium on keeping contracts and commitments brief and short-term. They also give continuing dominance to merchant and finance capital over any structural transition towards industrial capital.

In a later addendum to his model of Asian labour-intensive industrialisation, Sugihara made something of an exception for India. His model anticipated that, as in Japan, Asian governments would intervene to improve infrastructure, education, and skilling so that small-scale technological innovation would become a continuous process, guaranteeing rising worker productivity. In India, this process has proved very attenuated.[51] Rather than a viable alternative growth strategy, 'smallness' in south Indian textile manufacturing often appears more a strategy of survival under very difficult circumstances: those difficulties also create opportunities for capital to exploit the social vulnerabilities of a labour force, most of which is chronically poverty stricken and under skilled.

Notes

1   Maxine Berg, *The Machinery Question and the Making of Political Economy, 1815–1848* (Cambridge: Cambridge University Press, 1980); Maxine Berg, *The Age of Manufactures, 1700–1820* (London: Routledge, 1985); Maxine Berg, *Luxury and Pleasure in Eighteenth Century Britain* (Oxford: Oxford University Press, 2005); Maxine Berg, Felicia Gottman, Chris Nierstrasz, and Hannah Hodac, eds., *Goods from the East, 1600–1800: Trading Eurasia* (London: Palgrave, 2015).

2   Maxine Berg, 'Craft and Small-Scale Production in the Global Economy', *Itinerario* 37, no. 2 (2013): 23–45.

3   Tirthankar Roy, 'The Acceptance of Innovations in Early Twentieth Century Indian Weaving', *Economic History Review* 55, no. 3 (2002): 507–32.

4   Giorgio Riello and Tirthankar Roy, eds., *How India Clothed the World: The World of South Asian Textiles, 1500–1850* (Leiden: Brill, 2009).

5   B.R. Tomlinson, *The Economy of Modern India 1860–1970* (Cambridge: Cambridge University Press, 1993).

6 International Labour Office, *Women and Men in the Informal Economy: A Statistical Picture* (Geneva: ILO, 2018).

7 *Third National Handloom Census of Weavers and Allied Workers* (Delhi: National Council of Economic Research, 2011).

8 Jan Breman, *The Making and Unmaking of an Industrial Working Class* (Delhi: Oxford University Press, 2004).

9 Douglas E. Haynes, *Small-Town Capitalism in Western India* (Cambridge: Cambridge University Press, 2012); Tirthankar Roy, *Cloth and Commerce* (Delhi: Sage, 1996); with M. Liebl, *Hand-made in India* (Washington: World Bank, 2000).

10 Kaoru Sugihara, 'The Second Noel Butlin Lecture: Labour Intensive Industrialisation in Global History', *Australian Economic History Review* 47, no. 2 (2007): 121–54; Tirthankar Roy, 'Labour-Intensity and Industrialization in Colonial India', in *Labour-intensive Industrialization in Global History*, eds. Gareth Austin and Kaoru Sugihara (London: Routledge, 2013), 107–21.

11 Morris D. Morris, *The Indian Economy in the Nineteenth Century: A Symposium* (Delhi: Indian Economic and Social History Association, 1969).

12 K.N. Chaudhuri, *The Trading World of Asia and the English East India Company, 1660–1760* (Cambridge: Cambridge University Press, 1978).

13 Tomlinson, *Economy*.

14 David Landes, *The Unbound Prometheus: Technological Change and Industrial Development in Western Europe from 1750 to the Present* (Cambridge: Cambridge University Press, 1969).

15 Karl Marx, *Capital* (London: CreateSpace Publishing Platform, 2011), 1: 423.

16 A.K. Bagchi, *Private Investment in India, 1900–39* (Cambridge: Cambridge University Press, 1972).

17 Morris, *Indian Economy*; Gunnar Myrdal, *Asian Drama* (London: Penguin, 1968).

18 David Washbrook, 'The Indian Economy and the British Empire', in *India and the British Empire*, eds. Douglas Peers and Nandini Gooptu (Oxford: Oxford University Press, 2012), 44–74.

19 Tomlinson, *Economy*.

20 Karolina Hutkova, 'Technology Transfers and Organization', *Enterprise and Society* 18, no. 4 (2017): 921–51.

21 'A Century of Cotton Mills in India', *Economic Weekly*, 20 March 1954.

22 David Washbrook, 'India in the Early Modern Global Economy', *Journal of Global History* 2, no. 1 (2007): 87–111.

23 Roy, 'Acceptance'.

24 Rajnarayan Chandavarkar, 'Industrialisation in India before 1947', *Modern Asian Studies* 19, no. 3 (1985): 623–68.

25 Haynes, *Small-Town Capitalism*; Roy, 'Acceptance'; Roy, *Cloth and Commerce*; and also Roy, 'The Consumption of Cotton Cloth in India 1795–1940', *Australian Economic History Review* 52 no. 1 (2012): 61–84.

26 Roy, 'Acceptance'.
27 Ibid.
28 Mattison Mines, *The Warrior Merchants* (Cambridge: Cambridge University Press, 2010).
29 Santosh Mehrotra et al., 'Estimating India's Skills Gap on a Realistic Basis for 2022', *Economic and Political Weekly* 48, no. 13 (2013): 102–11.
30 Riello and Roy, eds., *How India Clothed the World*.
31 Roy, 'Labour-Intensity'.
32 M.K. Gandhi, *Hind Swaraj* (Delhi: Rajpal and Sons, New Edition, 2012).
33 Radhakamal Mukerjee, *The Foundations of Indian Economics* (London: Longman, 1916).
34 ILO, *Women and Men*.
35 Jeemol Unni, 'Wages and Incomes in Formal and Informal Sectors in India', *Indian Journal of Labour Economics* 48, no. 2 (2005): 311–17.
36 Bishnupriya Gupta et al., 'India and the Great Divergence', *Explorations in Economic History* 55, no. 1 (2015): 58–75.
37 Prasannan Parthasarathi, 'Re-thinking Wages and Competitiveness in the Eighteenth Century', *Past & Present* 158 (1998): 79–109; Prasannan Parthasarathi, *The Transition to a Colonial Economy* (Cambridge: Cambridge University Press, 2001).
38 Ravi Ahuja, 'Labour Unsettled', *Indian Economic and Social History Review* 35, no. 4 (1998): 381–404.
39 Karl Specker, 'Madras Handlooms in the Nineteenth Century', *Indian Economic and Social History Review* 26, no. 1 (1989): 131–66.
40 David Washbrook, 'Agriculture and Industrialization in Colonial India', in *Agriculture and Industrialization*, eds. Peter Mathias and John Davis (Oxford: Blackwells, 1996).
41 Christopher Baker, *An Indian Rural Economy, 1880–1955* (Oxford: Oxford University Press, 1984).
42 Breman, *Making*.
43 Janet Beckwith, 'Spinning a Yarn: The Effect of Labour Recruitment on Labour Coercion in the Indian Textile Industry' (unpublished MA thesis, University of Utrecht, 2015).
44 Tirthankar Roy, 'Economic Reforms and the Textile Industry in India', *Economic and Political Weekly*, 33, no. 32 (1998): 2173–81.
45 World Bank, *WITS: India Trade Statistics* (Washington: World Bank, 2013).
46 Kunal Sen, 'Where have all the Workers Gone?', *Economic and Political Weekly*, 50, no. 23 (2015): 108–15.
47 Rajnarayan Chandavarkar, *The Origins of Industrial Capitalism in India* (Cambridge: Cambridge University Press, 1994).
48 Washbrook, 'India'.
49 *Census of India*, 1991; *India Today*, 28 June 2018.
50 Roy, 'Acceptance'.

51 Kaoru Sugihara, 'The Quality of Labour in Industrialisation: India and
    Japan Compared', in *Democracy and Development in South Asia*, ed. Nobuko
    Nagasaki (Kyoto: Ryukoku University, 2005), 177–207.

5

An Outlook 'wrapped up in flannel': The Wool Textile Industry in Wales in the Early Twentieth Century

Pat Hudson

> I am a draper mad with love. I love you more than all
> the flannelette and calico, candlewick, dimity, crash and
> merino, tussore, cretonne, crepon, muslin, poplin, ticking
> and twill in the whole Cloth Hall of the world.[1]

Lovesick draper Mog Edwards muses over the 'hotwaterbottled' body of Myfanwy Price, dressmaker and sweetshop keeper, in *Under Milk Wood* (1954) by the Welsh poet Dylan Thomas. There can be no other ode to love with such rich reference to a stock of textiles, but the significance of Mog for the historian is that his 'emporium' in rural Wales was called 'Manchester House'. In the heart of the Welsh textile-manufacturing region, it was desirable by the 1940s, when Thomas was writing, to have a Lancashire connotation in order to sell cloth. This was neither new nor exceptional. Whether the fictional village of Llareggub (read it backwards) was based upon Newquay or upon Laugharne (Thomas lived and wrote in both) is a matter of debate,[2] but in both of these places the draper's shop, by the early twentieth century, was called Manchester House and the popularity of this name was notable in settlements throughout Wales.[3]

To understand why Welsh drapers and their consumers identified with Manchester rather than with their local textile centres demands study of the political and cultural, as well as the economic, context of making and selling woollen goods in Wales over the long term. The Welsh textile industry of the early twentieth century remained characterised by localized small-scale production units and by technologies and products that had changed little for more than a hundred years. This puzzled outsiders charged with undertaking surveys of the sector in the 1920s and 1940s, as we shall see. They found a backwater of skilled, conservative artisans, and workshops within a nation where the sector as a whole, centred on the merchanting hub of Manchester, was amongst the most advanced in the world. This chapter examines the circumstances and the logic underlying the durability and viability of small-scale structures in the face of large-scale change. In doing so it adds a further case study to a recurring emphasis in Maxine Berg's scholarship: the varieties of postindustrial as well as preindustrial small-scale organisations and structures of manufacturing to be found according to varied political, social, and cultural environments, and the nature of localised artisanal skills required to produce specialised products.[4]

The History of Welsh Textiles in a Rural 'Colonial' Society

Wool spinning and weaving, together with hand knitting, were central, alongside sheep farming, to the rural economy of Wales from the mediaeval period. Absentee landlords had little interest in improving their estates so textile by-employments became vital for cottagers and impoverished farm tenants. Alongside widespread part-time production for subsistence and local use, there was significant long-distance trade over the centuries, based on the production of particular Welsh cloths for a succession of international markets.[5]

However, throughout the early modern period all Welsh woollens for long-distance trade had to be sold through and finished by the (English) monopoly of the Shrewsbury drapers. This meant that the highest value-added process in the trade and thus much of the profit of the industry was not enjoyed in Wales. There is no doubt that the predominantly rural, semicolonial nature of the Welsh economy and society between the sixteenth and the early nineteenth centuries, and the Shrewsbury monopoly, held back development in the textile sector by restricting commercial enterprise and by limiting capital and credit supply compared with the more propitious environment of Lancashire and Yorkshire.[6]

Nevertheless, by the early nineteenth century, the Shrewsbury monopoly had been broken and commercial manufacturing, predominantly all-wool flannel, expanded. Production was centred in Newtown and Llanidloes where cloth halls were established and where carding and spinning began to be mechanised in small workshops and factories.[7] However, periodic overstocking crises in transatlantic markets, together with poor market accessibility meant that the mid-Wales commercial flannel industry was soon in trouble.[8] The region lacked a monied

Figure 5.1   Map illustrating the locations and transport links of the Welsh woollen industry in the nineteenth century.

middle class from which a strong and well-financed capitalist group might have sprung. Labour unrest from exploited workers who preferred better paid and more independent agricultural work, often with textiles as a domestic by-employment, aggravated matters.[9] The absence of local coal in mid-Wales added to difficulties by holding back mechanisation beyond what could be achieved by waterpower sites. However, most important in sending the mid-Wales flannel industry into the doldrums in the later decades of the nineteenth century was competition from Rochdale and Yorkshire in flannel markets. Such competition made it difficult for Welsh flannel to penetrate the Lancashire and Liverpool export markets newly opened to Welsh manufacturers by canal construction. The completion of the western branch of the Montgomeryshire canal to Newtown via Welshpool in 1821 brought the possibility of wider sales distribution and cheaper coal supplies for mid-Wales. But these new opportunities were matched by the greater ease with which Pennine flannels could enter the markets of mid-Wales. Such flannels were made by large-scale, mechanised, horizontally specialised mills in contrast to the generally much smaller, less specialised, and less technologically advanced enterprises of Wales. Pennine flannels also increasingly incorporated cotton, which made them highly competitive in price terms and contributed to a decline in popularity of all-wool Welsh flannel, particularly outside Wales.

Sales of high quality Welsh flannels direct to tourists and to British consumers further afield were aided for a time by Pryce Jones of Newtown, pioneer of mail order in Britain. Initially, he promoted only 'Real Welsh Flannel' to his extensive client list, but by the 1870s and 1880s, responding to consumer demand for cheaper more varied cloths, he was also selling flannels and other wool textiles from the north of England.[10] For most mid-Wales flannel firms the later nineteenth century brought bankruptcies and the emigration of workers.[11]

The Resurgence of the Industry in South Wales

From the 1860s or so a resurgence of commercial wool textile production occurred in south-west Wales, in a region of flannel making geographic-ally and socially distanced from Rochdale and Yorkshire competition; a region that concentrated on products and markets where northern flannels did not compete or find favour. By 1895 this regional shift had become very obvious with more than 300 mills in the Cardigan/Carmarthen/Pembrokeshire border area, which had not previously been a major centre of commercial textile manufacturing.[12] The industry concentrated in the valleys around the Teifi River, centred upon a cluster of villages in Llandysul parish. The speciality cloth remained all-wool flannel, but the industry largely turned its back on long distance and export markets to concentrate where it had a comparative advantage: supplying occupationally and culturally specific flannel and woollen clothing for the rapidly expanding working population of the south Wales industrial region. The coming of the railway to the towns and villages of south Wales in the 1860s created an efficient link to consumers in the Welsh coalfield and metal manufacturing region. Demand was boosted by the rapid growth of proletarian consumers: at its peak in 1913 the coal mining industry alone employed more than 230,000 men with perhaps a further 100,000 in other mining, quarrying, the metalliferous trades, and heavy engineering.[13] Slate and stone quarrying also expanded in Wales, alongside agriculture, further boosting the demand for all-wool outdoor work wear.

All-wool work clothes were warm in winter and cool in summer, good at wicking away sweat and repelling dirt and grit. They also had much lower flammability than clothes made of other fibres. Before the development of fire retardant synthetic safety work wear after World War II and the legislation of the early 1960s that insisted on its use, miners and metalworkers had to provide their own working clothes, and it was well known that all-wool flannel work shirts and miners' drawers had low combustibility and even produced a self-extinguishing char when ignited.[14] Loose, sweat-absorbing drawers could be worn in the depth and heat of underground coal seams, whilst collarless shirts, sometimes shorter at the front, to avoid getting caught by flames or in machinery, with open gussets under the arms for air circulation, provided some safety and comfort in tinplate and other factories where it was also common to clench a piece of wet flannel between the teeth to prevent singeing to the mouth and face.[15] Long, collarless flannel shirts were made in their thousands for agricultural workers and quarrymen, whilst triple-milled, almost waterproof, heavy coatings were also made for the all-year outdoor work common in Wales.

In addition, flannel skirts, aprons, shawls, and socks were produced by Welsh yarn and cloth manufacturers for female employments such as household work, the nursing of infants, coal sorting, market trading, and cockle picking.[16] Specialised male and female work wear thus under-pinned the domestic market of the industry between the late nineteenth and mid-twentieth centuries. Success in this period was promoted by a national revival that included a campaign to support Welsh industry (through nationalistic labelling and press campaigns in favour of Welsh textiles). The invention of a tradition of female Welsh national dress in the later nineteenth century (mostly in flannel), endorsed by the picturesque imaginings of tourists and demonstrated in a plethora of idealized photographs and postcards, added to the niche markets for Welsh all-wool clothing.[17] These factors ensured that particular sorts of Welsh garments remained in currency long after similar fabrics and styles had ceased to be fashionable elsewhere in Britain. Unlike flannel manufacturing in the north of England, the Welsh textile mills often made such garments themselves. They commonly incorporated sewing rooms and employed resident and outworking knitters and sewers to make up particular designs of work shirts, drawers, shawls, and other clothing geared to the needs of the working people of Wales.

By 1914, the success of the industry was thus underpinned by the demand for distinctively Welsh garments, work wear in particular, and was dependent upon the buoyancy of the heavy industries. The First World War initially disguised underlying instability, particularly for those firms that won contracts for the supply of military flannel uniforms. But in the ensuing slump, surplus stocks and high wool prices added to the difficulties of reverting to civilian production. It was during the postwar doldrums of the early 1920s that the sector became the focus of investigations yielding detailed evidence of the circumstances and the state of the industry.

The Jones Survey

The Oxford Agricultural Economics Research Institute undertook regional surveys of rural industries throughout England and Wales in the early 1920s. Anna M. Jones was responsible for the volume relating to Wales.[18] The project favoured rural manufacturing as a potential solution to industrial unrest and the decline of rural communities. There was more than a tinge of postindustrial romanticism in this approach. As one commentator suggested, the contributors 'might almost be writing with Herbert Read's *Art and Industry* open on their desks?[19] It was hoped that rural industries could help to create the 'complete rural community' and contribute to solving some of the social problems created, in town and country, by large-scale urban industrialisation:

> certain human advantages in rural industries may be set against the greater production of goods by the larger industrial units of the towns. In particular the smaller industrial concern enables a man to see the whole series and connexions between the making and using of an article, and brings his work into direct relation not only with his own life, but with that of the community of which he is a member. There is little or no distinction between producer and consumer, and one of the chief causes of present social conflicts is non existent.[20]

Jones identified 151 woollen factories, more than one hundred of which were in the south-west. At one extreme lay the large factories, dealing with the wholesale trade and employing between thirty and one hundred workers. At the other extreme were small factories run by the owner with one or two helpers and dependent upon their neighbourhoods for both raw materials and markets.[21] More than 60 per cent of firms still used only waterpower. This included all the smaller factories and a significant number of larger ones. The majority of larger factories had steam power and around ten had installed oil or steam engines to supplement waterpower.[22] Handweavers and small rural mills were found to have weathered the postwar instability better than the more commercialised parts of the sector.[23] But the primitive craft and community nature of such enterprises held little hope for longer term survival. Barter was still practiced and local farmers brought in their clip, all from the same Welsh mountain sheep, and expected it to be made up into a wide range of items from fine flannel to a heavy rug or overcoat.[24] It was Jones's opinion that as long as such mills used undifferentiated Welsh wool their sales would remain local and personal.

Problems for the majority of concerns were exacerbated by primitive technology, poor organisation, and out-of-date sales methods and fabric designs. There were few automatic mules. Instead, one or two spinning jacks were in use or a mule with only sixty to one hundred spindles. Handlooms remained common even in the most advanced factories. Often a large handloom was kept in service in each mill for making shawls, blankets, and *cathenni* (durable bed rugs). For plain weaving of flannels, the power loom, if run with the right yarn, appeared best for fineness and quality, but a significant amount of flannel was still woven on handlooms to suit Welsh outdoor work wear needs. [25]

Dependence upon waterpower was considered to be a problem because although it was suitable for spinning and carding it could be too uneven in force for weaving. None of the mills Jones surveyed used electric or hydroelectric power despite obvious advantages. It was suggested that insecurity of tenure of the mills may have prevented the investment necessary to install either hydro or steam power, harking back to an underlying problem suffered by the industry for centuries: lack of capital.[26]

Factories in the regional cluster in south-west Wales generally carried out most, if not all, the processes of manufacture under one roof although cloth was often sent away to be raised or finished, sometimes as far afield as Scotland. Flannel needed less finishing and was generally completed in the factory. Flannel was mostly sold in plain colours derived from the raw wool. If colour was required, it was most common to buy-in dyed yarns, often to make a stripe from the warp.[27]

Jones visited larger rural factories typically employing fifty to one hundred men and women. They used mostly English or foreign fine wool suitable for their main product: fine flannel. Mountain wool was *kempy*, suitable for *carthenni* or for coarse tweeds but not for flannels. There was thus no direct wool dealing with local farmers on the part of these larger mills. Some firms specialised in large shawls, some made yarn that was knitted on the premises into jumpers. Some made coats or 'costumes', one or two specialised in tweeds or suitings. Blankets were made in all factories. 'Reversible quilts'[28] often with characteristic Welsh geometric patterns found markets outside as well as inside Wales, often via tourist sales, but they required elaborate looms that had been installed only in some of the larger mills.

It was a matter of remark that the Welsh had never developed tweed production using local wools as the Scots had done. Jones put this down to lack of skill in dyeing in Wales arguing that Scottish 'homespun' tweeds found markets not because of superior wool or weaving quality but because of soft colourings from natural dyes. Welsh tweeds that were successfully produced and sold had usually been sent to Scotland for dyeing and finishing.[29] It was clear to Jones that it was the largely prole- tarian industrial demand for flannels, rather than tweeds, tourism, or other markets further afield, that determined the success of the industry particularly in the south-west. Unlike in Scotland, tourist markets were too often seen only as a source for the sale of surplus stock rather than an opportunity to develop high quality niche products.[30]

The availability and cost of labour was another problem faced by the industry. Textile factories established in the south Wales coalfield in the eighteenth century had been deserted because of the pull of better paid jobs in coalmining and iron manufacturing, in particular.[31] But even in the textile manufacturing centres the supply of waged labour could be a problem. Farms were family run and the rural waged workforce was limited.[32]

The Crankshaw Survey

William P. Crankshaw, former head of the Textile Department of the Royal Technical College in Salford was appointed, by the University of Wales, to survey the Welsh textile sector in 1925 and to recommend how a small fund might be applied to encourage the industry.[33] Crankshaw found 192 mills in operation.[34] More than half were in Cardiganshire and Carmarthenshire, and most firms had only one factory.[35] He visited 140 of these, confirming and extending Jones's findings.

Only twenty-six of the factories that Crankshaw visited employed more than twelve workers.[36] The median number of power looms was just thirty.[37] Twenty-one of the factories had only handlooms (between one and seven) and twenty-two of the power loom factories retained a handloom or two each. Crankshaw argued that concentrating the main processes in one factory was much more common in Wales than elsewhere because it had grown out of the practice of 'Undertaking' in the domestic system whereby wool was received from local farmers and made into cloths for their use.[38] The main concern was to provide a textile making service for the wool growing community.

Amongst the myriad of smaller establishments Crankshaw found processes and relationships that had changed little for two centuries. Water powered *pandies* (fulling mills) undertaking work for farmers as well as on their own account were common. Such mills generally produced plain cloths, flannel, and blankets though some made figured fabrics such as bedcovers and quilts. They sold cloth in local markets and fairs as well as on site and carried out dyeing and finishing in copper vessels over fires. Textile manufacturers frequently mixed textile employments with agriculture and fishing.[39] In one factory a butter churn ran alongside the textile machinery turned by the spinning machine shaft and cows were housed in the basement. Cheese presses were found in the finishing room of another mill.[40] Agriculture came first, and textile manufacturing was seen as a useful slack-season supplement to income. Often the premises were rented along with the farm: they were rarely owned by the manufacturers themselves.

Crankshaw was impressed by an array of eccentric but highly skilled craftsmen and women whose way of life had been little affected by the technological advances of the Industrial Revolution or by the commercialising thrust of British industry in the nineteenth century. One small factory was run by a recluse who lived amongst his books in a corner of his weaving room: 'The whole concern – building, machinery and owner would make a most attractive exhibit in the National Museum.'[41] At another mill three skilled sisters, who had been taught by their father, worked all processes from raw wool to finished cloths, alongside running a farm and a sawmill. He also found an old manufacturer who wove sonnets as well as cloth and who had won many bard's chairs at Eisteddfodau.[42]

One- or two-person mills undertaking only one process and tended by elderly people who were unable to interest their children in the business were common. The majority were 'decrepit and filthy', but one was spotless 'with roses growing up the walls and windows filled with ferns and flowering plants!' This was operated by two old ladies 'who still "undertake" for farmers as well as spinning on commission for weavers.'[43]

In no other commercial textile region of Britain, except perhaps for pockets in the Scottish highlands and islands, had such rural domestic structures survived. The mix of farming and textile manufacture, and the low overheads of waterpower and agricultural premises suggested to Crankshaw, as it had to Jones, that such small mills might continue

and thrive, producing specialist crafted items, with advantages of cost
and specialisation over larger manufacturers. But he was concerned
about the impact of competition from the power loom that had
restricted the handicraft industry to certain products.[44] Moreover, no
mills kept accounts and most found it impossible to ascertain the costs
of manufacture so that selling prices were fixed in an arbitrary manner.[45]

Factories of medium size represented the most promising group
for Crankshaw. These were family-based concerns with up to twelve
employees and some division of labour. They were run by younger
people, some of whom had had training in English or Scottish textile
colleges. In these establishments the machinery was newer. There were
generally one or two spinning mules, for example, and, although power
was mainly from water, some also had gas or oil engines. Some of these
concerns specialised in tweeds but often of 'Scotch' or Yorkshire design
rather than the old Welsh patterns. Two factories produced handloom
tweeds for niche markets.

Only five or six of the factories visited by Crankshaw would have
been classed as large outside of Wales, but the six biggest had half the
power looms in the principality, and all in this group were engaged in
mass production for wider markets. Most had specialised in government
flannel production during the war and some had been reequipped
for this, with the aid of government grants. However, the production
of 'angola flannel' incorporating between 25 per cent and 75 per cent
cotton, for military uniforms, weakened the industry in the longer
term by undermining the identification of Welsh flannel with all-wool
composition and by encouraging the installation of looms and other
machinery that could not easily be adapted for civilian all-wool products.
In addition, postwar government surplus stocks had lowered prices, and
strikes in the coalfields had damaged the demand for flannel work wear.
Many mills in this category were so depressed they were only partly
working or closed.[46]

An unusual feature of the Welsh woollen industry, identified by
Crankshaw, was that some mills in all size categories, but particularly
medium and large concerns, included hosiery making (mostly stockings)
and ran sewing rooms for making up (shirts, drawers, and other clothing)
on the premises and/or they put out these tasks to households in the
locality. Making up cloth into final products, alongside its manufacture,
was most common in towns where there was a better supply of female
labour. It provided an important solution to the problem of overstocking
bales of cloth. Machine-made hosiery makers had however to import
wools from England because Welsh knitting wool, although ubiquitous,
tended to be too uneven for machinery.

Crankshaw highlighted wasteful methods and inadequate super-vision and training of workers. A more surprising focus of his criticism was that it was common to find men occupied with a single narrow width loom running at only a moderate speed. He attributed this to the continuity of employment of former handloom weavers on power looms. In Yorkshire and elsewhere it was very unusual for former (male) handloom weavers to move into power loom weaving. Female and juvenile workers were initially preferred because they were more adaptable in the face of the new technology. Most weavers in south Wales were adult male ex-handloom weavers who could not conceive of being in charge of more than one loom. The double loom system (two looms in the care of a single woman), common in Yorkshire, was never found in Wales. The family-run nature of small mills had created a greater continuity of personnel from handloom to power loom and a legacy of conservatism and traditional working was the result.[47]

Crankshaw's Analysis of the
State of the Industry in the 1920s

Three circumstances that were responsible for the depressed state of the wool textile sector were identified. First, because the industry had long concentrated upon the domestic market and particularly upon the production of flannel and other wool textiles that were in mass demand amongst industrial workers of the coalfield areas, the interwar crisis in the heavy industries and the faltering purchasing power of the Welsh industrial population, had badly affected demand. Secondly, Crankshaw emphasised the impact of the high price of wool. Prices doubled between 1922 and 1925. This reverberated through all ranks of the industry. Larger concerns, including flannel manufacturers had to pay much higher prices for the wools that they purchased from England and further afield. Small and medium concerns that would normally work up wool belonging to local farmers, were often starved of this trade because farmers preferred to sell their wool direct for a profit whilst prices were inflated. Finally, Crankshaw stressed what had struck him most about the bulk of rural textile manufacturing in Wales: that it was seen primarily as an adjunct of farming. Where manufacturing was carried on in conjunction with agriculture, the ability to fulfil orders or to concentrate on quality was frequently thwarted by the seasonal interference of farming operations.

Changes in fashion, cheaper and more attractive fabrics, and ready-made garments, manufactured outside Wales, were seen as the most fundamental longer term problems for the industry. This was particularly so in the case of underwear where knitted cotton and merino wool vests, pants, and long johns were beginning to have an enormous effect on the demand for 'underwear flannel'. Furthermore, striped flannel shirting was being replaced by finer and lighter makes of wool or cotton mixtures that were beyond the capacity of the majority of Welsh factories to produce. Specialisation in flannel meant that the industry had no knowledge of the process of sizing which would enable it to use finer yarns and increase the productive capacity of looms. It was even unable to produce yarns suitable for its own hosiery industry. The declining popularity of linsey skirtings, woollen dress materials, aprons, and shawls, all of which had been central components of the dress of working women, added to the woes of the sector. The disappearance of the village tailor and the rise of the merchant tailor who was unwilling to make up customer's own cloth lowered demand for flannels and the introduction of ready-mades was killing the trade in Welsh tweeds.[48] Crankshaw concluded that the industry was chained by traditional methods and by an outlook 'wrapped up in flannel'[49]: 'the power to originate new effects and structures appears to be totally lacking'.[50]

His recommendations to support the industry were to give assistance in finding new markets, to promote the development of new fabrics and designs, and to sponsor technical education. Advice was needed about machinery, market information, better terms on which raw materials might be bought, cash payments instead of long credits, and a knowledge of bookkeeping and business methods. More attractive dyeing and more enterprise generally was seen as vital to promote the industry beyond local markets.[51]

In the following decade, with support from the Rural Industries Bureau, some new products were introduced and proved popular in wider national markets especially double weave bedspreads, furnishing fabrics, and some light tweeds. But the bulk of the industry remained deeply conservative and wedded to traditional lines of flannel work wear. When the Bureau employed Marriane Straub to go round mills in the 1930s introducing them to new designs she faced a sea of conservatism.[52]

The Rural Industries Bureau Reports, 1946–48

The Second World War renewed the demand for flannel and flannel mixes for the Ministry of Supply and Ordnance, creating an Indian summer for a handful of firms. However, the postwar slump in demand for flannels, accompanied by the continuation of wool rationing, caused a landslide of mill closures.[53] The Rural Industries Bureau conducted the last full survey of Welsh textile mills in 1946 (circulated 1947)[54] at a time when the size of the entire industry in South Wales 'probably approximates to that of a fairly large Yorkshire mill'.[55] Seventy-seven factories were identified and visited in 1946. Details of their history, machinery, the products made, and the markets served were noted. Only seventy were identified as functioning. Most continued to undertake several processes under one roof, forty-four carrying out spinning, weaving dyeing, and finishing. The mills together employed only 287 men and 219 women. Many had only a handful of workers and several continued alongside other enterprises, most commonly agricultural holdings.[56] There had been no major changes in the sorts of products made or in distribution and marketing since the 1920s. The 1947 report endorsed Crankshaw's pessimism about the future of the industry and its manifold problems of path dependency and conservatism. Most firms were selling traditional fabrics and finished products (particularly flannel shirts and blankets) via retail shops, tailors, and markets mostly in south Wales, and much confusion was caused by selling at the same price to the trade and direct to consumers.[57]

Several manufacturers sent their cloths to Yorkshire for finishing whilst others undertook the work themselves often with inadequate knowledge and inefficient equipment. The use of single-width looms and handlooms remained common. Double-width bedspreads therefore had to be sewn up the middle. Tweeds accounted for only 20 per cent of the production despite their potential for future sales compared with the dwindling markets for flannel. Although some firms had modernised their equipment and concentrated upon high quality tweeds, rugs, and scarves for the London market and the tourist trade, the great majority of mills had confined themselves to flannel or to knitting wool, and the future was predicted to be bleak.[58]

Conclusion

By the time that *Under Milk Wood* was being written, the textile industry of Wales offered little attraction to consumers or drapers like Mog Edwards. 'Manchester House' emporia were stocked with ranges of cloth in all manner of fibres and designs, most produced outside of Wales in a globalised trading system of mass production and consumption that the city of Manchester had come to symbolise since the Industrial Revolution. Such a system was far removed from the conservative and craft nature, the rural community culture, and garment specificities that had underpinned the textile industry of Wales for over a century. The enduring forms of Welsh textile manufacturing charmed academics like Jones and Crankshaw, encouraging a perception that they might

hold a key to rural regeneration, but it was already too late. Demand
for flannel work wear had been permanently undermined by crisis
and decline of the old staple industries, by competition from cheaper
colourful cottons and mixtures traded on international markets and by
ready-mades flooding agricultural and industrial Wales alike. Strong
cultural preferences for woollen garments and their association with
both occupational and nationalistic traditions were undermined by
increasing geographical mobility and information flow and by advertising and retailing innovations. Small-scale industrial structures had
proved resilient in the face of competition from larger scale and more
fully mechanised factories because they served well-established local
and regional consumer needs. But they could endure only so long
as the cultural, social, and economic circumstances of their existence
were preserved.

Notes

Chapter title quotes from William P. Crankshaw, *Report on a Survey of the
Welsh Textile Industry Made on Behalf of the University of Wales* (Cardiff:
University of Wales Press Board, 1927), 16.
1 'Throw away your little bed socks and your Welsh wool knitted jacket, I will
   warm the sheets like an electric toaster, I will lie by your side like the Sunday
   roast.' Dylan Thomas, *Under Milk Wood: A Play for Voices* (BBC broadcast 1954.
   London: Folio Society 1972), 18.
2 Thomas's map of Llareggub resembles both places. Dylan Thomas papers,
   National Library of Wales: Aberystwyth, Reference: NLW MS 23949E.
3 Manchester Houses included Barmouth, Lampeter Velfrey near Narberth,
   Llanfair Caereinion (Welshpool), Bridgend, Ammanford, Llandeilo,
   Newcastle Emlyn, Llandysul, Cardigan, and Milford Haven (where there
   was a Manchester Square). Cardigan had a Manchester House at 41 High St,
   the business of John James, draper, in the 1870s and 1880s. New Manchester
   House was then commissioned by James in 1884, a large stuccoed
   establishment on three floors with an array of shopfront windows. Glen K.
   Johnson, 'New Manchester House, Bridge Street', http://www.glen-johnson.
   co.uk/new-manchester-house-bridge-street (created 2 June 2013).
4 Maxine Berg, *The Age of Manufactures, 1700–1820: Industry, Innovation and
   Work in Britain* (London: Routledge, 2nd ed. 1994); Maxine Berg, 'Small
   Producer Capitalism in Eighteenth-Century England', *Business History* 35,
   no. 1 (1993): 17–39; Maxine Berg, 'Craft and Small-Scale Production in
   the Global Economy', *Itinerario* 37, no. 2 (2013): 23–45; Maxine Berg and

Pat Hudson, 'Rehabilitating the Industrial Revolution', *Economic History Review* 45, no. 1 (1992): 25–50.

5   J. Geraint Jenkins, *The Welsh Woollen Industry* (Cardiff: National Museum of Wales, 1969), 96–116; C.A.J. Skeel, 'The Welsh Woollen Industry in the Sixteenth and Seventeenth Centuries', *Archaeologia Cambrensis* 7, no. 11 (1922): 220–57; Chris Evans, *Slave Wales: The Welsh and Atlantic Slavery, 1660–1860* (Cardiff: University of Wales Press, 2010), 51–4.

6   Skeel, 'Welsh Woollen Industry', T.C. Mendenhall, *The Shrewsbury Drapers and the Welsh Wool Trade in the XVI and XVII Centuries* (Oxford: Oxford University Press, 1953); Jenkins, *Welsh Woollen Industry*, 119–26 and 183–6.

7   Jenkins, *Welsh Woollen Industry* 128–30; 'Llanidloes – The Flannel Makers 6: All Kinds of Welsh Flannels', Powys Digital History Project, http://history.powys.org.uk/history/llani/flan6.html.

8   C.A.J. Skeel, 'The Welsh Woollen Industry in the Eighteenth and Nineteenth Centuries', *Archaeologia Cambrensis* 7, no. 4 (1924): 1–38.

9   Jenkins, *Welsh Woollen Industry*, 148, 150, 167, and 200ff.

10 Ibid., 116–215. The Pryce Jones archive is held in the Powys County Archives. See Powys County Council, 'Archives and Family History', https://en.powys.gov.uk/archives. A small number of concerns in North and mid-Wales survived longer-term aided by tourist demand or by emulating cheaper Yorkshire-style mixtures: Pat Hudson 'Industrial History, Working Lives, Nation and Empire Viewed through some Key Welsh Woollen Objects', in *History after Hobsbawm: Writing the Past for the Twenty-First Century*, eds. John H. Arnold, Matthew Hilton, and Jan Ruger (Oxford: Oxford University Press, 2018), 160–83.

11 Jenkins, *Welsh Woollen Industry*, 154ff, 200ff.

12 Ibid., 247–308.

13 John Williams, *Digest of Welsh Historical Statistics*, 2 vols. (Cardiff: The Welsh Office, 1985); Arthur H. John, *The Industrial Development of South Wales, 1750–1850: An Essay* (Cardiff: Cardiff University of Wales Press, 1950); L.J. Williams and T. Boyns, 'Occupations in Wales, 1851–1971', *Bulletin of Economic Research*, 29 (1977): 71–83.

14 The ignition temperature of wool lies between 570 and 600 degrees centigrade compared with cotton at 255 degrees and synthetics in between. Wool also has a significantly higher limiting oxygen index and lower heat of combustion than cotton whilst it does not melt, drip, or stick to skin when ignited. International Wool Textile Organisation, 'Flame Resistance', https://www.iwto.org/flame-resistance.

15 I am indebted to Robert Prothero Jones, Curator, Heavy Industries, Museum of Wales for this and other information about work clothes in the metalliferous trades.

16 These were repeatedly fulled so they were durable and almost impermeable to water. For more on some of the specialised all-wool clothing of Wales see Hudson, 'Industrial History'.

17 For more on the expansion of flannel clothing as a response to these forces see Hudson, 'Industrial History'.

18 Anna M. Jones, *The Rural Industries of England & Wales. IV. Wales* (Oxford: Clarendon Press, 1927). Jones used further information from the survey in 'The Characteristics of Wool Production and Woollen Manufacture in Wales, in Relation to the Geographical Features of the Principality' (unpublished MSc, University of Wales, 1925).

19 Christopher Bailey, 'Rural Industries and the Image of the Countryside', in *The English Countryside between the Wars: Regeneration of Decline?*, eds. Paul Brassley, Jeremy Buchardt, Lynne Thompson (Woodbridge: Boydell Press 2006), 132–49.

20 C.S. Orwin, 'Preface', to Jones, *Rural Industries of England & Wales. IV. Wales*, v.

21 Jones, *The Rural Industries of England & Wales. IV. Wales*, 17 and 33. These figures represent an incomplete list according to Jenkins (*Welsh Woollen Industry*, 380). It is likely not to include establishments that were purely fulling mills making the numbers more comparable with those of Crankshaw (see below).

22 Jones, *The Rural Industries of England & Wales. IV. Wales*, 33–4.

23 Ibid., 13.

24 Ibid., 29.

25 Ibid., 26–7.

26 Ibid., 33–4.

27 Ibid., 23.

28 These became known as double weave bedspreads and were a mainstay of the industry amongst surviving firms in the 1960s and 1970s.

29 Jones, *The Rural Industries of England & Wales. IV. Wales*, 32. Crankshaw later suggested that tweeds had never taken root in Wales partly because local *kempy* wool needing to be sorted well and that only the better parts of it could be successfully used for tweeds. Crankshaw, *Welsh Textile Industry*, 12.

30 Jones, *The Rural Industries of England & Wales. IV. Wales*, 5.

31 Ibid., 7 and 9.

32 The 1921 census gave famers and graziers with their sons and daughters working on the farms of Ceredigion and Carmarthenshire as 5,613 and 8,878 respectively. The numbers of agricultural labourers were 2,766 and 3,558 respectively. This affected both the supply of labour for textiles and the home market. Jones, *The Rural Industries of England & Wales. IV. Wales*, 2.

33 The investigation was undertaken with the cooperation of the Rural Industries Bureau and financed largely by Sir Alfred Mond, MP for Carmarthen from 1924–28: Crankshaw, *Report on a Survey of the Welsh Textile Industry*. The survey was carried out in 1925–26.

34 Crankshaw, *Report on a Survey*, 2. The 1904 return of woollen factories

subject to Factories and Workshops Act of 1901 had identified 292 mills in Wales.

35 Crankshaw, *Report on a Survey*, 2.

36 As Crankshaw was most interested in visiting the smaller struggling mills, this probably underestimates typical size of concern in the Welsh industry overall.

37 His sample included some larger factories, one with 250 power looms in operation but this was an outlier (Holywell Mills, Flintshire). Crankshaw, *Report on a Survey*, 2–4.

38 Ibid., 5.

39 Ibid., 6–7.

40 Ibid., 7–9.

41 Ibid., 8.

42 Ibid., 8.

43 Ibid., 6.

44 Ibid., 6.

45 Ibid., 9.

46 The two largest mills, in North Wales, were less dependent on flannels than on 'Yorkshire-style' goods. Their productivity was aided by steam engines using coal from the North Wales coalfield. Crankshaw, *Report on a Survey*, 10.

47 Ibid., 11.

48 Ibid., 3.

49 Ibid., 16.

50 Ibid., 17.

51 Ibid., 16–19.

52 Marriane Straub (1909–1994) became one of the leading textile designers in Britain from the 1940s, famous, among other things, for her iconic upholstery designs for London Transport and fabrics for ocean passenger liners.

53 The National Archives, Kew (hereafter TNA), D4/1181: Rural Industries Bureau, 'Interim report on the Welsh Woollen Industry prepared for the Development Commission', by G.M. Dykes, 1946.

54 National Woollen Museum, Drefach Velindre: 'Rural Industries Bureau Survey of Welsh Mills', 1947. A technical report followed in 1948.

55 TNA, D4/1181: Rural Industries Bureau, 'Interim report on the Welsh Woollen Industry 1946', 2.

56 TNA, D4/1181: Rural Industries Bureau, 'Draft Report on the Welsh Woollen Industry 1948 (Technical Aspects and recommendations)', prepared by Mr G. Gaunt Technical Officer (Welsh Textiles).

57 TNA, D4/1181: Rural Industries Bureau, 'Draft Report on the Welsh Woollen Industry 1948 (Technical Aspects and recommendations)'.

58 TNA, D4/1181: Rural Industries Bureau, 'Interim report on the Welsh Woollen Industry 1946': 'Draft Report on the Welsh Woollen Industry 1948'.

PART TWO

The Age of Machinery: Technology, Human Capital, and Political Economy

6

Rethinking Protoindustry: Human Capital and the Rise of Modern Industry

Jan de Vries

The concept of protoindustry has been with us now for some fifty years.[1] When introduced it stood for the rise of a specific form of industrial production. It was organised neither in artisanal workshops, usually urban and regulated by guilds, nor in factories, equipped with machinery and directed by capitalist owners and managers. Rather, protoindustry relied on household labour, primarily rural, labouring within the home in the production of manufactured goods intended for sale in distant markets. This labour was organised by merchants, or merchant manufacturers, who commonly owned the raw materials and sometimes the tools and equipment used by the workers in their homes. Thus, protoindustry, as originally conceptualised by Franklin Mendels, acted as a bridge between urban-artisanal manufacturing and the factory system. Soon after, others, most notably Kriedte, Medick, and Schlumbohm, argued its importance as a powerful force in the transition from feudalism to capitalism.[2]

Protoindustry and Economic Growth Theory

When protoindustry first entered the economic historian's lexicon it was framed to fit the understanding of economic growth then prevailing among economists. Thus, it was inserted into a linear or stage-based narrative of movement from traditional to modern, or from feudal to capitalist societies. It focused on mass production, the large-scale production of simple, standard products for distant markets. It also emphasised the unskilled nature of rural industry and the growing supply of (nearly) landless labourers; before such labour could be gathered in factories and cities as a proper proletariat, it was organised and engaged in rural cottages.[3] Moreover, it placed much stock on the claim

108 JAN DE VRIES

that this organisation of rural labour in market-oriented production had
the social and cultural consequences historians and sociologists had long
associated with modern industry and urbanisation. Before there could
be a 'Making of the English Working Class' protoindustry had launched
the 'Un-making of the European Peasantry', whereby the traditional
constraints on family formation would give way to 'proletarian' fertility
behaviour (thereby accelerating the growth of a landless population),
and the traditional artisan guild organisation of manufactures would
lose its grip on industrial production.[4]

Finally, the concept of protoindustry promised to help resolve a
key puzzle in the theory of economic growth. The then prevailing
neoclassical growth models were driven by a rapid rise in the rate of
capital accumulation. Only through fixed capital formation could
improved technologies be introduced to production processes, but
this raised a major theoretical as well as historical question: how could
a low-income economy save enough to increase fixed capital investment
and, hence, the output of manufactures? Others had addressed this problem before, of course, notably Marx, Rostow, and Gerschenkron. But now
protoindustry suggested another avenue of approach: an intermediate
'labour-intensive path to industrialization' that economized on fixed
capital. All in all, the early advocates of protoindustry promised a great
deal – as did so many advocates of change in those years.

The passage of time has not been kind to the theory of protoindustrialisation. Empirical studies found far too much variation in the
demographic, institutional, and regional characteristics of protoindustrial zones to sustain the strong visions of the early theorisers. There are
sufficient postmortem accounts of the concept's theoretical shortcomings to allow me to be brief here.[5] Critics noted that the demographic
behaviour of rural industrial families did not lead to higher fertility
with any consistency, that rural industrial zones were not necessarily
innocent of guilds or other corporate controls on market relations, and
that for every protoindustrial zone that transitioned to modern industry
there were as many that failed to do so, or, indeed, persisted in their
protoindustrial structure deep into the era of modern industry.

Perhaps the most generally accepted critique of the protoindustrialisation literature is that it posited an excessive dichotomy between urban,
skilled, guild-organised artisanal manufacturing and rural, unskilled,
merchant-dominated proletarian manufacturing. There were, to be sure,
cautionary notes made by Mendels and others that this dichotomy was
a caricature – what economists prefer to call a stylised fact – but the
larger claims of the theory led inevitably to the assumption that rural
and urban industry were alternatives, that they were in competition

with each other, and that the triumph of protoindustry 'set the stage' for the next phase, factory industry.

In this context Maxine Berg's work on eighteenth-century English manufacturing stood out as a rallying flag for those who doubted the 'autonomy' of protoindustry, who sought to redress the neglect of urban manufactures, who sought to draw attention to the broad diversity of artisanal occupations in the pre-industrial economy, and, above all, sought to emphasise the importance of skill development in English and European manufacturing.[6] Her call was heeded, and in the past two decades much has been done to redress the balance. If the protoindustrialisation literature developed when economic theory was concerned primarily with aggregates of capital and labour, the new interest in artisanal skills has developed when economic theory is attentive to the importance of information, knowledge, human capital, and the institutions that foster the diffusion of knowledge and the nurturing of skills. Today the early modern world of artisans, craft workers, and their institutions cannot readily be dismissed as an obsolete survival. Rather, such phenomena should be seen as an intrinsic part of industrialisation at all stages of development into the modern era. This acknowledgement, in turn, sets the stage for a rethinking of protoindustry, one that stresses its interactions with the artisanal and urban economy more than its competition with it.

Berg was joined by several historians in reviving the study of artisanal production. Her own approach was to closely examine work and the organisation of work in a broad variety of trades, and not only those 'destined' for early mechanisation and factory organisation. She showed that English industrial growth was broadly based and that 'technical change started early and spread extensively through industry. Innovation was not necessarily mechanization. It was also the development of hand and intermediate techniques, and the wider use of and division of cheap labour. It was above all a conjuncture of old and new processes.' She went on to emphasise that 'industrialization was about work organization; decentralization, extended workshops, and sweating were equally new departures in the organization of production. There was no necessary progression from one to another; their relative efficiency depended on the economic context.'[7] Her approach converted a view of industrial history in stages (artisans to protoindustry to factories) to one involving an interacting complexity in which learning and adapting were central to both product and process innovation.[8]

These critiques, especially the new emphasis on labour skills and on the broad range of manufactures that characterised the long eighteenth century, fit nicely into new insights in economic theory emerging in the

late 1980s. The new 'endogenous growth theory' challenged the prevailing neoclassical theory that understood economic growth to be driven
primarily by 'exogenous' factors – the introduction of capital and the
technology it embodies into the production system. The new endogenous growth theory emphasised investment in human capital, innovation,
information, and knowledge as the most significant contributors to
economic growth. The theory also argues that these factors exert their
influence primarily through increasing returns to scale that are achieved
via positive externalities and the spillover effects of a knowledge-based
economy. Suddenly, skills, knowledge, organisation, and locality – the
issues Berg emphasised in her work – mattered. This led to further
developments to which we return below.

A New Protoindustry

Protoindustry became a wounded concept. It was often invoked only to
remind readers of its empirical shortcomings while its theoretical claims
lost their ability to impress. What has not happened is any assessment
of protoindustrialisation theory in the light both of contemporary
empirical knowledge and of current theories of economic growth. If
protoindustry had not been theorised in the 1970s, how would we seek
to theorise its characteristics today?

Any new, improved concept of protoindustry should be understood
as part of the larger mobilisation of labour that characterised Western
Europe in the seventeenth and eighteenth centuries and that elsewhere
I have referred to as an 'industrious revolution' and that Japanese scholars refer to as a 'labour-intensive path to industrialization'. It should
also be linked more closely than before to the long-term cultivation
and diffusion of manufacturing skills emphasised by S.R. Epstein and
Maarten Prak, which the latter calls an 'artisanal revolution'. Finally,
protoindustry's contribution to long-term growth should be evaluated in
a theoretical framework that is freed from fixations on binding exogenous constraints – whether capital, energy, or science – that long have
characterised neoclassical growth theory. This is a large agenda, of course,
and this contribution can only sketch out the intended path forward.

Proletarianisation

We can begin with the association of protoindustry with proletarianisation. The earlier emphasis on an altered logic to family formation
and its demographic impact had seemed plausible because of the rapid
growth of population experienced by many protoindustrial regions. A

new social class with a distinctly higher fertility rate than the old rural classes could explain this notable population growth. Indeed, it could do more than this; it could challenge the classical Marxian understanding of the emergence of a proletariat. Instead of expropriations, expulsions, and other acts of economic and judicial violence against a peasant world, protoindustrial theory suggested that the more important path toward proletarianisation was natural increase.[9]

The theory had focused on family formation and fertility, and had supposed that protoindustrial families were, or were well on their way to becoming, proletarians. Subsisting on their unskilled labour, they had little reason to delay marriage, as did farmers, artisans, and others whose livelihood depended on some form of capital. This proved not to be true with any consistency for the simple reason that households engaged in protoindustry were rarely true proletarians. Their industrial labour often required some skill and capital and they combined this with other pursuits.[10] Indeed, their commitment to protoindustrial labour was not irreversible.[11] Since they were not on a slippery slope leading inevitably to proletarianisation, they had little reason to abandon the demographic norms of the larger society.[12]

It is not surprising that early protoindustry theorists would suspect a profound change in marriage behaviour and a class-specific rise in fertility, for there is abundant evidence of a rapid growth of population in many regions of protoindustrialisation. A classic early study of the German territory of Saxony found that a four-fold increase of population between 1550 and 1843 was almost entirely accounted for by the growth of a class of cottagers, the region's subpeasants. The farmer class barely grew at all, and the town burghers increased very slowly. Indeed, Saxony's substantial cities did no more than hold their own as a percentage of the total population (table 6.1).

A similar process of change was documented for the Canton of Zürich, where Braun found that between 1634 and 1794 the population of the city grew by 80 per cent, that of the rural lowlands, dominated by farmers, grew by 60 per cent, while the uplands, where protoindustry spread, the population grew by 300 per cent.[13] Or, consider the Dutch province of Overijssel. There Slicher van Bath documented a doubling of the total population between 1675 and 1795. The cities grew by only 33 per cent, the farming districts by 64 per cent, while the district of Twente, a centre of rural textiles production, tripled in population.[14] Klep estimated that Brabant, in the southern Netherlands, more than doubled in population between 1702 and 1846 but that the urban population fell from 47 to 31 per cent of the total, while the rural proletariat (neither farmers or self-employed) rose from 28 to 43 per cent of the total.[15]

Table 6.1   Population of Electoral Saxony by occupation/status

	1550		1843	
	Population (in thousands)	% of total	Population (in thousands)	% of total
Burgher (town citizens)	116	26.7	300	16.2
Other urban residents	22	5.1	327	17.6
Total urban	138	31.8	627	33.3
Bauern (farmers)	215	49.5	250	13.5
Cottar (subpeasants)	20	4.6	869	46.8
Villagers, clergy, nobility	61	14.1	111	5.9
Total rural	296	68.2	1,230	66.2
Total population	434		1,856	

Source: Karlheinz Blashke, *Bevölkerungsgeschichte von Sachsen bis zur industriellen Revolution* (Weimar: Böhlau, 1967).

Regional studies of this sort are fairly abundant, and they led to several necessarily rough estimates of the growth of rural non-agricultural populations at the national and European levels. Necessarily rough because distinguishing full-time farmers and labourers from rural non-agricultural labourers requires strong assumptions. One is actually categorising labour time more than individuals. Wrigley offered estimates for England, France, and the Dutch Republic; Tilly proposed Europe-wide estimates for the 'proletarian' population, and Allen estimated the rural non-agricultural populations for nearly all European countries.[16] Pooling Allen's data for England, France, Germany, and the Low Countries confirms the pattern revealed by the more detailed examples just discussed (table 6.2).

The rapid growth of the rural non-agricultural population in the course of the seventeenth and eighteenth centuries may not have been caused primarily by the high fertility of proletarian couples, as the early protoindustrial theorists thought. It now seems likely that low rural mortality and migration between rural areas played a larger role. So long as industrial expansion required migration to the towns, the 'urban graveyard effect' kept population growth in check. Once protoindustry emerged to play a central role in industrial expansion, this check was removed and intrarural migration and natural increase combined to bring an often explosive growth to protoindustrial regions.[17]

The rural non-agricultural population is not synonymous with protoindustrial labour. In many regions its growth was buoyed by the

Table 6.2   Urban, agricultural, and rural nonagricultural population of Western Europe, 1600–1800

	Population in millions		Percentage of population	
	1600	1800	1600	1800
Agricultural	25.9	34.6	66.6	54.0
Rural nonagricultural	8.5	19.8	21.9	30.9
Urban	4.5	9.7	11.5	15.1
Total	38.9	64.1	100.0	100.0

Source: Robert Allen, 'Economic Structure and Agricultural Productivity in Europe, 1300–1800', *European Review of Economic History* 3, no. 1 (2000), 1–25.

proliferation of rural service providers and artisans. A more commercial agriculture generated demand not only for transport and iron mongering, but also bakers and shopkeepers, which complimented the growing specialisation in agricultural households. Moreover, the growth of protoindustry relied on improvements in the infrastructure of roads and waterways that connected the new sites of industry with urban merchants and markets. This and the increasing density of rural population in many regions allowed artisans normally associated with urban life to locate in the countryside. A growing population of bakers, tailors, shoemakers, butchers, coopers, etc. exploited the lower costs of rural location to supply urban markets. This weakened urban artisans economically, especially in the many small cities that blanketed western and central Europe. These rural craftsmen, hidden in plain sight, as it were, have rarely been studied directly.[18] What *have* attracted scholarly attention are the rural zones that came to supply large cities with specialised artisans, usually on a temporary or seasonal basis. In this way cities such as London, Paris, and Amsterdam were served by chimney sweeps, bakers, brick makers, and many other artisans and tradesmen.

Subpeasant Strata

The socio-economic group in which protoindustry could spread is what German scholarship calls *unterbauerliche Schichten* or the subpeasant strata.[19] They were – as Kriedte, Medick, and Schlumbohm demonstrated in Germany, Pfister demonstrated for Switzerland, and Viardi showed for northern France – not necessarily the poorest, most land poor of rural dwellers. For many, cottage industry was embraced as a means of 'returning' to full peasant status. Another compelling reason to decouple protoindustry from poverty is the frequent engagement of only some household members, and then only some of the time, in cottage industry. Moreover, the households often owned the required tools and more elaborate manufacturing equipment.[20]

From a distance the distinction between rural proletarians and 'subpeasant strata' may seem a subtle one. But up close it reveals its value, for it removes the teleology of proletarianisation from our topic and emphasises the multiple sources of economic support that potentially were available to subpeasant households. This, in turn, invites the historian to enquire into household agency: how families used their resources to optimise their economic and social outcomes. Those resources had their limits, to be sure, but they were often sufficient for individual skill development, family labour strategy, and community-level adaptive behaviours that made a difference. Where protoindustry had once been seen as a default position for those without skill or capital – an unlimited supply of labour at a subsistence wage – it now seems more fruitful to see it in a context of household strategy: labour intensification that increased household income, and, over time, improved the dexterity and discipline of labour as well as encouraging numeracy, literacy, adaptability, and even the development of managerial skills.

The Labour-Intensive Path

A basic assumption about England and Western Europe's path to modern economic growth, one reinforced by early protoindustrialisation theory, is that the path was smoothed by the European economy's greater capital-intensity and by its early economic specialisation and market dependence. The latter factors acted to erode the integrity of the land-holding peasant household, which led to proletarianisation: a low-skilled wage labour force that worked under the direction of others. Seen from a twenty-first-century rather than the mid-twentieth-century perspective, this formulation now appears reasonable only as *one* path. Indeed, East Asian economic historians have posited a 'labour-intensive path toward industrialization' that was pioneered by Japan and followed, with a considerable delay, by other East and Southeast Asian economies. The key difference between the capital and labour-intensive paths, apart from the difference in factor endowments, is the assumed 'strong markets' of the capital-rich west and the 'strong families' of the labour-abundant east. These strong families sought to overcome the resource-scarcity and limited factor markets they faced by heightened discipline over the labour of all household members, coordination of labour time across agricultural and industrial pursuits, and attention to the age and sex composition of the family, all with the aim of ensuring the long-term survival of the lineage. Through generations of such complex, 'rational' planning the East Asian peasant family acquired the human capital to grasp the new opportunities of the industrial age when, at length, they presented themselves.

There is much about this model that deserves critical scrutiny, but it has the singular virtue of allowing us to see European protoindustrialisation in a new way – through an East Asian lens, so to speak.[21] Its chief weakness derives from the fact that the dichotomy of a western (capital-intensive) and eastern (labour-intensive) path is overdrawn. The early modern differences were real but perhaps not decisive. The 'weak' European family structure was not so weak as to preclude the cultivation, by peasants and subpeasants alike, of the disciplined and industrious practices that honed business skills as well as intensified consumer aspirations. The original 'protoindustrial household' contributed to this exaggeration since it was presented as a unit of undifferentiated labour, poor and unskilled; the new 'subpeasant household' by contrast is a market actor, industrious, strategic, and, thus, becoming schooled by experience to accumulate human capital.

Regional Economics

A valuable aspect of protoindustrialisation theory, but one that was never developed very much, concerns its regional context. Early studies were primarily focused on explaining *where* protoindustry would emerge and flourish. They rarely examined the ways in which such zones were linked and integrated into larger regional economies and urban networks. Rather, they focused on the economic character of regions of protoindustry, seeking some common characteristics. Rural industry often spread in 'open' rather than 'closed' villages (i.e. those not dominated by a lord or corporate body), in pastoral rather than arable districts, and in upland areas rather than fertile valleys.[22] But not always. The failure to identify consistent locational predictors was one more sign of the theory's shortcomings. But, the more relevant predictors are summarized by two fundamental economic concepts: opportunity cost and transaction costs.[23] The opportunity cost (the best-paying alternative available to an individual contemplating rural industrial work) depends on the available non-industrial options. Thus, it varied by family member and could also exhibit strong seasonal variation. Transaction costs refer to all non-production costs of an economic activity. While a manufacturer may find that production costs, especially the cost of labour and taxes, are lower in the countryside, this advantage must be set against the transaction costs of transportation, distribution, monitoring, and enforcement, all of which will be higher in far-flung rural settings than within a city.

Protoindustry gained its advantage when the balance of the lower opportunity cost of rural labour and the higher transaction costs of rural production tipped in favour of the countryside, which it did in many parts of western and central Europe in the course of the seventeenth century. To understand when and where this tipping took place, we need to attend to both the supply of rural labour (shaped by opportunity cost) and demand for it (shaped by transaction costs).

Underlying both were factors to which the early protoindustrial theorists paid little attention but that are now thought central to the growth process. First, the opportunity cost of labour was strongly affected by an enlarged desire for money income. More of the household's labour entered the market economy in order to secure the advantages of specialisation in production and to purchase market-supplied goods. What I have called an 'industrious revolution' helped reshape the supply curve for rural industrial labour.[24] Second, the unit cost of rural labour in many regions fell as skill levels rose. Highly skilled crafts long remained urban monopolies, but the spread of literacy and numeracy and an intensified interaction between city and countryside allowed for significant improvements in the quality of rural production. Finally, the costs of coordinating and monitoring rural production and transporting raw materials and (semi) finished goods fell with transport improvements, the rising volume of rural manufactures and improved information flows.

Information was important to all three of these developments. Industrious workers were motivated, in part, by knowledge of new opportunities for both earning and spending their money and their skills were enhanced as their capacity for quality control and the intro-duction of marginal technical improvements rose. Their employers and/or buyers became more committed to rural production as their knowledge of rural markets and their local differences increased.

This brings us to the dynamic regional interactions of protoindustrial households, commercial agricultural producers, urban artisans and merchants. The spatial agglomeration of demand could lead to economies of scale as lowered marketing costs (made possible by increased trade volumes) raised the return to specialised production. In craft production 'the main sunk cost is the irreversible investment in acquiring the skills that make specialized workers more productive than unspecialized ones'.[25] Market integration encourages such an up-front commitment to invest in skill acquisition, but so does a thickening of consumer demand.

Consumer demand, in turn, will rise among specialised producers who, of necessity, come to depend on other specialists for a growing range of goods. It is apparent from this interactive account that coordination among multiple economic actors is required to achieve a major rise in production and increasing returns to scale.

An interactive process like this had stood behind the remarkably rapid growth of the Flemish textile towns in the eleventh to thirteenth centuries. An urban archipelago of specialised producers secured Europe-wide markets not because of dramatic technological advances but via a trade-induced shift to greater specialisation and fuller utilisation of capital and labour. The age of protoindustry experienced another such reorganisation of industry that led to increasing returns. What distinguished it from the rural industry that had preceded it – for cottage-based manufacturing was nothing new – was its incorporation in a reorganisation of industrial production on a much larger geographic scale than the artisanal town-based production of earlier centuries.

The crisis of urban industry that confronted manufacturers from Venice to Leiden in the first half of the seventeenth century, part of the larger 'crisis of the seventeenth century', acted as a catalyst by pressing merchant manufacturers to seek cost reductions. A second catalyst, gaining force over time, was the growing supply of new products – Asian luxuries, European emulations, 'populuxe' goods, distilled spirits, tobacco-related products – that supported denser networks of distributors and retailers and stimulated producers to develop a far more differentiated range of consumer goods.[26]

The first catalyst led the early protoindustrialisation literature to emphasise rural industry as an 'escape' from the high cost urban guilds, but this fails to capture the full story.[27] The second catalyst, now more fully in view, allows us to see that producers went well beyond simply avoiding the high costs of the towns and their guilds. They sought both reduced costs and increased product differentiation. The result can better be described as the fuller exploitation of 'roundaboutness' – the elaboration of steps in production (increasing the scope for intermediate goods production) to create value at minimal cost – in order to reach larger markets than had been possible in the old urban manufacturing tradition.[28]

Roundabout production methods not only reduced costs; they increased the differentiation of final goods, allowing versions of goods to be marketed at what we today would call multiple 'price points'. That is, the industrial sector in the century or so before the advent of the classical Industrial Revolution was more varied and market-sensitive than it had been in previous centuries.

In sum, the growth of protoindustrial zones was part of a larger set of adaptations to new opportunities that also involved urban artisans, commercial farmers, merchants, and urban and international consumers. This went further in England than elsewhere in Europe in part because of its greater market integration but also because the artisan tradition there had achieved a high level of skill which supported a high level of innovation – both product and process innovation.

Human Capital and Technical Innovation

The causes of that high skill level and its implications for the Industrial Revolution that was yet to come remain topics of intense debate. In the old protoindustry literature, these questions could be sidestepped. Protoindustry made possible a large increase in the volume of manufactured output by unlocking a large volume of underutilised labour. Neither skill-augmentation nor technological innovation figured in the story; it was enough that labour should be cheap and abundant.

The new concept of protoindustry no longer claims that it was the 'first phase of (modern) industrialization,' one that sweeps the old artisan tradition aside. Rather, it is an integral part of a broader process of economic intensification in which new supplies of market-oriented labour, increased demand for an expanded range of goods, improved dissemination of information, and reduced transportation costs all interact. The augmentation of useful knowledge and of the skills and competences to act on new market opportunities stands at the centre of economic growth in the century before the classical Industrial Revolution – indeed, it remained critical until well into the nineteenth century. Consequently, the most important issue concerning labour was not whether it was cheap or dear but whether it was productive – whether it embodied more human capital that before. In the seventeenth and eighteenth centuries, this occurred via two broad tracks: craft skills and general manufacturing competence.

The role of craft guilds in increasing human capital in industry and encouraging innovation has attracted much attention and debate since Larry Epstein, in his examination of the institutional foundations of artisanal innovation, concluded that they were critical to long-term technical progress and, of equal importance, to the diffusion of 'best practice' across Europe. Just as agricultural historians have come to understand that Europe's food production in the early modern era was limited not by hard technological constraints but by the strength of incentives to adopt long-known techniques, so Epstein argued that 'it was not technological constraints as such that hampered the pre-modern economy, but the underutilization of available technologies.[29] Epstein argued that the practices of craft guilds in most of Europe facilitated skill creation via apprenticeship training, the broad recruitment of new artisans (resisting monopolisation of skills by closed social groups), and the encouragement of the long-distance circulation of skilled workers.[30]

Maarten Prak takes such claims a step further in proposing the existence of a long-term rise in European labour quality that he calls an 'artisanal revolution.' This gradual revolution led to the guild-supported creation of 'pools of skill': communities of craftsmen that developed and transmitted the tacit knowledge of how to fabricate goods. This tacit knowledge was diffused – from Italy to Upper Germany to the Low Countries and, later, to the British Isles – by the circulation of craftsmen, abetted by national rivalries. This last step was critical not only to raise labour quality in peripheral areas, but also to improve skills via competition.[31]

Prak agrees with Berg about the importance of a 'broad-church' conceptualisation of the process of industrialisation. The artisanal revolution can be traced through a stream of process and product innovations not only in textiles and metallurgy but also in such crafts as printing, papermaking, glassmaking, clock, watch, and lock making, shipbuilding, and coach making. Prak emphasises that the technological advances scattered across several centuries in many branches of manufacture were 'the unintended outcome of craftsmen going about their normal business.'[32]

One should now take this argument one step further. Human capital in the form of sophisticated craft skills emphasised by Epstein, Prak, and Berg came to be complemented by human capital in the form of 'manufacturing competence' (dexterity, stamina, numeracy, and responsibility among other characteristics of a productive industrial work force). If the former remained a characteristically urban form of human capital, the latter was developed in the most successful rural zones of protoindustry, and these competencies were nurtured within the 'subpeasant strata.'[33]

This important point is given credence by a recent county-level study of factors that might account for the state of English industrial production observed in 1831, at the end of the classical Industrial Revolution era. The 1831 industrialisation levels in forty-two English counties were correlated with possible causal factors as measured in 1760. The proximity to coal had no explanatory power (although proximity to waterpower did). Low wages in 1760 explained a portion of the differential industrialisation of English counties. But far more important explanatory factors were the density of rural population (measured by the ratio of population to farmland in 1760) and the ratio of small to large farms. The concentration of small farms was itself a good predictor of better nutrition and greater height, which were associated with basic measures of human capital, literacy, and numeracy. In short, areas of dense rural population, where protoindustry was usually widespread, were the best predictor of later industrialisation. The early protoindustrialisation theories sought a direct link: protoindustrial activity would lead to factories. What now appears more plausible is an indirect link: protoindustry led to human capital formation, particularly in manufacturing 'competency', and this was conducive to further industrialisation.[34]

In the eighteenth century, in England more than on the European continent, the artisan tradition had attained a high level of skill in many domains and had shown a notable interest in product innovations to cater to an expanding consumer market. Simultaneously, domestic production coordinated by merchant-manufacturers had expanded the volume of production and had entered new fields with the improvement of worker skills and the reduction of transaction costs. Moreover, the artisan workshop and the domestic cottage did not function in isolated economic spheres. They had always been linked, but over time the connections became closer. Falling transaction costs allowed merchants to pursue extensions of the division of labour and 'roundaboutness' – dividing a complicated task into a succession of simpler processes, many of which lent themselves to the use of methods with which economies of scale can be achieved.

This sketch of long-term development on several fronts simultaneously, each interacting with the other, has its critics. Some are dubious, to say the least, that artisan guilds – rent-seeking institutions at their core – really acted to diffuse skill and nurture innovation.[35] And, more fundamentally, doubts have been expressed that the achieved high levels of human capital – however it was amassed and diffused – could have led, via the 'normal business' of artisans and manufactures, to the technologies of the Industrial Revolution, establishing the foundations for sustained, modern economic growth. Just as earlier theorists of the Industrial Revolution invoked the hard barriers of capital, land, and energy supplies as blocking the pathway to endogenous modern economic growth, so now an 'epistemic barrier' is posited, that blocked the pathway.[36] Joel Mokyr, who makes this case most fully, stated flatly that 'Artisans could not expand the epistemic base of the techniques they used … In other words a purely artisanal knowledge society will not create a cluster of macroinventions that revolutionised production from the foundation.'[37]

The incontrovertible fact that today's economy could not exist without a major science-led expansion of the epistemic base lends Mokyr's 'hard limits' narrative a high degree of plausibility. His argument reduces artisanal skills to a second order of importance. He concedes, however, 'Without artisanal skills ... the insights of natural philosophers would have had no economic impact.'[38] And in another work he gives further ground in arguing that British science was not far advanced over that of Continental Europe, especially France but 'that the higher quality of workers, especially in the right tail of the skill distribution ... meant that it was much easier for their engineers, technicians, and skilled workers to adopt the new techniques and install, operate, and maintain the equipment in which it was embodied.' He and his co-authors conclude that the deeper causes of British manufacturing precocity 'have to be sought in the reasons for the higher quality of its workers.'[39] The causal arrow is now more difficult to detect.

Conclusion

Proponents of the human factor in economic history, especially those who are attentive to the development of human capital and the diffusion of knowledge and information, have, since the 1980s, received important support from developments in economic theory (especially from endogenous growth theory) and developments in contemporary economic life. But, they have always faced resistance from the advocates of hard barriers that stand between two worlds separated by the 'Industrial Revolution.' This revolution deserves its capital letters because it achieved a once-and-for-all transformation by surmounting a formidable limiting barrier. Over time, powerful arguments have been made in support of the critical role of capital accumulation, an agricultural revolution lifting Malthusian limits, the exploitation of fossil fuels, and a scientific revolution extending society's mastery of nature. All of these achievements seem to trump arguments focused on human capital deepening, information thickening, and market expansion because they represent heroic breakthroughs that are up to the task of accounting for the barrier-breaking character of the Industrial Revolution.

But it is now clear in a way that was not yet evident a generation ago that the miracle of the Industrial Revolution resides not so much in an initial acceleration (which, in any event, now seems less dramatic than it once did) but in its very long continuation. Economic growth was substantial before the era of the Industrial Revolution, and, indeed, science-based innovations were not major contributors to sustained growth until after that era. It is possible that long-term growth – based on labour intensification, expanding consumer demand, higher skills, improved access to information, fuller utilisation of available knowledge and resources – channelled human ingenuity toward the enrichment of the fund of propositional knowledge. This would sustain growth through our own time. However, before this new phase of modern economic growth, the ingenuity of the craftsman and the competence of protoindustrial labour – and, hence, protoindustry – held a central place in early modern economic development.[40]

Notes

1   The term was coined by Franklin Mendels in a PhD thesis of 1969 and in his influential article of 1972, 'Proto-industrialization: The First Phase of the Industrialization Process', *Journal of Economic History* 32, no. 1 (1972): 241–61. However, even before this publication, Charles and Richard Tilly recommended it as a concept of great research potential in 'Agenda for Economic History in the 1970s', *Journal of Economic History* 31, no. 1 (1971): 184–98. Soon afterward, the term featured prominently in hundreds of articles and dozens of books. Terms such as rural or cottage industry, putting-out and *verlagssystem*, and home handicraft had all preceded it, of course, but they did not suggest a theory or promise a historical analysis.

2   Peter Kriedte, Hans Medick, and Jürgen Schlumbohm, *Industrialization before Industrialization* (Cambridge: Cambridge University Press, 1981 [or. German ed. 1979]). Even earlier, Hans Medick, 'The Proto-industrial Family Economy', *Social History* 1, no. 3 (1976): 291–315.

3   Industrial labour's unskilled and undifferentiated character drew on the influential work of W. Arthur Lewis, 'Economic Development with Unlimited Supplies of Labour', *Manchester School* 22 (1954): 139–91.

4   Examples include David Levine, *Family Formation in an Age of Nascent Capitalism* (New York: Academic Press, 1977); Medick, 'The Proto-industrial Family Economy'; Rudolf Braun, 'Early Industrialization and Demographic Change in the Canton of Zurich', in *Historical Studies of Changing Fertility*, ed. Charles Tilly (Princeton: Princeton University Press 1978), 289–334.

5   Early critical and sceptical reviews include Donald C. Coleman, 'Proto-industrialization: A Concept Too Many', *Economic History Review* 36, no. 3 (1983): 435–48; R. Houston and K. Snell, 'Proto-Industrialization?: Cottage Industry, Social Change, and Industrial Revolution', *Historical Journal* 27, no. 2 (1984): 473–92; Myron Gutmann and Rene Leboutte, 'Rethinking Proto-industrialization and the Family', *Journal of Interdisciplinary History* 14, no. 3 (1984): 587–607. See also Sheilagh Ogilvie, 'Proto-industrialization

in Europe' *Continuity and Change* 8, no. 2 (1993): 159–79 and essays in Sheilagh Ogilvie and Marcus Cerman, eds., *European Proto-industrialization* (Cambridge: Cambridge University Press, 1996).

6   Maxine Berg, *The Age of Manufactures, 1700–1820* (London: Fontana, 1985); Maxine Berg, Pat Hudson, and Michael Sonenscher, eds., *Manufacture in Town and Country before the Factory* (Cambridge: Cambridge University Press, 1983); Maxine Berg, ed., *Markets and Manufacture in Early Industrial Europe* (London: Routledge, 1991).

7   Berg, *Age of Manufactures*, preface and 316–17. Other contributors included Pat Hudson, Michael Sonnenscher, Charles Sabel, and Jonathan Zeitlin.

8   Maxine Berg, 'The Genesis of Useful Knowledge' *History of Science* 45 (2007): 123–34. Here she argues that an artisanal 'economy of imitation' pushed innovation forward.

9   Charles Tilly, 'Demographic Origins of the European Proletariat' in David Levine, ed., *Proletarianization and Family History* (Orlando: Academic Press, 1984), 1–85.

10   Osamu Saito, 'Proto-industrialization and Labour-intensive Industrialization: Reflections on Smithian Growth and the Role of Skill Intensity' in Gareth Austin and Kaoru Sugihara, eds., *Labour-Intensive Industrialization in Global History* (London: Routledge, 2013), 85–106.

11   For a thorough review of these issues, see Jürgen Schlumbohm, 'Labour in Proto-industrialization: Big Questions and Micro-answers' in *Early Modern Capitalism. Economic and Social Change in Europe, 1400–1800*, ed. Maarten Prak (London: Routledge, 2001), 125–34.

12   Liana Viardi, *The Land and the Loom: Peasants and Profit in Northern France, 1680–1800* (Durham: Duke University Press, 1993); Ad Knotter, 'Problems of the 'Family Economy': Peasant Economy, Domestic Production and Labour Markets in Pre-industrial Europe' in *Early Modern Capitalism*, ed. Prak, 135–60.

13   Rudolf Braun, *Industrialisierung und Volksleben: die Veränderungen der lebensformen in einem ländlichen Industriegebiet vor 1800* (Zürich: E. Rentsch, 1960).

14   B.H. Slicher van Bath, *Samenleving onder spanning: Geschiedenis van het platteland in Overijssel* (Assen: Van Gorchum, 1957).

15   Paul M.M. Klep, *Bevolking en arbeid in transformatie: een onderzoek naar de ontwikkelingen in Brabant, 1700–1900* (Nijmegen: Socialistiese Uitgeverij Nijmegen, 1981).

16   E.A. Wrigley, 'Urban Growth and Agricultural Change: England and the Continent in the Early Modern Period' *Journal of Interdisciplinary History* 15, no. 4 (1985): 696–702; Charles Tilly, 'Demographic Origins of the European Proletariat' in *Proletarianization and Family History*, ed. Levine, 1–85; Robert Allen, 'Economic Structure and Agricultural productivity in Europe, 1300–1800' *European Review of Economic History* 3, no. 1 (2000): 1–25.

Tilly guesstimated that Europe's proletariat grew nearly sixfold between
1500 and 1800 and that 88 per cent of that growth was accounted for by
rural proletarians.

17 Jan de Vries, *European Urbanization, 1500–1800* (London: Methuen,
   1984), 221–45.

18 An exception is found in the excellent study of the small German city of
   Schwäbisch Hall by Terence McIntosh, *Urban Decline in Early Modern
   Germany: Schwäbisch Hall and Its Region, 1650–1750* (Chapel Hill: University
   of North Carolina Press, 1997).

19 The concept of subpeasant strata is based on the work of the Swedish
   anthropologist Orvar Löfgren who introduced the concept of 'peasant
   ecotype'. This social formation contains peasants proper – capable of acting
   as commercial farmers – as well as subpeasants. The latter has a foot in the
   agricultural economy (indeed, inheritance, marriage, and other good fortune
   could restore the other foot to that economy) but must seek other sources of
   support. They are, he argued, not definable as units of production, are more
   dependent on supra-regional markets, and are particularly influenced by
   their wage relationship with the peasant strata. Michael Mitterauer applied
   Löfgren's concepts to historical studies, emphasising the varied sources of
   support of subpeasant strata, including wage labour in agriculture, industrial
   production, and cultivation of their own garden plots. O. Löfgren, 'Peasant
   Ecotypes. Problems in the Comparative Study of Ecological Adaptation',
   Ethnologia Scandinavica 4 (1976): 100–15; M. Mitterauer, 'Peasant and Non-
   Peasant Family Forms in Relation to the Physical Environment and the Local
   Economy', *Journal of Family History* 17 (1992): 139–59; Knotter, 'Problems of
   the "Family Economy"', in *Early Modern Capitalism*, ed. Prak, 135–60.

20 Viardi, *The Land and the Loom*; Ulrich Pfister, *Die Zürcher fabriques.
   Protoindustrielles Wachstum vom 16. zum 18. Jahrhundert* (Zurich: Chronos,
   1992); Peter Kriedte, Hans Medick, and Jürgen Schlumbohm, 'Proto-
   industrialization Revisited: Demography, Social Structure and Modern
   Domestic Industry', *Continuity and Change* 8, no. 2 (1993): 217–52.

21 Kaoru Sugihara, 'Labour-intensive Industrialization in Global History: An
   Interpretation of East Asian Experiences', in *Labour-Intensive Industrialization*,
   eds. Austin and Sugihara, 20–64; Osamu Saito, 'An Industrious Revolution
   in an East Asian Market Economy? Tokugawa Japan and Implications for
   the Great Divergence', *Australian Economic History Review* 50, no. 3 (2010):
   240–61. My criticisms are presented in Jan de Vries, 'Industrious Peasants in
   East and West: Markets, Technology and Family Structures in Japanese and
   Western European Agriculture', *Australian Economic History Review* 51, no. 2
   (2011): 107–19, and Jan de Vries, 'The Industrious Revolution in East and
   West', in *Labour-Intensive Industrialization*, eds. Austin and Sugihara, 65–84.

22 A particularly exhaustive inventory of all German rural industrial districts

(*Gewerbelandschaften*) was made by Karl-Heinrich Kaufhold. He identified no fewer than 39. Karl-Heinrich Kaufhold, 'Gewerbelandschaften in der frühen Neuzeit (1650–1800)', in *Gewerbe- und Industrielandschaften vom Spätmittelalter bis ins 20. Jahrhundert*, ed. H. Pohl (Stuttgart: F. Steiner Verlag Wiesbaden, 1986), 112–202.

23 Ogilvie was, I believe, the first to bring order to this aspect of protoindustrialisation theory. See Sheilagh Ogilvie, 'The Beginnings of Industrialization', in *Germany. A New Social and Economic History. Vol. II. 1630–1800*, ed. Sheilagh Ogilvie (London: Hodder Education, 1996), 118–36.

24 Jan de Vries, *The Industrious Revolution: Consumer Behavior and the Household Economy, 1650 to the Present* (Cambridge: Cambridge University Press, 2008), 71–2, 96–104.

25 An interesting account of this dynamic process, with applications to agriculture rather than industry, is found in George Grantham, 'Contra Ricardo: On the Macroeconomics of Pre-industrial Economies', *European Review of Economic History* 3, no. 2 (1999): 199–232. The quotation is from 217.

26 Here, too, the contribution of Maxine Berg is critical. Her explorations of the new world of consumer goods include Maxine Berg and Elizabeth Eger, eds., *Luxury in the Eighteenth Century. Debates, Desires and Delectable Goods* (Basingstoke: Palgrave Macmillan, 2003); Maxine Berg, *Luxury and Pleasure in Eighteenth Century Britain* (Oxford: Oxford University Press, 2005); Maxine Berg et al., eds., *Goods from the East, 1600–1800: Trading Eurasia* (Basingstoke: Palgrave, 2015).

27 Myron Gutmann, *Toward the Modern Economy. Early Industry in Europe, 1500–1800* (Philadelphia: Temple University Press, 1988). This ambitious analysis of industrial history interprets protoindustry as the product of a 'second crisis of urban industry'.

28 Allyn Young, 'Increasing Returns and Economic Progress', *Economic Journal* 38 (1928): 527–42. See also, Saito, 'Proto-industrialization', 97.

29 S.R. Epstein, *Freedom and Growth: The Rise of States and Markets in Europe, 1300–1750* (London: Routledge, 2000), 7.

30 S.R. Epstein, 'Transferring Technical Knowledge and Innovating in Europe, c. 1200–c. 1800', in *Technology, Skills and the Pre-modern Economy in the East and the West*, eds. Maarten Prak and Jan Luiten van Zanden (Leiden: Brill, 2013), 25–68.

31 Maarten Prak, 'Technology and Human Capital Formation', in *Technology, Skills, and the Pre-modern Economy*, eds. Prak and Van Zanden, 18.

32 Ibid.

33 Kelly, Mokyr, and Ó Gráda speak of Britain's 'higher quality of workers, especially in the right tail of the skill distribution', 384 and of productive ability and dexterity in Britain being 'more skewed than elsewhere, so there was a much larger density in the right tail', 364. Here, I argue that

the artisanal human capital of the right tail of the skill distribution was
complimented by the manufacturing competence further to the left, in
the centre of that distribution. Morgan Kelly, Joel Mokyr, and Cormac
Ó Gráda, 'Precocious Albion: A New Interpretation of the British Industrial
Revolution', *Annual Review of Economics* 6 (2014): 364, 374.

34 Morgan Kelly, Joel Mokyr, and Cormac Ó Gráda, 'Roots of the Industrial
Revolution', University of Warwick, CAGE working paper no. 248 (2015).

35 For a vigorous critique of the 'good guild' literature see Sheilagh Ogilvie,
The European Guilds: An Economic Analysis (Princeton: Princeton University
Press, 2019).

36 In *The Culture of Growth: The Origins of the Modern Economy* (Princeton:
Princeton University Press, 2017) Mokyr argues that a cultural
transformation – changing the beliefs and values of elites – was necessary to
establish the basis for a later 'Industrial Enlightenment' that could produce
and disseminate the propositional knowledge that enabled an industrial
revolution. It was not sufficient, as many economic historians have argued,
to establish efficient institutions. The root problem was not inadequate
incentive structures, it was insufficient scientific knowledge. Another study
emphasising the primacy of scientific discovery is Margaret C. Jacob, *The First
Knowledge Economy: Human Capital and the European Economy, 1750–1850*
(Cambridge: Cambridge University Press, 2014).

37 Ibid., 273.

38 38 Mokyr, *Culture of Growth*, 274.

39 Kelly, Mokyr, and Ó Gráda, 'Precocious Albion', 384.

40 For a fuller discussion of this approach to economic growth across the divide
of the Industrial Revolution see Jan de Vries, 'Economic Growth before
and after the Industrial Revolution: A Modest Proposal', in *Early Modern
Capitalism*, ed. Prak, 177–94.

7

Machinery, Labour Absorption, and Small Producer Capitalism in the Comparative History of Industrialisation

Osamu Saito

Introduction

Much has been said about the 'machinery question' and about non-factory forms of production in the English Industrial Revolution. The former was first raised by David Ricardo when he announced his change of mind in the third edition of his *Principles* and questioned whether labour-saving machinery caused technologically induced structural unemployment or if its higher productivity caused increased demand for products and hence for labour to produce them.[1] Subsequently, the 'machinery question' has been revisited by economic theorists. Questions concerning nonfactory forms of production came to the fore with the 'gradualist' and the 'alternative path' approaches to the study of industrialisation in the 1980s.[2] Maxine Berg's small producer capitalism, an industrial growth path based on flexible specialisation and division of labour among small-scale, skill-intensive producers, was a contribution to the latter.[3]

However, these two lines of research have so far been carried out independently of each other. This chapter discusses the relationship between them, which involves two tasks. One is to place the concept of small producer capitalism in a wider context of structural change associated with the Industrial Revolution and ask if it was really an alternative path to factory industrialisation. The other is to bring John Hicks's theoretical attempt to reformulate Ricardo's analysis of the machinery effect back into historical context.[4] Hicks restated Ricardo's thesis as a question of why it took so long to restore the balance between the new machinery's negative and positive effects on employment. It was the skill- and labour-intensive machinery sector that reabsorbed labour released from the machine-using sector. However, there were many other industries and trades that absorbed labour. Historians should question the relationship between those sectors that absorbed labour and those that released labour, and since the effects of machinery were most pronounced on female employment, this release–absorption issue ought to be explored as a gender question.

To undertake these tasks, this chapter uses historical occupational statistics provided by the International Network for the Comparative History of Occupational Structure (INCHOS).[5] I use the INCHOS's sector-specific, gender-specific labour force statistics for four countries to explore changes in the size of employment, release and absorption, and withdrawal from the labour market, separately for men and women.

The Issues

The basic facts about the English Industrial Revolution are now reasonably clear. While it was a period of structural change, average annual rates of per capita output growth were not impressive. The growth rate of aggregate output rose towards the end of the period but population increase also accelerated from the mid-eighteenth century, supplying abundant labour for a growing economy. Thus, despite an unmistakable increase in manufacturing output, economic growth on a per capita basis stayed low until the 1830s, and real wage growth remained stagnant for an even longer period.[6] Thus, when the factory emerged the growth industries were surrounded by thick layers of labour-using trades, most of which took the form of putting-out, workshops, and sweating.[7] The factory replaced some of those trades but many ended up with sweated labour. In between, argues Berg, there was a path she labelled small producer capitalism.

Her small producers consisted mostly of producers of consumer goods, such as buckles, buttons, cutlery, and watch-chains. Yet a cursory look at Birmingham's industrial structure reveals that manufacturers supplying edge tools and scissors to other producers also occupied an unmistakable place in the city's occupational structure. Moreover, the region developed a 'division of labour between processing and intermediate manufacture in the hinterland, and finishing and assembly in the centre.'[8] Sargant Florence once identified a general framework of 'productive sequences' from extraction to processing and assembly, and then to distribution. Historically, according to him, 'machines were first applied to the processing manufactures, cotton and wool textiles, rather than clothing; iron and steel, rather than engineering.' This was because the processing industries, whose products are generally homogenous, could enjoy 'economies of scale.'[9] It is therefore unsurprising to find skilled manufacturers taking on the new consumer markets where design, ornamentation, and fashion were so important and beyond the capabilities of machinery alone. However, small producer capitalists included mechanical engineering enterprises. They were skilled and adaptive, and it was they who produced machines and tools for other producers. Given the definitional equation that gross output can be divided up into interindustry transactions, fixed capital formation, consumption, and exports, it is to be expected that mechanical engineering enjoyed larger shares of interindustry transactions and fixed capital formation than other manufacturing industries. This can be substantiated from an input–output table for the UK in 1935 for which figures are more reliable than a century earlier. According to Tibor Barna's estimates,[10] personal consumption was unimportant for engineering, and the remaining products were either bought up by other industries or went to fixed capital stocks or exports. This was in contrast with clothing, an industry where consumer markets were central. They sold its largest share to other producers, both domestic and overseas, although nothing went to fixed capital. In the early phase of industrialisation, it is engineering that was 'the chief manufacturing contributor to capital formation'. Moreover, the small engineering producers played a key role in industrial 'swarming' with interlinked trades such as in the Birmingham and Black Country industrial complex of the 1930s.[11] While small producer capitalism was not an alternative to machine-based mass production, this swarming functioned as an absorbent of skilled labour in early industrialisation.

Turning to Hicks's reformulation of the machinery effect on employment, we find a different set of issues. Despite the consensus that macroeconomic performance was not spectacular with a variety of non-factory production organisations occupying an unmistakable place in the economy of the day, the impulse that mechanisation produced should not be underestimated. Hicks's exposition has turned our attention to the structural readjustment process that the introduction of labour-saving machinery necessitated. 'Economists have throughout been aware of these facts, but they could always be dismissed as consequences of labour immobility. New techniques are bound to diminish the demand for some sorts of labour, and to increase the demand for others.' But, asks Hicks, 'What is the net effect on the demand for labour as a whole?'[12] While the amount of labour required to operate a new machine was reduced, that of labour required to build it tended to increase.[13] He made it clear that asking why the absorption of labour was so delayed would go a considerable way towards a better understanding of the Industrial Revolution. What he did not realise was that the effects were gender-specific. Demand for female labour diminished whereas the demand for male labour increased.

Now all this can be set in a context of occupational structure. According to the Cambridge Group's tentative estimates for England and Wales,[14] the share of secondary-sector employment was already higher than 40 per cent by 1710. The sector's share in total output kept expanding, and the introduction of machinery in manufacturing meant a further impetus to this output growth but not necessarily to the sector's labour force growth. The primary sector's share in the labour force was declining from the level of about one-half to one-third of total male employment over the eighteenth century, suggesting that, given a high level of population growth, a substantial number of workers were released from the countryside. However, the secondary sector does not seem to have absorbed much of this excess supply as its share increased only marginally during that period. In textiles, for example, the ratio of labour to capital declined dramatically with mechanisation. Spinning jennies and mules are said to have taken away a large number of jobs from female workers (the Ricardian machinery effect). These women may or may not have been left unemployed, but what became 'an alternative to mechanisation' was certainly the employment of cheap female labour.[15] In the next section, I address these questions by exploring the labour force statistics.

Structural Change

In this and the next sections, I make full use of the new INCHOS data for England and Wales, Belgium, Japan, and Italy.[16] Belgium embarked on industrialisation several decades after England, but with an almost identical set of growth industries, i.e. textiles, iron, and coal, while Japan and Italy represent the experience of latecomer industrialisers of the period c. 1870–1940. I begin with the analysis of changing sectoral shares and female ratios derived directly from estimates of the labour force and its growth between benchmark years in the four countries. Table 7.1 sets out the results for the primary, secondary, and tertiary sectors with both sexes combined.

A first measure of industrialisation is the share of the secondary sector in the labour force (line 4). In all four countries this measure increased as the primary-sector share declined (line 1). But the level of the secondary-sector share was higher in the early industrialisers than in the latecomers. The latter's levels in the 1930s were well below the levels the former had achieved in the early nineteenth century. However, it is evident that the slope of the upward industrialisation trend

Table 7.1 Sectoral shares and growth of the labour force: England and Wales (1710–1871), Belgium (1846–1910), Japan (1874–1935), and Italy (1901–36)

Sector	England and Wales			Belgium		Japan			Italy	
Shares and growth measures	1710	1817	1871	1846	1910	1874	1909	1935	1901	1936
Primary sector										
(1) Sectoral share (%)	48	32	17	41	23	70	58	45	62	52
(2) Female share	0.36	0.22	0.22	0.31	0.32	–	0.43	0.44	0.38	0.38
(3) Absolute increase (%)		13	–13		0		–10	–9		–6
Secondary sector										
(4) Sectoral share (%)	38	44	47	42	45	13	19	23	21	26
(5) Female share	0.39	0.29	0.25	0.42	0.25	–	0.32	0.24	0.33	0.25
(6) Absolute increase (%)		52	51		50		55	37		50
Manufacturing										
(7) Sectoral share (%)	34	36	38	37	37	–	15	18	17	17
(8) Female share	0.44	0.34	0.32	0.46	0.32	–	0.39	0.30	0.41	0.33
(9) Absolute increase (%)		40	39		31		–	32		33
Tertiary sector										
(10) Sectoral share (%)	14	24	35	37	43	17	22	32	30	33
(11) Female share	0.45	0.48	0.46	0.37	0.43	–	0.36	0.32	0.30	0.33
(12) Absolute increase (%)		41	45		50		55	72		56
Total labour force										
(13) Sectoral share (%)	100	100	100	100	100	100	100	100	100	100
(14) Female share	0.38	0.31	0.32	0.37	0.32	–	0.39	0.36	0.36	0.34
(15) Absolute increase (%)		0.5	1.4		0.9		0.5	0.8		0.4

Measures
Sectoral share: % of the total labour force
Femal share: proportion of females in the total labour force
Absolute increase: % of the total absolute increase between two benchmark years
Rate of growth: average annual rate (%) of growth in the labour force between two benchmark years

Sources: England and Wales (1710 and 1871) from Leigh Shaw–Taylor and E.A. Wrigley, 'Occupational Structure and Population Change', in The Cambridge Economic History of Modern Britain, I: 1700–1870, edited by Roderick Floud, Jane Humphries, and Paul Johnson (Cambridge: Cambridge University Press, 2014), table 2.6, 68. I am grateful to the authors for allowing me to use their research. Data for other countries are derived from the unpublished manuscripts by Buyst, Saito, and Settsu, and Danielle and Malanima for Saito and Shaw-Taylor, eds., Occupational Structure (forthcoming).

remained rather shallow, if not completely flat, everywhere. It becomes even clearer with the share of manufacturing as an alternative measure of industrialisation (line 7). Given the historiography of the Industrial Revolution, this may appear surprising.

A second measure makes use of the absolute increase in the labour force between two benchmark years and is expressed as a percentage of the sum of all sectoral absolute increases. It shows, within the total increase, how many went to which sector. Note that the total increase was largely a product of population growth. For all the cases examined in the table, the average rate of population growth was in fact not negligible (line 15). It is probable that the sectoral absolute increase takes a positive value even when the sectoral share is declining. This was indeed the case for the English primary sector between 1710 and 1817, but in the following period, as well as in the other three countries the measure took a negative value (line 1). It is in this period that the rural sector released a good deal of labour, which was absorbed by the other two sectors. In Japan and Italy the proportion of workers who went to the tertiary sector was somewhat higher than the proportion absorbed by the secondary sector, while it was the other way round in England and Wales (lines 5 and 11). In the English case, however, the percentage of workers absorbed by the secondary sector declined from the pre-1817 to the post-1817 period (line 5). The same can be said about those who went to manufacturing (line 8).

Another measure shown in the table, the female share in the sectoral labour force, reveals that the above findings were gender specific. For both manufacturing and the entire secondary sector, this measure exhibited a substantial decline. With industrialisation, employment opportunities for women declined in manufacturing and the impact of decline was particularly strong in the English and Belgian cases (lines 6 and 9). It was the service sector that absorbed a large proportion of the increased supply of female labour, where the female ratio in most cases tended to rise (lines 11 and 12).

Gendered Patterns

All this suggests that any analysis with both sexes combined is likely to conceal important gender biases with respect to the machinery effect on industrial employment. In the English case, moreover, the masculinisation of the agricultural labour force progressed (line 3),[17] which must have acted as an extra pressure on the female labour market in general. Unfortunately, both changes took place before modern occupational censuses were taken. This constraint led Shaw-Taylor and Wrigley to make bold assumptions relating to how the female shares changed between 1710 and 1851: they assumed that noticeable changes took place in agriculture, clothing, and textiles only. In agriculture more women left the sector than males. So did females in textiles, but in clothing the pattern was the opposite.[18] It is worth noting that while the masculinisation of agricultural employment was an English phenomenon, similar trends in clothing and textiles were also found in Belgium between 1846 and 1910.

Let us have a closer look at this Belgian case. There, the demise of the rural linen industry occurred in the mid-nineteenth century, enabling us to assess the size of labour release from textiles as well as from the countryside. The task is to estimate how many women lost employment opportunities at sectoral and subsectoral levels by comparing a counterfactual size of the supply of labour with the actual situation in 1910. Suppose, first, that the labour force in the primary and textile sectors increased at the same annual average rate as for the total male labour force, at 1.0 per cent, and, second, that the female shares in 1910 remained unchanged from 1846, at 0.31 in the primary and 0.69 in textiles. This gives us hypothetical numbers of female workers in the two sectors in 1910: 491,000 and 436,000 respectively. The comparison with the actual numbers in that year (261,000 and 159,000) indicates that the numbers of women who had to seek employment elsewhere were 229,000 and 277,000 respectively.

Table 7.2 presents the results of this gender-specific exercise for the three major sectors plus manufacturing and its subsectors across the four countries. The figures show the difference between the hypothetical size of labour supply and the actual situation expressed as a percentage of the hypothetical total supply of labour. The minus sign indicates labour release and the plus sign labour absorption. In England and Wales between 1710 and 1851, for example, 23 per cent of the total male absolute increase was released by the primary sector (line 1), and this was absorbed by the secondary and tertiary sectors, 12 and 11 per cent respectively (lines 2 and 3); but it was the tertiary sector that absorbed a great deal of labour, both male and female, at the time of industrialisation (line 3).

Sharp contrasts exist between the male and female columns for both manufacturing and the entire secondary sector (lines 5 and 2). Without exception, the male measure took a positive and the female a negative value. Particularly drastic was what happened in textiles in the English and Belgian cases (line 7): the size of the negative values was large, accounting for much of the decline of employment opportunities in manufacturing. Such a dramatic decline did not take place in Japan and Italy. Even in labour-abundant countries, the introduction of

labour-saving technology from the West must have exerted an unmistakable pressure on employment; however, the employment of women in
Japanese textiles increased rather than decreased. The size of its increase
was marginal, but it suggests that Japan's textile manufacturers made a
conscious effort to operate the Western machinery with a labour-using
arrangement of a workforce of unmarried young women.[19] Again Italy
came in between. One may suggest that some of those who lost job
opportunities in textiles went to clothing, but this occurred only in
Belgium (line 6). There were some who went to other manufacturing
industries (line 10), but even there Belgian and Japanese women lost
employment opportunities. A vast majority of them were absorbed by
the tertiary sector (line 3).

The female column total deserves attention (line 4). The measure
indicates where the rest of women went after all the entry, release, and
absorption processes had been settled within the labour force. When
it takes a negative value, there were women who withdrew from the
labour market. This measure was negative in all the four countries, and
the size of withdrawal was larger in the English and Belgian cases where
the machinery effect had the greatest impact on female employment in
textiles. More than one in four English women withdrew, while it was
nearly one in five for Belgian women.

Turning to men, the figures for the secondary sector might suggest
that industrialisation offered them more job opportunities (line 2),
but the comparison with the figures for manufacturing (line 5) and
for the tertiary sector (line 3) implies that a considerable number of
men were absorbed into mining and construction, and also commerce
and transport, not necessarily into manufacturing. It is true that some
manufacturing industries absorbed a substantial proportion of male
labour (lines 8, 9, and 10), but the importance of non-manufacturing
groups of subsectors should not be underestimated in this respect.

Finally, a few comments on the growth of skill-intensive industries, particularly engineering. The industry's contribution to labour
absorption was not large (line 9), but the increase in the number of
machine- and toolmakers was rapid in the English and Japanese cases
and, to a lesser extent, in the Italian case.[20] Engineering occupied a
pivotal place: engineering firms were customers of iron and steel but
at the same time functioned as suppliers of intermediate inputs to
other manufacturers, thus enjoying 'economies of specialisation'.[21] This
points to the existence of a causal link between the rise of engineering
and subsequent growth performance of the economy. The link is well
known for Britain. For Japan too, its development in the interwar
years is said to have been conducive for the country's unprecedented

Table 7.2 Differences between the actual and the hypothetical size of labour supply expressed as a percentage of the total: England and Wales (1710–1851), Belgium (1846–1910), Japan (1906–35), and Italy (1901–36)

Sector	England and Wales 1710–1851		Belgium 1846–1910		Japan 1906–35		Italy 1901–36	
	Male	Female	Male	Female	Male	Female	Male	Female
A. Three sectors								
(1) Primary	-23	-33	-21	-17	-17	-16	-11	-13
(2) Secondary	12	-10	11	-18	6	-2	6	-3
(3) Tertiary	11	17	10	17	11	3	4	6
(4) Total	0	-27	0	-18	0	-15	0	-9
B. Manufacturing and its subsectors								
(5) Manufacturing	6	-10	3	-19	5	-2	4	-3
(6) Clothing	-1	-1	0	3	0	0	0	-3
(7) Textiles	-1	-12	-4	-20	1	1	0	-4
(8) Iron & steel, metal working, etc.	0	0	2	0	3	0	0	0
(9) Engineering	1	0	2	0	1	0	3	0
(10) Rest of manufacturing	7	2	4	-2	2	-3	2	3

Sources: See table 7.1.

Notes:
For the method of estimating the hypothetical supply of labour, see text. Percentage of the total is computed with the hypothetical total supply of labour being 100.
For England and Wales the calculation is made with 1710–1851, a periodisation different from table 1, because there is no point to conduct this gender-specific exercise by linking 1710 to 1817, for both of which female estimates are speculative (see Shaw-Taylor and Wrigley, 'Occupational Structure', 67–9).

growth from 1955 onwards.[22] The other issue concerns the typology of technological progress. If powered machinery capable of producing interchangeable parts and components were introduced, it would make the machinery industry more skill-saving and pave the way to mass production, which is what British engineers found when they saw American exhibits at the Crystal Palace, 1851.[23] If, on the other hand, they remained skill-intensive, then the manufacturing sector would be able to retain flexibility and adaptability in terms of both size and form of production organisation. The survival of the industrial districts, or 'swarming' in early twentieth-century Britain, that Marshall and Florence talked about, may have something to do with this skill-intensive, labour-using engineering tradition.

Discussion

In the early phase of industrialism, common forces were at work: population increase in the countryside and the machinery effect. Both acted as a supply-side pressure on the labour market for men and women, as a result of which they had to seek employment elsewhere. Thus, for example, Belgium faced a challenge posed by one million people looking for alternative jobs. Fifty-four per cent of the half million men found a secondary-sector job and the rest went to the tertiary sector. Of the half million women, 47 per cent found a service job while only a few per cent were absorbed by other manufacturing industries. The rest simply withdrew from the job market.

What happened to the English female labour market half a century previously appears to have been similar. Although the estimates for England and Wales in table 7.2 are too speculative at this stage, there are two village-level data sets showing a vivid picture of changes that took place in the rural labour market between 1782/90 and 1851.[24] Cardington, Bedfordshire, and the Dorset parish of Corfe Castle in the late eighteenth century were villages where cottage industries offered employment opportunities to women and children. Cardington's lace making was one of the few domestic industries that survived the Industrial Revolution, whereas Corfe Castle's spinning and knitting were wiped out by the mid-nineteenth century, just as in many other protoindustrial areas of this period. The contrast is reflected in the two villages' changing sex ratio of the population. The female ratio had been higher in both parish populations before the turn of the century, but while Cardington's male–female imbalance was marginally reduced during the period, in Corfe Castle there was an exodus of men and hence a sharp rise in the female ratio. If the Corfe case were representative of what a majority of

England's protoindustrial districts experienced, then the application of the formula used for table 7.2 would imply that three out of ten women who might have searched for an alternative job withdrew from the labour force.[25] Female jobs left in the marketplace must have mostly been in sweating and services and concentrated in urban areas, making it difficult for married women to combine work and family life.

The withdrawal of women from the labour force was found across the sample countries, and its level seems to have been inversely correlated with that of labour intensity in the country's leading industry. Why did those women withdraw? The Corfe case suggests that it was involuntary: since many of them stayed on in the countryside, they were forced to be idle once job opportunities disappeared. For those who left the village for towns, the situation was no different either – most of the jobs available there were not suitable for married women. Although an income effect might have been at work for those whose husband was in steady, better-paid employment, a majority must have involuntarily withdrawn in the urban sector too.

For men, there was no widespread withdrawal from the labour market. Male-dominant processing industries such as iron and steel employed less than one might expect and, hence, the pressure on real wages remained intense. But there were many labour-using industries and trades that offered a job. Particularly important was the availability of skilled jobs in manufacturing. Wherever a large market for skilled workers existed it made the absorption of excess labour easier and kept the industrial structure adaptable and flexible in the subsequent course of industrialisation. The concept of small-producer capitalism highlights the historical significance of this path, which is expected to have worked not just in the early phase of British industrialism but also for countries like Japan who chose a labour-intensive type of development strategy.[26] Finally, this brings us back to the gender question. If skilled men were better paid than other male workers, then it might have been one of the factors accounting for their partners' withdrawal from paid employment.

Notes

The author wishes to thank Leigh Shaw-Taylor for his generous support in the data preparation for this work.

1   Maxine Berg, *The Machinery Question and the Making of Political Economy, 1815–1848* (Cambridge: Cambridge University Press, 1980), chapter 4. The third edition of David Ricardo's *Principles of Political Economy* was published in 1821.

2   Maxine Berg, 'Small Producer Capitalism in Eighteenth Century England',
    Business History 30, no. 1 (1993): 17–39. The most influential of all the
    gradualist literature is N.F.R. Crafts, *British Economic Growth during the
    Industrial Revolution* (Oxford: Oxford University Press, 1985) and that of
    the alternative path school Charles Sabel and Jonathan Zeitlin, 'Historical
    Alternatives to Mass Production: Politics, Markets and Technology in
    Nineteenth-Century Industrialization', *Past & Present* 108 (1985): 133–76. For
    a critical examination of these revisionist interpretations, see Maxine Berg
    and Pat Hudson, 'Rehabilitating the Industrial Revolution', *Economic History
    Review* 45, no. 1 (1994): 24–53.
3   Berg, 'Small Producer'. For Birmingham, see also Maxine Berg, 'Commerce
    and Creativity in Eighteenth-Century Birmingham', in Maxine Berg, ed.,
    Markets and Manufacture in Early Industrial Europe (London: Routledge,
    1991), 173–204; and Maxine Berg, 'Inventors of the World of Goods', in
    *From Family Firms to Corporate Capitalism: Essays in Business and Industrial
    History in Honour of Peter Mathias*, eds. Kristine Bruland and Patrick O'Brien
    (Oxford: Clarendon Press, 1998), 20–50.
4   John Hicks, *A Theory of Economic History* (Oxford: Clarendon Press 1969),
    149–54 and 169–71. See also John Hicks, 'IS-LM: An Explanation', in *Further
    Essays on Money and Growth* (Oxford: Clarendon Press, 1977), 184–90.
5   This research network is organised by Osamu Saito and Leigh Shaw-Taylor at
    the Cambridge Group.
6   Crafts, *British Economic Growth*; N.F.R. Crafts and C.K. Harley, 'Output
    Growth and the British Industrial Revolution: A Restatement of the Crafts-
    Harley View', *Economic History Review* 45, no. 4 (1992): 703–30; and Charles
    H. Feinstein, 'Pessimism Perpetuated: Real Wages and the Standard of Living
    in Britain during and after the Industrial Revolution', *Journal of Economic
    History* 58, no. 3 (1998): 625–58.
7   For the coexistence of various production organisations, see Maxine Berg,
    The Age of Manufactures: Industry, Innovation and Work in Britain, 1700–1820
    (London: Fontana, 1985); and Berg and Hudson, 'Rehabilitating', 42.
8   Berg, 'Small Producer', 33–4; Berg, 'Inventors', 27; and Berg, 'Commerce and
    Creativity', 181.
9   P. Sargant Florence, *The Logic of British and American Industry: A Realistic
    Analysis of Economic Structure and Government* (London: Routledge and
    Kegan Paul, 1953), 12, and for his framework of productive sequences, see 9;
    and Nathan Rosenberg, 'Capital Goods, Technology, and Economic Growth',
    Oxford Economic Papers 15, no. 3 (1963), 220.
10 Tibor Barna, 'The Interdependence of the British Economy', *Journal of the
    Royal Statistical Society: Series A* 115, no. 1 (1952), 52–3.
11 Florence, *Logic*, 11 and 85–6. His term 'swarming' has much resemblance to
    Alfred Marshall's 'industrial district'. See Berg, 'Small Producer', 26.

12 Hicks, *Theory*, 148–9.

13 A numerical exposition Hicks made assumes that with technological innovation, the number of labour units required to operate the machine is reduced from ten to eight, but the corresponding requirement to make it is increased from ten to fifteen. It is in period eleven when the initial levels of output and employment are recovered. Hicks, *Theory*, Appendix, 168–71.

14 Leigh Shaw-Taylor and E.A. Wrigley, 'Occupational Structure and Population Change', in *The Cambridge Economic History of Modern Britain*, I: *1700–1870*, eds. Roderick Floud, Jane Humphries, and Paul Johnson (Cambridge: Cambridge University Press, 2014): 53–88.

15 Berg, *Age of Manufactures*, 146.

16 Data source for England and Wales is the Cambridge Group's preliminary estimates used in Shaw-Taylor and Wrigley, 'Occupational Structure'. For the other three countries, the data are taken from unpublished manuscripts and appendix tables for the forthcoming book, Saito and Shaw-Taylor, eds., *Occupational Structure*. The authors for the three chapters are Erik Buyst for Belgium, Osamu Saito and Tokihiko Settsu for Japan, and Vittorio Daniele and Paolo Malanima for Italy. Note that the English occupational tables are currently in the process of revision. The updated version will appear in Shaw-Taylor's chapter for the forthcoming *Occupational Structure*. There are two major areas where revision is being made – age coverage (from 20-plus to 15-plus) and ways in which sectorally unallocated labourers are allocated; it is expected, therefore, that revised sectoral shares would not be very different from the current estimates. Note also that while subsectors are grouped together to make intercountry comparisons possible, there remains one disagreement: while 'commerce' for England and Wales, Belgium, and Italy consists of dealers and sellers, Japan's includes financial and some other services as well.

17 This was a consequence of the proletarianisation in eighteenth-century English agriculture. See Shaw-Taylor, 'Agrarian Capitalism'.

18 Shaw-Taylor and Wrigley, 'Occupational Structure', 68–70.

19 According to Kiyokawa, the cotton mill, operated with technologically superior ring-frames on a shift work arrangement, turned out to be more labour-intensive than the mule-equipped mill. The factory was compatible with high labour intensity. Y. Kiyokawa, 'Technology Choice in the Cotton-spinning Industry: The Switch from Mules to Ring Frames', in Minami Ryoshin, K.S. Kim, F. Makino, and J. Seo, eds., *Acquiring, Adapting and Developing Technologies: Lessons from the Japanese Experience* (New York: St Martins Press, 1995), 85–111.

20 The average annual rate of growth in the engineering labour force was 2.6 per cent for England and wales, 1817–71; 1.8 per cent for Belgium, 1846–1910; 5.7 per cent for Japan, 1909–35; and 2 per cent for Italy, 1901–36

(calculated from the same data in table 7.1). Except for Belgium, the growth of engineering was faster than that of iron and steel.

21 Rosenberg, 'Capital Goods', 220.
22 H.B. Chenery, S. Shishido, and T. Watanabe, 'The Pattern of Japanese Growth, 1914–1954', *Econometrica* 30, no. 1 (1962): 98–139.
23 Nathan Rosenberg, ed., *The American System of Manufactures: The Report of the Committee on the Machinery of the United States 1855, and the Special Reports of George Wallis and Joseph Whitworth 1854* (Edinburgh: Edinburgh University Press, 1969), Introduction.
24 Osamu Saito, 'Who Worked When: Life-time Profiles of Labour Force Participation in Cardington and Corfe Castle in the Late Eighteenth and Mid-Nineteenth Centuries', *Local Population Studies* 22 (1979): 14–29.
25 In the Corfe case, men's propensity to out-migrate was so high that, to estimate a hypothetical supply of female labour, I used the actual size of female population aged 15 and over. This population size stood at 1,024 in 1790 and 4,645 in 1851, and the corresponding number of women in employment at 385 and 575 respectively. From the hypothetical supply of female labour in 1851 (1,746 = 4,645×0.38), the proportion of those who could not find a job is estimated to have been 0.32 (= [1,746–575]/[4,645–1024]).
26 Osamu Saito, 'Proto-Industrialization and Labour-Intensive Industrialization: Reflections on Smithian Growth and the Role of Skill Intensity', in *Labour-Intensive Industrialization in Global History*, eds. Gareth Austin and Kaoru Sugihara (Abingdon: Routledge, 2013), 85–106.

8

The Mechanisation of English Cotton Textile Production and the Industrial Revolution

Patrick Karl O'Brien

The Great Divergence, the First Industrial Revolution, and the Mechanisation of Cotton Textile Production

Debates about a chronology for the 'Great Divergence' in standards of living between Europe and Asia, as well as recent 'reconfigurations of the first Industrial Revolution' as a conjuncture in global economic history, return attention toward the mechanisation of industry. For analyses of differences between Europe and Asia and the specificities of a British Industrial Revolution, there is a significant corpus of historical research on famous machines that transformed possibilities for the production of cotton textiles in Hanoverian Britain, which might clarify and settle parts of the argument.[1]

By 1851 a sequence of improvements to macroinventions had led to the relocation of the cotton textile industry from the Orient to the Occident, an extraordinary acceleration in the growth of its output, and pronounced declines in the costs of producing cotton and thereafter woollen, linen, silk, and many other varieties of yarn and cloth. This history has not been settled because both economists and historians lack a theory of technological progress that might explain this famous and precocious case of mechanisation.

Meanwhile, the first Industrial Revolution turns out to have been a less pronounced discontinuity than traditional interpretations suggested. Several historians have dismissed it as a misnamed episode. That seems premature because even the macroeconomic discontinuities remain clear enough. Although as a widely diffused national event it did not come on stream until well into the nineteenth century, which is several decades later than Ashton's classical narrative supposed or as Deane and Cole's and subsequent attempts at quantification claimed.

Cliometric interpretations insist that, within manufacturing, productivity growth was confined, before the second quarter of the nineteenth century, to basic metallurgy, textiles, and above all to cotton yarns and fabrics. As late as the 1830s, the ongoing mechanisation of cotton production and the concentration of all the processes involved in the preparation, spinning, weaving, and finishing of cotton cloth into steam-powered factories, located in towns, still represented an example (even for other textile industries) to emulate.

In many ways that view of the first Industrial Revolution reads like an old story in which cotton textiles were represented in Schumpetarian terms. That reconfiguration has been contested by historians, whose research on regions, protoindustrialisation, and transformations in the organisation of numerous traditional handicraft techniques and processes leads them to construct narratives dominated by more rapid and broadly based sequences of improvements to industrial technologies.[2] Debate continues. For purposes of this chapter, the 'cliometric painting' of the Industrial Revolution (together with unsatisfying attempts from economics to 'endogenise' explanations for technological breakthroughs) provides a justification for re-examining the sequence of famous machines, processes, and improvements that emerged between the times of John Kay's flying shuttle (1733) and Richard Roberts's power-loom (1822).

In 1835, Baines recalled 'that all those inventions have been made within the last seventy years' and proclaimed, 'that the cotton mill presents the most striking example of the dominion of human science over the power of nature of which modern times can boast.'[3] If historians and economists could offer some kind of general explanation for the inventory of machines that transformed the manufacture of cotton cloth over the century from 1733, they might be on the way to communicating greater understanding of a 'prime mover' behind British and European industrialisation and offer insights into origins for a 'Great Divergence' between West and East, which had probably emerged in the seventeenth century and became stark by 1914.

Three General Theories of Technical Change

Innovations in cotton textiles comprehend all new techniques introduced to manufacture an imported organic material (cotton fibres) into finished (bleached, dyed, and printed) cloth. Between 1733 and 1822 the list of mechanical innovations and improvements is long, and it is difficult to reconstruct the entire flow of technological knowledge, applied through time. Taxonomies imposed on surviving patent data divide 'product' from 'process' innovations and differentiate 'macroinventions' from 'adaptations' concerned to modify machines or chemical processes, in order to bring them into efficient day-to-day use.[4]

Major inventions and subsequent improvements, which ultimately revolutionised four separable processes involved in the manufacture of cotton textiles, appeared haphazardly over more than a century. When Baines wrote his eulogy, the production of cotton cloth had been transformed from a handicraft protomanufacture (using some crude machinery, powered by muscles, water, and animals) into a mechanised, steam-driven, urban industry concentrated in factories rather than households. Craftsmen and women had made cloth for millennia, but this uplift in productivity occurred over a short span of time. The rate of transformation within and across stages of production was so rapid, the locus so geographically contained in one county, and its initial applications so concentrated upon one fibre, that the 'English revolution in cotton textiles' continues to be recognised as a, if not *the*, seminal episode in histories of technology.

But can we explain it? Only, I will argue, by focused historical research upon the machines and the men who 'conceived', 'assembled', and 'developed' them and with scepticism towards claims that the transformation of cotton textile production could, more or less, be explained with reference to evolving economic contexts that depended either upon the growth of consumer demand, inelastic supplies of labour, or sequences of challenge and response. All three theories relating to context are theoretically ambiguous without firm empirical foundations. They are but parts of a wider narrative that accords recognition to the role of human agency.

Demand for Technological Progress

Demand-led explanations for technological progress continued to appear long after Rosenberg analysed their inconsistencies and listed the evidence required for their validation.[5] Surely the existence of a desire for knowledge that will generate cheaper, more appealing, or higher quality products was something approximating to a constant for centuries of history? Alternatively, if (as this thesis implicitly posits) some intensification of propensities to consume cottons occurred prior to the technological breakthroughs in the eighteenth century, are not historians required to demonstrate when, how, and why such expenditures rose perceptibly through time or somehow became stronger in some countries, regions, or markets compared to others?[6] Responding to this challenge they have, however, developed a general thesis about 'the rise of material culture', which makes the valid point that there is more to consumption than incomes and prices.[7] Economic growth certainly required households who were not only able but 'willing' to spend more on the 'superfluities' of the day, to diversify their diets, to admit novelties to their homes, to fashion their attire, to emulate the consumption patterns of their betters, to maintain expenditure in the face of adverse fluctuations in real incomes, and to convert leisure into industrious work in order to find the money to consume more 'stuff'.[8] Devoted as most Anglo-American historians are to English exceptionalism, some are not convinced that the rise of material culture came conveniently on stream shortly after the Restoration. However this period coincides (inconveniently for any testable version of the thesis) with several supply side forces including higher rates of investment in transportation and distribution networks, an uplift in expenditures on naval power for the protection of oceanic commerce, and an upswing in agricultural productivity, which started around the same time.[9]

Nuanced versions of demand-led theories of technological progress that depend more upon changes in tastes and fashions initiated as a response to an influx of imported cottons from India are easier to document and illustrate.[10] There should certainly be space for analysis of the creation, widening, and deepening of demand, but this should be placed alongside the protection of the kingdom's domestic market and the shift to more open colonial markets, together with parliamentary regulations and protections to help us explain the rise of an embryonic household-based industry producing cotton yarns in Lancashire. Coordinators of domestic production were certainly aware of the tensile strengths, lengths, and other properties of raw cotton for purposes of carding, roving, spinning, and weaving cotton yarns compared to other natural fibres. Merchants and finishers of 'cottons' also recognised that this fibre absorbed and retained colours and prints more appealing to consumers than silks, woollens, and linens. Cotton cloth and fabrics could be adapted to a greater variety of uses, conditions, and climates as well as to the established preferences of consumers for other natural fibres.

Once British, American, and European consumers appreciated and learned more about the qualities and properties of cottons, the pace of substitution for other fabrics accelerated and the demand curve shifted to the right. Demonstration, bandwagon, and fashion effects certainly flowed from imports from the East and shifted the volume of cotton consumption up to a level where incentives became strong enough to promote import substitution.[11] Thereafter, domestic production of cloths embodying mixtures of cotton with other yarns attained levels of know-how that created conditions for a trajectory towards mechanisation. But just how far 'a shift in tastes, for novelties, fashion and luxuries' associated with cottons without (or even with) protection might have carried the production of English cotton textiles has not been measured by historians.[12] Baines concentrated on the steam-powered mechanised cotton mills of his day (1835) as 'the dominion of human science and technology over nature', because he recognised that shifts in the supply curve surely mattered far more than cycles or trends in the mix of linen and cotton yarns in the production of fustian demanded niche markets in the kingdom and its colonies in the Americas.[13]

Labour-Saving Machinery

Inelastic supplies of labour continue to attract debate among historians analysing the rise of the cotton textile industry. Businessmen complained for decades about high levels of wages paid to English, compared to Irish, French, and other workforces. Recent, and incomplete, programmes of research on wage rates paid to builders' labourers and craftsmen (measured in grams of silver per day) show they were higher in English towns than most other large cities on the mainland and had since the mid-seventeenth century risen sharply relative to prices of inputs (wood, iron, nonferrous metals, and bricks for the manufacture of capital goods). Higher wages and cheaper energy (coal) have retained their status as outstanding comparative advantages for a first Industrial Revolution.[14]

Nevertheless, there is no statistical evidence that supplies of industrial labour for production of cotton textiles in north-western England became increasingly inelastic between the times of Kay and Roberts. On the contrary, the anxieties of Anglican clergymen and the writings of mercantilists confront problems of unemployment among the poor. After mid-century when population growth accelerated and food prices began their upward climb, the supply curve of 'hands' presumably became more elastic as women, children, and other migrants moved in ever larger numbers into urban labour markets. But no economic historian debating technology and the Great Divergence has suggested that cotton's transition to a fully mechanised industry might be explained by elastic supplies of cheap labour.

On the contrary, by rejecting suggestions for the precocious mechanisation of the cotton industry based upon insecure proxies for levels and trends in real product wages paid to female labour engaged in spinning of cotton yarn, Styles has reconstructed the local market for spinners in which a Lancashire weaver of cottons, James Hargreaves, 'invented' a prototype machine (the jenny) that gradually mechanised the spinning of cotton yarns from fibres of a specific quality imported from the Americas. That machine, by way of its incorporation into another mechanical trajectory based upon spinning with rollers (the water frame), consolidated the mechanisation of several tasks involved in the preparation and spinning of cotton fibres (by mules) into yarns that continued to be woven by traditional handicraft methods and after a long lag by power looms.

Styles' forensic analysis of the geographically confined context in which the jenny first emerged elaborates on a local and inelastic supply of female labour engaged in spinning cotton yarn from fibres imported across the Atlantic in merchant ships subsidised by public investment in the Royal Navy. Craftsmen like Hargreaves and Crompton were located in Lancashire and engaged with weaving cloth that embodied yarns spun with varieties of fibres derived from cotton and flax, and embodied qualities that appealed to consumers with higher incomes located in the kingdom, its American colonies, and markets on the mainland of Europe.[15]

The Challenge and Response Model

The popular Challenge and Response Model (repeated in countless books, lectures, and undergraduate essays since it was mentioned in a memoir about Cartwright [1859], suggested in a biography of Crompton [1859], and elaborated by Ellison's book *The Cotton Trade of Great Britain* [1886]) draws ultimately upon standard early nineteenth-century histories of the cotton industry by Guest (1823), Baines (1835), and Ure (1836).[16] Ellison's book differs from earlier accounts by making explicit links between the advent of the shuttle and the challenge posed to and solved by mechanical engineers who confronted an evolving sequence of imbalances in production processes.[17] Ellison cites Guest to assert that the 'imbalance between hand spinning and hand weaving worsened significantly after the invention of the Fly Shuttle … a contrivance which enables the weaver to turn out twice as much cloth as before in a given space of time'.[18]

Ellison inaugurated a tradition of explanations for the sequence and timing of innovation across all four major processes in the production of cotton cloth. His 'model' implicitly posits that the diffusion of a new technique by affecting one stage of production sets up pressures for responses (either down or upstream) to deal with intensified demands for inputs or (as the story of Cartwright's invention of the power loom shows) with increased incentives to utilise cheaper supplies of cotton yarns.[19]

Ellison's story ends with Robert's loom and his automated mule but begins and becomes linear with Kay's shuttle. It has been 'emplotted' to persuade us that the shuttle intensified demands from weavers for yarns, satisfied after a lag of more than three decades by spinning machines invented by Wyatt and Paul, Hargreaves, Arkwright, and Crompton. The improvement and diffusion of their inventions then supposedly produced a surfeit of yarn, which prompted a search for powered looms, 'solved' in engineering terms by an Anglican clergyman in 1785 and 'resolved' commercially (after a protracted state of learning and development that extended over several decades) by Richard Roberts in 1822, who sized the warp and placed the loom in an iron frame.[20]

For this story to work as a progression of technical challenges and responses, the narrative should proceed from an initial state and on through several subsequent sequences of disequilibrium. But no evidence has been provided that the shuttle could have launched the sequence posited by simplistic versions of the model. Its competitive advantages seem to have resided more in its capacity to upgrade the smoothness and quality of narrow cloth, rather than in labour-saving properties that could have led to anything like a doubling in industry-wide demands for yarn.[21] It did not, moreover, even appear in the fustian industry much before mid-century and its diffusion around that time coincided with the development and production of high quality cotton velvets and velveteens prominent among rising exports for Africa and which substituted for light cotton fabrics previously supplied from India.[22]

Apart from the problem of long and unexplained lags, patents and other data provide no statistical support that the search for innovations shifted systematically in any clear direction following the introduction of the flying shuttle. On the contrary, they show that the proportion of recorded innovations which can be classified as designed to raise the productivity of labour engaged in the preparation of fibres and spinning of yarn for weaving declined from 46 per cent of the total before the appearance of Kay's wheeled flying shuttle, 1720–33, to 23 per cent between 1734 and 1753.[23] Furthermore, and just three years before patenting his shuttle, Kay developed a machine to spin and dress worsted thread, suggesting a desire on his part to address mechanical problems in general rather than a perception of profitable opportunities arising from a widely perceived need to relieve bottlenecks in weaving.

Manipulators of statistical techniques would be hard put to manufacture convincing evidence drawn from an imperfect dataset for 'systematic clustering' denoting the sort of patterns of search and success in inventive activity posited by conceivable versions of a challenge and response model. Annual figures for patents and other data for textile innovation display no discernible tendencies to 'cluster' around preparatory processes following the invention and diffusion of major breakthroughs in weaving. Nor is there evidence for the concentration upon manufacturing processes (concerned either with the weaving or the finishing of cloth) over the years that succeeded the diffusion of Hargreaves' spinning jenny, Arkwright's water frame, Crompton's mule, and Cartwright's loom.

Historians of technological change cannot avoid reading the engineering *detail* contained in patent specifications. On inspection there is some tendency for innovations to appear *prima facie* as improvements to, or substitutes for, macroinventions.[24] Several minor adaptations to the shuttle appeared in the 1740s. While a seemingly concerted surge of innovations for the manufacture of yarn followed hard upon Arkwright's all-inclusive carding and spinning patent of 1775. Over the next four years fifteen spinning machines appeared, of which eight were patented.[25] In the late 1770s Crompton developed the mule in order to deal with the problems he encountered in producing yarn of Indian quality, either on a spinning jenny or by rollers.[26] This same pattern followed Cartwright's designs for prototype power looms. Within a decade sixteen 'improvements' to his machine appeared. Half of them were patented.[27] Opportunities for profit presented by the emergence into the public domain of machines that worked in engineering terms prompted a search for further improvements (and/or stimulated differentiation in order to undermine a patentee's monopoly rights) rather than to promote any discernible reallocation of expenditures on research and development to alleviate bottlenecks up or downstream.

The Political and Geopolitical Contexts for the Mechanisation of England's Cotton Textile Industry

The first Industrial Revolution is now represented as an example of relatively slow unbalanced industrial growth, but this still includes a role for technological progress in cotton textiles. This demands that the macroeconomic background for the early transformation of that industry be sketched into a picture that will place the accumulation of mechanical knowledge and the outstanding achievements of English inventors of textile machinery at its centre. Unless their inventions could just as easily have emerged on a plausible spectrum of European locations (to flag a view entertained by Nick Crafts) then there must have been some features of the economy and culture of England that made it a 'more probable' site for innovations in cotton textiles between the Treaties of Utrecht (1713) and Vienna (1815) than, say, Holland, France, Saxony, Spain, Switzerland, and (as research into the Great Divergence has now made us aware) of several protoindustrial regions of India, China, and Japan.[28] Five features of the island economy (two within and three beyond its shores) can be elaborated to suggest that the location and timing for the technological breakthroughs that occurred in England between 1733 and 1822 cannot, however, be represented as merely random.

Firstly, the scale and scope of textile production located within the realm was already large by the late seventeenth century, and the industry continued to expand and diversify its output over the following century. By 1660 Britain and Ireland manufactured almost the entire range of textiles: woollens, linens, silks, cottons, fustians, and a variety of mixed yarns and cloths.[29]

Secondly, (and this assertion is attracting statistical comparisons) the English workforce may have included a higher proportion of relevant skills and knowledge in metallurgy, carpentry, precision engineering, clock and tool making, machine design, etc., than workforces on the European mainland. Josiah Tucker thought so and asserted 'we may aver with some confidence that ... parts of England ... exhibit a specimen of practical mechanics scarce to be paralleled in any part of the world'.[30] How, when, and why the English economy accumulated the human capital required to innovate and sustain improvements in mechanical engineering is, however, still not settled either in theoretical or historical terms.[31] Investigations into small samples of traceable names who registered patents for inventions or improvements for differentiated products for the British textile industry between 1688 and 1851 has not suggested that this segment of the English skilled workforce can be represented as a 'definable resource', separable from larger populations. Traceable patentees have not emerged as a 'distinctive' subgroup in terms of social status, education, residence, religion, politics, or linkages to networks for the exchange of scientific and mechanical information.[32]

Meanwhile three familiar 'exogenous' histories contextualise the progress of cotton textile production within England and derive credibility from histories of the political economy of imperialism. Firstly, the functional reaction of parliament to the threat posed to the country's indigenous textile industries from the rapid penetration of the home market by cheaply made but increasingly desirable cotton cloth imported from India and China between 1660 and 1721 has been well analysed.

In contrast to the reactions of other European governments, tariffs and other barriers erected to protect woollen, silk, and linen industries emerged slowly and then evolved into a framework for protection that allowed for the development of an English fustian industry from which the indigenous manufacture of pure cotton cloth eventually emerged.[33]

Fustian consisted of a mixed fabric woven from cotton wefts (made in Lancashire) and linen warps (imported mainly from Ireland but also from Scotland and the Baltic). In the reign of William III (r. 1689–1702) his ministers formulated policies for the pacification of England's rebellious Catholic province that included subsidies for an Irish linen industry, which they hoped would provide employment for dispossessed peasants and might placate Irish merchants and manufacturers after Parliament had legislated in 1697 to close English home and imperial markets to Irish made woollen yarns and linens.[34] These policies worked, and for decades Ireland supplied warps of linen yarn for the rapid development of fustian manufacturing in Lancashire. Eventually inelasticities in imported linen yarn supplies and instabilities in delivery (occasioned by mercantilist warfare on the Irish Sea, 1740–48 and 1756–63) and the vacillations of Parliament gave rise to expectations within the fustian industry that more secure and profitable opportunities could be realised from the manufacture of cloth from warps and wefts of cotton yarns spun entirely within Lancashire.[35]

Third, such expectations could only have been heightened by the extension of cotton cultivation first to British plantations in the West Indies, the Portuguese colony of Brazil, and later on to former southern colonies of America. Meanwhile, French competition on European markets for sugar intensified, following the exploitation of new and fertile plantations on Haiti, and provided an incentive to diversify production and exports from the Caribbean into cotton fibres. Indeed any food or industrial crop that could be grown cheaply on tropical soils anywhere in the Americas (utilising African slaves) promised returns from investment in plantations, in trade and shipping as well as the manufacture of cheaper textiles. As Britain moved into a position of naval hegemony among European powers and successfully exploited the economic potential of the growing Atlantic economy, opportunities to integrate cotton textile production across the domestic economy and the empire began to look increasingly profitable and more immune from risk than almost anywhere else on the mainland.[36] Furthermore, the counts and longer staples derived from cotton plants cultivated in the Americas turned out to be more amenable for mechanical spinning than fibres derived from the varieties of plants cultivated in India and China.[37]

From Necessary to Necessary and Sufficient Conditions

Structural preconditions and the political economy of English mercantilism help to explain why an embryonic or protocotton textile industry in England had by 1688 climbed to a 'plateau of possibilities' from where breakthroughs in technology might (with hindsight) be represented as more probable than random and more significant than changes in taste and fashion?

Nevertheless, elaborations of contexts are some way from emerging as a necessary and sufficient explanation for technological breakthroughs in the manufacture of cotton textiles. That remains the case because macroinventions were conceived and constructed by particular people at given moments in time. Unless and until the fundamental breakthroughs that occurred in the mechanisation of textiles (or indeed for the manufacture of any other commodity) can be convincingly analysed as a clear transformation of context into content, analyses of innovations in technology may have nowhere to go but back to biography.[38] Famous names have long been associated with macroinventions. Unless we believe with William Petty that 'innovation is undiscovered plagiarism' that association must first be verified.[39] Then the argument moves logically to reconnect the lives and the work of England's celebrated cotton textile inventors to the networks and contexts in which they operated.

Definitions of Macroinventions and Microimprovements

Mantoux and his generation of economic historians recognised that some artefacts, technical designs, and machines could be regarded as very much more important for the long run transformation of the textile industry than others.[40] They wrote about machines in ways that modern engineers would recognise as discontinuities or leaps forward that Mokyr relabelled as 'macroinventions'. The term is a useful reminder that prototype models provided 'essential' foundations for the accumulation of useful knowledge and future technical advances. The emergence and diffusion of machines as functioning models set new technical parameters, posed focused questions, and placed the search for improvements upon more steeply inclined trajectories. If and when such models emerged in the right spaces and social networks with potential for development, they represented a challenge and stimulus to local communities of businessmen, projectors, technologists, and other experts concerned with the exploitation of useful and profit-able knowledge. They recognised that prospects had changed and that the time had come for developing, interpreting, and testing a new machine in order to make it routinely functional and, above all, commercially viable.

Ideally, historians should present evidence for sequences of machines as they evolved in a form that recognises and dates the appearance of macroinventions by citing particular models that over time transformed 'technical possibilities' for the performance of specific handicraft actions and processes. Information of this kind could underpin a quantified history of technology by locating machines that engineers would recognise as 'radically new' and graph the familiar stages from invention through development to diffusion. For example, Cartwright's prototype model for a power loom which appeared in 1784 transformed prospects for automating or mechanising the operations and judgements performed by handloom weavers using established technologies. If we possessed relevant data we could graph productivity ratios for long spans of time and locate a conjuncture in the yards of fustian, woollen, or cotton cloth woven per hour by a skilled adult male weaver utilising the state-of-the-art handloom before Cartwright's loom appeared in 1785. Unfortunately, available estimates of labour productivity for weaving cloth are limited. Any graphs that could be drawn would be nothing more than 'synopia' for the kind of pictures economic historians would be pleased to draw if they possessed productivity data upswings, machine by machine for long spans of time.[41]

Biographical Narratives and Macroinventors

Post hoc it looks reasonably clear that conditions and contexts for the transformation of an industry manufacturing cottons as mixtures of cotton and linen yarns were in place in north-western England by, say, the 1740s. Historians of technology have recognised seven prototypes and operational machines associated with the endeavours of Kay, Wyatt and Paul, Hargreaves, Arkwright, Crompton, Cartwright, and Roberts that continued to be classified as inventions that appear to have been recognised by contemporaries as significant for a trajectory leading to the emergence of the first mechanised textile industry in the world.[42]

For historians of technology the inclusion of agency in narratives requires far less persuasion than has long been the case for historians of modern economic growth. When the latter reluctantly resort to biography, they tend to import theory from psychology, seek security in rhetorically persuasive vocabularies from evolutionary biology, and toy with notions of congenial spaces from geography, or resort to economic distinctions between macro- and microeconomics. Imported metaphors can be memorable, but it is not clear that they help us understand problems of agency and creativity. Macro seems to be little more than a Schumpeterian term for network technologies embodying potential for increasing returns to scale and scope and for the generation of technological spin-offs. Are Darwinian analogies to evolutionary mutations and species transformations heuristic? Speed of motion did not develop from breeding faster horses: what is the conceptual force of spatial metaphors compared to historical contexts and social networks as headings for analysis?

Psychology offers theories and evidence designed and calibrated to elucidate the cognitive characteristics of people selected as creative that purport to be based on experimental tests that claim to expose such personal traits as intrinsically motivated, self-confident, undaunted by failures, curious, zealous, imaginative, manipulative, and exploitative. Predictably there are documents that have exposed such traits in the biographies of the eight inventors of textile machinery cited above. But biographies also reveal that they did not find expression in Crompton's talents as a violinist, in Cartwright's tedious poetry, or in the business acumen of Kay and Roberts. Is there any reason to suggest that creative people are alike in those respects that leads posterity to represent them as creative? Indeed these rather elastic personality characteristics derived from psychometric databases of creative individuals may also have been present in much larger groups of comparable populations alive at the time.[43]

There is, however, a virtual library of contextualised biographies in print that includes historical research into the familial, social, and cultural networks to be placed alongside the economic spaces inhabited and exploited by this mere handful of inventors. Such a literary format and literature remains enlightening to contemplate and confront with a venerable and answerable question: *how it came to pass* that these men (with help from others) mobilised their very own and the social resources required to produce prototype machines that evolved to constitute the foundations for a global cotton textile industry located in Lancashire?[44]

Turning first to their social origins the historical evidence suggests that none of these remarkable men came from families at lower ends of the status and income scales. Only the Reverend Edmund Cartwright and Louis Paul moved in social circles that could be depicted as beyond the borders of the textile industry. With the possible exception of Hargreaves, this group would, by the standards of the day, be recognised as educated, although not one was a member of any of England's famous scientific

societies and the macroeconomic spinning machines were invented by
weavers of cotton yarns.[45]

Unfortunately, almost no evidence survives (in the form of letters,
diaries, reflexions, observations) that could provide historians with
insights into *how* prototype machines for the preparation of spinning,
weaving, and finishing cotton fibres into yarns and cloth were initially
conceived and by way of a process of experimentation assembled into
operational models for the rolling and spinning of yarns and weaving
of cloth. Rollers were already used for the manufacture of silk, paper,
and metals. While machinery that could help spinners produce more
than a single strand of yarn at a time had been around in China in the
fourteenth century and was patented in England in 1678, 1723, and 1755.[46]

Arkwright and Cartwright embarked on a costly process of developing operational machines as 'projectors', imbued with optimistic
beliefs that machines would perform these operations more effectively.
Their backgrounds, occupations, and quotable proclamations suggest
that confidence in the 'power of machinery' may have penetrated
more widely and deeply into British society than elsewhere in Eurasia.
They also appreciated that they had to recruit artisans to transform
'imaginative insights' into potentially operational machines. Louis Paul
entered into partnership with John Wyatt (a Birmingham mechanic) to
explore with evident success the possibilities of spinning with rollers.
Their acrimonious partnership ultimately failed.[47] As a weaver from
Blackburn, Hargreaves surely envisaged possibilities for a machine that
could spin more than a single strand of yarn at a time? Nevertheless,
he migrated to Nottingham and collaborated with a joiner to develop
improved versions of his jenny.[48] Arkwright (a barber and wig maker)
exploited the skills of several craftsmen in his Lancashire network. Yet he
too moved to Nottingham in search of the skills and dexterity required
to construct a frame that used rollers to simultaneously card and spin
cotton fibres into yarns.[49]

Neither the jenny nor the water-powered frame could produce
cotton yarns for warps as well as wefts of the qualities that satisfied
the aspirations of the Bolton weaver, Samuel Crompton.[50] He told Sir
Joseph Banks (a Fellow of the Royal Society) that, kept by his mother, he
conducted experiments over a six-year period that combined mechanisms from the jenny and the frame to construct the aptly named 'mule'
which matured into the prototype machine for the spinning of cotton
fibres into high quality yarns (warps as well as wefts), first in Lancashire
and in time other regions throughout the world.[51]

The history of mechanisation of cotton textile production comes
to a plateau with a sequence of weaving machines designed by the
Reverend Edmund Cartwright and brought to a level of higher and

more sustained efficiency by Richard Roberts, an artisan who turned his hand to the solution of mechanical problems across an extraordinary range of industries, including textiles.[52] Cartwright conceived of the first prototype loom 'from a basic principle that there could only be three movements which were to follow each other in succession and there would be little difficulty in repeating them. Full of these ideas he immediately employed a smith and a carpenter to carry them into effect.'[53] Further developments of his first 'rude piece of machinery' took place in Manchester with the help from unknown but 'superior workmen' from whence he, an Anglican theologian, patented four operational looms in 1787–88.[54]

Between the times of Kay and Cartwright none of these men could access firms to supply specialised skills in mechanical engineering to realise their 'conceptions' for spinning fibres into yarns or weaving yarns into cloth.[55] They relied on artisans available in Manchester, Birmingham, and Nottingham and men with the skills and dexterity of Roberts who could turn their hands to making machinery for multiple industrial processes.[56]

The investment required to transform notions or initial designs into a routinely functional machine was beyond the means personally available to any member of the group, except Cartwright. Not one of this group lacked networks of friends, relatives, partners, and patrons to support their endeavours. After seven years of engagement with a range of machinery, Cartwright had run through all of his own and most of his family's money. The Cartwrights lost a fortune by investing in the genius born into their enlightened clan.[57] None of the inventors of the machines that initiated Britain's Schumperteian process of mechanisation, that led eventually to the replacement of India and China on world markets for cotton textiles, became affluent from their indispensable contributions to the rise of this paradigm industry to a position of hegemony, apart that is from Richard Arkwright, whose 'talents' for purloining and exploiting the ideas of others have been well documented. Roberts, 'the greatest mechanic of the nineteenth century', died in poverty.[58]

Conclusion

Historians acquainted with a library of scholarly literature analysing the precocious transition of the English cotton textile industry to its leading position in world production and trade will know that the process was not linear but marked by the emergence into the public domain of a sequence of prototype machines that provided foundations for modifications, improvements, and learning by use before they became commercially viable.

The celebrated inventors discussed in this chapter certainly exude confidence in their abilities to solve the problems involved in the mechanisation of the distinct processes involved in the manufacturing of cotton cloth. Along with many other men residing in European market economies, they proceeded to exploit their ideas and hoped to make money. What is more striking, however, is their faith and persistence in seeking mechanical solutions to problems of production. Biography offers an approach to understanding them by reconstructing the economic, social, and cultural networks that surrounded their endeavours. It undermines 'ways of knowing' common in economics and economic history that find contexts for creativity both necessary and sufficient. It restores credibility to beliefs held by their contemporaries about this tiny group of creative men whose inventions transformed an industry at the core of the first Industrial Revolution.

These British engineers were creative partly because they just happened to be born in one of the most advanced and geopolitically aggressive of a range of successful market economies located along the coasts of the Eurasian land mass. They also inhabited a religious culture permeated by a scientific cosmology that extolled and sustained an optimistic attitude towards the comprehension of the natural world and that generated a 'frenzy for improvement', commented frequently upon by a stream of visitors to the Isles from the mainland. However, they leave an unfinished debate in global history on the Great Divergence with a Eurocentred question. Could a comparable group of innovators with similar ideas about the power and potential of machinery have emerged and revolutionised the cotton textile industries of India, China, and Japan at this time?

Notes

My thoughts on mechanisation have been heavily influenced by collaborations many years ago with Philip Hunt and Trevor Griffiths on an ESRC-funded research project.
1 Maxine Berg, *The Machinery Question and the Making of Political Economy, 1815–1848* (Cambridge: Cambridge University Press, 1980); Maxine Berg, *The Age of Manufactures: Industry, Innovation and Work in Britain, 1700–1820* (London: Fontana, 1985).
2 Pat Hudson, 'Industrial Organization and Structural Change', in *Cambridge Economic History of Britain*, I: *1700–1870*, eds. Roderick Floud and Paul Johnson (Cambridge: Cambridge University Press, 2004), 28–56.

3 Edward Baines, *History of the Cotton Manufacture of Great Britain* (London: Fisher, 1835–36), 28.

4 Trevor Griffiths, Philip Hunt, and Patrick O'Brien, 'Inventive Activity in the British Textile Industry', *Journal of Economic History*, 52, no. 4 (1992): 881–906.

5 Nathan Rosenberg, *Inside the Black Box. Technology and Economics* (Cambridge: Cambridge University Press, 1982).

6 Beverley Lemire, *The Fashion's Favourite: The Cotton Trade and the Consumer in Britain* (Oxford: Oxford University Press, 1991).

7 Lorna Weatherill, *Consumer Behavior and Material Culture in Britain, 1660–1760* (London: Routledge, 1988).

8 John Brewer and Roy Porter, eds., *Consumption and the World of Goods* (London: Routledge, 1993).

9 Patrick O'Brien, Trevor Griffiths, and Philip Hunt, 'Technological Change during the First Industrial Revolution: The Paradigm Case of Textiles', in *Technological Change: Methods and Themes in the History of Technology*, ed. Robert Fox (Amsterdam: Harwood Academics, 1996), 155–76.

10 Maxine Berg, 'From Imitation to Invention: Creating Commodities in Eighteenth Century Britain', *Economic History Review* 55, no. 1 (2002): 1–30; and John Styles, 'Fashion, Textiles and the Origins of the Industrial Revolution', *East Asian Journal of British History* 5 (2016): 161–89.

11 Maxine Berg, 'New Commodities, Luxuries and Their Consumers in Eighteenth Century England', in *Consumers and Luxury in Europe, 1650–1850*, eds. Maxine Berg and Helen Clifford (Manchester: Manchester University Press, 1999), 63–85.

12 Giorgio Riello, *Cotton: The Fabric That Made the Modern World* (Cambridge: Cambridge University Press, 2013).

13 Giorgio Riello, 'Trade, Consumption and Industrialization: Cotton Textiles in the Long Eighteenth Century' (unpublished paper presented to Nuffield College, Oxford, workshop Global Cotton as a Case of Precocious Globalization, 2017).

14 Robert C. Allen, 'The High Wage Economy and the Industrial Revolution: A Restatement', *Economic History Review* 68, no. 1 (2015): 1–22.

15 John Styles, 'Fibres, Yarns and the Invention of the Spinning Jenny' (unpublished paper for World Economic History Congress, Boston 2018).

16 Trevor G. Griffiths, Philip Hunt, and Patrick O'Brien, 'The Curious History and Imminent Demise of the Challenge and Response Model', in *Technological Revolutions in Europe: Historical Perspectives*, eds. Maxine Berg and Kristine Bruland (Cheltenham: Edward Elgar, 1998), 117–37.

17 Thomas Ellison, *The Cotton Trade of Great Britain* (New York: Frank Cass, [or. Ed. 1886] 1968).

18 Ibid., 15.

19 Margaret Strickland, *A Memoir of Edmund Cartwright* (Bath: Adams and Dart, 1971), 7–10.

20 Richard Hills, *Life and Inventions of Richard Roberts, 1789–1864* (Ashbourne: Landmark Publications, 1993).

21 Akos Paulinyi, 'John Kay's Flying Shuttle: Some Considerations on His Technical Capacity', *Textile History* 17, no. 2 (1986): 149–76; and Harold T. Wood, 'The Inventions of John Kay, 1704–70', *Journal of the Royal Society of Arts* 60 (1911–20): 73–86.

22 Stanley Chapman, *The Cotton Industry in the Industrial Revolution* (London: Macmillan, 1972).

23 Griffith, Hunt, and O'Brien, 'The Curious History', 126–33.

24 Sean Bottomley, *The British Patent System during the Industrial Revolution, 1700–1852* (Cambridge: Cambridge University Press, 2014).

25 Robert S. Fitton and Alfred P. Wadsworth, *The Strutts and the Arkwrights, 1758–1830: A Study of the Early Factory System* (Manchester, Manchester University Press, 1958); and Robert S. Fitton, *The Arkwrights: Spinners of Fortune* (Manchester: Manchester University Press, 1989).

26 Harold Catling, *The Spinning Mule* (Newton Abbot: David and Charles, 1970).

27 Patrick O'Brien, 'The Micro Foundations of Macro Inventions: The Case of the Reverend Edmund Cartwright', *Textile History* 28, no. 2 (1997): 201–33.

28 N.F.R. Crafts, 'Industrial Revolution in England and France. Some Thoughts on the Question "Why England was First"', *Economic History Review* 30, no. 3 (1977): 429–41; and Peer Vries, *State Economy and the Great Divergence: Great Britain and China, 1680s–1850s* (London: Bloomsbury, 2015).

29 Eric Kerridge, *Textile Manufactures in Early Modern England* (Manchester: Manchester University Press, 1985).

30 George Shelton, *Dean Tucker and Eighteenth Century Economic and Political Thought* (Basingstoke: Macmillan Press, 1981), 53.

31 Gillian Cookson, *The Age of Machinery: Engineering the Industrial Revolution, 1770–1850* (London: Boydell & Brewer, 2018).

32 Ralf Meisenzahl and Joel Mokyr, 'The Rate and Direction of Inventive Activity during the Industrial Revolution, Revisited', in *The Rate and Direction of Inventive Activity Revisited*, eds. Josh Lerner and Scott Stern (Chicago: Chicago University Press, 2012), 443–79.

33 Patrick O'Brien, Trevor Griffiths, and Philip Hunt, 'Political Components of the Industrial Revolution: Parliament and the English Cotton Textile Industry, 1660–1774', *Economic History Review* 44, no. 3 (1991): 395–423.

34 Julian Hoppit, ed., *Parliaments, Nations and Identities in Britain and Ireland, 1660–1850* (Manchester: Manchester University Press, 2003).

35 Trevor Griffiths, Philip Hunt, and Patrick O'Brien, 'Scottish, Irish and Imperial Connections: Parliament, the Kingdoms and the Mechanisation of Cotton Spinning in Eighteenth Century Great Britain', *Economic History Review* 61, no. 3 (2009): 625–50.

36 Robert S. Du Plessis, *The Material Atlantic. Clothing, Commerce and Colonization in the Atlantic World* (Cambridge: Cambridge University Press, 2016).

37 Giorgio Riello and Prasannan Parthasarathi, eds., *The Spinning World: A Global History of Cotton Textiles* (Oxford: Oxford University Press, 2009).

38 Patrick O'Brien, Trevor Griffiths, and Philip Hunt, 'Theories of Technological Progress and the British Textile Industry from Kay to Cartwright', *Revista de Historia Economica* 14 (1996): 533–55.

39 William Petty, *A Treatise on Taxes and Contributions* (London: N. Brooke, Cornhill, 1662), 19.

40 Paul Mantoux, *The Industrial Revolution in the Eighteenth Century: An Outline of the Beginnings of the Factory System in Britain* (London: Methuen, 1964).

41 Robert E. Allen, 'The Hand-Loom Weaver and the Power Loom: A Schumpeterian Perspective', *University of Oxford Discussion Paper in Economic and Society History* 142 (2016).

42 George W. Daniels, *The Early English Cotton Industry* (Manchester: Manchester University Press, 1920); and Jon Stobart, *The First Industrial Region: North West England* (Manchester: Manchester University Press, 2004).

43 Margaret Boden, ed., *Dimensions of Creativity* (Cambridge, Mass: MIT Press, 1994).

44 Alfred P. Wadsworth and Julia de L. Mann, *The Cotton Trade and Industrial Lancashire, 1600–1780* (Manchester: Manchester University Press, 1931).

45 Christopher Aspin and Stanley Chapman, *James Hargreaves and the Spinning Jenny* (Helmshore: Helmshore Local History Society, 1964); Fitton, *The Arkwrights*; Thomas Midgley, *Samuel Crompton 1753–1827: A Life of Tragedy and Service* (Bolton: Corporation of Bolton, 1927); Michael Rone, 'Samuel Crompton, 1753–1827: A Biographical Note and Appreciation', *Textile Recorder* (1927).

46 O'Brien, Griffiths, and Hunt, 'Theories of Technological Progress.'

47 David Bates, 'Cotton Spinning in Northampton. Edward Caves Mill, 1742–61', *Northampton Past and Present* 9 (1996): 237–51.

48 Christopher Aspin, 'New Evidence on James Hargreaves and the Spinning Jenny', *Textile History* 1 (1968): 119–31.

49 Fitton, *The Arkwrights*.

50 Gilbert French with an Introduction by Stanley Chapman, *Life and Times of Samuel Crompton* (Bath: Adams and Dart, 1970).

51 H. Catling, *The Spinning Mule* (Newton Abbot: David and Charles, 1970); and Midgley, *Samuel Crompton*.

52 William Radcliffe, *Origins of the New System of Manufacture, Commonly called Power Loom Weaving and the Purposes for which This System was Brought into Being* (Stockport: James Lomax, 1828); and Hills, *Life and Inventions*.

53 Guest, *Compendious History*, 45.

54 O'Brien, 'Micro Foundations'.

55 Cookson, *Age of Machinery*.

56 Hills, *Life and Inventions*.

57 Strickland, *A Memoir*; and O'Brien, 'Micro Foundations'.

58 Fitton, *Arkwrights*.

9

An Automatic Technology
in British Industrialisation

Kristine Bruland and Keith Smith

In a number of her works, Maxine Berg emphasised the centrality of machinery to the Industrial Revolution and to economic thinking around it, yet she also undercut the 'heroic' myths of technological change that continue to plague accounts of industrialisation. Maxine showed on the one hand the importance of industries (such as small metal products) that deployed rather simple technologies and on the other the importance of work organisation rather than simply technology in such major activities as textiles.

This chapter continues the discussion of organisation and technology by exploring the history of one the world's first significant automatic technologies, the so-called 'self-acting mule'. This invention automated textile spinning in the 1820s and became one of the most important industrial technologies of the modern era. But it spread only slowly into use. Our argument in this chapter is that to understand the adoption of this technology it should be seen in its social context and not just as a technical artefact. The evolution of technologies involves complex social processes of conflict, negotiation, compromise and adaptation. The key technologies of industrialisation cannot be understood in isolation from these social dimensions, and as a result the impacts of even major innovations are often far slower to appear than is commonly believed.

'A New Epoch in the Capitalist System'

The automatic or 'self-acting' mule was invented and patented in 1825 by the Manchester engineer Richard Roberts who was part of an important group of machine tool producers in Manchester.[1] We know a considerable amount about the circumstances of the invention and innovation: Roberts initiated the inventive process at the request of manufacturers who were seeking a solution to labour conflict with skilled spinners.[2] It was a major advance, both in the technology of textile production (then as now one of the world's most important industries) and also in terms of technical principles. It took the macro-inventions earlier discussed by Patrick O'Brien a step further: Roberts succeeded in something that many people believed to be impossible, namely automation of the process of cotton spinning. It became possible to replace an entire category of labour skill with a machine. The device itself was a complex and sophisticated one: it integrated large-scale power use with delicacy and accuracy of operation, based on the first significant industrial application of error-actuated servo control (a feedback process that detected and immediately corrected any malfunctioning).[3]

By 1825 the textile industry was already central to the British economy, so this was no ordinary invention, and Richard Roberts's achievement was immediately acclaimed by contemporaries. The *Manchester Advertiser* spoke at the time of 'a success ... so decisive, as to astonish even those who were acquainted with the extraordinary talents of the inventor.'[4] Later, more analytical observers echoed these sentiments: Andrew Ure, in *The Philosophy of Manufactures*, somewhat overdoing the classical metaphors, spoke of the automatic mule as 'this Herculean prodigy ... sprung out of the hands of our modern Prometheus at the bidding of Minerva ... to strangle the Hydra of misrule.'[5] In volume I of *Capital* Karl Marx characteristically went a step further, tersely making a very large claim: 'the self-acting mule ... opened up a new epoch in the capitalist system.'[6]

Slow Diffusion

Against this background we might expect the self-actor to have been welcomed with open arms by textile entrepreneurs. Yet it appears to have diffused slowly. Ultimately the automatic mule became the basic technique of the British cotton spinning industry. However, it was at least twenty to thirty years before it accounted for a substantial part of industry output. In some key parts of the textile process, namely fine-count yarns, the diffusion process took half a century. This is a puzzle, since on the face of it the machine had plain technical advantages that would have translated into significant economic superiority. In particular it involved a major productivity advance, producing between 20 and 25 per cent more output in a given period than the hand-mule technique, without loss of quality.[7]

Moreover there were probably no informational lags among potential adopters: entrepreneurs were well informed and seemed to have had a clear need for the machine. Some evidence for this lies in the scale of the innovative effort: there were at least six substantial attempts prior to Roberts's success, which perhaps is an indicator of the perceived priority of the task. More important are the actual circumstances of the innovation. Roberts was a skilled and busy engineer who did not approach the development of the self-actor on a speculative basis; rather, this is a case of user-initiated innovation.[8] Roberts produced the device – after an initial reluctance to undertake the task – following specific and repeated requests by a group of Lancashire cotton masters, 'who ceased not to stimulate his exertions by frequent visitations.'[9] His firm (Sharp, Roberts and Co.) subsequently spent £12,000 in development costs, which suggests a solid, well-considered project facing the prospects of assured demand for the product.[10]

The machine offered significant cost reductions: Roberts had succeeded in automating the highest cost component of the cotton spinning process. Spinning by the hand-mule technique had required considerable skill and judgment by the operator.[11] The skilled high-wage spinning operative was now replaceable by a relatively unskilled machine minder, a fact emphasised by the manufacturers in their early publicity.[12] This in turn indicates a *prima facie* case for the economic superiority of the new device, since within the spinning process (itself the most expensive suboperation in yarn manufacture) wages were the largest single element in costs.[13] We might expect that the device would diffuse rapidly, a prospect that was indeed suggested by some contemporary observers. Baines in his *History of the Cotton Manufacture in Great Britain* (1835) spoke of the machine 'coming rapidly into use', with upwards of 200,000 spindles in existence, a number which he expected to be more than doubled in the course of the year.[14]

But this picture is not supported by other analyses. W. Cooke Taylor, writing in 1843 (i.e. nearly twenty years after the first patent) wrote that 'self-acting mules are very generally used in the mills where low numbers (i.e. coarse yarns) are spun, but we believe that they have not been found applicable to the spinning of finer yarns.'[15] Catling quotes writers in 1860 and about 1880 who suggest that the self-actor was diffusing into medium-fine yarn processes but concludes that 'in fact, many hand mules continued to be used even for medium-fine counts fifty years after the introduction of the self-actor.'[16] For the fine spinning area of Bolton, Boyson gives figures of 1,231 hand mules and 1,191 automatic mules in 1877; that is, less than 50 per cent of the mules in Bolton were self-actors, more than half a century after their introduction.[17]

Von Tunzelmann argued that by 1834 self-acting spindles accounted for about 3 per cent of total British spindleage, that it made no progress in superseding hand methods for fine-count yarns before the 1860s, and that even in the coarse-count yarns, which turned out to be best suited to the automatic mule, it did not account for the largest share of industry output until the 1850s and 1860s.[18] In the case of the self-acting mule, therefore, we have a device for which large claims are made, yet which diffused primarily into processes (coarse yarns) that account for a minority of total industry output. It was fifty years before it dominated output in the industry. What then were the possible reasons for this slow pace of diffusion?

Technical Inadequacies

One possibility is that the machine simply did not work as well as advertised. Stanley Chapman, in his *Lancashire Cotton Industry*, suggests that a technical reason 'kept the self-actor out of some districts, namely that for many years the winding accomplished by this machine was defective.'[19] Certainly there seems to have been output problems with the machine: William Graham, in evidence to a parliamentary committee on manufactures in 1833, said 'we have not been able to get anything like the quantity which the patentees stated we should get off our mules.'[20] James Montgomery, writing at about the same time, makes the usual obeisances to Roberts's inventive brilliance but continues on a more sober note: 'Whether, after a few years trial, it will be found practically efficient, remains to be proven …'[21] The existence of technical inadequacies should not be surprising. Very few innovations begin their economic life in technically complete form, a point that is crucial in understanding diffusion processes. But this does not mean that a technically incomplete innovation will not diffuse, perhaps quite rapidly; subsequent development may simply enhance an already established – if precarious – commercial feasibility. Many innovations – such as, for example early wool-combing devices – diffused relatively quickly even though they suffered severe technical limitations.[22]

It is this simultaneity of the technicalities and economics of automatic spinning that were discussed by Nick von Tunzelmann in his *Steam Power and British Industrialisation to 1860*. He took the view that the technical difficulties noted by Chapman and others posed no absolute technical obstacle to the operation of self-actors. By an ingenious use of available cost and output data he attempted to quantify the costs and benefits of self-acting versus hand mules, in an attempt to reconstruct the elements of a rational investment decision by an 1835 entrepreneur, spinning low-grade (no.25) yarn. This effort showed that on low-grade yarns the greater capital and power costs of the self-actor and greater operating costs in supervision and piecing, were off-set by decreased wage costs in spinning and the gains of extra output. On higher yarn counts breakages were more frequent, entailing increased ancillary labour by 'piecers' to maintain output. The argument was thus that the early diffusion of the self-actor was limited, by extra piecing (repairing) costs, to the minority of manufacturers producing low-count yarns. The shift that rendered the self-actor economic for higher counts was not based on technical improvements which lowered piecing costs but rather on a fall in power costs. The self-actor was a relatively power-intensive process, using 60 per cent more power than the hand mule. By 1850 power costs had fallen sufficiently to compensate for the greater piecing costs associated with the self-actor on higher quality yarns, thus making it an economic proposition.[23]

Wages and Labour Costs

It is useful to approach the next sections, which develop different ideas about the constraints on self-actor diffusion, via a brief consideration of questions raised by spinners' wage movements after the innovation of the self-actor. The key point is that automation did not produce the major wage savings envisaged, and the question is why?

Wage costs in spinning were very substantial, making up approximately 46 per cent of total costs: the mule was explicitly offered as a device to cut labour costs, and its diffusion depended on this. Such costs can be reduced in various ways, of course, either by an actual wage-cut or by output per person rising faster than the wage rate, or by a combination of the two. Von Tunzelmann's analysis very usefully separated these processes, suggesting that a reduction of £32.07 per annum per machine in spinning labour costs was necessary to render the self-actor economic, even for coarse yarns, independently of increased productivity.

This was, in fact, a very sharp reduction. For hand-mule spinners of coarse yarns, Wood's tabulation of earnings in the period 1804–33 suggests that average earnings, for an ordinary week's work, would be within the range of 25–35 shillings.[24] Using 25 shillings for purposes of calculation, however, annual spinning wages would be £65, and von Tunzelmann's figures would therefore imply almost a 50 per cent wage cut. There is some evidence that such cuts were achieved. The factory inspector L. Horner in a report of 31 December 1841 quotes 'B.Y., one of the proprietors': 'The former high rate of wages paid to the mule spinner induced many parties to try the self-acting head-stock … We have now

Table 9.1   Relative wages in cotton spinning, c. 1850

	Hand mules Shillings	Self-actors Shillings
Spinner or minder	35	30
Cypher	15	12
Middle piecer	10	
Little piecer	5 or 6	7
Gross earnings	65 to 66	49

Source: George H. Wood, *The History of Wages in the Cotton Trade during the Past Hundred Years* (London: Sherratt and Hughes 1910), 27.

a room worked on this principle. In 1838 the number of hands in this room was 24 and their united wages amounted to £22.2s. Now, with self-actors, and producing about 10 per cent more work, we employ 17 hands, and their wages amount to £7.19s.'[25]

But there is considerably more evidence to the effect that although spinning earnings declined they did not do so to the dramatic extent indicated above. Wood, for example, gives the table reproduced above, remarking that, 'rough though this generalisation is, I do not think it can be far wrong.'[26]

The obvious question we can pose via these figures is why did the self-actor fail to realise the major labour-cost savings that were envisaged for it? In particular, why do these figures show a very small fall in spinners' and minders' wages when it was precisely that group of workers whom the self-actor was designed to cheapen or replace?

Managerial Costs, Production Management, and the Diffusion of Mule-spinning

The reduction in direct spinning labour costs, which were such a crucial element in the economic advantages alleged to accrue from self-actor production, were associated in von Tunzelmann's analysis with an increase in supervision costs. What was entailed by this increase? Our argument is that this shift in the distribution of costs implied managerial transformations, which had a major effect on the pace of diffusion.

All techniques involve a managerial component; that is, all techniques require systems of production management that comprise not only the skills of assembly and operation of techniques but also of supervision and coordination of the labour force. Technological change and development is thus not simply a matter of a new device but rather of a collection of practices and skills in which the actual techniques are, as Peter Mathias put it, 'only the visible tip of a submerged mass of relationships.'[27]

This is certainly the case with the automatic mule, for the transition to automatic spinning – as it was originally envisaged – was not just a matter of inserting a new technique into a pre-existing system of production management. In fact, a radical structural transformation of that system was required. The suggestion we make here is that the possibility and costs of this managerial transformation were crucial to self-actor diffusion. In particular the risks and expense involved created a significant inhibition to diffusion. This led to the retention of a quasi-managerial role for the operative spinner, which in turn helps explain the problem noted in the section above, namely the absence of any success in decisively cutting spinning labour costs.

In his *Genesis of Modern Management* Sidney Pollard emphasised two main difficulties in early industrial management. These were, firstly, the recruitment of a labour force and its adaptation to the new rhythms of work. This difficult challenge was often met by the use of unfree labour – prisoners, workhouse inmates, and children, for example. Secondly there was the inadequacy – indeed the nonexistence – of supervisory techniques suitable for the management of anything beyond small groups of workers.[28] In yarn production an attempt was made to overcome these difficulties through a system – familiar in many early industrial processes – based on subcontracting and piecework: it was not the owner but the operative spinner who was responsible for the recruitment and supervision of ancillary labourers (who might well be members of his own family). He paid them out of his gross wages for the piece (measured by weight or length).[29] W. Cooke-Taylor, a contemporary commentator, wrote: 'It is obvious that the spinner is a very important workman when such mules as we have described are employed: on him depend not merely the machinery and its work, but the employment of the young piecers and the "scavengers" or "cleaners", who are constantly employed in removing the waste cotton or "fly".'[30] In fact, in some cases the spinner's own employment depended on his ability to find ancillary labourers.[31]

The hand-mule spinner thus had both operative and managerial roles in production. The operative skill of the hand-mule spinner consisted primarily in his ability to guide the winding of the 'cop' package; his replacement was thus technically effected by Roberts's cybernetic winding device. But what was to replace his managerial functions, which were linked with his technical operations? The answer, of course, is that there was no adequate replacement for the spinner *qua* production manager, as William Lazonick has shown in several detailed studies. The spinner was replaced by a 'minder' who retained the 'traditional' managerial role of the spinner. Even though the minder was paid less than the hand-mule spinner, the dream of the self-actor inventors – to replace utterly the adult, male, union-member operative – was not achieved in Lancashire. Lazonick's argument is that replacement of the old minder–piecer system of production control by a 'multipair' system would not necessarily have resulted in lower unit labour costs.[32]

This problem was exacerbated by an intensely competitive industrial structure, which gave firms little margin of error if they wished to construct new managerial systems. Lazonick concludes, 'In the transition to the self-actor in the 1830s and 1840s, minders were able to retain a dual role as both operative and supervisor, not because they collectively forced this hierarchical division of labour on capitalists, but because capitalists had no leeway to experiment with new divisions of labour, particularly given the need for close supervision of younger workers.'[33]

Lazonick's work is essentially a study of the reasons for the perpetuation of the hand-mule division of labour into the self-actor era; his temporal scope is fairly wide, and he does not, therefore, discuss questions concerning the rate of diffusion of the self-actor at all. But the managerial problems which he describes, and the inadequacy of prevailing production management techniques generally, would also have operated as a constraint on self-actor diffusion because they nullified the realisation of the full labour-cost economies which were the principal *raison d'être* of the automatic mule. Systems of production management are complementary inputs to the machine itself. Absence of such inputs can significantly hinder both innovation and diffusion of new technologies.[34]

In this perspective, the complementary input of a management system must have involved considerable costs and risks that would, moreover, have been very difficult to forecast. Although in 1830 no one knew how to go about constructing production management systems for complex production processes, there were alternatives available. But in the transition between one system and another, the risk of failure may have been high; in a highly competitive industry the consequences of failure in an attempt to construct a new management system would have been catastrophic. It is not difficult to envisage entrepreneurial calculations that, comparing such costs with an imputed managerial cost within the operative spinner's wage, might conclude that the labour-cost advantages claimed for the self-actors were illusory. This would of course undercut one of the two main supports (the other being increased output) of alleged self-actor superiority.

As Lazonick points out, the multipair system of mule operation ('an overlooker managing 6 to 8 pairs of mules tended by piecers') was tried at least once in Manchester but, more importantly, was the basic form of self-actor management in the USA (where 'top-down hierarchical control prevailed and internal subcontract systems were virtually unknown') as well as in Scotland where, moreover, women were the usual operatives.[35] What factors, then, would have formed the parameters of any decision to change the supervisory structure in Lancashire?

The most important factors, we would suggest, were the labour costs, and the regularity and continuity of output, associated with the minder–piecer supervisory arrangement. If this system broke down, then entrepreneurs would have a strong incentive to replace it. But here we have a paradox: it was precisely the breakdown of this system, or at least a seemingly intractable problem within it, which provided the impulsion to the innovation of the self-actor. Why, then, did the minder–piecer system regain, as it were, viability *after* the innovation of the self-actor? And what effects might this have had on the diffusion of the self-actor?

The Self-actor as a Deterrent Weapon

'This invention confirms,' wrote Andrew Ure of the self-actor, 'the great doctrine ... that when capital enlists science in her service, the refractory hand of labour will always be taught docility.'[36] Hand-mule spinning was, as we have emphasised, organised around the central technico-supervisory role of the spinner; spinners were relatively highly paid and well organised, with their own craft union that also controlled a subordinate piecers' union.[37] They were, in the early nineteenth century, well-organised and willing to mount major strikes over pay or to protect their control over working arrangements, conditions of entry, and so on.[38] Their turbulence was a byword: 'The spinners knew their strength,' wrote Cooke-Taylor, 'and, though they received very large remuneration, frequently turned out for higher wages'; Tufnell speaks of their 'uncontrolled and despotic sway.'[39] One such strike, in Hyde, in 1824, was the direct impulse for the invention of the self-actor, as Roberts testified to the House of Lords select committee on 19 May 1851: 'The self acting mule was made in consequence of a turn-out of the spinners at Hyde, which had lasted three months, when a deputation of masters waited upon me, and requested me to turn my attention to spinning, with the view of making the mule self-acting.'[40]

Edward Tufnell, writing in 1834, was quite clear as to the nature of the self-actor, its objectives, and the likely course of events: 'The introduction of this invention will eventually give a death blow to the Spinners' Union, the members of which will have to thank themselves alone, for the creation of this destined agent of their extinction. It is now rapidly coming into use; other advantages, besides the great one of escape from the dictation of the workmen, are found to attend it; and in a few years the very name of the working spinner, as well as the follies and oppression of their combination, will only be found in history.[41]

The self-actor was thus developed as a weapon, the effectiveness of which to entrepreneurs would be gauged by the extent to which it played a part in defusing the endemic struggles between spinners and masters that had characterised cotton manufacture. But the effectiveness of weapons does not necessarily reside in their being used. In the age of deterrence we know, or at least we fervently hope, that the mere existence or even possibility of existence of a weapon may be sufficient to condition a struggle in such a way that its actual use might not be necessary. Could this have been the case with the automatic mule? This aspect of the self-actor was certainly acknowledged at the time of its invention. The clearest formulation of the 'deterrent' aspect of the self-actor came from Roberts himself, giving evidence concerning patent policy to a parliamentary select committee: 'when the machine was once made (the masters) would have considered their purpose as being answered, that is, that it would have been a rod in pickle (tool for punishment) for the workmen.'[42]

The workers responded to this threat, according to Rose, 'in such a manner that must even be pleasing to their employers. Measures have been perfected that will in future prevent the delinquency of individuals.' He suggested the spinners should respond to the self-actor with the same self-disciplinary measures.[43] For the threat from the self-actor was a real one, according to H.A. Turner: 'In 1836 ... the Preston spinners ... struck for a ten per cent advance. But this strike was particularly disastrous. It not only exhausted the union after three months, but led to the introduction of the self-actor (which was already working in some sixty English mills) to the rising north Lancashire spinning centre: while over a quarter of the Preston spinners were dismissed.'[44]

Ashworth notes, apropos of the Preston strike, the fact that 'in two of the factories, a few self-acting mules, or spinning machines, were substituted for common mules, thereby dispensing with the services of the spinners.'[45] A contemporary writer in the *Edinburgh Review* of 1838 repeated this: 'The boasted efficiency and power of the Cotton-Spinners Association has led to such an extensive establishment of machinery in that department of trade, both in Lancashire and Lanarkshire, as promises soon to supersede the human hand altogether in the spinning department. The patentees for the self-adjusting mule – that is, the machinery which dispenses with the spinners – are from the late strikes so overwhelmed with orders that one now given cannot be executed for *five years*.'[46]

The self-actor was of course far from the only element or weapon in the struggle between worker and capitalist in the textile industry after 1830. But it is the case that the period following the invention of the self-actor was one of quiescence and defeat for the spinners: 'a combination of the competitive threat (from the self-actor), of exhaustion from their previous defeats, and finally of recurrent and deep depression from 1837 to 1834, left the hand-mule spinner much subdued.'[47] Roberts himself had no hesitation in claiming that the self-actor was owed the credit for the subjugation of the spinners: 'The consequence of this has been, that the turn-outs have almost entirely ceased in the spinning department.' – (Roberts) If the hand-spinners ever turn out now, they are seldom allowed to resume work.'[48]

A concrete example of the threat faced by the spinners is provided by the program for self-actor installation given by William Graham, a Glasgow cotton master, to a parliamentary commission:

5398. Are you aware of any cotton spinning works where the proprietors are turning out the old machinery in consequence of a combination of workmen, and introducing self-acting mules? – We are doing it ourselves.

5399. Are you doing it to any extent? – With every mule that we have. We have a few mules that women are fit for, and we do not know whether we can adapt them to the self-acting mules, but if we can, we will even turn out the women to introduce those mules.

5400. What difference will that make in the number of men you employ? – Only about 22 men.

5401. Out of how many? – We shall dismiss all the spinners, all the men that are making those exorbitant wages.

5402. Will you not require some men to manage the self-acting mules? – None; a spinner at present has two piecers under him, we shall still employ two piecers, and to one of those piecers we may be obliged to give a couple of shillings more than the spinner gives him at present.[49]

The suggestion is, therefore, that the innovation of the self-actor undercut the grounds for its own diffusion. By providing a new element in the struggles between entrepreneurs and operative spinners, by shifting the balance of power in favour of the former, it may have helped in the construction of an economic environment in which its diffusion was less urgent. Andrew Ure certainly thought this: he saw the self-actor as 'a creation designed to restore order among the industrious classes ... The news of this Herculean prodigy spread dismay through the Union, *and even long before it left its cradle*, so to speak, it strangled the Hydra of misrule.'[50]

Conclusion

Fifty years after its invention, the automatic mule had become one of the core technologies of the British textile industry; it was also extensively used in the USA and became a key technology in Japan's entry into mechanised textile production.[51] By the last quarter of the nineteenth century major producers of the self-actor technology, such as the engineering firm Platt's of Oldham, were exporting up to about 60 per cent of their output, to all continents of the world.[52] In the case of the automatic mule we are dealing, therefore, with a radical technological innovation of international economic significance.

Diffusion, however, happened very slowly. This was largely for two reasons. On the one hand, skilled male spinners played not only a technical role in production but also a disciplinary, managerial role. They could be supplanted technically but not managerially. Secondly, they responded to the threats posed by the self-actor with a reduction in wage pressure and reductions in challenges to mill owners.[53] This countervailing strategy obviated the original aim of the innovation, which was to automate them out of existence.

The history of innovation in British industrialisation is only in part a history of radical, technically advanced machines. These machines often do not have the epoch-changing impetuses that are claimed for them because they diffuse slowly and because the economic outcomes that are heralded for them only appear many decades after their introduction. This has implications for the timing of industrialisation, which is slower and more hesitant than often believed. But the character of industrialisation must also be in question because the control and management methods of industrial capitalism were only slowly developed, through drawn-out negotiation and conflict.

Notes

1   Gillian Cookson, *The Age of Machinery: Engineering the Industrial Revolution, 1770–1850* (Woodbridge: Boydell & Brewer Press, 2018), 105.

2   Kristine Bruland, 'Industrial Conflict as a Source of Technical Innovation: Three Cases', *Economy and Society* 11, no. 2 (1982): 91–121.

3   Robert Allen has argued that the self-actor developed out of a path-dependent process that began with the spinning jenny. This should not however downplay the engineering creativity of Roberts's achievement. Robert C. Allen, 'The Industrial Revolution in Miniature: The Spinning Jenny in Britain, France, and India', *Journal of Economic History* 69, no. 4 (2009): 922.

4   *Manchester Advertiser*, November 1825, cited in H. Rose, *Manual Labour, versus Brass and Iron: Reflections in Defence of the Body of Cotton Spinners, Occasioned by a Perusal of Mr Robert's Self-Acting Mule* (Manchester: J.Pratt [printer] 1825), 2. See also, for example, James Montgomery, *The Theory and Practice of Cotton Spinning: or, The Carding and Spinning Master's Assistant* (first ed. 1832; Glasgow: J. Niven, 1886), 198, 204 for praise in similar terms.

5   Andrew Ure, *The Philosophy of Manufactures* (London: Charles Knight, 1835), 367.

6   Karl Marx, *Capital, Vol. 1* (London: Harmondsworth, 1976), 563.

7   G.N. von Tunzelmann, *Steam Power and British Industrialization to 1860* (Oxford: Oxford University Press, 1978), 188.

8   The importance of user-producer interaction as success-factor in innovation is emphasised by Eric von Hippel, *The Sources of Innovation* (Oxford: Oxford University Press, 1989).

9   Ure, *Philosophy of Manufactures*, 367.

10 Charles Singer, et.al., *A History of Technology*. vol. IV: *The Industrial Revolution c. 1750 to c. 1850* (Oxford: Clarendon Press, 1958), 288.

11 Harold Catling, 'The Development of the Spinning Mule', *Textile History* 9, no. 1 (1978): 45.

12 Advertisement quoted in Andrew Ure, *The Cotton Manufacture of Great Britain* (London: Charles Knight, 1836), 2: 156.

13 Catling, 'Development of the Spinning Mule', 48. Kurt Neste gives figures concerning the costs of a spinning mill of approximately 5,000 spindles, c. 1860: weekly current expenses are £35 9s 3d, of which £15 2s 4d consists of depreciation, machine maintenance, rent, and taxes, and £16 2s 5d is paid in wages (the residual covers minor sundry items). Kurt Neste, *The Mule Spinning Process and the Machinery Employed in It* (Manchester: John Hewood and London: Simpkin and Marshall, 1865), 91–2.

14 Edward Baines, *History of the Cotton Manufacture in Great Britain* (London: H. Fisher, B. Fisher, and P. Jackson, 1835), 207–8.

15 W.C. Cook-Taylor, *The Handbook of Silk, Cotton and Woollen Manufactures* (London: Richard Bentley, 1843), 151–2.

16 Harold Catling, *The Spinning Mule* (Newton Abbot: David & Charles, 1970), 51.

17 Rhodes Boyson, *The Ashworth Cotton Enterprise* (Oxford: Oxford University Press, 1970), 75.

18 von Tunzelmann, *Steam Power*, 188.

19 Sydney J. Chapman, *The Lancashire Cotton Industry* (Manchester: University Press, 1904), 70.

20 British Parliamentary Papers (hereafter BPP), *Industrial Revolution: Trade*, 2 (1833), 5481.

21 Montgomery, *Theory and Practice*, 205.

22 Bruland, 'Industrial Conflict', 66.

23 Ibid., 67.

24 George H. Wood, *The History of Wages in the Cotton Trade during the Past Hundred Years* (London: Sherratt and Hughes, 1910), 22–3.

25 BPP, *Reports of the Inspectors of Factories, for the Half-Year Ending 31 December 1841: Industrial Revolution, Factories*, 7 (1842–47): 86. See also evidence from the same manufacturer, 28.

26 Wood, *History of Wages*, 27.

27 Peter Mathias, *The Transformation of England: Essays in the Economic and Social History of England in the Eighteenth Century* (London: Methuen, 1979), 37.

28 Sidney Pollard, *The Genesis of Modern Management: A Study of the Industrial Revolution in England* (London: E. Arnold, 1965), esp. chapter 5.

29 Ibid., 51–65; William Lazonick, 'Industrial Relations and Technical Change: The Case of the Self-acting Mule', *Cambridge Journal of Economics* 3 (1979): 232–3.

30 Cooke-Taylor, *Handbook*, 151–2.

31 BPP, *Industrial Revolution: Factories*, 1, 8795.

32 Lazonick, 'Industrial Relations', 232–3, and 243. See also William Lazonick, *Competitive Advantage on the Shop Floor* (Cambridge, MA: Harvard University Press, 1990).

33 Lazonick, *Competitive Advantage*, 257–8.

34 Nathan Rosenberg, *Perspectives on Technology* (Cambridge: Cambridge University Press, 1977), 81.

35 Lazonick, 'Industrial Relations', 237 and 243. See Isaac Cohen, *American Management and British Labor. A comparative study of the cotton spinning industry* (New York and London: Greenwood Press, 1990).

36 Ure, *Philosophy of Manufactures*, 368.

37 Sidney and Beatrice Webb, *History of Trade Unionism* (London: Longman's Green and Company, 1926), 6–7. See also Bruland, 'Industrial Conflict'.

38 See Herbert A. Turner, *Trade Union Growth, Structure and Policy* (London: Allen & Unwin, 1962), 76, for an account of the major actions.

39 Cooke-Taylor, *Handbook*, 151; Edward C. Tufnell, *Character, Object and Effects of Trades Unions* (London: James Ridgway & Sons, 1834), 13.

40 BPP, *Inventions general*, 1 (1829–5): 1334. That the strike in 1824 was the impulse for the invention of the self-actor was a view widely held. See for example James Wheeler, *Manchester: Its Political, Social and Commercial History* (London: Whittaker, 1836), 538.

41 Tufnell, *Character*, 108–9.

42 BPP, *Inventions, General* I (1829–51): 1366.

43 Rose, *Manual Labour*, 2.

44 Turner, *Trade Union Growth*, 74–5.

45 H. Ashworth, *An Inquiry into the Origin, Progress and Results of the Strike of the Operative Spinners of Preston, From October 1836 to February 1737* (Manchester: John Harrison [printer], 1838), 9–10.

46 *Edinburgh Review*, vol. 67 (1838): 254–5. Emphasis in original.

47 Turner, *Trade Union Growth*, 74–5.

48 BPP, *Inventions General, I*, (1829–51): 1334.

49 BPP, *Industrial Revolution, Trade* 2, (1833): 323.

50 Ure, *The Philosophy of Manufactures*, 367. The emphasis is ours.

51 American use of the automatic mule is covered thoroughly in Cohen, *American Management and British Labor*. For a study of the mule in Japan see G. Saxonhouse, 'A Tale of Japanese Technological Diffusion in the Meiji Period', *Journal of Economic History* 34, no. 1 (1974): 149–65.

52 Kristine Bruland, *British Technology and European Industrialization* (Cambridge: Cambridge University Press, 1989), 150–2.

53 See Louise Purbrick, 'Ideologically Technical: Illustration, Automation and Spinning Cotton around the Middle of the Nineteenth Century', *Journal of Design History* 11, no. 4 (1998): esp. 278. G.N. von Tunzelmann, 'Time-saving Technical Change: The Cotton Industry in the English Industrial Revolution', *Explorations in Economic History* 32, no. 1 (1995): 12.

PART THREE

The Age of Luxury:
Consumption, Imagination,
and Desire

10

Leo Africanus Presents
Africa to Europeans

Natalie Zemon Davis

In 1550, a remarkable book about Africa, *La Descrittione dell'Africa*, came off the Giunta press in Venice, as the first volume of Giovanni Battista Ramusio's celebrated series of *Voyages*. It had been written by an African, Ramusio assured his readers: Giovanni Leone the African, 'Giovan Lioni Africano'.[1]

In fact, for most of his life its author had been called al-Hasan ibn Ahmed ibn Muhammad al-Wazzan.[2] Born in Granada around 1486–88, Hasan al-Wazzan had been taken by his family to Morocco around 1492, at the time of the Catholic conquest of his ancestral land. After his studies he became a diplomat, and in that capacity and on occasion as a trader, he visited polities all over Morocco. By caravan he crossed the Sahara to the Land of the Blacks ('le terre de li Nigri', as he translated into Italian the Arabic 'Bilad al-Sudan') and made stops among other places at Timbuktu and Gao, where he met the great Songhay emperor Askia Muhammad, and Agadez, from which town a Tuareg elite ruled over their slaves and the black people of the countryside. His duties took him to the Berber kingdoms of Tlemcen (present-day Algeria), Tunisia, and on to Cairo, from where he made *hajj* and then travelled to the Ottoman court at Istanbul.

In the summer of 1518, on his way by sea from Cairo back to Morocco, his boat was seized by a Spanish Christian pirate, Pedro de Cabrera y Bobadilla. Realising what a find he had made, Bobadilla decided not to seek ransom for al-Wazzan nor sell him as a slave but instead make a gift of the diplomat to Pope Leo X, then in the midst of urging a crusade against the Ottoman Turks. Incarcerated at the Castel Sant'Angelo, al-Wazzan was catechised, baptised by the pope, and given the names Joannes Leo (Giovanni Leone). Now free from prison, though dependent on Christian favour, Giovanni Leone thought of himself in Arabic as Yuhanna al-Asad, or even better, as he signed a 1524 Arabic manuscript, 'Yuhanna al-Asad al-Gharnati [the Granadan] previously named al-Hasan ibn Muhammad al-Wazzan al-Fasi [of Fez]', suggesting the multiple identities he carried around during his Italian years.[3]

By the end of five years in Italy, Giovanni Leone had mastered Italian and Latin sufficiently to venture writing seriously in those languages. He had been peppered with learned queries about Africa and Islam but surely also with questions about harems and baths and other intimate matters that fired European curiosity. He had listened to Egidio da Viterbo's sermons attacking Hagar and Ishmael; he had seen maps of Africa in printed editions of Ptolemy with woodcuts of headless persons in the interior and the word 'ANTHROPHAGI' (cannibals) etched in the southeast; he had undoubtedly heard or read assertions about the monstrous, the extremes in breeding and climate, and the unceasing and restless changeability of Africa. Further he had by now had the chance to see parts of the Italian world other than the circles of high churchmen and learned men. Slaves were performing domestic duties in some of the great households that Giovanni Leone visited as part of his own scholarly service in Rome: free 'Moors', such as 'Susanna the Moor' ('Susanna mora') and 'Giamara the Moor' ('Giamara mora'), lived in the Campo Marzio neighbourhood where Giovanni Leone spent his first years, along with artisans, tradespeople, and prostitutes. Some of these 'Moors' were people of colour, brown or black – the word *moro* could refer at that date to a person with dark skin as well as to someone from North Africa – and many of the slaves and freed persons had been brought up as Muslims.[4] By 1525, Giovanni Leone had also travelled beyond Rome: he had lived for a time in Bologna and Viterbo, had visited Florence, and had been as far north as Venice and as far south as Naples. His social and visual experience of life in a Christian land had widened and offered him a frame in which to present Dar al-Islam and the Africa he knew to Europeans.

The great work of Giovanni Leone's Italian years was his manuscript on Africa, which he titled *Libro de la Cosmographia et Geographia de Affrica* and whose colophon bore the date 10 March 1526.[5] He presumably had some Arabic travel notes for his years crisscrossing Africa, restored to him after his captors had emptied his diplomatic pouches, but much of the text was composed in his lively though simplified Italian, and he sometimes apologized for his 'weak memory'.[6] The resulting book was a mixture of genres, like so many others in the Arabic geographical tradition: geography, travel account, ethnography, and history were entwined together with occasional asides of autobiography and literary commentary. After a general introduction on geography, weather, customs, and health, Giovanni Leone organised his book around the different regions of Africa that he knew and concluded with an overview of Africa's rivers, flora, and fauna.

The world of Africa that emerged from Giovanni Leone's manuscript of 1526 undermined the clichés circulating about its peoples in European texts of the early sixteenth century. To be sure, Giovanni Leone reproduces in his introduction some stereotypes long traditional in North Africa itself, calling his Maghreb 'the most noble part of Africa … the people white and reasoning' and saying that 'the inhabitants of the Land of the Blacks … lack reason … and are without wits.'[7] But once he gets into his story, he portrays a range of behaviour and culture, from what he considers highly civilized to the brutish, in *all* the regions. Timbuktu, for example, has a splendid mosque and palace, artisans and merchants sell goods from all over the world, and prosperous citizens enjoy music and dance. Scholars, preachers, and judges are held in high esteem there, and manuscripts in Arabic are the hottest item of trade at the market.

Two copies of the manuscript of the *Geographia de Affrica* were circulating in Venice after the sack of Rome in 1527, when its author seems to have returned to North Africa and Islam, retaking his Arabic name and North African garb and basing himself in Tunis. When the Venetian humanist Giovanni Battista Ramusio decided to publish the manuscript as the opening to his multivolumed *Navigazioni e Viaggi*, he edited the text extensively so as to make its author and in some cases his Africa more acceptable to Christian European readers. Among other changes, Ramusio turned Giovanni Leone's simple but lively Italian into a complex and literary language; he changed Giovanni Leone's self-presentation as an Arab man of letters into that of an historian following professional rules; he strengthened Giovanni Leone's occasional negative statements about the Land of the Blacks; he inserted words to make explicit that the author of the text was a Christian.[8]

Africa as Site of Artisanal Production

Let us here follow one theme in the Africa book of Giovanni Leone (I will continue to call him mostly by his Italian name, since that was the name he used for his readers), a theme that would inform Europeans about one of the 'civilized' rhythms of life in African communities and the products that were part of that life. What did Giovanni Leone have to say about the artisans in different regions of Africa, what they made, what their products looked or felt like, and who acquired them?

In asking such a question, we follow the pioneering studies of Maxine Berg on early modern material culture, its manufacture and exchange across oceans and continents.

Such topics were little treated in the published literature on Africa available in Europe in al-Wazzan's day. Joannes Boemus's *Omnium gentium mores*, with its long section on Africa, first appeared in 1520. It had only a few words to say about animal pelts used to cover privy parts, wooden javelins, and stone weapons in a leather bag, along with longer accounts of people like the 'Ichthiophagi', who were in the shape of humans but lived like beasts in cliffs near the ocean.⁹

Portuguese writings of travel and conquest, some of them circulating only in manuscript, take readers more concretely to items produced in African lands near the coast. Thus, the captain of one of Henry the Navigator's caravels brought fishing nets back from a 1436 voyage south of Cape Bajador (in present-day Western Sahara). They were made from the bark of a tree, which could be spun into strong cords without adding any flax: 'something new to note for us in Spain', was the comment of the chronicler Gomes Eanes de Zucarara.¹⁰ In 1455–57, the young Venetian Alvise Cadamosta commanded one of Henry's caravels as far south as Gambia and beyond and later wrote up his *Navigations* in Italian. Though some of the rumours he reported are full of fancy, he did describe the cotton garments of men and women in the coastal region of Senegal and how they marvelled at the woollen cloth in his Spanish-style clothes, which amazed them even more than his white skin.¹¹ And to give one more example, in 1498, after Vasco da Gama had rounded the Cape of Good Hope and had passed Port Natal, his diarist recorded what the Portuguese had seen in a community where they were welcomed for a five-day stop for water. The villagers' weapons were long bows and arrows and spears with iron blades. The hilts of their daggers were of tin; the dagger sheaths of ivory. Copper ornaments were twisted around their arms and legs and in their hair. They prized linen cloth and were glad to exchange their copper for it.¹²

Sebastian Münster's *Cosmographia*, first published in Basel in 1544, put together the traditional stereotypes with the newer travel accounts. Giovanni Leone's Africa book was still circulating only in manuscript, and Münster had not seen it. In his pages on Africa, Münster drew first on Boemus, repeating stories that went back to Herodotus, seeing Egypt as a land of inversions (women went out to trade, men stayed home to spin), and including a chapter on 'the wondrous and monstrous creatures found in Africa', illustrated with headless humans and the like.¹³ Then Münster turned to 'New Africa, that is, to its recent investigation', and reproduced the findings of Alvise Cadamosta, whose *Navigations* had been published in translations in 1507 and afterward. So readers learned of the biweekly fairs in coastal Senegal where women and men traded cotton and cotton cloth, palm mats, foods, arms, and small amounts of gold.[14]

Revealing the African World of Goods

This is the world of African objects and their producers and users that Giovanni Leone opened for European readers with much greater breadth and detail, and without the constant assumption that European articles were always better.[15] As a travelling diplomat and occasional merchant, al-Wazzan would have been attentive to the look of products and their estimated value. Moreover, his family name, al-Wazzan, meant 'the weigher' in Arabic; his father and grandfather may both have been associated with the *muhtasib*, the supervisor of transactions at the *souk* (market), including those concerning weights and measures. He knew the workings of markets and fairs.

The textile trades – spinning, weaving, and dyeing cloth, and the making of garments, bed clothes, and other household items – took the time and energy of the largest number of artisans throughout Giovanni Leone's Africa. Linen and canvas were produced both in major centres like Fez (520 ateliers) and Tunis, and in villages in the Rif Mountains. Cotton cloth was made at Cairo and Timbuktu but also in small towns throughout Egypt, Tlemcen and the 'big village' of Djenné in the Land of the Blacks. Flocks of sheep yielded fleece for looms producing woollen cloth in Fez and Constantine, and also in towns and villages throughout Morocco and on the island of Djerba. Silk cloth was woven in Fez and the Mediterranean port of Cherchell, its production the work of Granadan émigrés, Giovanni Leone proudly noted, who had developed the planting of mulberry trees.[16]

The spinners of thread (or winders in the case of silk) were always women. Giovanni Leone recalled the skill of the women of Tunis: they let their spindles fall from their windows or some other high spot in their houses, and the result was thread 'well stretched, well twisted, and regular' and 'perfect linen sold all over Africa.'[17] Most weavers in Fez were men working in large industrial workshops, but Giovanni Leone reported a few places where women were weavers. Such was Figuig, a Berber oasis near the Atlas Mountains in eastern Morocco, where women wove woollen blankets for beds 'so thin and delicate they appeared to be silk.' They were much sought after at the markets in Fez and Tlemcen.[18]

Of the products from all these looms, garments were those most often described by Giovanni Leone, for he took clothing seriously as a mark of status and also knew that Europeans were curious about what people wore. Indeed, proper dress had been important in his past life as a diplomat, and a change in garments was part of his conversion to Christianity. He introduced basic garments early on in presenting the regions of southern Morocco. In coastal Haha, an area of traders and herders, men wore an ample woollen garment called *al-kisa* wrapped closely around their body. The cloth resembled that used for blankets in Italy, he remarked to his readers. Underneath it, they tied a small woollen cloth around their loins. In places where linen was available, a shirt might be worn underneath as well. Around their heads they wound in a distinctive fashion a long woollen cloth, stained with walnut dye.[19] Giovanni Leone added a second basic garment as he spoke of the towns and villages in the Tedle, a region of the High Atlas Mountains: the burnoose, *al-burnus* (again he gave the word in Arabic). This hooded cloak was beautifully made by women in the area and was here dyed black. Merchants came from afar to the Tedle's main market town to buy burnooses, which Giovanni Leone said could now even be seen in Italy and Spain.[20]

Giovanni Leone went on to show variations in these patterns. Shorter garments and simpler headdress were signs of lower status. The male miners and herders in villages in the Anti-Atlas wore a short, tightly cinched woollen shirt without sleeves; winegrowing villagers in the Rif Mountains dressed in a short hooded garment of wool with black and white stripes. Meanwhile, the women in these rural families went without veils.[21] In the kingdom of Tlemcen, Berber peasants dressed in 'a short garment of thick cloth'. The busy male artisans in the city of Tlemcen were garbed honestly in a short garment, and instead of a turban, most of them wore a smooth cap.[22]

The dress of wealthier families in Fez, Tunis, and Cairo was more sumptuous and received more attention from Giovanni Leone. In Fez, the men of high status wore 'foreign wool' (perhaps 'foreign' from Italy). They layered themselves: an undershirt, a garment over it with half-sleeves, linen breeches or pants, then a large robe sewn down the front, and over all, a burnoose adorned with the trimmings and tassels found in the Fez market. On their heads they put first a small cap (they were like the nightcaps of Italy, explained Giovanni Leone, except without the space for the ears), and then a turban of linen, wound under their beard and twice around their head. Men of more modest status wore only the undergarment and a burnoose, with a simple bonnet, while the poor went around in a garment and burnoose of coarse white local wool. Learned men were distinguished by the wide sleeves on their robes, rather like those, he pointed out to his readers, worn by men of high station and office in Venice.[23]

As for the women, the merchants selling cloth for their garments were among the richest of Fez. The women also layered themselves: first, a belted chemise or shift of good cloth, which was all they might wear in their dwellings in the hottest of days; then a robe of fine woollen cloth or silk, sewn down the front and with wide sleeves. When they went out, they added long pants, a voluminous cape covering their whole person, and a linen veil for the face leaving space for their eyes.[24]

For the well-dressed men and women of Tunis, 'Africa's most remarkable city', Giovanni Leone concentrated on the distinctive features of headdress. Here even artisans wore turbans, as did the merchants and men of learning: large turbans with a cloth hanging from them at a special angle. Military men and others serving the sultan wound their turbans without the hanging cloth.[25] The women, well dressed and adorned, used two pieces of cloth, one wound round the forehead, the other covering the hair and the face below the eyes so voluminously that they appeared to have 'a giant's head'. Still Giovanni Leone had been able to smell their perfumes as he passed them on the streets.[26]

The clothing of Egypt and of Cairo's prosperous families in particular had, in Giovanni Leone's telling, a narrower silhouette and a different mix of textiles from the garments of Fez. No burnooses here but rather for men an outer garment sewn close at the neck, then open to the ground and with narrow sleeves. In the summer the garment was silk or cotton with colourful stripes, in the winter, fine wool with cotton padding. Their turbans, made of cloth from India, were large, however, befitting men of high station. The woman's garment also had tight sleeves, and whether of fine wool, linen, or cotton was beautifully embroidered. Her costly headdress was tall and narrow, and when she went out in Cairo's busy streets she was covered with a veil of fine Indian cotton and wore on her face a black mask woven from hair, which allowed her to look out at people without being recognised herself.[27] (One can imagine women readers in Venice fascinated by this description.)

Meanwhile in Djenné in the Land of the Blacks, the people were 'courteous and well-dressed', so Giovanni Leone recalled (Ramusio later left out the 'civili'): the men wore blue or black cotton and draped a large cape over their heads, black if they were traders, artisans, or farmers, white if they were imams or judges. Likewise the men of Timbuktu were 'well-dressed in black or blue cotton', also wearing the European cloth brought to town on the merchant caravans from the Maghreb. The

Timbuktu women marked status by veiling, the slave women going with faces uncovered, the other women covering with one of the cotton cloths produced by local weavers. (For some reason, Ramusio cut Giovanni Leone's reference to the men's garb in Timbuktu, while retaining his account of the women.)[28]

The naked black African, so prominent in the European imagination, made an infrequent appearance in al-Wazzan's Africa. The farmers and shepherds in the countryside around the Songhay capital of Gao were 'ignorant' people: 'it would be hard to find one of them who could read or write within a hundred miles.' (European readers would, of course, recognise similar illiteracy among their own peasant populations.) They wore sheepskin in the winter, and in the summer, only a little cloth over their private parts.[29]

Leather, Jewellery, Wood, and Ceramics

The sheepskin garment of the countryfolk near Gao takes us to a second area of African production described by Giovanni Leone, that of leather. Tanning of sheep, goat, and cattle skin was found in many parts of Africa, but our author wrote most about the regions he knew best and which were, in fact, celebrated for their leather: many parts of Morocco – from the southern Sous to the northern Rif – and the kingdom of Tunisia. The handsome leathers tanned from goatskin at Tiyout, on a plain near the Anti-Atlas, for instance, found their way to the many leather craftsmen in Fez, who produced shoes, saddles, garments, pouches, and sheaths for knives and sabres. Production went on locally in many areas as well: Giovanni Leone mentions saddles made in a village on the Atlas slopes and sandals made from sheepskin by the village shoemakers of Gober in the Land of the Blacks. The sandals were 'similar to those worn in ancient times by the Romans', and were sold in Timbuktu and Gao.[30] Among the everyday objects he described were the large, skin water bags slung over the camel's back on his caravan trips, and the smaller ones, fancily decorated and borne by the water-sellers in the streets of Cairo. And among the fine objects were the saddles made in Fez: three layers of leather were artfully placed on top of one another. They were 'truly excellent and marvellous', as one could see in those exported to Italy itself.[31]

Many African artisans were drawn to the foundries, furnaces, forges, hammers, and other tools of the metal trades. Of the mines supplying metals to these workshops, Giovanni Leone mentioned only the silver, iron, and copper mines in mountainous and desert areas of Morocco, along with iron mines in Tlemcen and gold purchased from the Land of the Blacks.[32] But he remarked on the presence of founders, casters, blacksmiths, and goldsmiths in many regions from the Atlas Mountains to desert oases, and he noted their handiwork from the needles, nails, sabres, and spurs at the Fez market to the great cauldrons for sugar-boiling in Egypt to the golden bridles and bits he saw on the royal horses in Bornu.[33]

Especially interesting were the Jewish goldsmiths mentioned by Giovanni Leone in the towns and mountains of Morocco, in oases in the desert, like Segelmesse, on the way to the Land of the Blacks, and in Cairo. Jews also worked as founders and smiths in towns and villages that Giovanni Leone passed through; he saw them, for instance, producing hoes and sickles in the Atlas Mountains not far from Marrakech. But much of the jewellery sold at the souks in North Africa and in the desert came from their hands. (Giovanni Leone explained Jewish predominance by a Muslim law placing conditions on the sale of gold and silver.)[34]

Wherever he was, he had an eye for the jewellery women wore. In Fez, he could see it up close: the large gold earrings encrusted with precious jewels, undoubtedly worn in his own family, the heavy golden bracelets on each arm, and for the less wealthy, earrings, bracelets, and leg rings in silver. In the villages and plains of Morocco, where the women were not covered, he described silver earrings, bracelets, and rings (several on a hand); in a High Atlas mountain he called 'Ideucacal', the more prosperous women wore heavy silver earrings, sometimes four at once, along with silver on their fingers, arms, and legs, while the poorer women had to be satisfied with jewellery of iron or brass.[35] Finally there were the wealthy women of Cairo, 'magnificent with jewels', which he had managed to see despite their veils; they wore them in garlands around their forehead and neck.[36] One can imagine the Venetian women's envy on hearing of such adornment.

On two other kinds of artisanal products, wood and ceramics, Giovanni Leone gave report almost exclusively from North Africa. Europeans could read in his pages about fine combs of boxwood, made in the Atlantic town of Salé and sold throughout the sultancy of Fez, as well as combs for carding wool. They could learn of master woodworkers producing beams, plows, wheels, and mill parts as well as pails that would be used to measure grain and other such products sold in the markets. And there were the talented craftsmen who sculptured the fine wooden doors inside the Fez houses and made the great painted armoires where Fez families stored their bedclothes and their valuables.[37] From his past, he recalled the pulpit – the *minbar* in Arabic – at the celebrated Bu 'Inaniya madrasa in Fez, made of intricately carved

ebony and ivory.[38] Giovanni Leone thought Italians would also enjoy
hearing about the wooden shoes made for Fez gentlemen to wear
when the streets were muddy. They were most durable when made
from mulberry wood; they were more elegant when made from walnut
or the wood of an orange tree. With iron soles and a leather fastener
prettily decorated with silk, these wooden shoes cost anywhere from
one to twenty-five ducats.[39]

For pottery, Giovanni Leone evoked the kilns and potting sheds
in different parts of Morocco and Tunis. In Fez, he recalled both the
unglazed white bowls, basins, and pots made and sold cheaply on the
east side of town near the city wall and the beautiful coloured vases and
pots on display at the major market, some of the finest glazes coming
from the potters in a little town not far away at the foot of the Middle
Atlas. The potters of the Mediterranean town of Sousse furnished Tunis
and many other towns along the coast with bowls, jugs, and vases.[40]
Especially, he never tired of telling Italian readers about the stunning
coloured tiles and tile mosaics found on the walls of the mosques,
madrasas, fountains, and houses in North African towns.

Markets

As suggested by the vases of Sousse, Giovanni Leone talked of the
artisanal products of Africa not only as they were used and worn but
as they were exchanged as wares and moved through trade routes. He
described in detail the spatial arrangement of the souks in Fez, by craft
and by status (never had he seen a market 'with so many people and
things for sale, neither in Africa, Asia, nor Italy' as at the one on the
outskirts of Fez). Tlemcen, Tunis, and Cairo had similar arrangements.[41]
For smaller towns, he told Italian readers both of weekly regional
markets and of the movement of goods from the Maghreb and Egypt
to the Land of the Blacks and back. For example, traders from the
prosperous oasis of Oufran below the Anti-Atlas acquired European
wools and local linens at the port of Agadir (occupied by Portuguese
since 1505), they then added these textiles to their caravans loaded with
copper vessels made by their own artisans from nearby copper mines
and crossed the desert to Djenné and Timbuktu where they bought
dyed cotton cloth to bring back north. Italian readers would enjoy
Giovanni Leone's report of the high price of Venetian cloth in the
market at Gao.[42]

Meanwhile he also reminded them that European merchants were
buying African goods at Mediterranean ports. He mentioned the special
funduqs at Tlemcen and Tunis, hotel/warehouses to accommodate

Genoese, Venetian, Catalan, and other Christian merchants; other travellers had seen the traders' *funduqs* at Alexandria crammed with merchandise.[43] He recalled the boats from Venice, Genoa, Apulia, Sicily, Dubrovnik, Portugal, and from as far away as England crowding the docks of Alexandria. Economic historians have told us of the African cotton, wool, and fabrics being loaded on the boats at the North African ports, of the leather hides, of the dried fruits, olive oil, and wax, of the gold, ivory, and ostrich feathers, brought north on caravan routes across the Sahara – to give only a partial listing. Giovanni Leone talked not only about textiles and hides being exported to Europe but, as we have heard, even about certain garments and leather products.[44]

Finally, Giovanni Leone provided vignettes of the play of artisanal products in everyday life. In his student years, he had spent two days in an isolated and 'uncivilized' farming settlement in the High Atlas, whose inhabitants rarely saw merchandise from elsewhere. All the young men marvelled at his white mantle, white being the colour students wore. Presumably it was the material and the cut that were new to the mountain dwellers (Giovanni Leone did not call it a burnoose), and each of them had to rub it between his fingers. By the time he left, his cloak was 'dirty as a kitchen rag.' But he was richer by a horse, for one of the young men persuaded him to exchange his sword worth a ducat and a half for this mountain steed worth ten.[45]

Another Africa

Giovanni Leone/Hasan al-Wazzan presented to European readers the many sides to life in the different regions of Africa. His was a story of contrasts, both among regions and within regions, and of connections, including those made by the widespread practice of Islam. Many of his pages were devoted to bloodshed: wars and destruction among peoples and polities within Africa, and between the Muslim Arabs and Berbers of North Africa and the Christians of Spain and Portugal. But there were also peaceful tales, including the ones I have followed here, of the articles produced by craftsmen, their use in everyday life, and in exchange. In its specificity this account could offer European readers both affinity to Africans and also ways to react to difference without constantly weighing on a European scale of 'savagery' and 'civilization.'

Quotations from Ramusio's edition of the *Descrittione dell'Africa* and from its French, Latin, and English translations abound in many a book in the later sixteenth century and afterward.[46] Usually such reference was prompted by some special European interest or curiosity; the extent to which the *Description of Africa* had a deeper impact on European understanding and sensibility is a matter that goes beyond the bounds of this chapter. We can get a clue to the status of al-Wazzan's book as a witness to Africa by Ramusio's own series: the *Description of Africa* had pride of place as the opener to volume one, but it was followed on the next pages by Cadamosto's *Navigazione*.[47]

Let us conclude with a limited inquiry about impact, that is, the use of Giovanni Leone's word-pictures of African garments by a European artist eager to depict them.[48] He is the unknown creator of the engravings in the 1556 French translation of the Africa book, published by Jean Temporal in Lyon, the only edition of the book during the sixteenth century to have images. Several of the pictures appear on the same page with Giovanni Leone's descriptions of the garments worn in Fez and other parts of Morocco and in Cairo. The artist used precise motifs in the text to fuel his visual imagination and create figures of human vitality and presence. The woollen *al-kisa* of the Haha is here scanty rather than voluminous as Giovanni Leone had said of it, but it is tightly wrapped to the body of the young man with his spear (figure 10.1); the head covering has fewer windings than Giovanni Leone had described, but it does leave the top of the head bare. This is not a 'realistic' picture of the herders and traders of the Haha, but it does show the artist imagining a vigorous youth in a region that Giovanni Leone had said was marked by petty local war.

Similarly, in 'Acoutremens de ceux de Fez' (Garments of the [men] of Fez), the prosperous man of Fez on horseback (figure 10.2) is not wearing the burnoose that Giovanni Leone had detailed as the overgarment for men's outside wear. He carries a spear rather than the sword we would expect for a merchant. But his garments are layered, his coat is seamed down the front and has wide sleeves, his turban has a double wrap under his chin. If the pleasing designs on the rider's coat are the artist's playful imagining of what fine European cloth would look like in Fez or what he thought would look decorative in his picture, nonetheless he has tried to represent a determined North African man on a fine steed.[49]

The dress of the well-born couple of Cairo (figure 10.3) has this same mixture, with motifs drawn directly from Giovanni Leone's account, such as the headdresses, and others supplied by the artist's visual exercise and reflection, put in motion by the text. They are probably among the most appealing images to the European viewer, though the wife is here depicted without the mysterious black mask described by Giovanni Leone in his book, a mask which, he said, concealed her identity but allowed her to look at others.[50] The artist gave a partial face cover to a woman only in a second picture (figure 10.4), though she is an isolated and somewhat stealthy figure.[51]

Figure 10.1   Engraving of 'Costumes des hommes Marocains', from *Historiale description de l'Afrique* (Lyon: Jean Temporal, 1556).

Such peaceful pictures, like Giovanni Leone's book itself, coexisted with violent times. Wars and sacking continued, as did piracy and enslavement, and the condemnation of infidels and idolaters was heard on all sides. But nourishing the possibility of other kinds of relations is no small accomplishment of this African Muslim, present for a time in Renaissance Europe.

Figure 10.2 'Engraving of Acoutremens de ceux de Fez', from *Historiale description de l'Afrique* (Lyon: Jean Temporal, 1556).

Figure 10.3   Engraving of 'Habits des habitans du Caire', from *Historiale description de l'Afrique* (Lyon: Jean Temporal, 1556).

Figure 10.4 Engraving of 'Autre sorte d'habit des femmes d'Egypte demeurans au Caire', from *Historiale description de l'Afrique* (Lyon: Jean Temporal, 1556).

Notes

I thank the Walters Art Museum for allowing the reproduction of materials originally published as 'Leo Africanus' Presents African to Europeans, in *Revealing the African Presence in Renaissance Europe*. Joaneath Spicer, ed. (Baltimore: The Walters Art Museum, 2012), 60–74.

1 The quotations are drawn from the modern edition: Giovanni Battista Ramusio, ed. *La descrizione dell'Africa di Giovan Lioni Africano*, in *Navigationi et Viaggi*, ed. Marica Milanesi (Turin: Giolio Einaudi, 1978), 1: 19–460, cited as Ramusio, *Descrizione*.

2 For an extensive treatment of and full bibliography on al-Hasan al-Wazzan, see Natalie Zemon Davis, *Trickster Travels: A Sixteenth-Century Muslim between Worlds* (New York: Hill and Wang, 2006).

3 Al-Hasan al-Wazzan and Jacob Mantino, Arabic–Latin–German dictionary, ms 398, Manuscritos árabes, Real Biblioteca del Monasterio de San Lorenzo de El Escorial, 117b–118a.

4 D. Gnoli, ed., 'Descriptio urbis o censimento della popolazaione di Roma avanti il Sacco Borbonica', *Archivio della R. Società di Storia Patria* 17 (1894): 420–5.

5 *Libro de la Cosmogrophia* [sic] *et Geographia de Affrica*, V.E. ms 953, Biblioteca Nazionale Centrale, Rome, hereafter cited as CGA.

6 CGA 19r ('secundo la debil memoria del prefato compositore'); Ramusio, *Descrizione*, 39 (changes to 'questo è quanto m'è rimaso nella memoria').

7 CGA 2r; Ramusio, *Descrizione*, 20.

8 Ramusio also changed al-Wazzan's frequent use of 'he' and 'the author' (or compiler, 'il compositore') for self-reference to the first person thus eliminating a distancing device that the author had carefully inserted into the manuscript.

9 Joannes Boemus, *The Fardle of Facions Conteining the Aunciente Maners, Customes and Lawes of the Peoples Enhabiting the Two Partes of the Earth Called Affrike and Asia* (London: John Kingstone and Henry Sutton, 1555; facsimile edition: Amsterdam: Theatrum Orbis Terrarum and New York: De Capo Press, 1970), F 1r, F3r, F8v.

10 Gomes Eanes de Zurara, *Chronique de Guinée*, trans. Louis Bourdon and Robert Ricard (Dakar: IFAN, 1960), 77.

11 Alvise Cadamosto, *Relation des voyages à la Côte occidentale d'Afrique d'Alvise de Ca' da Mosto, 1455–1457*, ed. Charles Schefer (Paris: Ernest Leroux, 1895), 80–1, 115.

12 [Alvara Velho], *A Journal of the First Voyage of Vasco da Gama*, trans. E.G. Ravenstein (New Delhi and Madras: Asian Educational Services, 1995), 17–18.

13 Sebastian Münster, *Cosmographiae Universalis Libri VI* (Basel: Heinrich Petri, 1559), 1151–2.

14 Münster, *Cosmographiae Universalis*, 1128, 1157–8. Cadamosto, *Navigations*, xiii–xvii, 114–15.

15 On production and trade in the Mediterranean, see the classic study of Fernand Braudel, *La Méditerranée et le monde méditerranéen à l'époque de Philippe II*, 2nd ed., 2 vols. (Paris: Librairie Armand Colin, 1966), especially vol. 1.

16 CGA 291v; Ramusio, *Descrizione*, 294.

17 CGA 321r; Ramusio, *Descrizione*, 322.

18 CGA, 362r; Ramusio, *Descrizione*, 359 (Ramusio added 'tanto sottili e delicati'; CGA just said 'paron di seta').

19 CGA 46r; Ramusio, *Descrizione*, 70.

20 CGA 104r, 110v, 111r; Ramusio, *Descrizione*, 127–8, 133–4.

21 CGA 81v, 236r; Ramusio, *Descrizione*, 107, 247.

22 CGA 274r, 281r; Ramusio, *Descrizione*, 280–1, 286.

23 CGA 163v–164r; Ramusio, *Descrizione*, 183. Burnoose trimmings: CGA 155v; Ramusio, *Descrizione*, 176.

24 CGA, 164r–v, 166v; Ramusio, *Descrizione*, 183, 185. Merchants selling women's garments, CGA, 155v, Ramusio, *Descrizione*, 176.

25 CGA, 321r–v; Ramusio, *Descrizione*, 321–2.

26 CGA, 324v; Ramusio, *Descrizione*, 324.

27 CGA 394r–v, 414v–415r; Ramusio, *Descrizione*, 390–1, 412.

28 CGA 379v [Rauchenberger, *Johannes Leo*, 270].

29 CGA 384r–v [Rauchenberger, *Johannes Leo*, 288], 290; Ramusio, *Descrizione*, 381.

30 CGA 60v, 93v–94r, 384v [Rauchenberger, *Johannes Leo*, 290]; Ramusio, *Descrizione*, 86, 118, 381.

31 CGA, water bags: 415v, saddles: 154v ('per excellentia'); Ramusio, *Descrizione*, water bags: 412–13, saddles: 175 ('eccellenti e mirabili').

32 CGA 81r, 98r, 257v, 283v–284r; Ramusio, *Descrizione*, 89 , 107, 122, 265, 289.

33 CGA 154r–159r, 390r [Rauchenberger, *Johannes Leo*, 314], 404v; Ramusio, *Descrizione*, 175–9, 386, 401–2.

34 CGA 47v, 49r, 52v–53r, 61r, 78r, 82v, 87v , 353r, 357r, 407r; Ramusio, *Descrizione*, 71, 73, 78, 86, 104, 108, 112, 351, 355, 404.

35 CGA 56r–v, 60r, 86v, 96v, 112r, 164v , 257v; Ramusio, *Descrizione*, 81, 85, 111, 120, 134, 183–4, 266.

36 CGA 415r; Ramusio, *Descrizione*, 412.

37 CGA 128r–v, 138v, 158r, 292r; Ramusio, *Descrizione*, 151, 161, 178–9, 295.

38 CGA 142r; Ramusio, *Descrizione*, 164.

39 CGA 157v–158r; Ramusio, *Descrizione*, 178.

40 CGA 148v, 149v, 159r, 260v, 329v, 370r; Ramusio, *Descrizione*, 170–1, 269, 328, 365.

41 CGA 190r; Ramusio, *Descrizione*, 201.

42 CGA 351r–v (Oufran), 379r (Djenné), 380v–381r (Timbuktu), 384r (Gao) [Rauchenberger, *Johannes Leo*, 268, 274, 276, 288]; Ramusio, *Descrizione*, 350, 376, 378, 381.

43 CGA 279v, 320v; Ramusio, *Descrizione*, 285, 321.

44 CGA 399r; Ramusio, *Descrizione*, 395–6.

45 CGA 76v–77r; Ramusio, *Descrizione*, 102. Once again, Ramusio replaced al-Wazzan's third-person reference to 'il compositore' by the first person.

46 On the impact of Giovanni Leone's Africa book, see Zhiri, *L'Afrique*, and Oumelbanine Zhiri, *Les sillages de Jean Léon l'Africain: XVIᵉ au XXᵉ siècle* (Casablanca: Walalda, 1995).

47 'Delle navigazioni di messer Alvise da Ca'da Mosto, gentiluomo veneziano,' in *Navigazioni* vol. 1, Ramusio, 473–535.

48 On the interest in depicting the clothing of non-Europeans in the Renaissance and the other uses of pictures of garments, see Ulinka Rublack, *Dressing Up: Cultural Identity in Renaissance Europe* (Oxford: Oxford University Press, 2010), esp. 125–75 and 177–209.

49 *Historiale description de l'Afrique* (Lyon: Jean Temporal, 1556), 150: 'Acoutremens de ceux de Fez.'

50 *Historiale description*, 353: 'Habits des habitans du Caire.'

51 *Historiale description*, 354: 'Autres sorte d'habits des femmes d'Egypte, demeurans au Caire.'

11

Trade Cards and the Art of Selling Manufacture, c. 1680–1800

Helen Clifford

Introduction

The paperback edition of McKendrick, Brewer, and Plumb's *The Birth of a Consumer Society*, brought out a year after its first publication in 1982, bears on the front cover a picture of a goldsmith's trade card, signed as engraved by 'W. Hogarth' (figure 11.1).[1] The picture is pivotal to the argument of the book, which hangs on the importance of advertising between 1750 and 1800 during which the authors state, 'people learned to think in terms of products to be bought and sold'. It is ironic that the trade card chosen to adorn the front of the book has long been commonly agreed to be a forgery.[2] Another, more common, problem of dealing with the medium of advertising is that from the seventeenth century, the word itself shifted from denoting just the written notification of information to the sophisticated promotion of products involving the manipulation of imagery as well as of words. Not only contemporary consumers but also historians have been caught out by the persuasive power of the advertisement, and the corollary pitfalls of seduction and deceit.

The choice of image for the front of *The Birth of a Consumer Society* has further things to tell us about how advertising, and specifically the trade card, has been employed and interpreted within historical research and writing. Although the trade card is not by Hogarth it was created in the eighteenth-century, probably in the 1790s, and draws on the style of early to mid-century examples including those authenticated as by Hogarth, who started his working life as a silver engraver and commercial artist.[3] The design of the card balances the activities and skills of manufacturing (to the left – two men working before a furnace, one raising at a steady,

Figure 11.1   Supposed trade card of Peter De la Fontaine, goldsmith, Litchfield Street, London. Forgery, etching, London, 1790s.

the other annealing) and retailing (to the right – a bewigged shopkeeper and his boy supervise two ladies and a gentleman who handle various items of silverware before a counter) and at the fulcrum a floor to ceiling dresser loaded with goods, where making and retailing unite. The visual equilibrium is mirrored in the accompanying text. The address of 'Peter De la Fontaine Goldsmith' is given as at the shop sign of the Golden Cup, in Soho, London, and we are informed that he 'Makes & Sells all Sorts of Gold & Silver Plate'.[4] Whether 'real' advertising or not, this trade card reflects eighteenth-century attitudes and represents the lost half of

the story of commercialisation, that is, recognition of the importance
of making in the art of selling. Despite its cover, *The Birth of a Consumer
Society* does not deal with this part of the story, but its unprecedented
influence on the writing and study of history has resulted in a 'headlong
preoccupation with consumption and consumer culture' over the past
generation, at the expense of manufacture.[5] As a result, studies of trade
cards have focused on their role in consumption.[6] It was not until the
publication of *Material Goods, Moving Hands: Perceiving Production in
England, 1700–1830* in 2014 by Kate Smith that a major attempt was made
to reconnect making with selling. In her exploration of how individuals
understood the production process in the ceramics industry she argues
that manufacturers and retailers strove to control not only public access
to the sites but also the image of production. It was a battle, she asserts,
that was only won at the end of the eighteenth century. One of the
sources she uses are trade cards, showing how ceramic retailers invoked
ideas of geographical distance, images of the sea, ships and the exotic
juxtaposed with sturdy warehouses and workshops, to visually locate
the retailer as the pivot through which goods were made available to the
consumer.[7] What can trade cards offer the historian to map this change
and beyond the confines of the ceramics industry? The aim here is to
create a more nuanced and subtle appreciation of changing attitudes
to manufacture in advertising through an analysis of the words and
pictures incorporated in trade cards.[8]

The Foundation Stone
of Commercial Printed Graphics

Trade cards which emerged in the early 1600s, known at the time as
shopkeepers' bills and used to attract and remind customers, both
current and potential, of a business, have been called 'the foundation
stone of commercial printed graphics', spawning as they did billheads,
compliments slips, labels, handbills or leaflets, posters, price lists, and
entries in trade directories.[9] They were an illustrated medium from
the start, beginning as letterpress and woodcut or wood engraving but
swiftly adopted the techniques of copperplate and steel engraving, as
well as etching, and from the early nineteenth century lithography.
They are a precociously early, seductive, if enigmatic, source. More
attractive than their more numerous handwritten counterparts, rarely
dated but sometimes dateable through the purchases noted on them or
more problematically through style, they have been a focus particularly
for English collectors from the time of their first appearance, from
Samuel Pepys (1633–1703) and John Bagford (1650–1716) onwards.[10] As the

engraver George Bickham (1684–1758) claimed, they were part of a print culture in which 'Use and Ornament Unite in One.'[11] It was their very ornament, their visual appeal, that was responsible for their salvation from destruction.

Strategies of Design

Different visual devices were adopted by the owners of businesses who thought it worth paying 8 shillings per 500 for a trade card.[12] We can identify some of the options, and problems, using one of the largest collections made, by Ambrose Heal (1872–1959), whose 16,000 examples were donated in 1960 to the British Museum, adding to an existing 6,000 collected by Sarah Banks (1744–1818). The majority relate to London, although a small number survive that were commissioned by provincial businesses. For example of the 239 cards related to purveyors of hosiery (dealers in stockings) in the Banks and Heal Collection, only five represent businesses beyond London: Birmingham, Bristol, Newcastle, and Norwich. However only fifty-one are illustrated on the online catalogue and therefore easily available for visual comparison and analysis.[13] Although the detection of any chronological progression in these design choices is hampered by the problems of dating trade cards, there is an identifiable overall pattern common to all trades, moving from the use of shops signs only (early 1600s to 1720s), to shops signs with decorative cartouches, one of the earliest being Hogarth's own, the sign giving way to the display of goods and the depiction of work and sales shops (1720s to 1760s), to the rejection of signs, goods, and manufacturing and retailing scenes in favour of classical figures and settings (1760s to 1820s). Although these changes reflected broader stylistic shifts, from baroque to rococo to neoclassical, the banning of hanging shop signs in the City of London in 1762, and the following year in Westminster (as part of a campaign, begun in Paris in 1761, to tidy up increasingly crowded urban streets) prompted shopkeepers to rethink how they represented themselves and their businesses in graphic terms, as numbers replaced symbols as the means to identify an address. While some hung on to their earlier identities, others used both sign and number, many more experimented.

The pictorial aspect of these trade cards is however only half the story. If we look at the wording of the fifty-one illustrated hosiers' trade cards, nineteen refer to selling only and seven to making only, while twenty-two make no reference to either, relying on the visual device, and giving name, address, and trade only for information. Hosiers seem to have preferred selling over making in the wording of their trade cards. But how representative is this pattern of wording for other trades? Turning to Heal's illustrated *London Goldsmiths*,[14] which draws on 331 trade cards from eighteen different collections, the most common written description of the activities of a goldsmith on his (more rarely her) card is that he (or she) 'Maketh & Selleth', or later 'Makes & Sells'. Of the eighty cards illustrated, dated between 1702 to 1790 in the book, two thirds include this phrase.[15]

While goldsmiths, silversmiths and jewellers, cabinetmakers, carvers, coach makers and pewterers' cards have a predilection for the phrase 'Make & Sell',[16] purveyors of chinaware, hosiery, and hardware rarely do. There appears to be a marked preference within the luxury trades relating to metalware and furniture for emphasising making in both words and image, and for innovation in the design of advertising. An explanation for the latter lies in the close relationship between the metal and furniture trades with engraving and printing. From the evidence of signed trade cards Michael Snodin has shown how the core designs created between the 1730s and 1750s, the most prolific period of trade card production, can be connected with the silver engraver and printmaker Henry Copland (c. 1710–1752), 'the virtual inventor of the English rococo trade card'.[17] His early cards predate the earliest rococo pattern book, Mathias Lock's *Six Sconces* (1744)[18], and were mostly for goldsmiths and allied traders like Mary Owen, jeweller and goldsmith,[19] William Kidney, assayer and plate worker[20] (both 1739/40), and Thomas Gardner, goldsmith and watchmaker (c. 1741)[21], whose card was probably the prototype for at least twelve other cards of the same design.[22] Copland collaborated with Lock to publish *A New Book of Ornaments* in 1752, in which many of the designs reflect trade card prototypes. Silver and furniture associated trades were in the van of trade card design as their trades involved the engravers that made them, and they were the craftsmen innovators. Their work linked two-dimensional conceptual design with the world of three-dimensional objects, connecting art and artefacts.[23]

We know, of course, that what we see does not necessarily represent reality. Trade cards, like other advertising, imply a desirable ideal, here that making was performed at the site of retail, when in fact we know from other sources that often it did not. For example, although the London goldsmiths John Parker and Edward Wakelin (in partnership 1761–70) advertised on their 1761 trade card that they 'Make & Sell all Sorts of Jewels & curious work in Gold & Silver' from their premises in Panton Street, off the Haymarket, we know from their account books from this time that nothing was made on the premises, it was subcontracted out.[24] Yet making in word and image in this trade, and others in the luxury sector, is what the shopkeeper felt the customer wanted to see.

Selling Making

Having identified strategies of selling in both word and image, it is now time to look in more detail at how manufacture was represented. Looking across the trades it is possible to discern four distinct approaches. The first and earliest depict a person or people at work, the second appears from the 1720s when scenes of manufacture were made subsidiary to the main design and placed within an elaborate frame usually at the bottom.[25] The third focuses on a machine, either static or in operation. The fourth type emerges in the 1770s when the depiction of manufacture and machines was suborned to a classical ideal with, for example, instead of men or women at work, putti or cherubs wielding tools, where the act of labour was removed from reality. Any attempt to create a neat chronology however is complicated by the fact that earlier forms persisted into the later eighteenth century and businesses kept the same design across decades.

Possibly the earliest surviving trade card to show making is a vigorous woodcut for Jacob Stampe of Hounsditch, 'Callico Printer', c. 1680–85, depicting a man printing calico at a table, accompanied by a boy preparing the wooden pattern blocks with colour (figure 11.2).[26] Why did Stampe choose this image? First, perhaps he could not resist the pun on his own name, and secondly, he was maximizing the importance of the act of printing calico in London, in a period when the English were competing with Indian made calicoes. He clearly felt that his customers might be swayed to buy his goods because he was printing them in his own workshop. It was the act of home manufacture that is central to his message to the consumer. From the scarcity of surviving trade cards for calico printers it appears that Stampe was innovative and unusual investing in this type of advertising, it is even possible that, as a printer, he carved the wood cut for the trade card himself.[27] The device of using a scene of manufacturing continues into the eighteenth and nineteenth centuries, for example the glass cutter, china, glass, and earthenware manufacturer Lawrence Dorgan, operating from Aldersgate Street, London from the later eighteenth century, chose a trade card depicting seven men busily at work grinding glass in his factory.[28] It was only the processes of glass engraving and grinding that were depicted, and *never* ceramic production, on trade cards for businesses that manufactured and retailed both glass and china.

The next design step appears in the etched and engraved card of the printers William (1690–1756) and Cluer (1715–1775) Dicey c. 1736–56, although probably first employed by their predecessor John Cluer, William's brother-in-law (d.1736).[29] While the Maiden's Head, their shop

Figure 11.2   Trade card of Jacob Stampe, calico printer, Houndsditch, London.
Woodcut c. 1680.

sign in Bow Churchyard, dominates the top of the trade card which
advertises 'Shop-keepers Bills are curiously Engrav'd On Copper-Plates',
the card is grounded with two vignettes showing a letterpress used
for printing woodcuts as well as type to the left, manned by two men,
with two others setting type, and a rolling press for copper-plates to
the right, with a man operating the press, and a customer checking the
sample.[30] The business was very entrepreneurial selling patent medicines
(Dr Bateman's Pectoral Drips and Daffy's Elixir), as well as cheap prints,
chapbooks, and newspapers. The card implies a busy workshop with lots
of staff, underpinning the promise that 'all manner of Business Printed
with the greatest Expedition'. The dense expertly engraved ornament
demonstrates skills of design and layout. Scenes of manufacture were
incorporated within the new rococo cartouches of the 1730–1750s, like
that of Maydwell & Windle, glass sellers in the Strand, London, c.1750–56
which incorporates two men at a cutting machine to the left and on
the right another at work at a grinding machine, with an elaborate
curlicued cartouche dripping with cut glass chandeliers above and the
royal arms at the top.[31]

From where then did these images of manufacture derive? As Celina Fox has noted there is no tradition, or at least no surviving examples, in England for the depiction of craftsmen at work like the German, *Standebuch* or *Book of Trades*, produced in Nuremberg in 1567 with woodcut illustrations by Jost Amman, or Borduurder's *Mensschelyke beezigheeden* (Human Occupations) published in Holland in 1695. While Joseph Moxon's *Mechanick Exercises*, published in parts between 1677–84, illustrates tools to assist in understanding what he called the 'language' of each craft, for example a workbench with vices, a steady and anvil, and the furnace with bellows for the blacksmith, he does not show men or women at work. The exceptions were guild-based publications, like the frontispiece to *A Touchstone for Gold and Silver Wares of 1677* by the working goldsmith William Badcock (1622–1698) and an invitation to Goldsmiths' Hall, of 1741, which depicts not a single workshop but different specialisations within the trade in separate vignettes signed by A. Kirk and J. Kirk.[32] Six years later, John Hinton's monthly *Universal Magazine of Knowledge and Pleasure*, addressed to the 'gentry, merchants, farmers and tradesmen', was launched, which included in the early volumes, engravings of trade processes, including weaving, gold and silver refining, and clock and watch making among others. The images of manufacture on trade cards were a genre in their own right that predated and, it could be argued, influenced these later forms of illustration.

A Fascination with Technical Ingenuity

The third stage of design moved the visual focus from the makers to the machinery used in manufacture, placing it centre stage on the trade card. A good example of this is the card for 'Jones, Copper Plate maker' in Shoe Lane, London c. 1786 (figure 11.3).[33] A man turns the large wheel of the 'New Invented Machine for Polishing Copper Plates for Callico Printers ... which makes them exceeding smooth & level'. The text is set in a fashionably floral and curvaceous cartouche, which balances the starker formality of the press and is given a sense of movement via its operator. The technical drawing of the polishing machine is of a hybrid genre borne of fashion print and patent drawing.[34] From 1734, detailed descriptions of inventions registered in patents, including drawings, had become routine if not almost compulsory and patent drawings were often replicated in trade cards. For example, the pen, ink, and watercolour drawings for John Joseph Merlin's 1773 patent for a 'newly invented ... spring jack' to a Dutch oven[35] is the source for his engraved advertisement-cum-trade-card of the same year.[36] The enthusiastic response to the founding of the Society for the Encouragement of Arts,

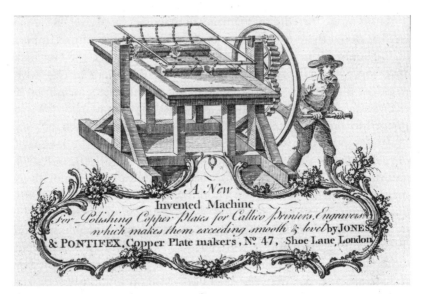

Figure 11.3   Trade card of Jones & Pontifex, copper plate makers, Shoe Lane, London,
c. 1786.

Manufactures and Commerce in 1754 was testimony to 'A fascination
with technical ingenuity and improvement, commercial innovation and
enterprise ... shared by an indiscriminate mix of talents and ranks'[37] (in
fact the very audience to whom advertising was addressed). There was an
enhanced consciousness of the importance of drawing for commercial
purposes in the first half of the eighteenth century. As a result there was
increasing familiarity with depictions of machines, by artists and by
consumers. Clearly the depiction of a machine was meant to convey a
sense of importance. To be 'scientific' or technical was an indicator of
modernity and a mark of credibility and value.[38]

    The entrepreneurial flair of Richard Jones (d. 1788) was enhanced
by his apprentice William Pontifex (1766–1851), who joined him in
partnership in 1786, the date of the trade card. Pontifex was an ingenious character; in 1799 he and his brother took out a patent for an
improvement to copper stillheads which feature in later trade cards[39] and
ran several copper-related businesses.[40] Pontifex's card, c. 1790,[41] shows
a response to changing style and combines a simple oval cartouche
depicting four men beating copper, set above neoclassical swagged bell
husks and examples of his products, a stillhead and a fashionable tea
urn. His trade card reveals how diverse trades could be connected by
the coppersmith, as they supplied 'Brewers, Distillers, Calico-printers,
Dyers, Sugar-bakers, Engravers and West India planters', and how they
could be set within a decoratively fashionable and unifying context.

The Arts of Industry Rejected

While Kate Smith argues that towards the end of the eighteenth century manufacturers and retailers wrested control over the image of manufacture, this needs to be set in a wider perspective and in the context of the battle that was being fought between the cerebral and the manual in the field of art. When Joshua Reynolds became the first president of the newly founded Royal Academy of Arts in 1769, he used his annual discourses addressed to the students to demonstrate how the aims and endeavours of commercial artists, represented by the Royal Society of Arts, Manufactures and Commerce, were in direct opposition to those of fine art and artists. He reminded his audience that 'mechanical felicity' while amusing in its 'minute neatness' and 'imitation' was but a shadow to the substance and 'grandeur of ... ideas', the manual labour involved in depicting reality would always be second to universal truths and the grand idea. This was all part of a longer 'narrative of the progressive mastery of mind over matter', which inculcated, as Jules Prown observed, 'a mode of hierarchical ordering in the way in which we evaluate human activities and experiences, privileging that which is cerebral and abstract over that which is manual and material.'[42] As a result 'antique' cherubs and putti, classically draped figures, and gods and goddess supplanted craftsmen with rolled up sleeves in the workshop on trade cards. The art historian John Barrell explains the wider absence of the image of manufacture and the maker in art, in his exploration of the visualising of the division of labour through an analysis of W.H. Pyne's *Microcosm, or A Picturesque Delineation of the Arts, Agriculture & Manufacture* (1806–08).

The adoption of neoclassical design on trade cards, which air-brushed out human labour, coincides with the period in which 'tradesmen, manufacturers, and the newly-wealthy came under ... prolific literary attack' from novelists and moralists in the 1770s and 1780s who insisted on the impossibility of their full conversion to gentility.[43] James Raven argues that the movement against manufacturing 'upstarts' was also fuelled by the increasing mystery of industrial operations. He notes that whereas earlier in the century visitors had been welcomed to visit factories and manufacturing sites, Mrs Thrale complained that in Birmingham in 1787 'they would not show their Manufactures', Byng Viscount Torrington was barred from Arkwright's mills in 1790, Faujas de Saint-Fond was not allowed to enter the chemical works at Prestonpans, while Fanny Burney was discouraged from inspecting a pin factory in Gloucester on 'account of its dirt'.[44] In London, where skilled labour was plentiful, the growing complexity of subcontracting meant that it would have been impossible to see the manufacture of a commodity from design to retail

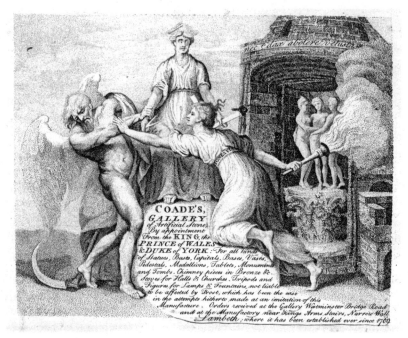

Figure 11.4   Trade card of Coade & Sealy, Gallery Westminster Bridge & Manufactory
Lambeth, engraved by Samuel Rawle, 1814.

on one site. Manufacturers instead encouraged curious customers to
visit 'galleries', rather than factories and workshops, where they could
orchestrate their own image more selectively.

Eleanor Coade (1733–1821) tapped into this fashion by marketing her
new 'twice fired stone' launched c. 1769, in classical context. Rather than
inviting customers to her manufactory in Lambeth, where the secrets
of the recipe might be leaked, she opened a gallery in Westminster in
1799. The Coadestone doorway to this gallery depicted an open kiln,
in front of which the figure of Time is defeated by the vitrifying aid
of the female figure of Fire (figure 11.4).[45] It was engraved and used as
the frontispiece to the *European Magazine* (volume 41) in 1802. Like the
eminent sculptors who supplied Coade with models, the engraver of the
card, Samuel Rawle, also exhibited at the Royal Academy. The design
for the doorway however can be traced back far earlier and appears
on Coade's trade card, the work of the ceramic modeller John Bacon
(1740–1799) who worked for Coade from 1769 and was awarded a gold
medal for his work by the Royal Academy two years later.[46] Once again
it is the trade card design that comes first, that sets the trend.

Trade cards, as miniature examples of the engraver's art, stood between the worlds of the academy and commerce. Their makers, though often unnamed jobbing engravers, were also sometimes celebrated artists, and many signed their works. Trade cards were part of a wide and growing print culture that is largely forgotten today. While the mass of everyday print has been lost, it is the rarer, more expensive art prints that survive in greater numbers, skewing our vision of that culture,[47] making it difficult to appreciate 'how pervasive such pieces were in the literary and visual cultures of the period,' but also explaining why so many illustrated trade cards survive.[48]

Conclusion

The depiction of manufacture on London trade cards had few historical examples to draw upon, and engravers created their own genre of representation, in a commercial art form that influenced the wider world of advertising, connecting it with the world of art. Tradesmen who chose to highlight the importance of manufacture in word and image were dominated by goldsmiths, cabinet makers and carvers, glassmakers and printers (of calico, copper plates, books, and beyond), who had close ties with the craft of engraving, and it was the engravers who were in the van of advertising. These were luxury trades dominated by subcontracting, where the retailer took on the role once adopted by the patron of taste. Where skilled labour had to be coordinated, but cost had to be limited and the customer kept at a distance from the maker, the image rather than the reality of production was deployed. Yet choosing to depict manufacture did not necessarily indicate success in a business but more often the pressures of competition, inspiring innovation in graphic design. Jacob Stampe's attempt to challenge the dominance of East India calicoes, the hosiers who adopted the stocking frame in their trade cards at the moment the industry was in decline in the metropolis, and pewterers who were failing to compete with tin-plate and cheap pottery and glass, adopted more innovative advertising to attract the attention of customers.[49] Attention to manufacture within advertising reveals very different approaches over time and trade, creating a complex but dynamic picture of the art of selling.

Notes

All trade cards referred to in this paper are from Banks and Heal Collection at the British Museum unless otherwise stated.

1 There are several copies of this trade card: Cc,2.260, Cc,2.261, Cc2,262, 1868,0822.1644, 1868,0313.1, Heal,67.115, and Banks,67.63.

2 Heal, 67.115 was long viewed with suspicion by Hogarth scholars and omitted from their catalogues raisonnés. George Steevens (1736–1800) attributed it to William Henry Ireland, whose father published *Graphic Illustrations of Hogarth* (1794). See Mark Jones et al., eds., *Fake? The Art of Deception* (London: British Museum Press, 1992), 156–9.

3 The design of the card draws heavily on one that Hogarth created for his sisters c. 1725, who ran 'the Old Frock Shop' in Little Britain, London, see Heal,40.62 and Heal,40.64. As Julie Anne Lambert has noted, Hogarth 'is known to have designed about 30 trade cards, and is also reputed to have painted shop signs', and his own trade card is thought by some to be his earliest dated work. See Julie Anne Lambert, *A Nation of Shopkeepers* (Oxford: Bodleian Library, 2001), 47.

4 No goldsmith of this name appears in the records of the Goldsmiths' Company or any other contemporary sources. A captain of this name was convicted for forgery and transported to Virginia in 1752, see *Newgate Calendar*, Part II, 1780 edition.

5 Beverly Lemire, 'The Power of "Things" in Eighteenth-Century Societies', *Eighteenth Century Studies* 50, no. 3 (2017): 341.

6 For example Maxine Berg and Helen Clifford, 'Selling Consumption in the Eighteenth Century: Advertising and the Trade Card in Britain and France', *Cultural and Social History* 4, no. 2 (2007): 145–70; Philippa Hubbard, 'Trade Cards in 18th-Century Consumer Culture: Movement, Circulation, and Exchange in Commercial and Collecting Spaces', *Material Culture Review* 74–75 (2012): 30–45.

7 Kate Smith, *Material Goods, Moving Hands: Perceiving Production in England, 1700–1830* (London: Routledge, 2014), 63–9.

8 Ibid., 75.

9 Maurice Rickards, *The Encyclopedia of Ephemera* (London: British Library, 2000), 148.

10 Collections of continental trade cards are very rare but see the collection of trade cards held at Waddesdon Manor. The Rothchild Foundation, https://waddesdon.org.uk/the-collection/research-publications/trade-cards/.

11 George Bickham, *The Universal Penman* (London 1733–41, republished New York: Dover Pictorial Archive Series, 1968).

12 From Lambert, *A Nation of Shopkeepers*, 45, using trade card of J. Rozea, Letter-Press and Copper Plate Printer, London c. 1790.

13 British Museum collection search tool: http://www.britishmuseum.org/ research/collection_online/search.aspx.

14 Ambrose Heal, *The London Goldsmiths: 1200–1800* (1953, Newton Abbot: David and Charles Reprint, 1972).

15 The alternatives were 'Buys & Sells' or to give a list of goods.

16 E.g. John London coachmaker, VAM, E.4937-1927.

17 Michael Snodin, 'Trade Cards and English Rococo', in *The Rococo in England*, ed. Charles Hind (London: V&A Museum, 1986), 82–103, 84. His earliest signed and dated trade card was for Benjamin Rackstrow, 'Figure-Maker' in Fleet Street, 1738, Heal,28.187, replacing an earlier one of 1720 illustrated with the shop sign only, see Heal,28.186.

18 M. Heckscher, 'Lock and Copland: A Catalogue of the Engraved Designs', *Furniture History* 15 (1979): 1–34.

19 Heal,67.305.

20 Heal,67.247.

21 Heal,39.33.

22 Snodin, 'Trade Cards', 87, same design used until 1790s.

23 Pamela H. Smith, Amy R.W. Meyers, and Harold J. Cook, eds., *Ways of Making and Knowing. The Material Culture of Empirical Knowledge* (Chicago: University of Chicago Press, 2017).

24 Heal,67.311 and Heal,67.310. Helen Clifford, *Silver in London: The Parker and Wakelin Partnership, 1766–1770* (London: Yale University Press, 2004).

25 VAM, E.858-1997, engraved by Robert Clee, see Hilary Young, 'An Eighteenth-century London Glass-cutter's Trade Card', *Apollo* (February 1998): 41–6.

26 Heal,41.7.

27 The only other trade card for a calico printer in the Banks and Heal Collection is c. 1760 for C. Hooker, eschewing images for text only Heal,41.3.

28 Heal,37.21.

29 Banks,99.12 and Heal,59.56.

30 See Sheila O'Connell, ed., *London 1753* (London: British Museum, 2003), 95, cat. I.77.

31 Heal,66.44, see also earlier trade card of Weatherby, Crowther, Quintin, and Windle, Heal,66.75 with interior of glass house featured at top, partnership dissolved 1751.

32 Ashmolean Museum, Department of Prints and Drawings. John Kirk engraved his own trade card, see Banks,59.104. This design was replaced the following year by one which replaced scenes of making with cherubs representing Justice and Virtue, Henry Copland, British Museum C,2.586.

33 Banks,58.22.

34 Alain Pottage, *Figures of Invention: A History of Modern Patent Law* (Oxford: Oxford University Press, 2010).

35 Patent No.1032, 29 January 1773 in Anne French et al., *John Joseph Merlin: The Ingenious Mechanick* (London: Greater London Council, 1985), 66, cat.no. B6.

36 Ibid., cat.no. B7, 67

37 Celina Fox, 'Art and Trade – from the Society of Arts to the Royal Academy of Arts', in *London 1753*, O'Connell, 18.

38 Maxine Berg, 'Inventors of the World of Goods', in *From Family Firms to Corporate Capitalism: Essays in Business and Industrial History in Honour of Peter Mathias*, eds. Kristine Bruland and Patrick O'Brien (Oxford: Oxford University Press 1998), 15.

39 Banks,85.127.

40 Aquatint of *An interior view of William and Russell Pontifex and E. Goodwin's copper and brass works at 46–8 Shoe Lane showing men at work* (London: W.H. Pyne and J.C Nattes, c. 1806).

41 Banks,85.82.

42 Jules David Prown, 'Material/Culture: Can the Farmer and the Cowman Still Be Friends?', in *Art as Evidence: Writings on Art and Material Culture*, Jules David Prown (New Haven and London: Yale University Press, 2001), 235.

43 James Raven, *Judging New Wealth: Popular Publishing and Responses to Commerce in England 1750–1800* (Oxford: Clarendon Press, 1992), 239.

44 Quoted in ibid., 233–4.

45 Heal,106.7

46 The design was pirated by the engraver Richard Carpenter, sometime after 1785, for Baverstock's china and glass warehouse near St Paul's, reversing the image, removing the Three Graces in the kiln and replacing them with dishes, a tureen, and models, adding an address, misspelt, in Paris, see Banks,77.22.

47 Anthony Griffiths, *The Print before Photography: An Introduction to European Printmaking 1550 to 1850* (London: The British Museum, 2016).

48 Kevin Murphy and Sally O'Driscoll, eds., *Studies in Ephemera: Text and Image in Eighteenth-Century Print* (Lewisburgh: Bucknell University Press, 2013), 2.

49 The company had more than 200 members in 1600, and twice as many at the end of the seventeenth century, when the domestic use of pewter reached its peak. See Peter R.G. Hornsby, Rosemary Weinstein, and Ronald F. Homer, *Pewter: A Celebration of the Craft 1200–1700* (London: Museum of London, 1989), 12.

12

Old and New Luxuries in Town and Country in the Eighteenth-Century Habsburg Netherlands

Johan Poukens and Herman Van der Wee

On 7 April 1724, the estate of the late Henricus de la Rue, former bailiff of Grimbergen near Brussels, was auctioned.[1] Such public auctions were not exceptional in the countryside of Brabant, but this one drew the attention of an unusually large number of wealthy buyers due to the high social status of the deceased. The auctioned furniture was indeed of an exceptional quality. It included fifty-two chairs, some covered with leather ('Spanish chairs'), others with cloth and velvet. There were also ten tables, including three hard wooden ones, another one made of walnut, and one inlaid with slate (*schalietaefel*). The gold leather hangings were sold together with thirty-seven paintings and some printed chimney cloths (*gedruckte schouwkleden*). Also at auction were two cabinets with glass doors, a wardrobe, a pantry, a buffet, two desks, four lavish bedsteads (*ledikanten*) and a bedframe (*campagnekoets*) with coloured and printed hangings.

The belongings of de la Rue were luxurious by contemporary rural standards. They could withstand comparison with the types of furniture and decorations commonly found in the drawing rooms (*saletten*) of noble families in nearby towns such as Antwerp, Brussels, or Leuven.[2] These were typical 'old luxuries', a term coined by Jan de Vries to characterise changes in the appearance and appreciation of luxury. However, according to de Vries, starting in the Dutch Republic during the second half of the seventeenth century, 'old luxuries' gave way to 'new luxuries'. Old luxuries were expensive objects appreciated for their high intrinsic value, whereas new luxuries were cheaper and less durable objects that were appreciated for their novelty, design, and fashion. Moreover, new luxuries served different functions and different owners. Whereas aristocratic families used conspicuous consumption of old luxuries to socially distinguish themselves, new luxuries appealed to the urban middle class for socialising purposes. The shift from old to new luxuries resulted in the lowering of financial and moral barriers, which previously inhibited access to luxury for nonelite households.[3] As such, it was a necessary precondition for a second concept proposed by de Vries, that of the 'Industrious Revolution'.[4]

The Industrious Revolution was the result of a set of interrelated changes in decisions over consumption and production at the household level. In short, starting in the second half of the seventeenth century, de Vries observes that households in north-western Europe started to reallo-cate both their supply of labour and their demand for goods increasingly towards the market. According to de Vries, an intensification of labour was induced by desire for consumption beyond the necessaries of life. The additional income from this intensification stimulated demand for new types of furniture, clothing, and foodstuffs.[5] The Industrious Revolution, he observes, was not just an urban phenomenon. In densely urbanised north-western Europe, rural households also could and would participate in the new urban consumer culture.[6]

This chapter investigates the diffusion of new standards in taste and comfort during the eighteenth century in the provincial town of Lier near Antwerp and in its rural hinterland. The middling classes of Lier became increasingly preoccupied with decorating and furnishing their homes with the new luxuries for the entertainment of friends and guests.[7] Some probate inventories of middling class households present a veritable catalogue of the new luxuries. They allow us to comparatively analyse the spread of the new luxuries by constructing a quantitative index of the ownership of these objects and by suggesting the motivation for their acquisition.

The Town of Lier and Its Hinterland

In the eighteenth century, Lier was a provincial town of about 6,000 inhabitants and functioned as a commercial and industrial hub for its rural hinterland. Lier was famous for its flourishing brewing industry, *Caves* being its prime beer exported to the entire Habsburg Netherlands. During the first half of the century, the town was affected by the general urban crisis in the region. Its recovery after 1748 was fuelled by a renewed expansion of brewing for export and by a rapidly expanding protoin-dustrialisation.[8] The hinterland of Lier stretched mainly to the east of the town, an area with sandy soils and small-scale mixed agriculture. Most farms were small to very small. According to a 1747 survey, 63 per cent of the farms did not have a horse and cultivated less than five hectares (the lower boundary of a permanently self-sufficient holding in the area). The small size of their holdings notwithstanding, many peasants were able to sell some of their products on the Lier market such as dairy products (mostly butter) and vegetables. The introduction and expansion of potato cultivation for subsistence during the second half of the eighteenth century gave to peasants, even with modest holdings, the opportunity to market some arable crops (mostly wheat and maslin, a mixture of wheat and rye). They took advantage of the agricultural innovations of the period to raise and diversify the output of their holdings.[9]

Probate Inventories

Our sample derives from the archives of the aldermen's two courts of Lier and vicinity (*Bijvang*).[10] The courts took care of the orphans in their jurisdiction. When a deceased parent left minors or disabled children, according to the customary law of Lier and vicinity, an inventory of his or her belongings had to be made within six weeks after death in order to facilitate the division of the inheritance between the surviving parent and the children. The inventory was assessed by two sworn appraisers and recorded by the town's secretary in the presence of two aldermen.[11] The appraisers carefully listed most of the movables (clothing was often excluded) of the household. Debts owed by, and to be paid to, the deceased were also specified. Immovable property on the contrary was never evaluated but sometimes mention was made of it with the term *pro memorie*.

Extant inventories should in principle represent a random group of households. Many scholars however agree that households at the top and bottom of the social scale are under represented.[12] In the case of Lier, for example, the top group could withdraw from the obligation by appointing guardians in their testaments, whereas in the bottom group several poor did not possess anything and others were exempted because the cost of the inventory surpassed the value of their belongings.[13] The alleged over representation of middle-rank households is confirmed by the social distribution of inventories in our sample and is more evident in surviving urban inventories than in the rural ones (table 12.1). However, on the whole, the bias does not distort the analysis pursued because it is primarily concerned with a class-by-class comparison of possessions. We divided the sample into three socio-economic categories according to the social power scheme (SOCPO scheme) and compared the categories with a stratification of the population by the same criteria.

The SOCPO scheme is a social classification based on occupation.[14] It can quite easily be applied to probate inventory samples because

Table 12.1   Social distribution of the probate inventories sample (in percentage)

Social status	Urban		Rural	
	Household sample	Population (1755)	Household sample	Population (1747)
Lower income groups	47	68	45	53
Middle income group	43	25	48	43
Elite	10	7	7	4

Source: Probate inventory sample (SAL, OA, nos. 1833–84; OG, nos. 72–4); Population census of 1755 for Lier (Vorst, State Archives, *Officie Fiscaal* no. 373); Poll tax of 1747 for the '*Bijvang*' (Beveren, State Archives, *Oud gemeentarchief Nijlen*, no. 39; Vorst, State Archives, *Staten van Brabant: Cartons*, nos. 400–1).

the occupations practiced in the household of a deceased parent are sometimes mentioned in the introduction of the inventory but usually can also be inferred from the listed types of tools, stocks, and cattle. A weaver, for instance, can be identified by his loom, and a tailor is recognisable from the combination of scissors, yardstick, and pressing iron (*persijzer*). In the social power scheme, occupations are grouped into social power levels according to their economic and cultural power. Economic power is determined by skill, authority, and, for the self-employed, the scale of their enterprise; cultural power is determined by the manual or nonmanual character of labour and by social status (noble titles for instance). For households in the agricultural sector, the size of the holdings is also considered as a source of their economic power. The size of the agricultural holdings of households in our sample was inferred from the possession of cattle and horses since there was a linear correlation between landholding and livestock ownership. Elements from both dimensions of power are combined into five social power levels that can be reduced to three classes reflecting income groups.[15]

Ownership of Luxuries

We created an index of fourteen objects to measure changes in the diffusion of luxuries and novelties in Lier and its rural hinterland. The index method was first used by Lois Green Carr and Lorena Walsh for measuring changes in consumption patterns in Saint-Mary's County (in the English colony of Maryland, North America) during the eighteenth century. Carr and Walsh constructed an index of amenities consisting of twelve nonessential objects that made life more enjoyable.[16] Because indices are a crude but effective instrument for revealing differences in the ownership of selected goods between periods, locations, and social groups at an aggregate level, their method was quickly adopted by other historians of material culture.[17] For her study of the French region of Meaux, for example, Micheline Baulant constructed an index of the standard of living (*indice de niveau de vie*) on the basis of eighty-six objects divided over five categories (basic objects, private life, comfort, luxury, and cultural refinement). Typical new luxuries such as hot drinks (tea, coffee, cocoa), exotic spices, ceramics, drinking glasses, knives, forks, and paintings were in the cultural refinement (*civilisation*) category, whereas the luxury category represented the old luxuries with objects such as horses, carriages, and valets.[18] The challenge in the creation of any index is selecting the appropriate goods. The full range of objects in our luxuries index is presented in table 12.2. They were carefully selected with regard to regional circumstances and the limitations of our source. Wigs, for instance, were excluded from the index because they were considered as part of the clothing that was often left out of the inventory. Moreover, our index is an index in its simplest form. All items are assigned equal weights. A pewter teapot and an elaborate tea set of fine China porcelain both count for one in the index. The scores hence reflect only the introduction of new objects.

Figure 12.1 shows the mean urban and rural index numbers for the inventory sample in intervals of twenty-five years. The full lines represent the mean for all households and the error bars indicate the difference between the mean index numbers of the lower income households (lower bounds) on the one hand and the middle income and elite households (upper bounds) on the other hand.[19] The graph shows that during the eighteenth century the index numbers in general increased regardless of location or social status. In the countryside, the change was gradual up to the last quarter of the eighteenth century, when the mean index number suddenly jumped upwards, in contrast to the urban index that had already increased quickly during the second quarter of the century. Thereafter, however, the urban index stagnated. The final result was some convergence between town and countryside at the level measured by the index numbers. During the first quarter of the century, the urban index number was a fourfold of the rural, but by the last quarter it was only double the rural index number. Generally speaking, households from all layers of rural society added new objects to their belongings, but at the same time socially determined differences persisted and even were aggravated. Moreover, at the end of the eighteenth century lower income rural households – agricultural labourers and smallholders with one or two cows – owned a greater variety of goods than the rural middle income and elite households – tenant farmers with horses, craftsmen, retailers, and a few office holders – did

Table 12.2 Evolution of ownership of selected luxuries in Lier and its hinterland, 1695–1795 (%)

Object	Social status	Urban				Rural			
		(1)	(2)	(3)	(4)	(1)	(2)	(3)	(4)
Chimney cloth	Lower	37	56	62	31	0	3	18	19
	Upper	76	88	77	27	9	12	26	41
Chocolate	Lower	0	5	0	0	0	0	0	0
	Upper	5	23	21	12	0	0	0	0
Clock	Lower	0	0	4	15	0	0	0	14
	Upper	11	10	13	35	0	3	13	48
Coffee	Lower	11	12	7	15	0	0	0	5
	Upper	16	35	36	62	0	2	0	17
Delftware	Lower	70	76	60	88	38	58	39	62
	Upper	66	85	74	69	52	53	50	55
Fork	Lower	19	49	73	73	17	13	30	76
	Upper	45	79	87	62	15	22	17	76
Glass	Lower	48	63	71	77	4	18	12	41
	Upper	68	87	92	73	24	34	24	52
Hot drinks refinement	Lower	7	24	33	23	0	3	0	0
	Upper	32	71	59	42	3	2	4	3
Mirror	Lower	93	80	71	77	8	13	18	22
	Upper	97	98	92	92	15	17	26	31
Picture	Lower	56	54	56	62	0	5	0	8
	Upper	84	88	74	88	12	9	9	17
Silverware	Lower	0	7	9	4	0	0	0	0
	Upper	34	27	23	19	9	3	2	3
Spice	Lower	41	59	44	73	4	3	3	19
	Upper	66	90	74	81	15	12	22	24
Table linen	Lower	93	90	73	62	29	43	24	27
	Upper	97	100	95	96	36	45	39	52
Tea	Lower	0	46	89	100	0	0	15	62
	Upper	5	88	97	100	3	3	35	79
Tinware	Lower	89	83	82	85	67	50	45	70
	Upper	100	100	97	100	70	76	85	97

Legend:
– Lower status are lower-income households, upper status are middle-income and elite households.
– (1)=1695–1719; (2)=1720–1744; (3)=1745–1769, (4)=1770–1795

Source: Probate inventory sample (SAL, OA, nos. 1833–84; OG, nos. 72–4).

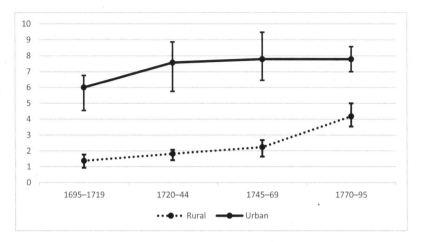

Figure 12.1   Mean index numbers of ownership of luxuries in Lier and its hinterland, 1695–1795.

a century earlier. The difference between the rural mean index numbers therefore rose from 1.1 to 1.5. In the town of Lier an opposite movement can be observed. The social gap had also widened in the town during the second quarter of the eighteenth century but thereafter lower income households – labourers and skilled craftsmen – bridged part of the gap with the better-off households, the retailers, and the liberal professions.

The shift from old to new luxuries is immediately visible from the decline in the ownership of silverware in urban areas and the tremendous increase in the incidence of pots, cups, and saucers for hot drinks. Expensive and conspicuous silverware was a textbook example of an old luxury.[20] Silver plates, mustard jars, pepper boxes, and salt shakers were traditionally mostly found in inventories taken from members of the urban elite but gradually disappeared from their tables. At the other end of the luxury spectrum, from the second quarter of the eighteenth century onwards, evidence of the consumption of hot drinks, tea in particular, quickly became common in urban inventories. Pots, cups, and saucers for tea appeared also in 70 per cent of the rural inventories but only during the last quarter of the century. Coffee gained some popularity in town during the same period, but at that moment appliances for preparing coffee and cups and saucers for drinking it were still uncommon in rural inventories. This is even truer for cocoa, which in the eighteenth century was still entirely absent in rural inventories. In town too it remained an elite pleasure. Generally, the adoption of hot drinks in Lier and in its rural hinterland conformed to the general north-west European pattern of a quick spread to urban households during the second quarter of the eighteenth century and a slow diffusion in the countryside by the end of the century.[21] Parallel to tea and coffee, ownership of containers for pepper and other exotic spices also spread in Lier and to a lesser extent in the countryside.

Fine, glazed earthenware (generally called *gleiswerk*) is another typical example of a new luxury. It was not only cheaper than pewter but also better suited for displaying taste because of its colourful decorations.[22] By the beginning of the eighteenth century such fine earthenware became fairly common in the town of Lier. In the countryside, these ceramics were only gradually complementing coarse earthenware and especially pewter tableware. Nevertheless, the appearance of fine ceramics in inventories of the countryside, in particular in those of the better-off income groups, increased by 63 per cent during the eighteenth century. The use of glass at the table increased too and added further to the breakability of tableware. The fork was another innovation in tableware. Similar to tea, forks spread quickly in urban households from the second quarter of the eighteenth century onwards. The rural population also caught up, albeit rather slowly, during the last quarter of the century.

Thus, with a clear time lag there was some convergence between town and countryside in the ownership of the new types of tableware. As far as decorations were concerned, on the contrary, differences between town and countryside remained visible. Whereas a large majority of the urban middle-income group owned one or more paintings in the eighteenth century, they were unusual in the countryside. Rural households preferred mirrors, chimney cloths, and clocks. This preference was typical of about 30 per cent of the rural population at the end of the eighteenth century but was socially skewed towards the middle-income and elite households.

Reasons for Acquisition

The socially and spatially determined patterns by which the consumption of new luxuries spread, suggest that emulation might have been an important driver of consumer change. The concept of emulation, fundamental in Neil McKendrick's pioneering account of the 'Consumer Revolution', draws from the work of Thorstein Veblen and Georg Simmel.[23] Both emphasised that low-class consumers were motivated by social aspirations to imitate the conspicuous consumer behaviour of the better-off classes. This imitation set in motion a new cycle of consumer innovation by elites seeking new means to differentiate themselves from those down the social scale. It must be said that de Vries is critical of emulation as the primary motivation for the acquisition of new luxuries.[24] Rather than looking upward, he argues, households looked forward. For de Vries, it was not emulation but innovation that was the most important driver of consumer change. This leaves much more room for agency by nonelite consumers and brings us to Marina Bianchi's concept of the 'active consumer' as a framework for understanding the motivation of rural households for acquiring new luxuries. In line with Tibor Scitovsky, Bianchi argues that consumers are innately motivated by the pursuit of novelty. Novelties only become widely accepted, however, if they were also familiar in appearance or in function.[25]

The spread of the fork could serve as an example for the diffusion of novelty via emulation. According to Norbert Elias, the courts in the early modern period initiated a 'civilizing process' in table manners by starting the use of forks, among other new types of tableware: from that moment it trickled down in society. In Brabant, the first forks effectively seem to have been used in the homes of the courtly elite in Brussels at the beginning of the seventeenth century.[26] A careful analysis of the mentions of forks in inventories from urban nonelite households, however, shows that other factors were at work during the emulation process: forks owned by the lower- and middle-income groups were not made of silver but predominantly made of pewter instead.[27] A similar social factor has to be taken into account when looking at the evolution of the consumption of hot drinks. Although at the beginning of the eighteenth century cocoa was the preferred drink in the circles of the Lier urban elite, it was not the expensive cocoa but the cheaper tea and later coffee which spread down the social scale. Thus not only taste was at work here but also income and wealth. The increasing frequency of fine, expensive, and elaborate tea services in Chinese or Japanese porcelain in urban elite inventories also suggest that the elite, by using such sophisticated and expensive services, wanted to distinguish themselves from households of lower rank.[28] These examples illustrate not only how the dichotomy between the old and new luxuries was far from simple, but they also show that the acquisitive behaviour of the lower- and middle-income groups, as far as tableware was concerned, was not determined by social aspirations alone but depended on other factors such as income and wealth.[29]

The inventories of smallholders and agricultural labourers also offer little evidence in support of such an easy emulation process. Milk jugs, sugar pots, and rinsing bowls (*spoelkommen*), instrumental in the ritualised sociable consumption of tea, for example, were almost entirely absent in their homes. We therefore propose the hypothesis that the slow diffusion of the new luxuries in the countryside from the late eighteenth century onwards has to be understood within the framework of a traditional way of rural life. John Styles has argued that the use of fashionable dress in the English countryside during the eighteenth century was still intricately linked with the festive calendar.[30] In the accounts of contemporary observers of everyday life in the Habsburg Netherlands we equally regularly find remarks that the consumption of luxuries in general and new luxuries in particular was an event of Sundays, High Days, and the annual fair (*Kermess*). These luxuries not only included clothing but also special food and drinks.

The French priest Lesage, who in the eighteenth century visited the Brabant countryside, observed that it was only during Sundays and during festivities that rural families put on their best dress to attend mass at church and visit the tavern afterwards.[31] He did not go into detail about the appearance of their clothing. That they were slowly adopting fabrics with new luxury characteristics such as cotton is evident from the essay of the Italian count and statistician Giovanni Arrivabene. He related that wives of rural labourers wore woollen or linen dresses during the week, but on Sundays they gradually began to wear cotton dresses, caps, and scarfs or cloaks.[32] Exemplary evidence from our inventories concerning the rural hinterland of Lier corroborates that the best pieces of clothing were reserved for Sundays.[33] It also shows that the wives of agricultural labourers and smallholders by the end of the eighteenth century already owned cotton dress accessories such as aprons, caps, and scarves.

On Sundays, they not only wore better clothes but also drank better beer and ate better food than during the week. Even throughout the week the quality of daily food improved in general in the countryside: it consisted increasingly of rye bread, butter, milk, and potatoes. On Sunday, rural people also started consuming meat regularly, in particular salted pork. According to the aforementioned Arrivabene, agricultural labourers, however, only served fresh beef and wheat bread during the annual fair (*Kermess*).[34] We did not find explicit references to the material of tableware used at these occasions, but we did find evidence in probate inventories that contradicts everyday use of fine earthenware. In the countryside, the appraisers mostly encountered coarse earthenware in the scullery (*op de mose*) where dishes were washed. The incidence of fine earthenware in the scullery was limited to only 6 per cent of the rural inventories with fine earthenware. So we can reasonably suppose that festivities were the moments for taking the finer earthenware from the shelves if such items were available in the house.

The examples given in this study illustrate how the consumption of the new luxuries in the countryside remained limited to special occasions and highlight their specific sociability dimension. Next to the parish church, the tavern was at the heart of village life.[35] Contemporary observers remarked that the rural population of Brabant in general enjoyed frequent and long visits to the village tavern after attending church.[36] Hans Medick, among others, has stressed the importance of sociocultural reproduction for the rural lower income groups through public sociability and the display of luxury and conspicuous consumption on these occasions.[37] Foreign travellers equally noticed that in Brabant people in the countryside gave great attention to their public appearance.[38] It seems reasonable to assume therefore that the acquisition of new luxuries by agricultural labourers and smallholders was to a significant degree motivated by their desire to uphold their status in the community on Sundays and at moments of festivity.[39]

Conclusion

The extension of commercial networks and of market-oriented labour during the eighteenth century broadened the scope of goods available to urban and rural households. New luxuries such as hot drinks, hitherto the prerogative of urban households, spread slowly but clearly to the countryside, even reaching some households of agricultural labourers and smallholders by the end of the century. Finer earthenware and glass tableware became part of the material belongings of the rural better-off households and even, albeit more slowly, of some rural labourers and smallholders. In this way the rural classes of Brabant conformed to what emerges from the literature as a general northwest-European pattern.

Recent studies, however, emphasise that the motivation for acquiring new luxuries in the countryside as well as in towns differed according to social status. For the urban higher income groups the new luxuries served the old function of luxury consumption as a means of distinction vis-à-vis the lower income groups. For the majority of the rural population, on the other hand, the new luxuries remained firmly rooted in their traditional sociability. The shift from old to new luxuries in this group was integrated into their social traditions: loyalty to the church, pleasure in the tavern, and participation in the festivities of the village were the main determinant factors. But they did open a new world of goods and pleasures. Tradition, in this case, did not curb innovation.

Notes

1 Leuven, State Archives, *Schepengriffies Brussel*, no. 3721 (7 April 1724).

2 Brecht Dewilde and Johan Poukens, 'Confraternities, Jansenism and the Birth of a Consumer Society in 17th–18th Century Leuven', in *Religion and Religious Institutions in the European Economy, 1000–1800*, ed. Francesco Ammannati, Fondazione Istituto internazionale di storia economica F. Datini Prato. Pubblicazioni. Serie 2: Atti delle settimane di studio e altri convegni 43 (Florence: Firenze University Press, 2012), 671–93; Bruno Blondé and Veerle De Laet, 'New and Old Luxuries between the Court and the City: A Comparative Perspective on Material Cultures in Brussels and Antwerp, 1650–1735', in *A Taste for Luxury in Early Modern Europe: Display, Acquisition and Boundaries*, eds. Johanna Ilmakunnas and Jon Stobart (London: Bloomsbury, 2017), 39–57.

3 Jan de Vries, 'Luxury in the Dutch Golden Age in Theory and Practice', in *Luxury in the Eighteenth Century: Debates, Desires and Delectable Goods*, eds. Maxine Berg and Elizabeth Eger (Basingstoke: Palgrave, 2003), 41–56; Jan de Vries, *The Industrious Revolution: Consumer Behavior and the Household Economy, 1650 to Present* (Cambridge: Cambridge University Press, 2008), 44–70.

4 Sheilagh Ogilvie, 'Consumption, Social Capital, and the "Industrious Revolution" in Early Modern Germany', *Journal of Economic History* 70, no. 3 (2010): 311–12, 320.

5 Jan de Vries, 'Between Purchasing Power and the World of Goods: Understanding the Household Economy in Early Modern Europe', in *Consumption and the World of Goods*, eds. John Brewer and Roy Porter (London and New York: Routledge, 1993), 85–113; Jan de Vries, 'The Industrial Revolution and the Industrious Revolution', *Journal of Economic History* 54, no. 2 (1994): 249–70; de Vries, *Industrious Revolution*, 122–86.

6 Jan de Vries, 'Peasant Demand Patterns and Economic Development: Friesland, 1550–1750', in *European Peasants and their Markets: Essays in Agrarian Economic History*, eds. William N. Parker and Eric L. Jones (Princeton: Princeton University Press, 1975), 179–266; Ilja Van Damme, 'Mensen doen dingen, steden niet: Interview met historicus Jan de Vries', *Stadsgeschiedenis* 4 (2009): 207–16.

7 Johan Poukens and Nele Provoost, 'Respectability, Middle-Class Material Culture, and Economic Crisis: The Case of Lier in Brabant, 1690–1770', *Journal of Interdisciplinary History* 42, no. 2 (2011): 159–84.

8 Erik Aerts and Herman Van der Wee, *Geschiedenis van Lier: Welvaart en samenleving van het ontstaan van de stad tot de Eerste Wereldoorlog* (Lier: Gilde Heren van Lier, 2016).

9 Herman Van der Wee, 'The Agricultural Development of the Low Countries

as Revealed by Tithe and Rent Statistics, 1250–1800; in *Productivity of Land and Agricultural Innovation in the Low Countries*, eds. Herman Van der Wee and Eddy Van Cauwenberghe (Leuven: Leuven University Press, 1978), 1–23; Johan Poukens, 'Tout à la fois cultivateurs et commerçans: Smallholders and the Industrious Revolution in Brabant', *Agricultural History Review* 60, no. 2 (2012): 153–72.

10 Lier, Municipal Archive (hereafter SAL), Oud archief (hereafter OA), nos. 1833–1884; Oud gemeentearchief (hereafter OG), nos. 72–4.

11 Guillaume Philémon De Longé, 'Coutumes de la ville de Lierre et de sa banlieu', in *Coutumes de Kiel, de Deurne et de Lierre*. Coutumes du pays et duché de Brabant: Quartier d'Anvers 5 (Brussels, 1875), 411–701; Aerts and Van der Wee, *Geschiedenis*, 61.

12 Anton Schuurman, 'Things by Which One Measures One's Life: Wealth and Poverty in European Rural Societies', in *Wealth and Poverty in European Rural Societies from the Sixteenth to the Nineteenth Century*, eds. John Broad and Anton Schuurman (Turnhout: Brepols, 2014), 23.

13 SAL, OA, no. 2013 (24 May 1732); De Longé, 'Coutumes la ville de Lierre', 582. See also, Philippe Godding, 'Le contrôle des tutelles par le magistrat dans las Pays-Bas méridionaux', in *Het openbaar initiatief van de gemeenten in België: Historische grondslagen (Ancien Régime). Handelingen* (Brussels: Credit communal de Belgique, 1984), 557–68.

14 Erik Thoen and Eric Vanhaute, 'The "Flemisch husbandry" at the Edge: The Farming System on Small Holdings in the Middle of the 19th Century', in *Land Productivity and Agro-Systems in the North Sea Area (Middle Ages–20th Century): Elements for Comparison*, eds. Bas J.P. Van Bavel and Erik Thoen (Turnhout: Brepols, 1999), 276–7, 287, 291.

15 Bart Van de Putte and Andrew Miles, 'Social Classification Scheme for Historical Occupational Data: Partner Selection and Industrialism in Belgium and England, 1800–1918', *Historical Methods* 38 (2005): 61–92; Bart Van de Putte and Erik Buyst, 'Occupational Titles? Hard to Eat, Easy to Catch', *Belgisch Tijdschrift voor Nieuwste Geschiedenis* 40 (2010): 7–31; Bart Van de Putte and Patrick Svenson, 'Measuring Social Structure in a Rural Context: Applying the SOCPO Scheme to Scania, Sweden (17th–20th Century)', *Belgisch Tijdschrift voor Nieuwste Geschiedenis* 40 (2010): 249–93.

16 Their 'amenities index' includes earthenware, bed or table linen, table knives, forks, fine earthenware, spices, religious and secular books, wigs, clocks or watches, pictures, and silverware. Lois Green Carr and Lorena S. Walsh, 'Inventories and the Analysis of Wealth and Consumption Patterns in St Mary's County, Maryland, 1658–1777', *Historical Methods* 13 (1980): 81–104; Lois Green Carr and Lorena S. Walsh, 'The Standard of Living in the Colonial Chesapeake', *William and Mary Quarterly* 45 (1988): 135–59.

17 Schuurman, 'Things', 26–8.

18 Micheline Baulant, 'L'appréciation du niveau de vie: Un problème, une
    solution', *Histoire & Mesure* 4 (1989): 299–301. Indices similar to those of
    Carr and Walsh and Baulant were used in Gloria L. Main and Jackson
    T. Main, 'Economic Growth and the Standard of Living in Southern New
    England, 1640–1774', *Journal of Economic History* 48, no. 1 (1988): 27–46;
    Christian Dessureault, John A. Dickinson, and Thomas Wien, 'Living
    Standards of Norman and Canadian Peasants, 1690–1835', in *Material
    Culture: Consumption, Life-Style, Standard of Living, 1500–1900*, eds. Anton
    Schuurman and Lorena Walsh (Milan: Università Bocconi, 1994), 95–112.
19 Median index scores for all households followed the same trajectory and
    were generally very close to the mean. The median rural score rose from 1 in
    1695–1719, to over 2 in 1710–44, and 2 in 1745–69 to 4 in 1770–95. Urban
    median scores were 6, 8, 8, and 8 respectively.
20 Blondé and De Laet, 'New and Old Luxuries'.
21 Lorna Weatherill, *Consumer Behaviour and Material Culture, 1660–1760*
    (London: Routledge, 1988), 88; Johan A. Kamermans, *Materiële
    cultuur in de Krimpenerwaard in de zeventiende en de achttiende eeuw:
    Ontwikkeling en diversiteit* (Wageningen: Afdeling Agrarische Geschiedenis,
    Landbouwuniversiteit, 1999), 121; Hester C. Dibbits, *Vertrouwd bezit:
    Materiële cultuur in Doesburg en Maassluis 1650–1800* (Nijmegen: Socialistiese
    Uitgeverij Nijmegen, 2001), 321, 326; Amy Barnett, 'In with the New: Novel
    Goods in Domestic Provincial England, c. 1700–1790', in *Fashioning Old
    and New: Changing Consumer Preferences in Europe (Seventeenth–Nineteenth
    Centuries)*, eds. Bruno Blondé and Ilja Van Damme (Turnhout: Brepols,
    2009), 83; Bruno Blondé and Wouter Ryckbosch, 'Arriving at a Set Table:
    The Introduction of Hot Drinks in the Urban Consumer Culture of
    the Eighteenth-century Southern Low Countries', in *Goods from the East,
    1600–1800: Trading Eurasia*, eds. Maxine Berg, Felicia Gottmann, Hanna
    Hodacs, and Chris Nierstrasz (Basingstoke: Palgrave, 2015), 309–27.
22 Blondé and Ryckbosch, 'Arriving at a Set Table', 316–17.
23 Neil McKendrick, John Brewer, and John H. Plumb, *The Birth of a Consumer
    Society: The Commercialisation of Eighteenth-Century England* (Bloomington:
    Europa, 1982), 9–33.
24 De Vries, *Industrious Revolution*, 46–52. Other critiques of emulation as a
    driver for consumer change can be found in Stana Nenadic, 'Middle-Rank
    Consumers and Domestic Culture in Edinburgh and Glasgow 1720–1840',
    Past & Present 145 (1994): 123–25; Marina Bianchi, 'Taste for Novelty and
    Novel Tastes: The Role of Human Agency in Consumption', in *The Active
    Consumer: Novelty and Surprise in Consumer Choice*, ed. Marina Bianchi
    (London and New York: Routledge, 1998), 69.
25 Bianchi, 'Taste', 74–6.
26 Veerle De Laet, *Brussel binnenskamers: Kunst- en luxebezit in het spanningsveld
    tussen hof en stad, 1600–1735*, *Studies Stadsgeschiedenis* 8 (Amsterdam:

Amsterdam University Press, 2011), 151–2; Bruno Blondé, 'Tableware and Changing Consumer Patterns: Dynamics of Material Culture in Antwerp, 17th–18th Centuries', in *Majolica and Glass from Italy to Antwerp and Beyond: The Transfer of Technology in the 16th–Early 17th Centuries*, ed. Johan Veeckman (Antwerp: Stad Antwerpen, 2002), 298–9, 301; Bruno Blondé, 'Cities in Decline and the Down of a Consumer Society: Antwerp in the 17th–18th Centuries', in *Retailers and Consumer Changes in Early Modern Europe. England, France, Italy and the Low Countries*, eds. Bruno Blondé and Ilja Van Damme (Tours: Presses Universitaires François-Rabelais, 2005), 43–4.

27 The frequency of silver cutlery was 68 per cent in urban inventories from the elite and 29 and 9 per cent respectively in middle and lower income group inventories. In the countryside, almost no silver forks were encountered. See also, De Laet, *Brussel binnenskamers*, 151–2; Ryckbosch, 'A Consumer Revolution', 246–7.

28 Jon Stobart, *Sugar and Spice: Grocers and Groceries in Provincial England, 1650–1830* (Oxford: Oxford University Press, 2012), 242–53; Blondé and Ryckbosch, 'Arriving at a Set Table', 315.

29 Blondé and De Laet, 'New and Old Luxuries', 50–1.

30 John Styles, 'Custom or Consumption? Plebeian Fashion in Eighteenth-Century England', in *Luxury in the Eighteenth Century: Debates, Desires and Delectable Goods*, eds. Maxine Berg and Elizabeth Eger (Basingstoke: Palgrave, 2003), 103–15; John Styles, *The Dress of the People: Everyday Fashion in Eighteenth-Century England* (New Haven and London: Yale University Press, 2007), 319.

31 Rita Van Damme, 'De Zuidnederlander in reisverhalen van de tweede helft van de achttiende eeuw (1748–1795)' (unpublished Master's thesis, Leuven, 1964), 124.

32 Giovanni Arrivabene, 'Enquête sur l'état des paysans de la commune de Gaesbeek', *Recueil encyclopédique belge* 4 (1834): 239.

33 For instance, 'The husband dressed his best for church in a coat with some silver buttons' ('Item de man zoals hij op zijn best naar de kerk gaat met enige zilveren knopen aan zijn kamizool'), SAL, OG, no. 73 (7 August 1752).

34 Charles Joseph Fortune d'Herbouville, *Statistique du département des Deux-Nèthes* (Paris, 1802); Jan Lodewijk Van Aelbroeck, *Werkdadige landbouw-konst der Vlamingen, verhandeld in zes zamensprаken, tusschen eenen grond-eigenaar en zijnen pachter* (Gent, 1823), 93; Joseph Fernand de Lichtervelde, *La bêche, ou La mine d'or de la Flandre oriental: Ouvrage, ou l'on trouve les détails des principes suivis de culture, de l'emploi des engrais, de l'éducation du bétail, de gouverner les laitages, ainsi que de tous autres objets pratiques* (Gent, 1826), 34; Arrivabene, 'Enquête', 246.

35 Robert Muchembled, 'De kroeg als trefpunt', in *België in de 17de eeuw: De Spaanse Nederlanden en het prinsbisdom Luik*, ed. Paul Janssen (Gent: Dexia Bank; Snoeck, 2006), 355–62.

36 Thomas De Wolf, 'De visie van reizigers op Brabant en Mechelen (1701–1800)' (unpublished master's thesis, Gent, 2004).

37 Peter Kriedte, Hans Medick, and Jürgen Schlumbohm, *Industrialization before Industrialization: Rural Industry in the Genesis of Capitalism* (Cambridge: Cambridge University Press, 1981), 64–73.

38 De Wolf, 'De visie.'

39 Alan Hutchinson, 'Consumption and Endeavour: Motives for the Acquisition of New Consumer Goods in a Region in the North of Norway in the 18th Century,' *Scandinavian Journal of History* 39, no. 1 (2014): 27–48.

13

Threads of Empire: Indigenous Wares and Material Ecologies in the 'Anglo-World', c. 1780–1920

Beverly Lemire

The threads of empire that bound together people and places took many forms. My focus is on the less celebrated materials, a small traffic when set against industrial and imperial manufactures, such as cotton. Let me first paint the scenario: hegemonic material culture spanned the 'Anglo-World' and beyond – Anglo-World being a term defined by James Belich as including metropole and settler colonies aligned by language and customs.[1] By the nineteenth century cotton from plantations and factories defined this era, part of the nexus of the Industrial Revolution, a central paradigm of time and place.[2] The common industrial threads marking Anglo-World networks were the fruits of rationality, mechanisation, standardisation, efficiency, and profit, founded on capital investment, slave and waged labour, and imperial structures, celebrated by a British contemporary as 'unparalleled in the annals of the world.'[3] Monumental new technologies of production underpinned imperial policy and, thereafter, preoccupied generations of economic historians, focused on heroics of industry and technology. The roles of women and children in this scenario only intermittently received attention in past historiography until the 1990s; similarly, their roles in augmented consumer practice are a more recent focus.[4] Importantly, these plantation and industrial systems also redefined material ecologies. Fibres and fabrics were dispatched as part of imperial vitality, a juggernaut of thread and cloth producing a distinctive material ecosystem.[5] Economic history should expand its focus to address natural and cultural ecologies more fully, reflected in historic objects and distinct systems of production and consumption.

Juxtapose the products of the nascent industrial system against the hybrid indigenous-made things that travelled these same networks. My focus is the myriad goods *made for the market* by colonised indigenous

peoples of northern North America, commercial flows far smaller in scale
than those pouring from factories to markets. Yet, these distinctive wares
added a critical diversity to the material ecology of the Anglo-World,
a diversity not yet fully assessed. Further, they materialised cultural
priorities distinct from those of western manufacturers. This chapter is
a preliminary consideration of these goods and their significance: arts
and crafts circulating in increasing quantities into the twentieth century,
arising from the land-based ecologies and indigenous knowledge systems
of Native American communities. Over the past generation, art historians demonstrated the significant artistry of indigenous creations.[6] The
world catalogue of noteworthy media was expanded beyond Eurasian
fibres, fabrics, and aesthetic materials to include North American objects
of cedar, birch bark, porcupine quill, and moose hair, among others. It
is important to recognise the full historic range of goods circulating
through the Anglo-World, including in Britain itself and among other
European nations. The traffic in indigenous-made fashions, furnishings, and accessories moved products from discrete material ecologies
through the imperial system. Indigenous-made fashions represent
ecologies of knowledge and these largely women-made goods signify
'a remarkable intellectual, technical, and artistic legacy.'[7] These commodities carried political weight as emblems of resistance to colonialism,
expressive of applied traditional knowledge in new forms, determined
insertions into international markets giving complex pleasure to buyers
not least through the 'Indianness' of the goods themselves. Moreover
these fashions were crafted amidst tightening imperial and colonial
administrative apparatus.

Perplexing Media, Innovative Fashions

Centuries of globalising trade moved products that enriched material
lives; indeed, many of these things arose from indigenous and
non-Western communities, commoditised as adjuncts of globalism and
domesticated in new realms over time. Once 'foreign', these became
accepted (even necessary) components of everyday life, eliciting habits
that shaped diverse world regions:[8] tobacco, cotton, tea, and sugar
epitomised this for some; mahogany, silk, tortoise shell, beetle wings,
and ivory for others. The list is long. They touched people of all ranks
and set new standards of taste. As Erika Rappaport observes for tea,
'the British Empire exerted power over land, labor, tastes, and the daily
habits of millions of people living in so many parts of the globe.'[9] In
Britain, this was part of 'being at home with the Empire', a concept
coined by Catherine Hall and Sonya Rose, with a materiality premised

on the 'connections across the globe ... in the context of unequal relations of power.'[10] These precepts were exemplified through material
culture, through goods circulating via global commerce and imperial
infrastructure. The resulting assemblages were typically ranked by elites
and political cognoscenti, not necessarily premised on the skills of the
makers or the qualities of the things themselves. The curation of things
by imperial denizens was often tied to theories of human hierarchies
throughout the West, including theories of 'race' and 'whiteness.'[11] Arts
that arose from non-Western locales and knowledge systems, particularly those from regions of settler colonialism, often elicited responses
rooted in priorities of imperial intent.[12] Nonetheless, the circulation of
wares made by colonised indigenous peoples defied simple racialism or
imperial policies. The indigenous arts and commodities that emerged
from colonial North America added critical complexity to the material
ecology of the Anglo-World, not least in Britain itself.

I use the term 'material ecology' in a historic context, stretching
concepts of 'ecology' for, as Timothy LeCain argues, the 'contemporary
idea of "ecology" is too pinched.' LeCain notes that human interactions
with things 'literally change our brains and bodies, or that we coevolve
and become entangled with powerful things, or simply that the cultural
and material are inextricably mixed in all sorts of unexpected ways.'[13]
LeCain urges historians to attend to more diverse phenomena such as
art, cooking, and music and to 'pay more attention to the history of
changes in the material environment.'[14] Indigenous ontologies likewise
include far wider precepts of the 'material.'[15] Economic historians must
also account for these dynamics.

America's indigenous peoples made objects within different natural
ecologies and cultural knowledge systems, resulting in many decorative traditions initially unknown to Europeans. Sherry Farrell Racette
describes many of the objects now resting in museums: 'objects encoded
with knowledge, although they are sometimes impenetrable and difficult
to understand ... Through the power of colour and design, the objects
in museum collections not only speak to a powerful aesthetic, they also
reveal critical information about the worlds and circumstances in which
they were created.'[16] Porcupine quills (dyed and flattened), moose hair
(brilliantly coloured), tree bark moulded into shapes, plus hides of many
kinds – soft textured or hard – were among the resources used to make
trade goods. Native Americans understood raw materials in the spiritual
context of the animal, rock, or plant, although only 'some are' animate,
as one Ojibwa elder explained.[17] Racette notes that within indigenous
communities 'Women were charged with the responsibility of visually
communicating that respect [through their arts].'[18] The predominantly

female workforce involved in crafting these wares also relied on the transfer of generational knowledge of how best to use resources to create the most satisfactory results. Skills persisted despite the surging pressures of colonisation, as design aesthetics evolved, suited to the tastes of makers, settlers, and metropolitan markets. Ruth Phillips argues that, 'In tailoring their wares ever more closely to the tastes and desires of prospective buyers, indigenous people learned a new vocabulary of the object and new ways of negotiating the semiotics of ethnic difference.'[19] Indigenous makers mastered a material dialogue.[20]

This innovative process can be seen in a pocketbook described as 'French' circa 1700, held in the Victoria and Albert Museum. Its components reflect debts to European and indigenous materials and skills, combining white satin, silk embroidery thread, and porcupine quills in an exceptional accessory that gleamed. Indigenous peoples on the northeast coast, the St Lawrence, and Great Lakes regions were among the great practitioners of quillwork, a medium that initially perplexed Europeans. Jesuits in New France described this medium in their early seventeenth-century correspondence.[21] French Ursuline Sisters established a monastery in Quebec City in 1639, among the prominent female religious that worked with proximate indigenous groups and enforced material standards emblematic of conversion. The sisters were deft embroiderers themselves, using the elements standard among European women: silk, beads, and gilt thread. Their indigenous students adapted these materials to their own decorative priorities; a blending took place.[22] Among the prominent Ursulines was Mère Sainte-Marie-Madeleine, born in 1678, with a French father and Wendat (Huron) mother. She mastered the media of both cultures and 'used her leisure to teach the young to embroider on silk, gold and bark.'[23] This is the context from which to assess the French pocketbook, a memento of exchange and innovation.[24]

Whether the maker of this pocketbook was Native American or not, its quillwork is symbolic of indigenous material culture and material ecology. This accessory also demonstrates an aesthetic that valued luminous shine, a feature treasured among indigenous peoples of north-east North America, articulated here through combined satin, silk embroidery thread, and porcupine quills.[25] Importantly, this fashion object carried indigenous-based knowledge to wider venues. It demonstrates the disruption of simple colonial categories and the increased material diversity within imperial systems through cultural work performed by indigenous women. Quillwork featured on countless useful and fashionable wares and these commodities were an increasingly important source of income for families and communities from

INDIGENOUS WARES AND MATERIAL ECOLOGIES

the late-eighteenth century onwards. Indigenous women performed these decorative and productive tasks, details of which were described by a later American aficionado of these arts: 'Sorting and coloring the quills, tracing the design on dressed skin or birchbark ... [and] embroidering [was] exclusively the work of [indigenous] women ... A woman who was skilled or had a natural gift for drawing would copy a design by freehand method, except that she had first made some measurements in order that the pattern should be in its proper place and proportions. Some even compose designs, both the forms and the arrangements of colours, and worked them out as they embroidered.'[26]

Quillwork was most commonly applied to hide and birch bark, producing distinctive object types whose motifs changed over time. Important scholarship has illuminated Asian influence on European material culture and design in the early modern and modern eras.[27] An equal effort should be made to unpack the complex interventions of indigenous materials from the Americas over this same period because influences were multidirectional. Although the volume of indigenous-made goods was in no way commensurable to other American or Asian commodity trades, the powerful meanings embedded in indigenous manufactures and the responses they provoked demand attention. Bark, for example, was well known as the substance used by North American indigenous peoples to make long-distance canoes: 'some of which ... are capable of containing two tons [of cargo]'.[28] Birch bark took on other roles in the making of souvenirs and fashionable notions.[29] By the late 1790s, when Irishman Isaac Weld toured the colonial polities around the Great Lakes and St Lawrence River, he heaped praise on the embroideries he saw: 'The embroidery upon their moccasins and other garments shews that the females are not less ingenious in their way than the men. Their porcupine quill work would command admiration in any country in Europe.'[30] Catherine Parr Traill, colonial settler, writer, and wife of a retired British officer, also recounted the range of goods available from local Anishinaabeg peoples – Ojibwa and others – in the region north of what is now Toronto where she settled with her husband. Traill exemplifies the mixed sentiments of colonists towards the indigenous women making and selling goods, despite the acknowledged quality of their wares. Racialism infused her commentary: 'The squaws are very ingenious in many of their handiworks. We find their birch-bark baskets very convenient for a number of purposes. My bread-basket, knife-tray, sugar-basket, are all of this humble material. When ornamented and wrought in patterns with dyed quills, I can assure you, they are by no means inelegant ... The Indians are acquainted with a variety of dyes, with which they stain the more elegant fancy-baskets and porcupine-quills. Our parlour is ornamented with several very pretty specimens of their ingenuity in this way, which answer the purpose of note and letter-cases, flower-stands, and work-baskets.'[31]

Figure 13.1 is an example of a tray decorated in geometric patterns with dyed porcupine quillwork, an object held in the collection of the Victoria and Albert Museum, London. It is wreathed in anonymity, the originating community is now unknown, though in all likelihood it was made by an artisan in the eastern region of what is now Canada. The Mi'kmaq, for example, resided in the Atlantic regions of Canada and the United States and Mi'kmaq women were notable exponents of quillwork. Surviving quillwork commodities, including large decorative furnishing, are held in museums throughout the Atlantic world, confirming the diverse flows of products made for the market. Figure 13.2 is a very different style of birch bark tray or plate, with striking flora, fauna, and figurative designs picked out in dyed moose hair. The shared pleasure of the tobacco pipe, among settlers and Native Americans, is whimsically presented. Equally notable is the wolf in the centre square, with a bird between its paws. The wolf is ascribed with powerful attributes (courage, loyalty, and strength) and is a clan name in many Indigenous communities. Birds are sometimes understood as carrying messages from the Creator. The combined utility and symbolic complexity in this artwork suggests the challenges faced by Native Americans and their responses to these pressures, employing design in ways unlikely to be understood by colonial consumers. Nonetheless, these arts found wide markets. This piece is part of the Peabody Essex Museum collection, dating from about 1840. Ephemera like this survive in public museums and private British collections, usually without provenance, evidence of 'counterflow' traffic in indigenous-made things, a trade too little studied. The aggregate flow of Native American-made commodities *moved against the tide of imperial manufactures* – thus, a counterflow product.[32] Figure 13.3, a heart-shaped pincushion from a Manchester museum, typifies such items, finding a niche in everyday imperial settings, now without attribution. The front of the pincushion is bark, embroidered with dyed moose hair in a fine floral pattern; the back is crimson silk. Dated about 1800, this small domestic ornament may have been a gift or travelled as cargo in a trunk from North America to its ultimate British user.[33] The needlework expresses the cultural continuity of indigenous female skills and the strategic creativity of communities of makers.

Quillwork, bark work, and moose hair embroidery required the combined skills of indigenous men and women, to harvest animals, plants, and trees and put the elements to use. These processes could not be mechanised. Moreover, the physical attributes of the processed

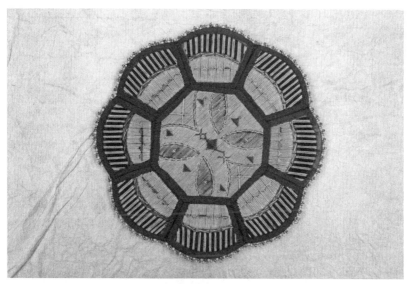

Figure 13.1   Porcupine quillwork tray, made in what is now Canada, by an anonymous Indigenous artisan, c. 1830–72.

Figure 13.2   Tray (birch bark and dyed moose hair), American School, c. 1840.

Figure 13.3   Elongated heart-shaped pincushion. Birch bark front
embroidered with moose hair in four colours. Back of crimson silk
bound in cream moose hair, 1770–1800.

materials emerged from deep traditional knowledge, including the dyes
that produced 'the most beautiful and brilliant colours imaginable; as
Isaac Weld testified about 1800. He noted that 'many of them [the dyes]
yet remain unknown [to Europeans], as do also many of the medicines
with which they perform sometimes most miraculous cures. Their dyes
and medicines are all procured from the vegetable world.'[34] Moose hair
embroidery uses the stiff hair from the mane or cheek, generally from
two to five inches long. These are assembled in bundles and dyed, after
which the hair is laid on the cloth, bark, or hide and couched with
fine stitches according to the design. These goods evoked praise and
puzzlement plus a deep curiosity from Europeans.

A century after Weld's description, another Euro-American eyewit-
ness called this work 'ingenious; a recurring comment among western
observers; he also repined at the secrecy surrounding traditional dyeing
techniques.[35] The indigenous arts circulating along Anglo-World
networks augmented demand for these wares. The material ecologies
and cultural traditions from which these goods emerged stood in

sharp contrast to the bales of cloth pouring out of British mills. The British Arts and Crafts Movement that emerged in the later nineteenth century is positioned as a critical creative response to industrialisation. Did the appeal of indigenous-made arts hold an appeal inspired by similar sentiments beyond the souvenir or the 'exotic'? Certainly, some indigenous communities responded to demand and produced goods in relatively large quantities, while other communities sold in small streams; their scale of production was in large measure determined by the materials they employed, its landscape of origin, available labour, and proximate networks plus the colonial constraints under which they lived.

Britain and the Indigenous (Material) Presence

The Wendat resided outside Quebec City, a regional capital city and the first major port on the St Lawrence River. The Wendat practiced many arts including moose hair embroidery, building production in response to the settler influx and the loss of their lands. They also took advantage of tourism and, strategically, Wendat leaders directed distribution including through Euro-American retailers with international ties.[36] Industrial exhibitions figured in their promotions, including at Quebec City, Montreal, and Paris. By 1859, this community manufactured twenty thousand mukluks and moccasins, many embroidered, plus quantities of embroidered wares of all qualities. In 1858, they earned an income of $34,000 by one report, a healthy commercial enterprise that evolved into the next century.[37] Indigenous producers in this region focused on well-known local markets plus occasional distant venues.[38] The earlier period around the Great Exhibition of 1851 confirms the entrepreneurship of indigenous makers, though it nearly went awry.

North-east Native American communities were familiar with regional exhibitions and, on hearing of the 1851 Great Exhibition in London, planned to sell at this venue, misunderstanding its more static purpose. Some indigenous objects *were* showcased among the assemblage from British North America, including 'Several embroidered [table] cloths ... the work of Indians at Niagara Falls ... formed with moose-hair, none of which is more than two inches in length.'[39] However, exhibitors did not sell from this venue. Yet, several groups of indigenous entrepreneurs travelled to London including a small party from Kahnawake, Quebec, near Montreal, who brought $3,000 worth of stock. Their misadventure was turned to advantage when it was widely reported, with readers directed to George Caitlin's Exhibition in Waterloo Place, where 'specimens of the articles ... may be seen and

purchased.'[40] London's *Morning Advertiser* boasted on the front page
that 'Iroquois Chiefs and Warriors' could be found at Caitlin's establishment, along with thousands of 'Mocasins [*sic*], Bags, Reticules, Caps,
Bracelets, etc, which they had intended for the Great Exhibition, [and]
are now being purchased by Ladies and Gentlemen, *from the Indians'
own hands*.'[41] This sale joined other periodic auctions of things 'by the
North American Indians', publicized in local newspapers, including the
'Grand Bazaar at Albion School' reported in a Lancashire periodical in
May 1867. The goods assembled by that genteel stallholder included 'a
fan made by Canadian Indians of the hair of the prairie turkey, with a
bird in the centre, and dyed by these inhabitants of the wilds of America;
moccasins also made by Canadian Indians of the skin of the Moose
Deer, and artistically ornamented.'[42] Sales of Native American arts and
crafts took place across the kingdom, goods were closely examined and
widely acquired, including moccasins.[43]

   In the nineteenth century, Hudson's Bay Company (HBC) employees carried small and midsize cargoes of indigenous wares back to
their homelands at the ends of their contract or when visiting family,
particularly to Scotland, the HBC's main recruiting site. But the HBC
constrained this traffic across the vast inland territory they administered.
In 1825, HBC servants were ordered to reduce the quantities of indigenous-made goods carried out of the western plains, with instructions
that 'no Servant or others leaving the [trading] country be permitted
to embark beyond 20 pairs of Indian Shoes, and that all such property
be subject to search.' Penalties were promised for infractions 'whither
[these were] denominated *presents, Curiosities* or *otherways*.'[44] These orders
were repeated almost annually, suggesting the porousness of their trade
routes and the profitability of these wares. Norbert Welsh, a Metis buffalo
hunter in the western plains, opened a store after 1885 and regularly
secured moccasins of various kinds from local indigenous makers. The
HBC was always keen to buy his stock, shipping quantities to England
to feed the fancy for this commodity.[45] This explains HBC hostility to
employees seen to infringe on their profits. But it also points to the ways
indigenous enterprise in this region was fenced off from larger markets,
unlike that of the Wendat outside Quebec City.

   Figures 13.4 and 13.5 illustrate the varied decorative techniques
applied by moccasin-makers. These images show finely crafted
east coast trade moccasins the like of which powered counterflow
commerce to Britain. Moccasins and other wares traversed imperial networks from many points on the North American continent,
finding buyers in distant lands. Moreover, public fascination with
moccasins – their weight, feel, decorative features, and rhetorical

Figure 13.4   Black chamois footwear embroidered with dyed moose/deer hair and porcupine quillwork, 1780–1800. Made in a First Nations community in the Eastern Great Lakes or by Haudenosaunee (Iroquois).

Figure 13.5   Shoes, made in the northern United States (?), 1850–79. Maker(s) unknown. Dark leather embroidered on the cuffs and vamps in five colours of moose hair, trimmed and lined with red silk.

prominence – encouraged this fashion. Ulinka Rublack notes the fascination with footwear among elite Renaissance men, 'as objects of cultural and historical significance: shoes reflected civilization in their technological advances, oddities and customs'.[46] This appeal persisted, though different priorities drove the purchase or collection of moccasins. This footwear was celebrated in fictional accounts of colonial adventures and, later, advertised across Britain and Ireland, ideal for comfort, style, and value while also redolent of imperial landscapes, materialized in this distinctive footwear. In 1920s advertisements for 'moccasin slippers' the guarantee of quality was the indigenous maker, as an Aberdeen advertiser made clear: 'Indian Moccasins ... Guaranteed Hand-Made by Indians of the Huron Tribe. Beautiful Goods'.[47] Thus a specialist trade grew into a structured, international commerce, rooted in Native American technologies.[48]

There was a bottomless appetite for imperial exotics, which indigenous travellers turned to their advantage as they could. The long-run presence of indigenous peoples in Britain is only now receiving due attention, an antidote to what Catherine Hall and Sonya Rose term 'a geographical imagination that bifurcated the political and economic space of empire into a bounded "home" ... physically and culturally separated from the colonised "other"'.[49] However, as Coll Thrush shows, the indigenous presence in London (and Britain generally) was incontrovertible: 'few in number but with cultural and political impacts far outweighing their head count'.[50] The same claim can be made for indigenous-made fashions, surrogates for a population under extraordinary pressure, memorialized in storied material ecologies. Indigenous arts were sold and displayed at industrial exhibitions throughout the British Isles, including in Scotland at the Caithness Industrial Exhibition in 1868[51] and the Mains and Strathmartine Industrial Exhibition in 1886, outside Dundee, with Native American manufactures displayed under the banner 'Rare Needlework'. The region of Caithness, along with the proximate Orkney Islands, was a main recruiting ground for the HBC. In addition to the commercial flows of indigenous goods, personal connections provided channels for these media. The indigenous works shown in exhibitions hearkened to family ties linking Britain with northern North America, including the many 'country marriages' of Scotsmen and indigenous women; the children often returned with their fathers to Scotland, carrying embroidered tokens from their mothers.[52] Indigenous-made objects in Britain signified the entangled relations of empire: tangible evidence of indigenous knowledge and spaces, reminders of blood relations, souvenirs of service or of imperial claims. These also signalled indigenous economic agency of great significance. I end this analysis with a tablecloth and a marriage.

Conclusion

In June 1878, Dunbar James Douglas, 6th Earl of Selkirk, wed Cecily Louisa Grey-Egerton near her father's estate in Cheshire, their guests embodying the administration of the British Empire. Dynastic occasions like this reveal what Emma Rothschild calls 'the inner life of empires', including the myriad roles of material culture.[53] These nuptials were a time for gifting, detailed in the local newspaper.[54] The imperial ethos of the gifts was the most notable feature of these offerings. Margot Finn addresses the power of 'colonial gifts' in consolidating imperial networks where identities were revealed and reinforced.[55] Luxurious trinkets were joined by embroidered furnishings and accoutrements, actual 'threads of empire', the antithesis of the factory-made goods that also powered the nation. Among these presents was a 'Scarlet cloth Canadian table cloth, worked and embroidered with moose hair',[56] a product of indigenous hands, sourced in part from North American ecologies. Such tablecloths were a particular fashion at the time and a British visitor's report from Wendake noted the moose hair embroidered tablecloths as 'extremely handsome, and are probably well-known in England.'[57] Fashionable and distinctive things kept the indigenous presence in view in the metropole and across provincial settings, in shop windows and domestic spaces, in the heart of empire and across colonial lands. Distinctive material culture and design aesthetics distinguished these products, critical adjuncts amidst the hegemonic systems of the age. Ultimately, numerous surviving items with this provenance found their way to museum collections across England, Scotland, and Ireland.

The counterflow goods in Britain held meanings that contrasted sharply with the output of factories and contrasted as well with the intended extirpation of indigenous peoples in settler colonies. Some might see the Native American goods landing in Britain as part of an extractive process of empire. Others acknowledge the ways imperial webs allowed unexpected opportunities beyond the intent of authorities, including in the deployment of arts and crafts made by indigenes.[58] Indeed, the enterprise of colonised people enabled them to employ media steeped in custom and tradition and to disseminate their applied knowledge, its materials, and storied arts. They adapted their output for a critical purpose. Though moose hair was sometimes stitched on industrially made cloth and moccasins were sometimes lined with silk, the artistry of these wares maintained a diversity of peoples as well as things. Imperial and industrial systems were thereby constrained. The embroidered tablecloths and countless moccasins moving through Britain embodied the active intervention of indigenous communities and the material ecologies they deployed.

Notes

1 James Belich, *Replenishing the Earth: The Settler Revolution and the Rise of the Anglo-World* (Oxford: Oxford University Press, 2009).

2 Giorgio Riello and Prasannan Parthasarathi, eds., *The Spinning World: A Global History of Cotton Textiles, 1200–1850* (Oxford: Oxford University Press, 2009); Beverly Lemire, *Cotton* (Oxford: Berg, 2011); Giorgio Riello, *Cotton: The Fabric That Made the Modern World* (Cambridge: Cambridge University Press, 2013); Sven Beckert, *Empire of Cotton: A Global History* (New York: Vintage Books, 2014); Robert Duplessis, *The Material Atlantic: Clothing, Commerce, and Colonization in the Atlantic World 1650–1800* (Cambridge: Cambridge University Press, 2015); Beverly Lemire, *Global Trade and the Transformation of Consumer Cultures. The Material World Remade, c. 1500–1820* (Cambridge: Cambridge University Press, 2018), chapters 2 and 3.

3 *Aberdeen Magazine, Literary Chronicle, and Review* 1 (1788–90) in *The British Cotton Trade, 1660–1815*, 4 vols, ed. Beverly Lemire (London: Pickering and Chatto, 2010), 4: 201.

4 Ivy Pinchbeck, *Women Workers and the Industrial Revolution* (London: Routledge, 1930); Maxine Berg and Pat Hudson, 'Rehabilitating the Industrial Revolution,' *Economic History* Review 45, no. 1 (1992): 24–50; Maxine Berg, *The Age of Manufactures 1700–1820: Industry, Innovation and Work in Britain*, 2nd ed. (London and New York: Routledge, 1994), especially chapter 7; Jan de Vries, *The Industrious Revolution: Consumer Behavior and the Household Economy 1650 to the Present* (Cambridge: Cambridge University Press, 2008); Jane Humphries, *Childhood and Child Labour in the British Industrial Revolution* (Cambridge: Cambridge University Press, 2010).

5 Riello, *Cotton*.

6 Ruth B. Phillips, *Trading Identities: The Souvenir in Native North American Art from the Northeast, 1700–1900* (Montreal and Kingston: McGill-Queen's University Press, 1998); Janet C. Berlo and Ruth Phillips, eds., *Native North American Art*, 2nd ed. (New York: Oxford University Press, 2015); Cynthia Lamar Chavez, Sherry Farrell Racette, and Lara Evans, eds., *Art Is Our Lives: Native Women Artists in Dialogue* (Santa Fe: School for Advanced Research Press, 2010).

7 Sherry Farrell Racette, 'Looking for Stories and Unbroken Threads: Museum Artifacts as Women's History and Cultural Legacy,' in *Restoring the Balance: First Nations Women, Community, and Culture*, eds. Gail Guthrie Valaskakis, Madeleine Dion Stout, and Eric Guimond (Winnipeg: University of Manitoba Press, 2009), 285.

8 Maxine Berg, *Luxury and Pleasure in Eighteenth-Century Britain* (Oxford: Oxford University Press, 2005).

9 Erika Rappaport, *A Thirst for Empire: How Tea Shaped the Modern World* (Princeton: Princeton University Press, 2017), 6–7.

10 Catherine Hall and Sonya Rose, 'Introduction: Being at Home with the Empire' in *At Home with the Empire: Metropolitan Culture and the Imperial World*, eds. Catherine Hall and Sonya Rose (Cambridge: Cambridge University Press, 2006), 5.

11 Nell Irvin Painter, *The History of White People* (New York: W.W. Norton & Company, 2010), esp. chapter 5.

12 Charles Dickens reflected these racialist theories, discussed in Coll Thrush, *Indigenous London: Native Travelers at the Heart of Empire* (New Haven: Yale University Press, 2016), 9–10.

13 Timothy J. Lecain, *The Matter of History: How Things Create the Past* (Cambridge: Cambridge University Press, 2017), 128.

14 LeCain, *Matter of History*, 133.

15 David C. Posthumus, *All My Relatives: Exploring Lakota Ontology, Belief, and Ritual* (Lincoln: University of Nebraska Press, 2018).

16 Racette, 'Looking for Stories and Unbroken Threads', 285.

17 Alfred Irving Hallowell, 'Ojibwa Ontology, Behavior, and World View' in *Readings in Indigenous Religions*, ed. Graham Harvey (London: Continuum 2002), 362.

18 Racette, 'Looking for Stories and Unbroken Threads', 287.

19 Phillips, *Trading Identities*, 261.

20 Lemire, *Global Trade*, chapter 6.

21 Reuben Gold Thwaites, ed., *The Jesuit Relations and Allied Documents: Travels and Explorations of the Jesuit Missionaries in New France 1610–1791*, vol. 1, *Acadia 1610–1613* (Cleveland: The Burrows Brothers, 1898), 279.

22 Natalie Zemon Davis, *Women on the Margins: Three Seventeenth-Century Lives* (Cambridge, MA: Harvard University Press, 1995), 96–7.

23 Quoted in Phillips, *Trading Identities*, 106.

24 Ibid., 106–7.

25 Ibid.; George R. Hamell, 'Strawberries, Floating Islands, and Rabbit Captains: Mythical Realities and European Contact in the Northeast during the Sixteenth and Seventeenth Centuries', *Journal of Canadian Studies/Revue d'Etudes Canadiennes* 21, no. 4 (1986): 75–6.

26 James Mooney (Ethnologist, Smithsonian Institution, 1885–1921), 'Note', in 'History of the Savage Peoples who are Allies of New France, by Claude Charles Le Roy, Sieur de Bacqueville de La Potherie', in *The Indian Tribes of the Upper Mississippi and Region of the Great Lakes …*, vol. 1, ed. Emma H. Blair (Cleveland: Arthur H. Clark Company, 1911), 327, n220.

27 Maxine Berg was prominent in these revisions. Maxine Berg, Felicia Gottman, Chris Nierstrasz, and Hannah Hodacs, eds., *Goods from the East, 1600–1800:*

Trading Eurasia (London: Palgrave, 2015); Maxine Berg, *Luxury and Pleasure*; Maxine Berg, 'In Pursuit of Luxury: Global History and British Consumer Goods in the Eighteenth Century', *Past & Present* 182 (2004): 85–114.

28 Isaac Weld, *Travels through the States of North America, and the Provinces of Upper and Lower Canada, during the years 1795, 1796, and 1797*, 2nd ed., vol. 1 (London: John Stockdale, 1799), 318.

29 Phillips, *Trading Identities*, 106–7.

30 Isaac Weld, *Travels through the States of North America, and the Provinces of Upper and Lower Canada, during the years 1795, 1796, and 1797*, 3rd ed., vol. 2 (London: John Stockdale 1800), 259.

31 Catherine Parr Traill, *The Backwoods of Canada: Being Letters from the Wife of an Emigrant Officer Illustrative of the Domestic Economy of British America* ... (London: C. Knight, 1836), 68, 169.

32 I use the term 'counterflow' in a manner similar to that of Michael Fisher, who described the counterflow of Indians from the subcontinent to England. Michael Fisher, *Counterflows to Colonialism: Indian Travellers and Settlers in Britain, 1600–1857* (Delhi: Permanent Black, 2004). Ruth Phillips first pointed out the movement of these goods to the UK. Phillips, *Trading Identities*.

33 Elongated heart shape pincushion. Platt Hall Gallery of Costume, Manchester Art Gallery, 1982.325.

34 Weld, *Travels through the States of North America*, 3rd ed., vol. 2, 259–60.

35 F.G. Speck, 'Huron Moose Hair Embroidery', *American Anthropologist* 13, no. 1 (1911): 1–7; Anne de Stecher, 'Souvenir Art, Collectable Craft, Cultural Heritage: The Wendat (Huron) of Wendake, Quebec', in *Craft, Community and the Material Culture of Place and Politics, 19th–20th Century*, eds. Janice Helland, Beverly Lemire, and Alena Buis (Farnham: Ashgate, 2014), 37–58.

36 Annette de Stecher, 'Wendat Arts of Diplomacy: Negotiating Change in the Nineteenth Century', in *From Huronia to Wendakes: Adversity, Migration, and Resilience, 1650–1900*, eds. Thomas Peace and Lathryn Labelle (Norman, OK: University of Oklahoma Press, 2016), 182–208; and Brian Gettler, 'Economic Activity and Class Formation in Wendake, 1800–1950', in Peach and Labelle, *From Huronia to Wendakes*, 151–4.

37 'The Last of the Huron', *The Middlebury Register* (Middlebury, VT) 16 February 1859; Gordon M. Sayre, 'Self-Portraiture and Commodification in the Work of Huron/Wendat Artist Zacharie Vincent, aka "Le Dernier Huron"', *American Indian Culture and Research Journal* 39, no. 2 (2015): 19–20; Gettler, 'Economic Activity and Class Formation in Wendake', 151–3.

38 Phillips, *Trading Identities*.

39 'The Great Exhibition', *John Bull* (London, England) 30 August 1851, 4. The skilful execution with this media often astonished viewers.

40 'North American Indians Sufferers by the Great Exhibition', *The Colonial Intelligencer; or, Aborigines' Friend* (London, England) 1 October 1851, 304.

41 'The Iroquois Chiefs and Warriors ...', *Morning Advertiser* 19 August 1851. My emphasis.

42 *Ashton Weekly Reporter & Stalybridge & Dukinfield Chronicle* (Lancashire), 5.

43 *Dumfries and Galloway Standard,* 14 May 1856, 1; *Liverpool Daily Post,* 8 November 1862, 9; *Alloa Advertiser* (Clackmannanshire, Scotland) 7 December 1867; *London Evening Standard,* 13 March 1889; *Bristol Mercury,* 22 August 1896, 8; *Freeman's Journal* (Dublin), 2, 4, and 6 October 1897, 1. For a 'Children's Exhibition and Sale of Work' including moccasins and snowshoes, *West Cumberland Times,* 26 April 1893, 4.

44 R. Harvey Fleming, ed., *Minutes of Council, Northern Department of Rupert Land, 1821–1831* (Toronto: The Champlain Society, 1940), 124, 159, 191–2, 222, n1 p124. I thank Prof. Gerhard Ens and John Cole for bringing this directive to my attention.

45 Racette, 'Looking for Stories and Unbroken Threads', 289. See also, *Norbert Welsh, The Last Buffalo Hunter* (New York: Thomas Nelson and Sons, 1939), 291–2.

46 Ulinka Rublack, 'Matter in the Material Renaissance', *Past & Present* 219 (2013): 56.

47 *Aberdeen Press and Journal,* 29 December 1926, 12.

48 Advertisements of moccasin 'slippers', in varieties of leather and finishings, include *Hastings & St Leonards Observer* (Sussex), 13 December 1924; *Derby Daily Telegraph,* 18 December 1924; *Aberdeen Press and Journal,* 12 December 1925 and 29 December 1926; *Cheltenham Chronicle,* 26 December 1925; *Southern Reporter* (Selkirkshire, Scotland), 31 December 1925.

49 Hall and Rose, 'Introduction', 25.

50 Thrush, *Indigenous London,* 3.

51 'Opening of the Caithness Industrial Exhibition', *John o'Groat Journal* (Caithness, Scotland), 5 March 1868, 2.

52 Alison K. Brown, with Christina Massan and Alison Grant, 'Christina Massan's Beadwork and the Recovery of a Fur Trade Family History', in *Recollecting: Lives of Aboriginal Women of the Canadian Northwest and Borderlands,* eds. Sarah Carter and Patricia A. McCormack (Edmonton: Athabasca University Press, 2011), 89–111.

53 Emma Rothschild, *The Inner Life of Empires: An Eighteenth-Century History* (Princeton: Princeton University Press, 2011).

54 *Cheshire Observer,* 6 July 1878.

55 Margot Finn, 'Colonial Gifts: Family Politics and the Exchange of Goods in British India, c. 1780–1820', *Modern Asian Studies* 40, no. 1 (2006): 205.

56 *Cheshire Observer,* 6 July 1878.

57 'Nine Months in America', *Exeter & Plymouth Gazette*, 25 February 1870; 'A Narrative of a Short Residence in Lower Canada …', *The New Monthly Magazine*, April 1868, 476.

58 Tony Ballantyne, 'The Changing Shape of the Modern British Empire and its Historiography', *Historical Journal* 53, no. 2 (2010): 451; Phillips, *Trading Identities*; Claire Wintle, 'Negotiating the Colonial Encounter: Making Objects for Export in the Andaman Islands, 1858–1920', in *Craft, Community and the Material Culture*, 143–60.

PART FOUR

The Age of Global Trade: Goods, Markets, and Trade

14

Who Knew How? Visual Representations of the Ceramics Production Process on Porcelain Vessels

Anne Gerritsen

This chapter discusses a set of illustrations of the manufacture of porcelain, depicted on the surface of porcelain vessels. My interest is in the intersection between knowledge of manufacturing a vessel and the production of that knowledge. In the case of the two eighteenth-century pieces of Chinese ceramics that feature in this chapter, a fish bowl from the Gemeentemuseum in The Hague and a terrine from the Groninger Museum in Groningen, the person who knows how to make a vessel is also the person who produces knowledge about how to make a vessel. The painter of the illustrations on the surface of the vessel is a maker, a craftsperson, someone who has the embodied knowledge that allows them to make the piece. At the same time, this person is also the creator of what we might term 'codified knowledge' in visual form that explicitly articulates the technology of making porcelain so that it can be transmitted at distance. This chapter seeks to argue that this combination of knowing and making in a single person that these objects represent is significant because it illustrates that eighteenth-century Europe was not the only place where this combination was possible, as some earlier scholarship has suggested.[1] Moreover, it reminds us of the importance of adding not only the knowledge about making objects but also the objects themselves to discussions about technological change and as a source for understanding the socio-economic implications of technological change.

This short chapter responds to one of the questions Joel Mokyr posed in *The Gifts of Athena*: 'Who knew that which was "known"?'[2] This was not intended to be an epistemological question, but a socio-historical question that could help explain when, where, and why the Industrial Revolution happened. According to Mokyr, so long as there was a divide between 'those who knew things' (i.e. the *savants*) and 'those who made things' (i.e. the *fabricants*)³ there could be no progress. In his view, the two groups only came together in what he termed 'industrial enlightenment' in Europe, and only after 1750, when 'the sharing of knowledge between those who knew things and those who made them' started to become 'a reality.'⁴ Mokyr proposed, in *The Enlightened Economy*, that a 'public culture of knowledge' emerged in eighteenth-century Europe, which allowed for the easy transmission and wide circulation of both the more abstract knowledge of the *savants* as well as the skills and crafts of the practitioners.⁵ This European particularity was contrasted with the period before this and with the circumstances in most other parts of the world where 'what the large majority of workers and peasants knew and believed mattered little as long as there were enough of them to do what they were told by those who knew more.'⁶

In the discussions that followed the various iterations of Mokyr's position, Liliane Hilaire-Pérez argued for the importance of including artisanal knowledge in the discussion and expanding the scope of the modes and genres of communication to be included in our analyses.⁷ Maxine Berg showed the importance of stretching 'Europe' beyond the geographical boundaries of Europe because the *savants* were also very interested in the useful knowledge that could be gathered in India, for example.⁸ But in principle, Mokyr's argument that something happened in Europe that could never have happened anywhere else stands. In fact, Mokyr stated explicitly that, apart from in medicine, in fields such as 'engineering, mechanics, chemistry, mining and agriculture, the savants and the fabricants in China were as far or further apart from one another as they ever were in Europe.'⁹ I would like to suggest here that the two porcelain depictions of making porcelain demonstrate that the coming together of *savants* and *fabricants* was also possible beyond Europe, in this case in eighteenth-century China where these two objects demonstrate at least the possibility that artisans were also participants in the production of knowledge about making. To substantiate this claim, I will begin by demonstrating that the textual tradition about porcelain production in seventeenth- and eighteenth-century China should be understood as codified knowledge and that the visual materials produced about the multiple steps required for the manufacture of porcelain should equally be considered 'codified knowledge.' This visual material, known as *tu*, (lit. illustration) about the manufacture of porcelain, which appeared over the centuries in many forms and on a range of surfaces, circulated between the imperial court, the site of manufactures, and the global art market, as Ellen Huang has shown. The two porcelain pieces under discussion here allow us to pay attention to the perspective of the artisan who both decorated the vessels and participated in the process of creating codified knowledge.

One of the key texts about the manufacture of porcelain in China is the 'Records of Jingdezhen ceramics' (*Jingdezhen taolu*). The information contained in this treaty was initially assembled by Lan Pu, who died in 1795. In 1815, Lan Pu's material was revised and supplemented by Zheng Tinggui, and in 1891 a further amended and illustrated edition appeared.[10] The 'Records of Jingdezhen ceramics' contains detailed information about the manufacture of porcelain that not only spans the late eighteenth and nineteenth centuries but also integrates information from much earlier written sources. By the late eighteenth century, Jingdezhen, the city in southern Jiangxi province where most of the porcelain production for the imperial court was located, had already been the focus of texts narrating the production processes for many centuries, including 'Notes of ceramics' (*Taoji*), a thirteenth-century description of the variety of goods that were produced in Jingdezhen and traded throughout the region and a detailed section of a sixteenth-century Jiangxi gazetteer with information about manufacturing processes, prices of raw materials, and quantities of production.[11] As early as the mid-nineteenth century, the text of 'Records of Jingdezhen ceramics' was also known in the West, through the 1856 translation into French by Stanislav Julien (1797–1873), entitled *Histoire et Fabrication de la Porcelaine Chinoise*.[12] In Berg's discussion of Mokyr's concept, she identified that 'useful knowledge' should include propositional as well as prescriptive knowledge – in other words, both the 'what' and the 'how' – moreover, that knowledge should be 'collective across society as a whole,' 'accessible,' and 'shared with others.'[13] On that basis, the information that was contained in these texts about the manufacture of porcelain was, I would argue, 'useful knowledge.'

The textual knowledge produced about the manufacture of porcelain was complemented by materials in visual form. The history of visual representations of the manufacture of porcelain goes back to Song Yingxing's *Tiangong kaiwu*, a title that can be translated as 'The works of heaven and the inception of things.'[14] This seventeenth-century text features detail on many aspects of the material world, including a chapter in six sections on aspects of ceramics manufacture. As Ellen Huang has discussed, the thirteen woodblock illustrations included in this text provide visual clues about ceramics production, including the moulding of clay, the making of tiles and jars, and the loading of the kilns.[15] The illustrations do not appear in a specific sequence, and of course these thirteen images do not illustrate all of the seventy-two separate steps in the ceramics manufacturing process that Song Yingxing described. In the eighteenth century, during the reign of the Qiánlong emperor (1735–96), several sets of illustrations that made up a single album were produced representing the manufacturing processes as separate steps. These could be viewed as a sequence, beginning with the preparation of the clay and the transport of raw materials, all the way to the final stages of packaging and transporting the finished pieces of porcelain. As scholars have pointed out, such illustrations are a specific genre, known as *tu*, 'technical images' which guided the viewer to action, as distinct from more descriptive visual genres such as paintings (*hua*) and images (*xiang*).[16] These *tu* often worked in conjunction with text and should be seen as instructive, regardless of whether they were representational (including, for example, drawings of agricultural implements or machines used for spinning and weaving) or diagrammatic (including, for example, symbolic representations of the transformative path to enlightenment, which required reflection and study). *Tu* were 'seen as capable of conveying a broad range of specialist knowledge and skills that were "technological" in the sense that they were meant to be of some kind of "practical" use.'[17] In that sense, then, these visual materials should also be understood as codified knowledge.

Some of these albums, three of which are extant today, were made explicitly for the emperor. They contained a sequence of twenty illustrations that were accompanied by explanatory descriptions produced in 1743 by Tang Ying (1682–1756), the court official who had spent several decades based in Jingdezhen as overseer of the imperial kilns.[18] While the albums of paintings produced at the imperial court were intended for the emperor and did not circulate beyond the court, Tang Ying's textual explanations of Jingdezhen's manufacturing process did circulate and received a new set of illustrations in the 1815 edition of the 'Records of Jingdezhen ceramics' mentioned above.[19] The sequence of illustrations begins with maps of Jingdezhen and continues with the fundamentals of the process, such as mining of the stone, preparation of the clay, shaping the various forms, adding underglaze decorations, glazing the wares, and placing the pieces in the kiln, interspersed with the various subsidiary processes, such as grinding down the cobalt pigment, making the saggars, and opening and closing the smaller kilns used for second-firing the enamel glazes. From the early seventeenth century onwards, then, both textual and visual knowledge about the processes of manufacture circulated throughout the Chinese empire.

Figure 14.1 is made up of two images that illustrate the shaping of ceramic vessels. On the right-hand side, in the foreground, a figure carries a long wooden plank over his right shoulder. The plank is bending

Figure 14.1   Illustrations from Lan Pu and Zheng Tingjian, 'Records of Jingdezhen ceramics' (*Jingdezhen taolu*), 1815, repr. 1891.

under the weight of the twelve or more bowls placed on top of the plank. In the open workshop space to his right we see a potter at work, with feet either side of the turning wheel, his back hunched forward, and his hands lifting the shape up from the wheel. A frame surrounds his wheel and a plank rests on top of the frame to allow the potter to place the finished shapes on the plank. Another worker seems to be rushing past, holding a larger shape in his hands. The left-hand image shows another open workshop space with three separate workstations. The figure to the right is kneading the clay, the three workers in the middle are together shaping a much larger vessel on a wheel, and to the far left of the shop another pot is being turned. To the right and left of the two workshops stand larger vats, on the right-hand side covered with lids. In the foreground, a figure seems to be working on a tall vase with a narrow neck. Trees, mountains, and rocks frame the workshops, suggesting a rural setting. The two characters in the lower right-hand corner of the image on the right read *zuo pi* (做坯), "making clay bodies."

The visual information about the production processes of porcelain also circulated in the West in the form of albums, made up of between six and fifty silk or paper leaves.[20] These albums for the overseas market included detail on the commercial processes that were not part of the visual story of imperial porcelain, including the painting of wares with

Figure 14.2   Porcelain fish bowl depicting the production of ceramics, 1730–50, Jingdezhen, China.

decorative elements of specific interest to overseas consumers such as foreign flags or ships, and the commercial transactions that happened around porcelain shops in Canton. Collectively, as Huang's important essay has shown, these sets of illustrations should be understood as part of the same continuum of visual information about the porcelain production process. The images of the manufacture of porcelain circulated in various forms, such as the albums of paintings created and annotated at the imperial court, the woodblock prints created in or near Jingdezhen, and albums of watercolours or gouache popular with consumers in Japan, Europe, and America.[21] Rather than seeing these as entirely separate media, genres, and markets, Huang argues that we should see these materials as part of a connected international art market, not one belonging 'only to the growing market for porcelain in Europe or America.'[22] Knowledge production about manufacturing processes emerges from circulation, exchange, and cultural interaction both within the Chinese empire and throughout the world.

The genre of visual depiction that receives only a very brief mention by Huang is the representation of production processes on porcelain.[23] The bowl in figure 14.2 is an example of this genre: a fish bowl made between 1730 and 1750, now held at the Gemeentemuseum in The Hague

Figure 14.3 A–B   Details of figure 14.2.

(Netherlands).[24] On the inside of the bowl the illustration of a bright carp suggests the use of the bowl for keeping fish.

On the outside, we see a series of scenes depicting aspects of the ceramics manufacturing process. The scenes are separated by wooden beams that make up separate workshop spaces. On the far left of figure 14.2, a seated person has his back towards us as he works on a vase-like shape placed before him. Some objects in unusual shapes are drying on a table in the same space, with what looks like saggars placed under that table. In the next workshop space, closer to the middle of the side of the pot facing the viewer, two workers are working side by side. Their backs are towards each other, but their faces are turned to suggest interaction between the two men. The figure on the left is shaping clay into mounds, two of which are placed on a small table by his side; on the right, a man bends over a higher table, kneading the clay. Next to them, in the middle of figure 14.3A, a man sits astride a framed pottery wheel, the stick used for pushing the wheel into motion placed across the frame. The black tool in his hands is used to sharpen the edges of the

Figure 14.4   Detail of figure 14.2.

base of the upturned bowl before him. On the left, in figure 14.2A, two
men face each other, one standing by a larger vat, holding a small cup
in his right hand, the other seated astride another wheel (figure 14.3A).

The other side of the bowl, out of sight in figure 14.2, shows the
bricked-up opening of the kiln, a pile of saggars, and a man carrying
two planks, loaded with finished bowls, towards the wooden frame of
drying racks (figure 14.4).

The black and white images do not do justice to the bright colours
of this fish bowl. The clay and the pots are a delicate yellow; the workers'
clothing is rendered in dusty pink, mauve, and turquoise green; the trees
are a vibrant green; and the bricks of the kiln a warm terracotta hue.
The floral pattern framing the scenes and surrounding the foot of the
bowl, as well as the lip on the inside of the bowl add further colourful
variety to the piece. Clearly, the bowl was made to be attractive; perhaps
it was intended as a centrepiece on a finely dressed dining table to
stimulate conversation? Punch bowls certainly fulfilled this function
on the eighteenth-century dining table, although the average punch
bowl was much smaller in height and diameter than this fish bowl.[25]
Wherever this fish bowl was placed, it was intended to be seen and the
detailed decorations were intended to communicate something about
the making of porcelain.

Knowledge is not merely about the mechanics of making; it is also
about visualisation and imagination, about translation and dissemination, about visual, verbal, and written languages.[26] Visual representations
do their work of communication in very different ways from textual
representations. There are further participants in that process of
communication, namely, the creator of the design and the actual painter
of the decorations on the pot. We know nothing about those two, and
yet, in the moment that we look at the work of a painter of ceramics
depicting the work of making ceramics, we adjust our gaze, as we might
do when looking at a painting of a painter's studio. The confluence
of the act and the depiction of the act tempts us into 'reading' the
information in the image in a different way. We imagine the painter

looking around his or her environment and using this view to inform the depiction. Of course, nothing is further from the truth. What we are looking at is shaped by the conventions of the genre, in this case of porcelain decorations. The red bat (*fu* in Chinese) flying past the entrance of the kiln is there because *fu* also means 'good fortune', and red is the colour of joy, as well as filling up an empty space. The seated animal that looks slightly like a dog is probably a deer (*lu* in Chinese), which also means 'emolument', and thus good fortune. The shapes of the clouds, rocks, trees, and flowers are all in line with conventional depictions, and thus, of course, they convey general messages rather than specific information about the natural environment of the kilns. Moreover, there are technological limitations to the possibilities of representation here. The colours of the bowl are determined not only by the artistic preferences of the painter but also by the palette of enamel colours available in Jingdezhen in the early eighteenth century. The level of detail is limited not by the level of knowledge of the painter but by the size of the brush, the size of the pot, and the eyesight of the painter.

And yet, there are some aspects of these details that are not bound by convention or technicality, that provide us with insight into the mind and hand of the painter. For example, the workers all have slightly different hats and hairstyles. There are various cotton hats as well as a straw hat; there are loose queues, knotted braids, as well as two workers with the queue wound around their heads, giving the appearance of a thin crown atop their otherwise shaven forehead. One of the workers is pressing a bit of tobacco in his pipe while he sits at the pottery wheel to sharpen the edges of the upturned bowl between his knees. The worker carrying the two planks with pots over his shoulder is using the tips of his fingers to control the movement of the planks, rather than the grip of his whole hand. These might seem irrelevant details, but they convey a message of personal insight and bodily experience to the inexperienced viewer. The message conveyed is that the viewer is the outsider, and the creator of the image is the insider. The creator of the image, therefore, is the one who has the knowledge about making; s/he is 'the one who knew how.'

The tureen in figure 14.5, made between 1750 and 1775 in Jingdezhen (China), illustrates these points. The painter created a decorative scheme on the surface of the terrine that follows the established conventions of such objects, with a geometrical pattern on the band around the edge of the lid and the terrine, and trees, rocks, and flowering bushes that formed part of the decorative repertoire of the porcelain painters. The composition of the scene also follows the conventions of the illustrations of porcelain production: workshop spaces with an open front under a

Figure 14.5   Lidded tureen, blue-and-white porcelain, decorated with a depiction of
the production of porcelain, 1750–75, Jingdezhen, China.

sloping roof, facing a central space where a rack allows for the drying
of the long planks of objects, with individual workers traversing the
space and performing a variety tasks, at different stations, alone or in
small groups. The illustration depicts technical know-how about the
variety of tasks and spaces, the production of different shapes and sizes,
different methods for carrying and drying, the multiple postures associated with the bodies of the labourers. It is not a painting or a symbolic
representation; instead, it is the kind of depiction that is associated
with action, as Francesca Bray has identified. It is codified knowledge,
in the sense that the information is conveyed by means of a formal
language of porcelain decoration, using an underlying 'grammar' in
the composition that allows for the communication of the detail. The
conventions of porcelain painting such as the smaller diagonal lines that
pass by the feet of the workers allow for the viewer to understand the
movement of bodies and objects between the different workstations,
to reflect on the frequency and repetitive nature of that movement, and
imagine the weight of the goods carried. The viewer's understanding of
perspective allows for the blue and white diagonal lines to represent the

undulating shapes of the roof tiles, the protection from bright sunlight and rain they provide and the difference between covered workspace and open space, where the sunlight is needed for drying the pieces. There is repetition in the postures, too: the standing figure whose brush is held at head height, touching an object on a stand before him or her appears on the lid, in the top workstation and again very near the foot-ring of the terrine, confirming the multiple workstations where similar tasks are performed. In each of these stations, the worker is facing the object to be painted positioned in the middle of a wider platform over a narrower stem, which conveys meaning about the necessity of space to produce a continuous decoration on a round object. The grammar, or the conventions of the genre, allow for the producer of the knowledge to convey the specifics regardless of the distances in time and space between producer and consumer of that knowledge.

Objects traded between Asia and Europe have conventionally been described as 'objects of encounter.'[27] The Victoria and Albert Museum devoted an entire exhibition in 2004 to such objects, aptly entitled 'Encounters: The Meeting of Asia and Europe 1500–1800.'[28] The term 'encounter', however, suggests separation, differentiation, and the primacy of initiation of contact between Asia and Europe. The encounters narrative served the field of global history well because it allowed for objects 'to provide a method of global history', and to serve as the mediators between global and local.[29] As the objects in this chapter demonstrate, however, objects are not isolated representations of one culture that convey their story to another. They are collaborative and multilateral products that move in the space that connects Asia and Europe and thus play a key role in the production and circulation of knowledge. More importantly, these objects allow us to see how the *savants* and the *fabricants* – the person who knew what and the person who knew how – come together in one. This one exceptional case may not be enough to counter the argument put forward by Mokyr, which rests on extensive and wide-ranging evidence. The existence of one counter example, however, suggests at the very least the theoretical possibility of the opposite of Mokyr's argument being true. The two objects discussed in this paper show that Europe was not the only place where this combination was possible; knowing and making can come together in a single person, in this case in eighteenth-century China.

Notes

1 This will be discussed in detail below, but in the first place, I refer here to the work of Joel Mokyr.
2 Joel Mokyr, *The Gifts of Athena: Historical Origins of the Knowledge Economy* (Princeton: Princeton University Press, 2002), 2. In a different publication, Mokyr's question was posed as follows: 'Who knew "that which was known" and how did they use it?' See Joel Mokyr, 'Long-Term Economic Growth and the History of Technology,' in *Handbook of Economic Growth*, vol. 1, part B, eds. Philippe Aghion and Steven Durlauf (Amsterdam: Elsevier, 2005), 1119.
3 Mokyr, 'Long-Term Economic Growth,' 1138.
4 Mokyr, *Gifts of Athena*, 35.
5 Joel Mokyr, *The Enlightened Economy: Britain and the Industrial Revolution, 1700–1850* (New Haven: Yale University Press, 2009).
6 Joel Mokyr, *A Culture of Growth: The Origins of the Modern Economy* (Princeton: Princeton University Press, 2017), 282.
7 Liliane Hilaire-Pérez, 'Technology as a Public Culture in the Eighteenth Century: The Artisans' Legacy,' *History of Science* 45, no. 2 (2007): 135–53; see also Maxine Berg, 'The Genesis of "Useful Knowledge"' *History of Science* 45, no. 2 (2007): 123.
8 Maxine Berg, 'Passionate Projectors: Savants and Silk on the Coromandel Coast 1780–98,' *Journal of Colonialism and Colonial History* 14, no. 3 (2013).
9 Joel Mokyr, 'King Kong and Cold Fusion,' in *Unmaking the West: 'What-If' Scenarios That Rewrite World History*, eds. Philip E. Tetlock, Richard Ned Lebow, and Geoffrey Parker (Ann Arbor: University of Michigan Press, 2006), 303; Kenneth Pomeranz, in his contribution to the same volume, argued more or less the same thing, claiming that 'as far as we know artisans were largely outside even such networks of scientific correspondence as were developing in seventeenth- and eighteenth-century China.' Kenneth Pomeranz, 'Without Coal? Colonies? Calculus? Counterfactuals & Industrialization in Europe & China,' in *Unmaking the West*, 260.
10 Lan Pu and Zheng Tinggui, *Jingdezhen taolu [Records of Jingdezhen ceramics]*, Jingdu shuyetang cangban, 1891.
11 For more detail on these texts, see, for example, Anne Gerritsen, 'Ceramics for Local and Global Markets: Jingdezhen's Agora of Technologies,' in *Cultures of Knowledge: Technology in Chinese History*, eds. Dagmar Schäfer and Francesca Bray (Leiden: Brill 2012), 164–86.
12 Stanislas Aignan Julien, trans., *Histoire et Fabrication de La Porcelaine Chinoise* (Paris: Mallet-Bachelier, 1856); for an English translation, see Lan Pu, *Ching-Te-Chen T'ao-Lu: Or the Potteries of China; Being a Translation with Notes and an Introduction by Geoffrey R. Sayer*, trans. Geoffrey Robley Sayer (London: Routledge and K. Paul, 1951).

13 Berg, 'Genesis of "Useful Knowledge"', 124; referring to Mokyr, *The Gifts of Athena*, 6–7.

14 Song Yingxing 宋应星, *Tiangong kaiwu* 天工开物 *[The works of heaven and the inception of things]* (1636; repr., Beijing: Zhongguo shehui chubanshe, 2004), 203–30.

15 Ellen C. Huang, 'From the Imperial Court to the International Art Market: Jingdezhen Porcelain Production as Global Visual Culture', *Journal of World History* 23, no. 1 (2012): 125–6.

16 Bray refers to *tu* as 'templates for action'. Francesca Bray, 'Introduction: The Powers of Tu', in *Graphics and Text in the Production of Technical Knowledge in China: The Warp and the Weft*, Sinica Leidensia, v. 79, eds. Francesca Bray, Vera Dorofeeva-Lichtmann, and Georges Métailie (Leiden: Brill, 2007), 2.

17 Peter J. Golas, *Picturing Technology in China – From Earliest Times to the Nineteenth Century* (Hong Kong: Hong Kong University Press, 2015), xix.

18 Peter Lam, 'Tang Ying (1682–1756): The Imperial Factory Superintendent at Jingdezhen', *Transactions of the Oriental Ceramics Society* 63 (1998–99): 65–82; For details on the three known albums, see Huang, 'From the Imperial Court to the International Art Market', 127–8.

19 Huang, 'From the Imperial Court to the International Art Market', 137.

20 Jane Sze and Caroline Lang, eds., *Trading China: Paintings of the Porcelain Production Process in the Qing Dynasty* (Hong Kong: Hong Kong Maritime Museum, 2015), 84–5.

21 Ibid., 143.

22 Huang, 'From the Imperial Court to the International Art Market', 144–5.

23 Ibid., 135.

24 The Gemeentemuseum fish bowl is one of only two known examples of this type. The other is a fish bowl with very similar decoration, dated 1735, sold by Cohen and Cohen. See Cohen and Cohen, Chinese export porcelain and oriental art, https://www.cohenandcohen.co.uk/objectdetail/772528/0/sold-chinese-export-porcelain-making.

25 Maxine Berg, *Luxury and Pleasure in Eighteenth-Century Britain* (Oxford: Oxford University Press, 2010), 72–3.

26 Katie Scott and Helen Clifford, 'Introduction: Disseminating Design: The French Connection', *Journal of Design History* 17, no. 1 (2004): 1.

27 See, for example, the introduction by Berg in *Goods from the East, 1600–1800: Trading Eurasia*, eds. Maxine Berg, Felicia Gottman, Chris Nierstrasz, and Hannah Hodacs (Basingstoke: Palgrave, 2015), 5; or, for another example, Nicholas Thomas et al., *Artefacts of Encounter: Cook's Voyages, Colonial Collecting and Museum Histories* (Honolulu: Otago University Press, 2016).

28 Anna Jackson and Amin Jaffer, eds., *Encounters: The Meeting of Asia and Europe 1500–1800* (London: V&A Publications, 2004).

29 Berg et al., *Goods from the East*, 4.

15

Factories before the Factory: The English East India Company's Textile Procurement in India and British Industrialisation, 1650–1750

Giorgio Riello

In his 1838 *A Dictionary, Practical, Theoretical and Historical, of Commerce*, the Scottish economist John Ramsay McCullock defined the term 'factory' in a way that was fast becoming outdated. He explained that starting in 1612, and following the example of the Portuguese and Dutch, the English East India Company (EEIC) established its first 'factory' in Surat 'to serve as depots – for the goods collected in the country for exportation to Europe.'[1] The name 'factory' derived from having a 'factor' in charge of trading ports used for the assembling, processing, packing, and eventual sending of Asian goods to Europe. Factories, McCullock explained, were central to the English and other European companies' 'schemes for monopolising the commerce' of India in the seventeenth and eighteenth centuries, especially that of textiles.[2]

Today, the term 'factory' has come to signify solely a place where commodities are produced replacing the terms 'mill' and 'manufactory' in the course of the nineteenth century. Yet, the use of the term factory to designate both a productive and a commercial space is no coincidence. This paper starts by considering recent literature that has emphasised the link between global commerce and the productive and economic transformation of the European economy that led to industrialisation. Particular attention has been given to the role that Asian goods procured in India (and handled through 'commercial' factories) played in stimulating innovation in Europe (and the subsequent rise of 'industrial' factories). This work has connected Asian manufactures to the technological and material transformation of European production in the classic era of industrialisation. By considering the case of Madras, this chapter extends these arguments by going back to the Indian factories and by showing how the several challenges the EEIC faced in the procurement of textiles provided a stimulus for the reconfiguration of manufacturing in Britain leading to the rise of a new type of factory: the large-scale mills of the Industrial Revolution.

Global Trade and Quality Products

Until the 1980s the literature on trade and on manufacturing remained rather separate. With the exception of theories that posited that eighteenth-century European trade – mostly in the Atlantic – was vital to capital accumulation needed to finance large-scale mechanised production, it was thought that British and European industrialisation relied on factors endogenous to their economic systems.[3] The acknowledgement of the large quantities of Asian goods imported to and consumed in Europe did little to revise established industrial narratives. By relying on supply-led models, economic historians remained reluctant to acknowledge the role that consumption played in reshaping production.

Since the late 1980s new research on the 'consumer revolution' and on the 'industrious revolution' has done much to revise these narratives. Jan de Vries, notably, linked consumer preferences to working hours and participation in the labour market especially by women. He extended the narrative of industrialisation to include decentralized, labour-intensive activities that increased household incomes used to purchase both necessities and what have been labelled as 'niceties', namely luxury goods that included Asian commodities.[4]

In the early 2000s, Maxine Berg proposed that Asian commodities such as Chinese porcelain, Indian textiles, and Japanese lacquerware reshaped not just the consuming habits of Europeans but also their ideas of products and, in consequence, their manufacturing practices. She explained that these 'exotic' commodities brought about a 'product revolution' in Europe and stimulated technological innovation as well as changing expectations among consumers and producers alike.[5] Indian calicoes were imported into Europe in their millions every year and accounted for perhaps a quarter of all textiles arriving in England in the eighteenth century. Beautifully printed and painted Indian cloths came to be coveted products by consumers, but they also fostered product innovation on the part of textile manufacturers and merchants. Thus, the story of how Britain became the nation of a cotton-textile revolution is strongly entwined with long-lasting attempts at imitating Indian cottons. This was not a simple process of import-substitution as development economists have long maintained but one of adaptation of products, familiarization of taste, and technological innovation.[6] The search for goods that could rival their Indian or Chinese counterparts led to the invention of new technologies, techniques, and processes that in turn

expanded into altogether new productive methods such as the use of
copperplate printing and new mordanting techniques for cotton textiles,
transfer-printing on porcelain, and new ways of producing lacquerware
unknown in Asia.[7]

The global trade in luxury goods had a profound impact on the
quality of the goods produced in Europe. From a material point of view,
Asian commodities were appreciated for their superior quality, be it the
translucent nature and thinness of porcelain compared to the opacity of
European earthenware, or the brightness and fastness of colour of Indian
chintzes compared to the fugitive and shadowy dyes of many European
woollens and linens. Both Maxine Berg and Prasannan Parthasarathi
have argued that the process of European industrialisation cannot be
interpreted as a simple search for cheaper methods of production or
increased productivity that allowed European producers to compete
against the low-wage economies of eighteenth-century India and China.[8]
Traditional cost-reducing models should be accompanied by an explanation of technological innovation and industrialisation resulting from
a search for quality.[9] The success of European industrially produced
commodities lay not just in their cheapness but also in being of as good
a quality as those produced in Asia.

Today the Industrial Revolution cannot be narrated as a separate
episode in the history of British or indeed European industrialisation.
Global history has promoted the view of a 'global industrial revolution'
shaped by trade. Yet there are two implicit drawbacks in this broader
narrative of economic development and global divergence. First, the
fact that Europe is presented as reactive to external challenges. There is
now sufficient ground to argue that there might have been an iterative
process in which both European and Asian products changed because
of world trade.[10] Notwithstanding the fact that Asian products were of
central importance to European innovation in eighteenth-century (and
indeed long before) European manufacturing, we know little about
their production and merchandising. Second, more agency needs to be
attributed to South Asia and its producers without falling into the trap
of assuming that Asian products were always matched perfectly with
European consumer demand or that their procurement was a smooth
business. Quite the opposite: the EEIC's correspondence and factory
reports detail the enormous challenges encountered by the company
in being supplied with the right type of cloth. The rest of this chapter
focuses on the EEIC's business operation at Fort St George in Madras,
one of the most important ports for the procurement of textiles by
the company during the second half of the seventeenth and the first
half of the eighteenth century. I am particularly interested in showing

how standards were central to the definition of quality. My argument here is that quality was central but that quality was as much defined by European producers and consumers as it was by Asian artisans and servants of the European companies in South Asia.

The Procurement System in India: The Case of Madras

Where did the Indian cotton cloth in demand among European consumers come from? Factories acted as information nodes and assembly points where commodities for trade back to Europe or to other parts of the Indian Ocean were checked, sorted, packed, and loaded on ships.[11] Production was carried out across vast areas in the hinterland with spinning employing literally millions of women and weaving hundreds of thousands of men in the different textile-producing areas of South Asia – and especially in Gujarat, the Malabar Coast, the Coromandel Coast, and Bengal. The organisation of production varied markedly, yet two features characterised the textile procurement business of the European companies. The first is that weaving was carried out in villages often specialised in the production of one or more types of cloth where weavers acted as independent artisans. Access by the East India companies was limited, something that they had acknowledged since their early days in India. On the Coromandel Coast, weaving villages were often scattered in the countryside and characterised by small communities sometimes totally employed in the weaving of up to 150 different varieties of cloth.[12] At other times procurement stretched inland, to larger communities: the 1772 census of the sizeable weaving town of Arani in Tamil Nadu, 150 kilometres inland from Madras, reveals that out of 246 households, ninety-nine were weaving cloth, sixty-eight were spinning cotton, and forty households belonged to the castes of the lomatties and chetties, which suggests that they were engaged in the trade of cloth.[13]

Access to productive places such as Arani was limited for Europeans, a feature shared with the production of most of the Asian commodities that they traded in. The Chinese porcelain, considered by Anne Gerritsen in this book, was produced hundreds of miles from the trading ports. Similarly Indian calicoes and chintzes were often woven in places far removed from trading ports. The second feature of the East India companies' procurement system was that they had to rely on a series of intermediaries, starting with commissioning agents operating from the major coastal centres often in partnerships. They in turn made use of other 'intermediary merchants' (or brokers – sometimes referred to as *delols*), who agreed the type of cloth to be produced, the quantity, price, and date of delivery. An intermediary might commission an order by using in turn a series of other intermediaries (sometimes known as *picars*) within the village itself who received a small commission around 1–2 per cent of the price. Other intermediaries might include gomastas (*gumashtas*) and head-weavers, who in their turn might employ sometimes up to a hundred weavers.[14]

These complex and geographically articulated relationships were regulated by contracts and cash advances. Cash advances were necessary to support weaving households during the months (up to six) when the cloth was being produced. If the production of cloth was dispersed and difficult to control, the finishing stages (dyeing, printing, and designing) were normally located nearer to the factories. In the 1670s, European traders reported that in Madras the division of labour in finishing was highly refined with dyers, woodblock cutting, and designing with charcoal on textiles located near the city.[15] This allowed to a certain extent customization of production to suit European tastes. Yet the fact that Indian printers had long been producing cloth for markets across the Indian Ocean did not mean that the requests of European traders always found ready acceptance: from the perspective of Indian producers, the European East India companies were just one group among the many buyers of cloth for international markets.

The chiefs ('factors') in charge of the factories were sent precise instructions and provided with musters (samples of the required cloth). A letter sent from the factory at Fort St George in Madras to the subfactory at Fort St David, a hundred miles south in Cuddalore, explained that musters were 'to shew you the goodness of the cloth, and the brightness of the Dye' though it was added that 'you must direct the Weavers when they make them to vary the checks that they may not be too many of one Pattern, and there must be no mixture of Red in any of them.'[16] The rise of calico printing in Europe from the last quarter of the seventeenth century has been interpreted as the rational response of the EEIC to the difficulties in being supplied with the right type of designs. As Europeans preferred lighter coloured backgrounds with small flowers, one solution was found in printing in Europe on white cotton cloth imported from South Asia. I have shown elsewhere that during the eighteenth century a large part of the EEIC textile cargo was composed not of printed textiles but of white and bleached Indian cloth that was destined for printing in places such as London, Orange in France, Mulhouse, and in several Swiss cities. European calico printing presented a technological challenge that was mastered through knowledge transfer from India and the Middle East in the course of the first half of the eighteenth century.[17]

The substitution of only one part of a chain of production relied on the purchase of semifinished goods (white and bleached cloth) in India. It allowed the production of designs suited to European consumers thus avoiding the long time (two years) needed to send an order to India and receive back the finished cloth. It also allowed domestic specialisation in the high value-added parts of the productive process.

As Maxine Berg demonstrated, the process of import substitution of Asian commodities in Europe was also one of imitation and innovation.[18] The ban enacted by most European governments on the import of Asian textiles (both Indian cottons and Chinese silks) might have provided the institutional framework and protectionism needed to develop a cotton industry in Europe. Yet there were other factors at play, one of which was the increasing price of cotton textile cloth procured in India. While purchase prices in India had been low throughout the first half of the seventeenth century, they increased markedly over the following century.[19] By the mid-1750s the Dutch East India Company (VOC) noted that the prices of *guines* cloth, *salampuri*, and other cloth had increased more than 50 per cent since 1690.[20] The same was the case for the EEIC: the 1690s had been admittedly a good decade when prices had been low and markups (the sale price in London divided by the purchase price in India) four times the purchase price. By the 1750s the price of cloth had more than doubled and the markup was down by 50 per cent.[21]

The problem of lower profit margins for the EEIC was resolved by increasing quantities to satisfy high demand in Europe. In the 1690s the company imported into England 2.3 million pieces of cloth per decade, by the 1750s this had increased to 5.6 million. The EEIC felt the pressure of this strategy on its procurement system in India. The EEIC's archives are replete with complaints about the rising cost of cloth and the inability to secure sufficient supplies. Competition between companies was a factor: the English complained that the VOC had better supply systems on the Coromandel Coast.[22] The Dutch Company had a factory at Pulicat, just thirty kilometres north of Madras, from where they traded a variety of fine *rumals, bethilles, gingams, taftas, chelas,* and *muris* from across the coast as far south as Nagapattinan, 300 kilometres south of Madras. From the Madras area itself, the VOC received the best chintzes available anywhere on the coast in terms of material and workmanship.[23] By the early eighteenth century, the French too were operating from the port of Pondicherry, creating even more pressure on supplies.[24]

The EEIC blamed increasing purchase prices and the difficulties encountered in being supplied with cloth not just on the increasing competition with other companies but also on the power of local

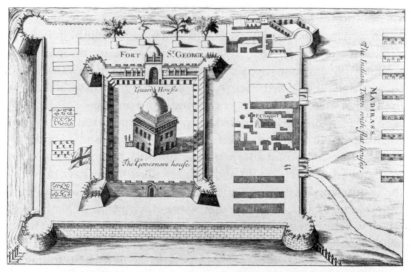

Figure 15.1   Plan of Fort St George in Madras, the English East India Company's
factory, established in 1644.

merchants. The original factory at Fort St George was small, measuring
around a quarter of mile in length and no more than one hundred yards
in width (figure 15.1).[25] Yet especially in the 1670s and 1680s the EEIC
significantly expanded its operations making its presence keenly felt in
the city of Madras. A new building for sorting cloth was added in 1683,
and in 1687 the company granted the city the status of a corporation.[26]

Such a growth was possible thanks to the presence of a large
merchant community with the capital necessary to procure millions
of yards of cloth per year.[27] The company would sometimes put up
notices at the factory gates inviting merchants to present samples from
their weavers.[28] Yet, this was no open market: in 1669, for instance, the
merchant Kasi Viranna (or Veeranna) was appointed chief merchant
of the EEIC in Madras. Over the following decade he was said to have
controlled a quarter of the EEIC's business in South Coromandel where
entire weaving villages were known as 'Viranna's villages'.[29] The EEIC
had little power against such a monopsony. The strong hand enjoyed
by the merchants can be appreciated in their response to a grievance
by the EEIC to which they flippantly replied that 'if the Honorable
Company would or could find other Merchants that could serve them
more cheap, with better goods, and more punctually, they should be
very glad thereof, for they could not'.[30]

Quality Standards and the EEIC
Procurement in India

It has been argued that increasing procurement prices in India, difficulties in being supplied with the required varieties of cloth, and the complexity of conveying design specifications provided the conditions for the development of a cotton industry in Europe. Yet, the explanation put forward for the increasing quality of both cotton yarn and cloth produced in Europe needs to be connected to the trajectory of procurement in India. I argue that the rigid standards of quality applied by the EEIC in India helped to shape the European market for cottons. Rather than importing large quantities of low quality cloth, the company retained high standards. This allowed Indian cotton textiles sold in Britain and North America to maintain stable sale prices in Europe at a time when textile prices more generally were declining.[31] Yet, this strategy had two unforeseen consequences for the development of a British cotton industry. First, by maintaining stable prices, it made it easier for local producers to compete with imported Indian cloth, supplementing rather than replacing the always limited supplies from South Asia. Second, the company created the opposite of a 'market for lemons,' excluding lower varieties that could have led to a general downward spiral of quality and prices.[32] High quality standards were instead upheld: the very standards that British producers eventually managed to attain.

Perhaps the question that needs to be asked is did the EEIC purposely pursue a strategy that privileged quality in its procurement? A tentative answer is that this was no strategy as such but a general rigidity in the EEIC's practices. For sure the company was very much aware of a general decline in quality due to increasing demand. In 1723 the Madras consultations, detailing the business of the factory, reported that merchants 'told us that it was impossible for them to pretend to furnish 4,000 Bales of Cloth which should all exactly answer musters, and that the utmost they can do is to keep their weavers as near as possible to them' and added that

the very large demand lately made has occasion'd the running the Cloth off the Loom so fast 'tis not practicable to keep them justly to the goodness of the muster. That they can always provide the quantity and much more, but that when they do so they cannot pretend to engage for the Goodness, Since it is certain that the People working in a hurry must be more careless and negligent than when they have more time; so that when this place provided

1,000 Bales per annum it was very easy to keep them up to the
Musters, but that now the demand is encreas'd to four times
that quantity it is not reasonable to expect it should be equal
in goodness.[33]

The company attempted to remedy this detrimental situation by
creating a quality classification system that was applied across all cloth
brought to the factory. This included at least three different levels of
quality (No. 1, 2, etc.) for each type of cloth provided by merchants.
Yet the EEIC archives are full of disputes between the company and
merchants. In 1674, for example, it was noted that the merchants had
no doubt 'that they can bring the Weavers to a more exact complyance',
though they insisted that 'whatsoever the kind or quality of the cloth
be, there is no dealing unless there be second and third sorts allowed
of, for what falls short of the perfection of the first; for as they buy so
they must sell'.[34] Clearly merchants felt obliged to accept cloth from
their weavers that was below standard. Yet the EEIC refused to receive
it, arguing that they could not sell inferior qualities as the VOC did: 'The
Dutch Company doo the same, but they vend most of their second and
third sorts in their Spice Islands, Jappon, Maccassar &c., parts of the
South seas, and send only their first sorts for Europe'.[35]

The checking of the quality of the cloth was one of the major
activities carried out in the EEIC factories. This was the job of the
'warehousekeeper' who had to ensure that the cloth delivered matched
the musters provided in terms of yarn count, finishing, and neatness
of work. Occasionally the governor and council would ask for bales of
different types to be taken into the consultation room to 'compare 'em
with the Musters'.[36] More commonly this was work carried out by sorters
who opened up entire bales to avoid being defrauded by having good
quality cloth placed on the top of the bale and cheaper sorts below.
They had also to check that the yarn count was the same across a single
piece of cloth as it was not uncommon for weavers to have a higher
count at the start of a piece continuing with lower counts for the parts
of the cloth that were folded.[37] Warehousekeepers had a difficult job:
they complained that all checks had to be done too quickly as there
was often little time before the cloth had to be loaded and in turn were
accused of accepting bribes from the merchants in order to have low
quality cloth accepted and marked as quality No. 1.[38]

Quality was not just a matter of the intrinsic characteristics of the
cloth or its yarn count. Measurements constituted a further area of
control as consistency of lengths and widths had to be carefully met: 'We
must remind you that you strictly keep your Merchants up to Lengths

and Breadths & goodness of Cloth' recommended one Company servant in Madras in 1722.[39] This was no trivial matter: consumers in Europe were used to very precise lengths and imported textiles had to conform to notions of quality and with the regulations imposed by law.[40] The correspondence of the French East India Company explains that only certain sizes were easily sold in France and advised factors in India to get hold of those 'types of cloth which we get painted in ordinary chittes for France, because of their [suitable] width', though the French admitted that the cheaper varieties 'which are hardly wider than these' might be suitable for the less demanding markets made of 'common people as well as for the American islands'.[41] Even when measurements had been agreed, it was explained, 'The same workers will differ in length – some will give 1 or sometimes 2 fingers more than that ordered, and others will give less'. The EEIC reached similar conclusions when it observed that 'a weaver cannot, with all the skill he hath, make a peece of bafta or stuffe soe thick and well wove, notwithstanding he have the same yarne and the same quantity, in the dry time as they can in the raines or wett time'.[42]

Quality was a problem faced by all European companies. Whilst there is not yet sufficient research to clearly distinguish the tactics adopted by different companies, one can cautiously conclude that the EEIC remained consistently opposed to accepting lower standards. In 1726 the Resident at Metchlepatam in Andhra Pradesh, 500 kilometres north of Madras, was told by his superiors in Fort St George that whilst they acknowledged 'the Difficulty you mention [that] you had to bring the Weavers to agree to the Company's Breadths of the Salampores' he had 'on no account admit of any under that Breadth, which must be full'.[43] A few years earlier the principle was stated as a matter of general practice in Madras itself: 'The Merchants there desire our leave for short cloth to be taken in, on a proportionable abatement. Resolv'd and Agreed that we don't indulge the taking in of any such cloth, but to keep to the Standard of their usuall lengths and breadths, unless in urgent necessity on dispatch of any ship to fill up a vacancy of Tonnage may justify our so doing'.[44]

Conclusion

This chapter has traced the relationship between the procurement of textiles by the EEIC in India and the development of a British cotton industry in the period 1650–1750. Focusing on Madras, it has shown how the quality of the cloth imported into Europe should not be taken as a given category. Quality, rather than productivity, remained a key issue for the development of a viable cotton industry in Britain and more generally in Europe. Yet, this chapter has shown how such 'quality' was the result of both a failure to procure larger quantities of India cloth and the EEIC's rigid practices in admitting only the highest standards of cloth. The road to a 'quality-driven' industrialisation did not therefore just rely on standards set by European consumers and the consequent action of producers in Britain, France, and elsewhere in Europe. It should also be connected to the complex system of procurement of textiles in India, the role played by local merchants and weavers, and the ways in which notions of quality were constructed and upheld by the servants of the EEIC in Asia.

Notes

1   John Ramsay McCulloch, *A Dictionary, Practical, Theoretical and Historical, of Commerce and Commercial Navigation* (London: Printed for Longman, Orme, Brown, Green and Longman, 1838), 521.
2   Ibid.
3   Patrick O'Brien, 'European Economic Development: The Contribution of the Periphery', *Economic History Review* 35, no. 1 (1982): 1–18.
4   Jan de Vries, *The Industrious Revolution: Consumer Behavior and the Household Economy, 1650 to the Present* (Cambridge: Cambridge University Press, 2008); Joan Thirsk, *Economic Policy and Projects: The Development of a Consumer Society in Early Modern England* (Oxford: Clarendon, 1978); Neil McKendrick, John Brewer, and J.H. Plumb, *The Birth of a Consumer Society: The Commercialisation of Eighteenth Century England* (London: Europa, 1982); John Brewer and Roy Porter, eds., *The World of Goods* (London and New York: Routledge, 1993).
5   Maxine Berg, 'New Commodities, Luxuries and Their Consumers in Eighteenth-Century England', in *Consumers and Luxury in Europe, 1650–1850*, eds. Maxine Berg and Helen Clifford (Manchester University Press, 1999), 63–85; Maxine Berg, 'In Pursuit of Luxury: Global History and British Consumer Goods in the Eighteenth Century', *Past & Present* 182 (2004): 85–142. See also John Styles, 'Product Innovation in Early Modern London', *Past & Present*, 168 (2000): 124–69; Maxine Berg, *Luxury and Pleasure in Eighteenth-Century Britain* (Oxford: Oxford University Press, 2005); Beverly Lemire and Giorgio Riello, 'East and West: Textiles and Fashion in Eurasia in the Early Modern Period', *Journal of Social History* 41, no. 4 (2008): 887–916.
6   Maxine Berg, 'From Imitation to Invention: Creating Commodities in Eighteenth-Century Britain', *Economic History Review* 55, no. 1 (2002): 1–30.

7   Giorgio Riello, 'Asian Knowledge and the Development of Calico Printing
    in Europe in the Seventeenth and Eighteenth Centuries', *Journal of Global
    History* 5, no 1 (2010): 1–29; Anne Gerritsen and Stephen McDowall,
    'Material Culture and the Other: European Encounters with Chinese
    Porcelain, ca. 1650–1800', *Journal of World History* 23, no. 1 (2012): 87–114.
8   Maxine Berg, 'Quality, Cotton, and the Global Luxury Trade', in *How India
    Clothed the World: The World of South Asian Textiles, 1500–1850*, eds. Giorgio
    Riello and Tirthankar Roy (Leiden: Brill 2009), 391–414; Prasannan
    Parthasarathi, 'Historical Issues of De-industrialisation in Nineteenth-Century
    India', in *How India Clothed the World*, Riello and Roy, 415–35; Prasannan
    Parthasarathi, *Why Europe Grew Rich and Asia Did Not: Global Economic
    Divergence, 1600–1850* (Cambridge: Cambridge University Press, 2014), xx.
9   For a classic productivity-increasing approach, though globally comparative,
    see: Robert C. Allen, *The British Industrial Revolution in Global Perspective*
    (Cambridge: Cambridge University Press, 2009).
10 Giorgio Riello, *Cotton: The Fabric That Made the Modern World* (Cambridge:
    Cambridge University Press, 2013).
11 Jan de Vries, 'Understanding Eurasian Trade in the Era of the Trading
    Companies', in *Goods from the East*, ed. Maxine Berg et al. (Basingstoke: Palgrave
    2015), 14–15. See also Emily Erikson, *Between Monopoly and Free Trade: The
    English East India Company* (Princeton: Princeton University Press, 2014).
12 K.N. Chaudhuri, 'The Structure of Indian Textile Industry in the
    Seventeenth and Eighteenth Centuries', in *Cloth and Commerce. Textiles
    in Colonia India*, ed. Tirthankar Roy (New Delhi: Sage, 1996), 44. See
    also Karuna Dietrich Wielenga, 'The Geography of Weaving in Early
    Nineteenth-Century South India', *Indian Economic and Social History Review*
    52, no. 2 (2015): 147–84.
13 Sinnappah Arasaratnam, *Merchants, Companies and Commerce on the
    Coromandel Coast, 1650–1740* (Delhi: Oxford University Press, 1986), 267–8.
14 The complexity of these intermediary systems derives from the fact that
    different organisations were in place in different areas of the country. See for
    instance Carla M. Sinopoli, *The Political Economy of Craft Production: Crafting
    Empire in South India, c. 1350–1650* (Cambridge: Cambridge University
    Press, 2003), 186; and Ian C. Wendt, 'The Social Fabric: Textile Industry
    and Community in Early Modern South India' (unpublished PhD thesis,
    University of Wisconsin–Madison, 2005), 145.
15 Mattiebelle Gittinger, *Master Dyers to the World: Technique and Trade in Early
    Indian Dyed Cotton Textiles* (Washington, DC: The Textile Museum, 1982), 61.
16 'To the Worsh. James Hubbard Esq. Deputy Governor & C. Council of Fort
    St. David, 10 July 1739', in *Letters from Fort St George, 1739*. vol. 23 (Madras:
    Printed by the Superintendent, Government Press, 1931), 31.

17 Giorgio Riello, 'The Indian Apprenticeship: The Trade of Indian Textiles and the Making of European Cottons', in *How India Clothed the World: The World of South Asian Textiles, 1500–1850*, eds. Giorgio Riello and Tirthankar Roy (Leiden: Brill, 2009), 309–46; Riello, 'Asian Knowledge'.

18 Berg, 'In Pursuit of Luxury'; Berg, 'From Imitation to Invention'.

19 On cloth prices on the Coromandel Coast see Kanakalatha Nukund, *The Trading World of the Tamil Merchant: Evolution of Merchant Capitalism in the Coromandel* (London: Sangam, 1999), esp. 181–2; and Chris Nierstrasz, *Rivalry for Trade in Tea and Textiles: The English and Dutch East India Companies (1700–1800)* (London: Palgrave, 2015), 171–4.

20 Om Prakash, *The New Cambridge History of India. Vol. II. 5: European Commercial Enterprise in Pre-Colonial India* (Cambridge: Cambridge University, Press 1998), 299.

21 Riello, *Cotton*, chapter 4; on price convergence and decreasing mark-up of Asian goods in Europe see Pim de Zwart, 'Globalization in the Early Modern Era: New Evidence from the Dutch-Asiatic Trade, c. 1600–1800', *Journal of Economic History* 76 no. 2 (2016): 520–58.

22 K.N. Chaudhuri, *The Trading World of Asia and the English East India Company, 1660–1760* (Cambridge: Cambridge University Press, 1978), esp. 245–53 and 299–305.

23 Prakash, *The New Cambridge History of India. Vol. II. 5*, 298–9.

24 Philippe Haudrère and Gérard Bouëdec, *Les Compagnies des Indes* (Rennes: Ouest France, 1999), 80.

25 John Fryer, *A New Account of the East India and Persia, Being Nine Years Travel, 1672–1681*, ed. William Crooke, 3 vols. (London: The Hakluyt Society, 1909), 1: 104. See also the print reproduced on the previous page.

26 H.D. Love, *Vestiges of old Madras, 1640–1800: Traced from the East India Company's Records*, 3 vols. (London: Murray 1913), 1: 471.

27 On the social segregation between the so-called 'white town' of six streets within the perimeter of Fort St George and the 'black town' of more than 100,000 people see Søren Mentz, 'Cultural Intersection between the British Diaspora in Madras and the Host Community, 1650–1790', in *Asian Port Cities, 1600–1800: Local and Foreign Cultural Interactions*, ed. Haneda Masashi (Singapore: National University of Singapore Press, 2009), 167.

28 Jeyaseela Stephen, *Oceanscapes: Tamil Textiles in the Early Modern World* (New Delhi: Primus Books, 2014), 135.

29 *The Travels of the Abbé Carré in India and the Near East, 1672 to 1674*, ed. Charles Fawcett with Richard Burn, 3 vols. (London: The Hakluyt Society, 1947), 605. See also Stephen, *Oceanscapes*, 123–4.

30 *Records of Fort St George: Diary and Consultation Book; Vol. 1. 1672–1678* (Madras: Government Press, 1910): 'Consultation in Fort St George 29 September 1674', 27.

31 Riello, *Cotton*, 108; Maxine Berg, "'The Merest Shadows of a Commodity": Indian Muslins for European Markets, 1750–1800; in *Goods from the East*, eds. Berg et al., 124–5.

32 On the original formulation of the 'market for lemons' see George Akerlof, "'The Market for Lemons": Quality Uncertainty and the Market Mechanism', *Quarterly Journal of Economics* 84 no. 3 (1970): 488–500.

33 *Records of Fort St George: Diary and Consultation Book, 1722–1724* (Madras: Madras Government Press, 1930), 145 (20 December 1723)..

34 *Records of Fort St George: Diary and Consultation Book; Vol. 1. 167–1678* (Madras: Government Press, 1910): 'Consultation in Fort St George 29 September 1674; 28.

35 Ibid.

36 *Records of Fort St George: Diary and Consultation Book, 1699–1702* (Madras: Madras Government Press, 1922), 39 (7 June 1700).

37 On the weavers' methods to conceal defects see Prasannan Parthasarathi, *The Transition to a Colonial Economy: Weavers, Merchants and Kings in South India, 1720–1800* (Cambridge: Cambridge University Press, 2011), 25–6. Eventually in the second half of the eighteenth century the EEIC introduced a double system of checks both by the merchants and in the factory. Ibid., 92–3.

38 *Records of Fort St George: Diary and Consultation Book; Vol. 11. 1692* (Madras: Government Press, 1917): 'Letter of John Nick, 5 July 1692; 27–9.

39 *Letters from Fort St George, 1722–1723.* Vols. 18 and 19 (Madras: Printed by the Superintendent, Government Press, 1931): 'To the Worship. [Will.m] Jennings Esq., Deputy Governor of Fort St David & C., Council, 9 March 1721–2; 7 (no. 9).

40 Philippe Minard, 'Réputation, normes et qualité dans l'industrie textile française au XVIIIᵉ siècle; in *La qualité des produits en France, XVIIIᵉ-XXᵉ siècle*, ed. Alessandro Stanziani (Paris: Belin 2004), 69–92.

41 Archives Nationales de France, Archives d'outre Mer (Aix-en-Provence), C2 67f, 189-189v, Ougly 18 December 1704. Cit. in Indrani Ray, 'The French Company and the Merchants of Bengal (1680–1730); in *The French East India Company and the Trade of the Indian Ocean: A Collection of Essays by Indrani Ray*, ed. Lakshmi Subramanian (New Delhi: Munshiram Manoharlal, 1999), 68.

42 William Foster, ed., *English Factories in India: Vol. 11. 1661–64* (Oxford: Clarendon Press, 1923), 112.

43 *Letters from Fort St George; Vol. 20. 1726* (Madras: Printed by the Superintendent, Government Press, 1931): 'To Mr John Sanderson Resident at Metchlepatam, 18 August 1726; 36 (no. 58).

44 *Records of Fort St George: Diary and Consultation Book, 1709–1711* (Madras: Madras Government Press, 1929), 129 (13 December 1710).

16

Botany as Useful Knowledge: French Global Plant Collecting at the End of the Old Regime

Sarah Easterby-Smith

In the 1780s or early 1790s, the French royal botanist and plant hunter André Michaux (1746–1802) wrote a proposal outlining a project to create a new plant nursery in the southern French port town of Bayonne. Copies were sent to his patron, the royal doctor and professor of botany Guillaume Le Monnier (1717–1799). Further copies of his proposal were probably also sent to other influential individuals in and around Paris: Michaux's objective was to gain royal approval – and funding – to support the creation of the garden, which would 'acclimatize a great number of [exotic] Plants.' The nursery would perform an essential job in enabling the successful introduction of new medicinal drugs, foodstuffs, and materials for the arts and manufactures, as well as plants whose 'economic use' was still to be established. Cultivating and studying nonnative specimens in a specialised location like the Bayonne nursery, Michaux concluded, would 'make the science of Botany more useful.'[1] As such, his proposed project fitted precisely into a broader objective professed by each of eighteenth-century France's successive governments: that of improving the economy through a process of gathering together the raw materials of commerce and then enhancing contemporary understandings of how these might be cultivated and subsequently turned into commodities. The explicit orientation of such initiatives towards developing practical expertise in the cultivation and use of plants places them firmly within the arena of what economic historians and historians of technology have termed 'useful knowledge.'[2] From a scientific perspective, the systematic study of these natural productions led to the development of an area of enquiry that is now known as economic botany.

Projects like that of André Michaux, and the others that will be discussed in this chapter, allow us to explore the ways in which scientific knowledge and economic concepts intersected in eighteenth-century France. My chapter focuses on how useful natural knowledge had to be developed in order to facilitate the plant transfers themselves. This was particularly important for plants sent to Europe from the east because they traversed much longer distances than those sent across the Atlantic, a space that has been considered much more extensively in the scholarship.[3] While France's colonial botanical gardens did enhance the chance of success at different stages of these transfers, slow and arduous oceanic travel nevertheless meant that the specimens' survival rate remained very low overall. Solving the practical problems posed by global botanical travel was a particularly urgent matter.[4]

I begin by assessing how useful knowledge has been understood within economic history and the history of science, and explore the ways in which economic ideas about mercantilism specifically influenced French natural history collecting. I then draw from a set of archival examples that connect metropolitan France to the Mascarenes, India, and China. Each introduces a very different kind of collector: a connoisseurial consul, a public-spirited ship's captain, and a royal plant hunter. Each exposes how useful natural knowledge featured within French initiatives to acquire or cultivate plants from the east. My three examples gesture towards the range of formal and informal institutions that variously facilitated or obstructed the transmission of useful natural knowledge about plants.

Useful Knowledge

Useful knowledge, as Joel Mokyr explains, refers to practical forms of knowing that combine the tacit and explicit dimensions of knowledge. Tacit knowledge, which is difficult to express in words or images, often seems informal and has often been discussed in relation to histories of skill. Explicit knowledge, on the other hand, may be codified and thus communicated more easily.[5] The history of useful knowledge is central to the history of technology in general; for eighteenth-century studies in particular, discussions have focused on understanding the processes that contributed to industrialisation and, eventually, to the Industrial Revolution.[6] The turn towards global history over the past years has placed debates about the emergence, distribution and accumulation of useful knowledge within a larger frame. The scholarship initially focused its attention on comparing industrial expansion in different parts of the world and paid little attention to useful knowledge specifically.[7] However, subsequent work, especially that by Maxine Berg, Parsannan Parthasarathi, Giorgio Riello, and others, has insisted on the centrality of useful knowledge to global economic development. Their work has reframed the debate, moving from comparative questions to studies of connectivity and exchange. Taken together, it has underlined the value of understanding the social connections and cultural contexts that were central to the development and circulation not only of manufactured goods but also of the techniques and practices that comprised useful knowledge. The result of such work is a series of fine-grained studies that have placed the histories of technological development within a wider geographical context of global exchange.[8]

The approach taken by the latter body of research is closely aligned with that developed recently within history of science, which tends towards the study of connections over comparison and towards micro-historical approaches. Working from the principles that information must move in order to become knowledge, and that knowledge is normally negotiated and reinterpreted rather than simply absorbed and assimilated, a wealth of publications have explored the roles played by intermediaries, mobile individuals, and portable objects in facilitating the transfer of information and development of new knowledge across cultures.[9] For eighteenth-century studies, developing a clear under-standing of the distinctions between colonial and noncolonial forms of connection that framed the exchange and circulation of information is key: the global condition of the eighteenth century was largely (though not entirely) framed by imperial dynamics. This work contributes to our understanding of how knowledge systems associated with one part of the world emerged as a result of engagement with those located elsewhere.[10] Recognition that the European accumulation of knowledge was in fact the product of global circulation and exchange ('dispersion', in Lissa Roberts's terms) radically alters the nature of any study of economic development and science.[11] Such a perspective encourages us to develop careful qualitative analyses of the relationships between local contexts and global frameworks.

French Natural History Collecting

The European science of botany was a major beneficiary of global exchange. Often characterised as one of the 'big sciences' of the eighteenth century, historians have shown how European governments invested considerable time, money, and effort into obtaining data about native and exotic plants. The useful knowledge derived from botanical study could lead to the improvement of agriculture, medicine, and manufac-tures in a domestic setting and in Europe's colonies and trading posts. Its clear potential to serve the utilitarian aims of economic development meant that the science came, over the course of the eighteenth century, to occupy a position at the top of many European states' agendas. Indeed, botany was so intertwined with eighteenth-century European colonial aspirations that phrases such as 'colonial botany' or the 'botany of empire' are now common historiographical idioms.[12]

Given that the scientific study of plants occupied a central role in supporting European colonialisms, we might therefore assume that the discipline evolved under the close supervision of the state during the eighteenth century. Historians James E. McClellan III and François Regourd have argued that France's absolutist government developed a kind of 'colonial machine', which directed and structured most of natural history research conducted in its colonies.[13] This mechanistic metaphor for the functioning of the absolutist French state is controversial and has been the subject of extensive historiographical debate.[14] Whether or not one agrees with their notion of a machine, the emphasis they place on mercantilism as an overall frame for old-regime French natural history collecting is apposite. This will be developed further here: as we will see, the link drawn by mercantilists between accumulation and power offered a key structuring device for many French collectors.[15]

Recent work in cultural intellectual history has explored the ways in which theories about political economy influenced data gathering projects, and vice versa. Fredrik Albritton Jonsson has examined the 'rival ecologies of global commerce' evident within eighteenth-century European scholarship of the natural world. These commercial ecologies did not necessarily divide along national lines, and most countries experienced robust debates about the best way in which to exploit the natural world. Old-regime France can be broadly characterised as mercantilist, but the advocates of mercantilism did not always agree with each other and faced strong competition from proponents of alternative economic theories, especially physiocracy.[16] Nevertheless, the mercantilist stress on accumulation – not just of bullion but also of information – retained a significant place within government policy and collecting practices.

As Jacob Soll has shown, the seventeenth-century royal institutions created under Jean-Baptiste Colbert such as the Bibliothèque du Roi (the King's Library) provided a bureaucratic structure within which new information could be collected. These institutions also acted as visible manifestations of the potency of the absolutist state. Princely collections had, of course, been associated with power long before Louis XIV and Colbert founded the Bibliothèque. But the connection between knowledge and power gained new pertinence, for Colbert believed that accumulated knowledge had a practical value for the state.

He therefore insisted that collections of books and manuscripts were integrated into government archives.[17]

Drawing from Soll, Stéphane Van Damme has argued that the logic that drove orientalist study in seventeenth- and eighteenth-century France was a form of 'intellectual mercantilism.' As Van Damme explains, 'manuscript research is clearly similar to a mercantilist conception of knowledge based on the desire to enrich the state, to feed the prosperity of the nation ... The abundance of manuscripts is the counterpart of an abundance of money in the discourse of librarians.'[18] Van Damme explored this relationship through a study of the activities of the orientalist scholar and traveller, Abraham-Hyacinthe Anquetil Duperron (1731–1805), whose methods for obtaining manuscripts underline the close connections between science, commerce, and politics in this period.[19] Mercantilism, then, was related to much more than economic activity alone.

Intellectual mercantilism encouraged the collection of naturalia, too. Indeed, Duperron's own brother Étienne-Jean Anquetil de Briancourt (c. 1727–1793), offers an instructive example and will form my first case-study. De Briancourt worked as a merchant (and eventually French consul) in the thriving Guajarati port city of Surat for the majority of the period 1758–79. A partial inventory of de Briancourt's possessions compiled in 1779 demonstrates, however, that he and his family engaged not only in trade but also extensively in scholarship. Their library contained more than a thousand European books, and they possessed an extensive collection of scientific instruments, mostly for the study of astronomy and electricity.[20] De Briancourt's letters to his patron in Paris reveal that he also gathered useful specimens of plants in a *jardin français* that was attached to his residence and attempted to import to Gujarat some of the most economically interesting specimens available, not least tea (*Camellia sinensis*).[21] However, Anquetil de Briancourt, like his brother, did not receive explicit direction from France's various intellectual institutions, except where *he* requested them. Writing to his patron in Paris in 1761, de Briancourt explained that 'Not being able to study anything here but nature, in order to examine it more profitably, I beg [you to] send me clear instructions, and some new memoirs [on natural history].'[22] His patron obliged when he could – though the disruptions caused by the Seven Years' War meant that little of what was dispatched actually reached de Briancourt.

The Anquetil brothers, then, did not act in *response* to directives from France, they *requested* them. They engaged in their studies primarily because they saw themselves as connoisseurs, and their activities formed part of an attempt to construct a reputation as a respectable scholar (each brother was unsuccessful, though for very different reasons). That their independent activities fit within the broad objectives of a mercantilist project of data collection is an indication of the cultural influence of that economic framework.

Closer inspection of their activities, however, also reveals the limits of intellectual mercantilism. The evidence found so far suggests that Anquetil de Briancourt does not seem to have delivered on the specifics. Although he mentioned in his letters to Paris that he was involved in plant acclimatisation projects and other useful experiments, he communicated nothing about the practical knowledge required for the successful execution of his schemes. His letters simply list the items he had obtained.[23] It is possible that there are further materials yet to be uncovered about de Briancourt's scholarly activity during his initial years in Surat. However, the impression currently offered by the sources is that de Briancourt was disengaged from practical matters. This seems strange because a number of instructions were published for overseas collectors in the eighteenth century that explicitly asked them to pay attention to practical questions concerning the nature of plants' growth and cultivation, information that was essential for successful transplantation projects.[24] Anquetil de Briancourt may, of course, have been ignorant of such details, especially if he delegated the task of cultivating his collected economic specimens to servants. It seems that, although de Briancourt understood the general orientation towards collecting and cultivating useful plants, he had either not been briefed on the more precise requirements that were developing within eighteenth-century botanical circles or – if he had been so instructed – did not care to fulfil them.

Utility and Collecting

Anquetil de Briancourt is an example of a collector whose ties with key metropolitan institutions were relatively loose. My second example invites us to consider the extent to which the people working within and around royal institutions in Paris were able to negotiate the internal structures, patronage relationships, and bureaucratic constraints that characterised metropolitan science in the late eighteenth century. It also underlines the importance of recruiting the right personnel for knowledge transfer. For this we return to Paris and specifically to a coterie of botanical patrons and gardeners connected to the Jardin du Roi.

In February 1788, a public-spirited sea captain named Captain Fournier[25] wrote to the Abbé Henri-Alexandre Tessier (1741–1837), director of the royal farms at Rambouillet. Fournier expressed his desire to serve his country by transporting useful vegetables to the Île de France (Mauritius) where they might be acclimatised for agricultural use. He explained that his ship would be only lightly loaded with goods at its next sailing and would therefore have sufficient space to carry live plants. His novel promise to provide adequate room and provisions for the transportation of living vegetables was almost unheard of. Tessier leaped into action, passing copies of the letter to the royal minister and fellow member of the Académie des Sciences, Chrétien-Guillaume Lamoignon de Malesherbes (1721–1793), to the minister of the navy, César Henri de La Luzerne (1737–1799), and to the head gardener of the Jardin du Roi (royal botanical garden), André Thouin (1746–1824). A six-week-long correspondence ensued, in which the men determined which vegetables should be sent to the Mascarenes, how to ensure that they survived the journey, and, crucially, how the whole enterprise was to be funded.[26]

This project is instructive on two points. Firstly, the letters expose the social and political complexity involved in obtaining support and funding among the institutions that comprised the absolutist state. André Thouin was at the heart of these negotiations and developed a convoluted play of veils in order to arrange funding for the project. In sum, he first presented the proposal to the director of the jardin, the Comte de Buffon. Once Buffon had been persuaded to back the project, Thouin then portrayed the whole enterprise externally as Buffon's initiative – not his own. He then negotiated with Luzerne for naval funding. Luzerne showed strong support for the project and was committed (in Thouin's words) to 'enriching our Colonies with the most useful productions of Europe and to bringing back in return those that could be of some use to France', but he was not willing to invest significant amounts of naval money in it. Thouin eventually secured an agreement that the navy would fund only the transportation expenses and that the Jardin du Roi must cover all other costs.[27] These intricate negotiations underline how, even for schemes that directly served the aspirations of the absolutist state, organising any initiative that involved multiple ministries was an extremely challenging affair.

The second element to draw from this example brings us squarely back into the realm of useful knowledge. Right from the start of the negotiations, Thouin insisted that the plants should not be entrusted to the captain alone. He explained to Luzerne that, 'long experience has unfortunately shown us only too often that their [plants'] preservation during journeys as long as this depends considerably on the care that is taken of them during the voyage and that in general sailors are rarely able

to administer this[.] I believe that to ensure the success of this consign-
ment we must entrust them to a young, active and intelligent gardener.'[28]
Thouin then reinforced his point with the calculated comment that
'the British have for a long time followed this method.'[29] His request to
appoint a gardener was accordingly granted.

As the quotation above suggests, Thouin's concern was that the plants
would not survive their journey to the Île de France unless a skilled
custodian cared for them. The gardener appointed was Joseph Martin
(fl. 1788–c. 1819), who had trained at the Jardin du Roi and who was
carefully instructed by Thouin prior to his departure on how to record
information that might contribute to the development of useful natural
knowledge. Thouin issued the young gardener with a set of pre-prepared
books in which he was to record detailed notes about every change that
he observed in the plants' growth during the journey. In sum, Thouin
very rapidly concocted a scheme that would not only transfer objects
but that would also enable the further development of that skill and
thus contribute to the accumulation of useful natural knowledge overall.
Joseph Martin's involvement was absolutely crucial: he possessed a
combination of skills and botanical understanding that would permit
him to learn as he travelled. Practical expertise was essential to the
successful collection of useful natural knowledge.

Ornamental Utility

Useful plants are not the same thing as useful natural knowledge. In
a context in which global plant transfers were unreliable and highly
dependent on practical expertise, the transfer of any kind of plant –
ornamental or 'useful' – could constitute a contribution to the overall
development of useful knowledge. My third example considers the
relation between these two categories, returning to André Michaux's
proposal for the acclimatisation nursery at Bayonne.

The 'useful' and the 'ornamental' have often been treated separately:
the study of utility has been located within economic history and histories of industrialisation; consideration of the 'beautiful' has been situated
within histories of design and especially garden history. Within an
eighteenth-century mercantilist framework, however, beautiful objects
performed a useful function, even though most were luxury items
that did not have an immediate economic use (beyond a few highly
priced sales to wealthy collectors). Stéphane Van Damme has shown
how French collectors operating within the parameters of intellectual
mercantilism prioritised quantity over quality and demonstrated a

clear preference for the aesthetically attractive.[30] That preference is an important reminder of the extent to which early modern collectors responded to the symbolic dimension of information collecting, and also how the desire for political prestige could act as a significant motivating force. Beautiful objects were thus easily assimilated into mercantilist collecting economies.

From a botanical perspective, collections of ornamental luxury items could contribute significantly to practical natural knowledge. André Michaux's proposal for a nursery at Bayonne is revealing of the way in which such useful knowledge was developed. In making a case for the nursery, Michaux drew a careful differentiation between the knowledge and methods required to grow 'uncultivated' (wild) plants and those that had already been grown in agricultural or horticultural contexts in the countries from which they had been sent. Using Chinese plants as examples, Michaux explained that the gardener in charge of the nursery must 'observe with all the more attention all the changes that arrive to an uncultivated plant ... which has always been abandoned to itself.' 'Cultivated' plants presented a striking contrast, however, for 'in these we can identify the stamp of subjugated nature'; he drew a direct comparison between these specimens and 'the domestic animals sent to us from China.' Michaux explained that exotic horticultural plants could be grown with ease in European gardens simply 'by subjecting them to the various methods used in our gardens, such as pruning, grafting, [and] growing on espaliers.'[31] Wild plants required very different kinds of treatment compared to their domesticated counterparts; understanding their distinct needs was essential to ensuring their successful acclimatisation. The two genres of plant could be differentiated from each other with ease, however, by an experienced, perceptive gardener.

Michaux's proposal was explicitly concerned with the cultivation of useful plants. However, the practical knowledge essential to the success of this project was derived from the pleasure garden. Michaux supported his observations by drawing from his own experience cultivating horticultural plants, discussing in particular ornamental Chinese flora that were grown in fashionable European *jardins chinois*. The useful and the ornamental were thus not opposed to each other: knowledge drawn from working with the latter could be applied to greater economic gain in cultivating the former. The useful natural knowledge developed from the manipulation of beautiful plants also, of course, served the values of symbolism and prestige.

Conclusion

This chapter has offered a brief exploration of the ways in which economic concepts and scientific practices could interact as part of the development of useful natural knowledge. It was inspired in part by Maxine Berg's 2013 article 'Useful Knowledge, the Industrial Enlightenment and the Place of India'.[32] In this, Berg makes a clear case for uniting economic history with history of science. I have developed some aspects of that approach here, drawing from each historiographical strand to consider how eighteenth-century economic concepts influenced the *practices* involved in the collection of scientific data.[33] Useful knowledge, understood here as a practical understanding of how plants should be cared for and cultivated, was essential to all eighteenth-century botanical collecting projects. The examples that I have discussed, however, gesture towards some of the problems and limitations that complicated its development.

Useful natural knowledge became associated with intellectual mercantilism, a culture that framed and encouraged Anquetil de Briancourt's scholarly activities in Surat. However, his example pointed towards the limits of this culture, for it seems that de Briancourt did not communicate practical knowledge to Europe. One part of the reason for this may be that, at least in the early 1760s, Anquetil de Briancourt had relatively loose ties with metropolitan French scientific institutions. As we saw in my second example, the metropolitan institutions certainly recognised the value of transferring the objects of useful natural knowledge but even in the 1780s this was undertaken on an ad hoc basis. The negotiations over Captain Fournier's plant transfer mission revealed the continuing presence of internal institutional rivalries that shaped the way in which such projects were organised and funded, and which undermine the historiographical metaphor of a smooth-running 'colonial machine'. Finally, André Michaux's proposal fits squarely within the culture of colonial collecting exhibited in my first two examples. Michaux's example is particularly helpful because it underlines that commodities that normally circulated within different economic circuits – the 'useful' and the 'ornamental' – could serve the same intellectual and practical goals. Even luxury items, then, could contribute to the development of useful natural knowledge.

From a broader perspective, the examples discussed in this chapter make a case for the value of paying attention to the lesser officials and middlemen within state imperial frameworks and trading companies. They underline, too, that although useful natural knowledge was central to the success of each project, its codification and communication still presented huge challenges. The survival of plants used in global botanical transfers depended almost entirely on the skill of the gardener to whom they had been entrusted or, in other words, on the accumulation and movement of the people who could carry useful knowledge with them.

Notes

1 Bibliothèque Centrale, Muséum National d'Histoire Naturelle, Paris (hereafter MNHN), MS357 Le Monnier, XX, André Michaux, 'Projet concernant l'etablissement d'une pépinière d'arbres et plantes étrangères dans les environs de Bayonne.' Undated document written in the late 1780s or possibly the early 1790s.

2 Maxine Berg, 'The Genesis of "Useful Knowledge", *History of Science* 14 (2007): 123–33; Maxine Berg, 'Useful Knowledge, "Industrial Enlightenment", and the Place of India', *Journal of Global History* 8, no. 2 (2013): 117–41.

3 James E. McClellan III and François Regourd, 'The Colonial Machine: French Science and Colonization in the Ancien Régime', *Osiris* (2001): 31–50; Christopher Parsons and Kathleen S. Murphy, 'Ecosystems Under Sail: Specimen Transport in the Eighteenth-Century French and British Atlantics', *Early American Studies: An Interdisciplinary Journal* 10, no. 3 (2012): 503–29; Londa Schiebinger, *Plants and Empire: Colonial Bioprospecting in the Atlantic World* (Cambridge, Mass. and London: Harvard University Press, 2004).

4 Sarah Easterby-Smith, 'Recalcitrant Seeds: Material Culture and the Global History of Science', *Past and Present*, Supplement 14 (2019): 215–42.

5 Joel Mokyr, *The Gifts of Athena: Historical Origins of the Knowledge Economy* (Princeton: Princeton University Press, 2002).

6 Peter M. Jones, *Industrial Enlightenment: Science, Technology and Culture in Birmingham and the West Midlands, 1760–1820* (Manchester: Manchester University Press, 2008).

7 The now classic example of this is of course Kenneth Pomeranz, *The Great Divergence: China, Europe, and the Making of the Modern World Economy* (Princeton: Princeton University Press, 2001).

8 Berg, 'Useful Knowledge'; Prasannan Parthasarathi, *Why Europe Grew Rich and Asia Did Not* (Cambridge: Cambridge University Press, 2011); Giorgio Riello, *Cotton: The Fabric That Made the Modern World* (Cambridge: Cambridge University Press, 2013).

9 Ursula Klein and E.C. Spary, eds., *Materials and Expertise in Early Modern Europe* (Chicago: University of Chicago Press, 2006); Simon Schaffer, Lissa Roberts, Kapil Raj, and James Delbourgo, eds., *The Brokered World: Go-*

Betweens and Global Intelligence, 1770–1820 (Sagamore Beach, MA: Science History Publications, 2009).

10 Sujit Sivasundaram, 'Sciences and the Global. On Methods, Questions, and Theory', *Isis* 101 (2010): 146–58; Kapil Raj, *Relocating Modern Science: Circulation and the Construction of Knowledge in South Asia and Europe, 1650–1900* (New York: Palgrave Macmillan, 2007).

11 Lissa Roberts, *"Le Centre de toutes choses"*: Constructing and managing centralization on the Isle de France', *History of Science* 52, no. 3 (2014): 322.

12 Yota Batsaki, Sarah Burke Cahalan, and Anatole Tchikine, eds., *The Botany of Empire in the Long Eighteenth Century* (Washington, DC: Dumbarton Oaks, 2016); Londa Schiebinger and Claudia Swan, eds., *Colonial Botany: Science, Commerce and Politics in the Early Modern World* (Philadelphia: University of Pennsylvania Press, 2005). See also Richard Drayton, *Nature's Government: Science, Imperial Britain, and the "Improvement" of the World* (New Haven and London: Yale University Press, 2000); Schiebinger, *Plants and Empire*; Spary, *Utopia's Garden*.

13 James E. McClellan III and François Regourd, *The Colonial Machine: French Science and Overseas Expansion in the Old Regime* (Turnhout: Brepolis, 2011), 24.

14 Loïc Charles and Paul Cheney, 'The Colonial Machine Dismantled: Knowledge and Empire in the French Atlantic', *Past & Present* 219 (2013): 127–63; Kenneth Banks, 'Communications and "Imperial Overstretch": Lessons from the Eighteenth-Century French Atlantic', *French Colonial History* 6 (2005): 17–32; Roberts, 'Le Centre'.

15 Much recent historiography emphasises the value of taking a decentred approach to thinking about eighteenth-century collecting and knowledge transfer, an approach with which I strongly agree. See Roberts, 'Le Centre'; John McAleer, '"A Young Slip of Botany": Botanical Networks, the South Atlantic, and Britain's Maritime Worlds, c. 1790–1810', *Journal of Global History* 11, no. 1 (2016): 24–43; Dorit Brixius, 'French Empire on the Ground: Plants, Peoples, and Knowledge in the Service of Eighteenth-Century Isle de France' (unpublished PhD dissertation, European University Institute, 2017).

16 Fredrik Albritton Jonsson, 'Rival Ecologies of Global Commerce: Adam Smith and the Natural Historians', *American Historical Review* (2010): 1342–63; Fredrik Albritton Jonsson, *Enlightenment's Frontier: The Scottish Highlands and the Origins of Environmentalism* (New Haven and London: Yale University Press, 2013); E.C. Spary, '"Peaches which the Patriarchs Lacked": Natural History, Natural Resources, and the Natural Economy in Eighteenth-Century France', in *Œconomies in the Age of Newton* annual supplement to vol. 35 *History of Political Economy*, eds. Neil De Marchi and Margaret Schabas (Durham and London, Duke University Press, 2003): 14–41.

17 Jacob Soll, *The Information Master: Jean-Baptiste Colbert's Secret State Intelligence System* (Ann Arbor: University of Michigan Press, 2009).

18 Stéphane Van Damme, 'Capitalizing Manuscripts, Confronting Empires: Anquetil-Duperron and the Economy of Oriental Knowledge in the Context of the Seven Years' War', in *Negotiating Knowledge in Early Modern Empires. A Decentred View*, eds. László Kontler, Antonella Romano, Silvia Sebastiani, and Borbála Zsuzsanna Török (Basingstoke and New York: Palgrave MacMillan, 2014), 109–28 (quotation from 114).

19 Van Damme, 'Capitalizing Manuscripts', 111–15.

20 Minstre des Affairs Étrangères, Nantes, 2mi 2153, Consulat de France – Comptes de commerce des navires, 1774–1784. 'Copie du Brouillon de la note d'une partie des effets de M. Anquetil, qu'il demandoit à M. Gambier (Tannoh, 8 Mars 1779)'.

21 Archives nationales de France (hereforth AN), 177 mi 198, Dossier 149, Papiers de Malesherbes, Pièces 15–18. Letters from Anquetil de Briancourt (Surat) to Malesherbes, April 1761; February 1762. It is not clear from the surviving archival materials whether Anquetil de Briancourt actually had true tea specimens. These were very difficult to obtain and would have represented a significant coup had he actually gained possession of such plants.

22 AN, 177 mi 198, Letters from Anquetil to Malesherbes, April 1761; February 1762.

23 AN, 177 mi 198, Letters from Anquetil to Malesherbes, April 1761; February 1762.

24 For examples see Parsons and Murphy, 'Ecosystems Under Sail'.

25 This Captain Fournier is not the same person as the Captain Fournier whom I discuss in Sarah Easterby-Smith, 'On Diplomacy and Botanical Gifts: France, Mysore and Mauritius in 1788', in *Botany of Empire*, eds. Batsaki *et al.*

26 MNHN, MS 47, 'Documents divers concernant les îles de France et de Bourbon'. Letters exchanged between 14 February and 1 April 1788.

27 MNHN, MS 47, 'Documents divers', Copy of letter from André Thouin to comte de La Luzerne, 14 February 1788.

28 Ibid.

29 Ibid.

30 Van Damme, 'Capitalizing Manuscripts'.

31 MNHN, MS357 Le Monnier, XX, André Michaux, 'Projet concernant l'etablissement d'une pépinière d'arbres et plantes étrangères dans les environs de Bayonne'.

32 Berg, 'Useful knowledge'.

33   One deviation away from Berg's initial discussion (which focuses on technology) is that I have maintained a focus on botany. Berg states that we need 'to reach beyond the broad core of research done in the 1980s and 1990s on empire and botany to enquire into the wider extension of Europe's enlightenment investigation of arts and manufactures' (119). This chapter reconsiders these earlier histories of botany in the light of more recent historiographical developments.

17

Frictions of Empire: Colonial Bombay's Probate and Property Networks in the 1780s

Margot Finn

This chapter complicates historians' conceptualisations of the flow of property and finance between colony and metropole on the subcontinent in the era of the English East India Company (EEIC).[1] It focuses on the accumulated assets of military personnel and civil servants below the level of the successful 'nabobs', whose excessive wealth unduly dominates historical representations of Anglo-Indian society.[2] Situating these property relations within transcontinental flows of persons, goods, and information, it contributes to a strand of historiography in which extended webs, circuits, and networks are conceived as fundamental economic engines. Inspired by a lively, ongoing dialogue between 'new' cultural historians of empire, global historians, and historically minded geographers, the 'networks of empire' approach has enriched national and metropole/colony models of British economic growth. By examining the limited mobility of property in Company Bombay, however, I suggest the need to elaborate networked models of empire to account for constraints on movement within imperial networks.

Friction and Flow

Economic historians debate the extent to which flows of capital, goods, and commerce from its empire to its metropolitan heartland promoted Britain's unprecedented expansion and prosperity in the modern period. Focused on institutional mechanisms and quantitative measures of performance, this debate has spawned an impressive literature on the balance of payments, contract enforcement, and the rise of the fiscal state.[3] Postcolonial historians, however, have increasingly critiqued approaches to empire that assume that economic outcomes reflect the transparent operation of market mechanisms and rational economic choices. As Alan Lester observes, 'capitalism cannot be thought of as having a logic or structure which exists somehow prior to or outside of culture.'[4] Rather, 'new' imperial historians argue that cultures of capitalism played formative roles in shaping imperial experiences. Many historians now situate colonial economic cultures within multilayered networks or 'geographies of connection', arguing that Britain and its colonies were 'knitted together within a global culture and political fabric' that encompassed not only the circulation of economic goods but also the exchange of discourses, information, people, and social practices.[5] Compared both to histories of empire that reify distinctions between colony and metropole and to more recent histories of colonial culture that have been preoccupied with discursive formations, the networks of empire approach promises an integrated field of play in which material histories of colonialism can be systematically recon-nected to histories of colonial power and difference.[6]

However, the networks model suffers from a tendency to focus on 'flow' – that is, fluid or unimpeded circulation. 'Flow' is the dominant modality of imperial networks as conceived by colonial historians. Lester thus underlines the circuits that linked Britain, the Cape colony, and New South Wales: 'Colonial and metropolitan sites were connected most obviously through material flows of capital, commodities and labour.'[7] The hydraulic metaphor of 'flow' succeeds in conveying the force and dynamism of imperial networks, their ability to cover and connect vast cultural and geographical distances. But it underplays the extent to which, in Frederick Cooper's words, 'economic and political relations are very uneven ... filled with lumps, places where power coalesces surrounded by those where it does not, places where social relations become dense amid others that are diffuse.'[8]

In this context, the concept of 'friction' elaborated by ethnographer Tsing offers an attractive tool for augmenting networked approaches to British imperialism. Tsing contests models of globalisation in which the 'flow of goods, ideas, money and people ... [is] pervasive and unimpeded', arguing that dominant analyses of global connection wrongly assume that 'motion ... proceed[s] entirely without friction'. Friction, in her analysis, is the space created by the contact between universalizing historical forces and specific cultural contexts. Tsing recognises that capitalism depends on 'global connections' that spread 'through aspir-ations to fulfil *universal* dreams', but underscores the limits of these flows, for 'this is a particular kind of universality: it can only be charged and enacted in the sticky materiality of practical encounters'. Friction, in this formulation, is the contact zone between capitalist (and other) universalisms and culturally specific historical actors. Crucially, friction for Tsing is a creative and productive place, one that can encompass (but is not confined to) resistance to network flow. Through friction, through interruptions to flow, new possibilities of global connection, social interaction, and political praxis are born. Networks, in this interpretation, feed continually upon the frictions that result from the 'uneven and awkward links' that compose 'globe-crossing, capital and commodity chains'. The rate as well as the substance of exchange within global networks depend upon the play of such 'sticky engagements', as she calls them. 'Friction is not just about slowing things down', Tsing concludes. 'Friction is required to keep global power in motion.'[9]

Tsing's conception of friction resonates with Hancock's arguments about eighteenth-century commerce. Focusing on Scottish merchants who enabled the production and circulation of Madeira wine in the Atlantic and the Indian Ocean worlds, Hancock too emphasises the need to juxtapose successful and failed exchanges within global networks and to understand these outcomes as connected (rather than purely antipathetic) phenomena. Eighteenth-century Madeira merchants compensated for the interrupted flows of goods and information caused by limited transportation and communication networks by grounding their economic transactions in personal relationships, most notably ties of family, kin, nation, and ethnicity. Fostering trust and reducing risk, these personal relations enhanced the flow of information among merchants. But they also provided a constant source of friction in mercantile networks, at times impeding communication and exchange. Family members and personal friends were less amenable to market disciplines than were employees with whom merchants had only contractual relations; kinfolk who relied upon implicit and customary agreements reduced merchants' ability to respond rapidly to new market opportunities and to make precise calculations of profit and loss.[10] Opposed and yet inextricably linked together in a dynamic relation, friction and flow constitute two sides of the same commercial coin in systems of circulation.

Whereas Tsing's model of circulation, friction, and flow privileges the political dynamics of economic networks, Hancock's research reminds us of the key roles played by social formations in exchanges between local and global contexts. In this, Hancock's approach resonates with Bruno Latour's conception of the social,[11] allowing us to see that global traders' social worlds were constituted and performed through their commercial networks, rather than existing prior to or outside these systems of circulation. In examining the flow of EEIC property in Bombay, I accept Tsing's emphasis on the creative potential of friction in global networks and also apply, to forms of colonial property, the 'sticky' qualities that Tsing associates with the inherent frictions of global encounter and that are central to Latour's model of performances of the social. Historians have extensively analysed the financial mechanisms that underpinned the large-scale flows of capital between India and Britain.[12] The pivotal role played in these transactions by indigenous Indian traders and merchants is also well attested.[13] Much less attention has been devoted to the more mundane processes by which company men transferred fortunes accumulated in India from Asia to Britain.[14] Remittances were a vital component of company servants' ability to establish marital families and thus to reproduce the colonial social order. They channelled from India capital resources by which Britons married, raised children, and purchased assets that included landed estates, Parliamentary seats, and stock in turnpikes, canals, and railways. Never a colony of settlement under company rule, India was an attractive investment to Britons only if wealth accumulated on the subcontinent could subsequently be repatriated home. The systems by which individuals remitted their wealth thus constituted essential components of the colonial networks that secured Britain's empire in India.[15]

Friction pervades these property transfers. Company men's reliance on long-distance networks of credit, the large gaps in their knowledge of the market conditions, and the company's own byzantine institutional conventions (as well as its mounting deficits) routinely disrupted the flow of property in colonial networks.[16] So too did the excessive mortality rates suffered by company men in India, which both ensured that Anglo-Indian property was constantly changing hands and disrupted the probate mechanisms by which its orderly transfer from India to Britain was intended to be effected.[17] The bills of exchange through which the bulk of these men's wealth was remitted to Britain were imperfect financial instruments. Hejeebu's systematic analysis of Bengal bills of exchange from 1746 to 1756, depicts remittances as flowing readily from India to Britain.[18] Underlining their 'coherent design', she represents bills of exchange as unproblematic conduits for the smooth transit of savings that 'operated like modern checkable deposits'.[19] In contrast, Mentz's analysis of trade in Madras, based on merchants' private correspondence and business accounts, highlights the constraints that confronted company servants eager to remit Asian fortunes. He notes that bills of exchange were only one among many mechanisms for remitting fortunes home. He identifies diamonds as especially effective vehicles for rapid remittances and also stresses the extent to which merchants were constrained by social and cultural expectations. Administering funds left in India by retired company servants offered EEIC officials lucrative opportunities to increase their

own wealth, but these transactions were often marked in Madras by friction rather than by flow: lapses in communication and prolonged delays
in the reconciling of accounts meant that these transactions extended
over years and even decades without full resolution.[20] These disruptions
to the flow of property cannot be adequately captured by economic
historians' concept of 'transactions costs', for friction functioned as a
productive force in the East India Company's colonial networks: it
created not only price differentials and impediments to trade but also
traction for transactions and opportunities for new social relations.[21]

Alexander Durham's Letter Book

The letter book of Andrew Durham, an EEIC surgeon whose private
correspondence illustrates both the intense frustrations and the productive potentials of friction in colonial networks, allows us to examine
friction and flow within remittance networks. Letter and account books
of individual merchants, as Hancock observes of Atlantic trade, 'reveal
a different perspective from the official records of the royal chartered
companies'.[22] Official company records fail to capture the full spectrum of traders' private transactions and are especially poor sources
of information about the interpenetration of economic endeavour by
political, social, and cultural factors.[23] Andrew Durham's letter book,
documenting private trade and estate administration in the Bombay
Presidency in the 1780s, provides a rare opportunity to assess the complex
and often fraught processes and relationships that accomplished the
circulation of company servants' assets from India to Britain.

First acquired by the British in 1662, Bombay rapidly rose to become
a flourishing centre of EEIC trade; military and political considerations
encouraged the company to shift its headquarters in western India
from Surat to Bombay in 1687.[24] Although it became India's premier
nineteenth-century port, Bombay languished in the eighteenth century,
experiencing a period of especially acute crisis in the 1780s. Private
trade continued to provide its European population with a wealth of
opportunities for accumulating capital, but Bombay's public finances
deteriorated sharply. Company merchants' determination to profit
from private investments diverted their attention from the sale and
reinvestment of official cargoes shipped annually from London; the
absence of countervailing revenue from territorial alliances with Indian
rulers added to Bombay's financial embarrassment.[25] By the 1780s, its
government was shackled by its public debts: only repeated recourse to
the extensive credit networks of the indigenous merchant and banking
community allowed this western outpost of the company to function as

a colonial enterprise.[26] Military campaigns against the Maratha powers exacerbated these problems. Civil servants' salaries went unpaid for months on end, and the company's investment in commodities such as pepper ground to a halt due to an acute shortage of both capital and credit. 'Whether the Company would retain any hold at all in western India was, in 1784, much in doubt', Nightingale observes.[27]

In this far from propitious context Andrew Durham sought to secure his own and his colleagues' fortunes through participation in Bombay's financial markets but rapidly found that frictions in these networks demanded that he place reliance as well on the sticky materiality of social relations. Durham joined the company's service as an assistant surgeon in 1768, retiring in 1790. Appointed a principal surgeon of the general hospital in 1784, he rose to become physician general of Bombay in 1787, and joined the presidency's military board in 1788. These positions gave Durham access to substantial capital resources.[28] His salary as physician general was £1,500 per annum, and his roles on the medical board brought him lucrative contracts for supplying Bombay's general hospital.[29] To these official duties and emoluments, he added two further, unpaid economic roles. He oversaw the management of the Indian assets of several company servants who had returned to Britain on furlough or retirement, and he served as an executor for many deceased Anglo-Indians' estates. The agents and executors who performed these vital roles were key nodal points in the networks through which property circulated in the Anglo-Indian world.[30] Analysis of Durham's efforts to manage the assets and to settle the estates of absent or deceased company men illuminates the pervasive impediments to 'flow' within the company's networks and illustrates the ways in which these frictions fed into and from colonial social formations.

Spanning from 1783 to 1791, Durham's 222-page letter book contains copies of his business letters to a wide variety of European correspondents.[31] Among its first entries is a letter to the widowed Mary Thomas of London. Mary Thomas – with whom Durham had no personal acquaintance – was the sister of Seth Lofthouse, an army captain who had died in Bombay Presidency in 1779, naming Durham as an Indian executor of his estate. The interval of four years between Lofthouse's death and Durham's letter is itself a significant reminder of the protracted nature of Anglo-Indian probate relations and the ensuing asymmetries of information that created friction in colonial networks. 'I am glad that you have received safe the attested copy of the late Capt[ai]n Lofthouse's Will and the account Current of his Estate', Durham began. 'I most earnestly wish that it had been equally easee [sic] for me to have transmitted to you the balance due to it, but even had I been sooner favored [*sic*] with your commands on that head, I should have found it impracticable? Multiple barriers hindered the movement of Lofthouse's property.

Lacking a power of attorney until nearly four years after Lofthouse's death, Durham had been incapable of remitting any income to England. But the absence of this legal document formed only a small part of the much larger obstacle course negotiated by company executors: as Durham patiently explained in his letter to Lofthouse's sister, the company's swingeing deficits posed a major impediment to the profitable transfer of these assets. While awaiting Mary Thomas's instructions from London, Durham duly collected the debts owed to her brother and invested the estate in Bombay treasury notes, bonds that bore a generous 9 per cent annual interest. But the very security of Bombay treasury notes precluded the orderly flow of property to Lofthouse's heirs. Since 1780, Durham explained, 'in consequence of almost half the European and Indian powers ... having united as if determined on the ruin of Great Britain ... neither Treasury Bonds nor drafts on ... [them] would be accepted ... and many who were under the necessity of raising money at all events were obliged to allow a considerable discount' to redeem them.[32]

Depicted in economic historians' accounts as reliable conduits for the flow of company capital, bills of exchange emerge instead from Durham's letter book as key sites of financial friction. By 1783, the discount charged for acceptance of Bombay bills had risen to over 40 per cent, and Durham was understandably loath to remit Lofthouse's estate, which he valued at just under thirty thousand rupees (or £3,000), at such a disproportionate loss. 'You now Madam must be convinced that I have not yet had it in my power to send you a single shilling, nor ever shall (should the discount continue on the Treasury)' he concluded.[33]

Andrew Durham's extensive probate correspondence repeatedly refers to the excessive transaction costs that marked financial dealings in Bombay. Again and again these letters also document the socially embedded familial and material strategies that he deployed to ensure the continued flow of property from India to Britain – strategies that are largely ignored in analyses by practitioners of the 'new' institutional economic history.[34] The emphasis of the second half of Durham's letter to Mary Thomas shifted from the impediments posed by politics and economics, to the potential relief from these obstructed exchanges offered by recourse to social formations and cultural processes. Having begun by focusing on legal instruments, bond issues, and interest rates, Durham turned to discuss networks forged by memorial keepsakes, trusted friends, and domestic sociability. He drew attention to the careful arrangements he had made for the transport to London of a portrait Lofthouse had left in his will to his sister. 'I shall be glad to hear of its getting [to you] safe and undamaged, which I have [every] reason to expect as Capt[ai]n Huddart who is a particular friend of mine, promised to be careful of it', Durham observed. Like the Madeira wine merchants studied by Hancock, Durham sought proactively to personalise his business relations, when compelled to do business with strangers.[35] Given the failure of formal legal and financial processes to yield up the deceased's assets, Durham adduced the personal ties of domesticity as appropriate mechanisms for expediting the remittance of Lofthouse's income to his principal heir, his niece. 'I took the liberty in one of my former letters to recommend Miss Thomas's coming to India as the speediest and perhaps the most advantageous method of being put in possession of her fortune', Durham reported. 'At that time I had it in my power to accommodate Miss Thomas agreeable to her expectations but the loss of a beloved wife that I have since sustained, puts it out of my power to renew my advice on that head.'[36]

Durham's offer of his own home in Bombay as a base from which Lofthouse's niece could attempt to prise her fortune from the company's coffers reminds us of the limited ability of financial instruments alone to effect capital flows in colonial Bombay. His correspondence identified social relations in Bombay as a twofold impediment to and enabler of the orderly transfer of company men's accumulated savings. His letter to Mary Thomas noted that the executors would charge the estate with a monthly payment of fifteen rupees to the credit of Lofthouse's former 'housekeeper'. Lofthouse's will makes it clear that this Indian housekeeper had in fact been his concubine and reveals a host of adhesive domestic affiliations that surrounded, constrained, shaped, and propelled the transfer of his Indian property within and beyond Bombay. He gave 'to my Girl wh[ic]h now lives with me w[hi]ch I call Mary her Portuguese name I do not know', the interest on 2,000 rupees from his company treasury bills for life, 'but should she have a child by me and she will swear it is mine', Mary was to receive for life the interest on 10,000 rupees from his estate, as long as the child remained alive. She also inherited . goods from Lofthouse that would secure her own future domestic comfort beyond his demise. 'I likewise give her six Tea Spoons six Table Spoons, her chest and clothes, one small table and 6 small chairs', the will continued, 'and a little slave girl named Theresa.'[37] Decisions about the flow of company servants' remittances, as Durham's letter book demonstrates, were shaped not only by 'rational' calculations of profit and risk but also by the friction imposed on the flow of capital by their entanglement in domestic and affective networks.

The enslaved Theresa was one among several living legacies that Seth Lofthouse sought both to circulate and to fix in place posthumously through his personal networks in Bombay. His will decreed that his friend Isaac Richardson was to inherit Lofthouse's sword, mathematical instruments, charts, and 'my Boy Manuel he [having] been a true and faithfull [*sic*] Servant to me [for] many years', with the proviso however that Richardson 'shall [have] him but not sell him.' The will gave Durham's co-executor, his fellow surgeon John Blakeman, 'my Boy Essia and my Gold Watch', animate and inanimate keepsakes that would render Lofthouse's memory palpably alive to Blakeman through the protracted financial transactions that would eventually culminate in the settlement of this estate. Lofthouse also tied Durham by adhesive property relations through this will. 'I likewise give to Mr Andrew Durham Surgeon being a Married man my Boy Sam his Wife and Family ... knowing him [Sam] to be a faithful good servant but [Durham is] not to sell him, likewise [I leave] my Chaise to Mr Durham!', Lofthouse instructed.[38] Anglo-Indian legacies such as these both were and were not property; they travelled in colonial networks that included but were not confined to capital and commodity chains. Colonial probate property, Seth Lofthouse's will suggests, was sticky property: its circulation or flow was calculated to create cohesion among European economic agents in a colonial context in which high transaction costs (created by constraints on the free movement of both money and information) were normative. This sticky human and material property, at once displaying flow and friction, was social in the creative, performative sense defined by Bruno Latour. Reflecting more than purely economic values, its halting, protracted circulation within local and transoceanic imperial circuits worked to constitute the sphere of colonial social and economic relations.

Conclusion

A broader analysis of the probate accounts of Andrew Durham and his circle of associates in the 1780s reveals the multiple ways in which 'friction', in the form of adhesive Anglo-Indian property relations, performed or constituted social relationships and thereby animated the EEIC's financial networks in Bombay.[39] Durham's letter book provides abundant evidence of his ability to work effectively within colonial institutional structures, to engage in complex economic transactions, and to make sophisticated calculations of profit and loss. But like the erstwhile colleagues whose flow of probate he managed, he perforce placed great reliance on personal relations of trust to bridge the vast geographical and temporal distances traversed by colonial property. Formal legal and economic institutions were present and fully operational in Bombay, but resort to them was entangled with transactions based on interpersonal relations predicated upon trust.

Notes

1   This chapter draws from arguments elaborated in Margot Finn, "'Frictions" d'empire: les réseaux de circulation des successions et des patrimoines dans la Bombay coloniale des années 1780; *Annales* 65, no. 5 (2010): 1175–204.

2   For the nabobs, see Tillman W. Nechtmann, *Nabobs: Empire and Identity in Eighteenth-Century Britain* (Cambridge: Cambridge University Press, 2010). For the great disjunction between the nabob stereotype and the normative economic experiences, see P.J. Marshall, *East Indian Fortunes: The British in Bengal in the Eighteenth Century* (Oxford: Clarendon Press, 1976).

3   For example, Javier Cuenca-Esteban, 'India's Contribution to the British Balance of Payments, 1757–1812; *Explorations in Economic History* 44, no. 2 (2007): 154–76; Santhi Hejeebu, 'Contract Enforcement in the East India Company; *Journal of Economic History* 65, no. 2 (2005): 496–523; Patrick O'Brien, 'Inseparable Connections: Trade, Economy, Fiscal State, and the Expansion of Empire, 1688–1815; in *The Oxford History of the British Empire; Volume II: The Eighteenth Century*, ed. P.J. Marshall (Oxford: Oxford University Press, 1998), 53–77; and Ralph A. Austen and Woodruff D. Smith, 'The Economic Value of British Colonial Empire in the Seventeenth and Eighteenth Centuries; *History Compass* 4, no. 1 (2006): 54–76.

4   Alan Lester, *Imperial Networks: Creating Identities in Nineteenth-century South Africa and Britain* (London: Routledge, 2001), 2.

5   Lester, *Imperial Networks*, 5; Natasha Glaisyer, 'Networking: Trade and Exchange in the Eighteenth-century British Empire; *Historical Journal* 47, no. 2 (2004): 451–76; Zoë Laidlaw, *Colonial Connections, 1815–45: Patronage, the Information Revolution and Colonial Government* (Manchester: Manchester University Press, 2005); and Kerry Ward, *Networks of Empire: Forced Migration in the Dutch East India Company* (Cambridge: Cambridge University Press, 2009).

6   Alan Lester, 'Imperial Circuits and Networks: Geographies of the British Empire; *History Compass*, 4, no. 1 (2005): 124–41; Claude Markovits, *The Global World of Indian Merchants, 1750–1947: Traders of Sind from Bukhara to Panama* (Cambridge: Cambridge University Press, 2000); Claude Markovits, Jacques Pouchepadass, and Sanjay Subrahmanyam, eds., *Society and Circulation: Mobile People and Itinerant Cultures in South Asia, 1750–1950*

(London: Anthem Press, 2006); and Kapil Raj, *Relocating Modern Science: Circulation and the Construction of Knowledge in South Asia and Europe, 1650–1900* (Basingstoke: Palgrave, 2007).

7   Lester, *Imperial Networks*, 6.

8   Frederick Cooper, *Colonialism in Question: Theory, Knowledge, History* (Berkeley: University of California Press, 2005), 91.

9   Anna Lowenhaupt Tsing, *Friction: An Ethnography of Global Connection* (Princeton: Princeton University Press, 2005), citations 5, 1, 6, 4, 6.

10 David Hancock, 'The Trouble with Networks: Managing the Scots' Early-Modern Madeira Trade', *Business History Review* 79, no. 3 (2005): 467–91, esp. 478–84. See also David Hancock, *Citizens of the World: London Merchants and the Integration of the British Atlantic Community, 1735–1785* (Cambridge: Cambridge University Press, 1995).

11 Bruno Latour, *Reassembling the Social: An Introduction to Actor-Network Theory* (Oxford: Oxford University Press, 2005), 204, 241–2.

12 John F. Richards, 'Imperial Finance under the East India Company, 1762–1859', in *Decentring Empire: Britain, India and the Transcolonial World*, eds. Durba Ghosh and Dane Kennedy (London: Sangan Books, 2006), 16–50.

13 See especially C.A. Bayly, *Rulers, Townsmen and Bazaars: North Indian Society in the Age of British Expansion, 1770–1870* (Cambridge: Cambridge University Press, 1983); and Lakshmi Subramanian, *Indigenous Capital and Imperial Expansion: Bombay, Surat and the West Coast* (Delhi: Oxford University Press, 1996).

14 For remittances, see Holden Furber, *John Company at Work: A Study of European Expansion in India in the Late Eighteenth Century* (Cambridge, MA: Harvard University Press, 1951), esp. 45–50, 79–80, 89–96, 114–28.

15 See Margot Finn and Kate Smith, eds., *The East India Company at Home, 1757–1857* (London: UCL Press, 2018).

16 These impediments to communication are discussed by Huw Bowen, *The Business of Empire: The East India Company and Imperial Britain, 1756–1833* (Cambridge: Cambridge University Press, 2006), 151–81.

17 For high mortality rates, see Philip D. Curtin, *Death by Migration: Europe's Encounter with the Tropical World in the Nineteenth Century* (Cambridge: Cambridge University Press, 1989).

18 Hejeebu, 'Contract enforcement', 511–13.

19 Ibid., 500, 503.

20 Søren Mentz, 'English Private Trade on the Coromandel Coast, 1660–1690: Diamonds and Country Trade', *Indian Economic and Social History Review* 33, no. 2 (1996): 155–73, esp. 171; Søren Mentz, *The English Gentleman Merchant at Work: Madras and the City of London, 1660–1740* (Copenhagen: Museum Tusculanum Press, 2005), esp. chapter 4.

21 Jacob Price, 'Transaction Costs: A Note on Merchant Credit and the Organization of Long-distance Trade', in *The Political Economy of Merchant Empires*, ed. James Tracey (Cambridge: Cambridge University Press, 1991), 276–97.

22 David Hancock, '"A World of Business to Do": William Freeman and the Foundations of England's Commercial Empire, 1645–1707', *William and Mary Quarterly*, 3rd series, 57, no. 1 (2000): 6. See similarly Toby Ditz, 'Shipwrecked or, Masculinity Imperilled: Masculine Representations of Failure and the Gendered Self in Eighteenth-century Philadelphia', *Journal of American History* 81, no. 1 (1994): 51–80, and S.D. Smith, 'The Account Book of Richard Poor, Quaker Merchant of Barbados', *William and Mary Quarterly*, 3rd series, 66, no. 3 (2009): 605–28.

23 See esp. Mentz, 'English Private Trade', 158 and Webster, *Richest East Indian Merchant*.

24 Holden Furber, *Rival Empires of Trade in the Orient, 1600–1800* (London: Oxford University Press 1976), 90, 92–4, 198.

25 Holden Furber, 'Trade and Politics in Madras and Bombay', in *Trade and Finance in Colonial India 1750–1860*, ed. Asiya Siddiqi (Delhi: Oxford University Press, 1995), 66–88, esp. 81–8.

26 Lakshmi Subramanian, 'Banias and the British: The Role of Indigenous Credit in the Process of Imperial Expansion in Western India in the Second Half of the Eighteenth Century', *Modern Asian Studies* 21, no. 3 (1987): 473–510.

27 Pamela Nightingale, *Trade and Empire in Western India, 1784–1806* (Cambridge: Cambridge University Press 1970), 13–14.

28 List of Company Surgeons, Bombay Presidency, British Library (hereafter BL), African and Asian Studies (henceforth cited as A&AS), IOR L/MIL/12/86: Andrew Durham, M.D.

29 D.G. Crawford, *A History of the Indian Medical Service 1600–1913*, 2 vols (London: W. Thacker, 1914), 2: 25, 473.

30 For probate, see esp. T. Arkell, Nesta Evans and Nigel Goose, eds., *When Death Do Us Part: Understanding and Interpreting the Probate Records of Early Modern England* (London: Leopard's Head, 2000); and Amy Louise Erickson, *Women and Property in Early Modern England* (London: Routledge, 1993).

31 Letter book of Andrew Durham, MD (1783–1791), BL, A&AS, MSS EUR C82 (henceforth cited as Durham letterbook).

32 Ibid., 27 December 1783.

33 Durham letter book, Durham to Mrs Mary Thomas, 27 December 1783, 3–4.

34 The foundation text for this institutionalist approach is Douglass C. North and Robert Paul Thomas, *The Rise of the Western World: A New Economic History* (Cambridge: Cambridge University Press, 1973).

35   Hancock, 'The Trouble with Networks', 480.

36   Durham letter book, Durham to Mrs Mary Thomas, 27 December 1783, 4–6.

37   Probate (14 February 1780) and Will (4 August 1779) of Captain Seth
     Lofthouse, in BL, A&AS, Bombay Wills and Estates (1776–1783), IOR P/416/98,
     p. 107–111. For Anglo-Indian bequests to Indian concubines and their
     children, see Indrani Chatterjee, 'Colouring Subalternity: Slaves, Concubines
     and Social Orphans in Early Colonial India', in *Subaltern Studies X*, eds.
     Gautam Bhadra and Gyan Prakash (Delhi: Oxford University Press, 1999),
     49–97; Durba Ghosh, *Sex and the Family in Colonial India: The Making of
     Empire* (Cambridge: Cambridge University Press, 2006); and C.J. Hawes, *Poor
     Relations: The Making of a Eurasian Community in British India 1773–1833*
     (Richmond: Curzon, 1996).

38   Ibid. For slavery in Bombay, see Holden Furber, 'Trade and Politics in Madras
     and Bombay', 87. The problematic relations between domestic slaves and
     property in Anglo-India is detailed in Margot Finn, 'Slaves out of Context:
     Domestic Slavery and the Anglo-Indian Family, *c.* 1780–1830', *Transactions of
     the Royal Historical Society* 19 (2009): 181–203.

39   See Finn, 'Frictions d'empire'.

Contributors

KRISTINE BRULAND is professor emeritus of economic history at the University of Oslo and was formerly professor of economic history at the University of Geneva. Her work focuses on the diffusion of technologies, especially during early industrialisation. Her publications include *British Technology and European Industrialization* (1989), and she has edited *Technology Transfer and Scandinavian Industrialisation* (1992) and (with Maxine Berg) *Technological Revolutions in Europe, Historical Perspectives* (1998). She has researched extensively on technological change and innovation. More recently she and David Mowery co-authored the chapter 'Technology and the spread of capitalism' in *The Cambridge History of Capitalism, Vol II, The Spread of Capitalism: From 1848 to the Present*, eds. Larry Neal and Jeffrey G. Williamson (eds.), (2014), 82–127.

HELEN CLIFFORD worked at the Victoria and Albert Museum and the University of Warwick and currently directs her own museum in Swaledale, North Yorkshire. She completed her PhD on the royal goldsmiths Garrard at the Royal College of Art. She is the author of *Silver in London: The Parker and Wakelin Partnership 1760-1776* (2004) and has curated major exhibitions including *A Treasured Inheritance: 600 Years of Oxford College Silver* (2004) for the Ashmolean and *The Story of Britain and Gold* (2012) for the Goldsmiths' Company, where she is a freeman. She has recently published a book on the silver of the Grocers' Company.

SARAH EASTERBY-SMITH teaches and researches modern European history at St Andrew's University. She was awarded her PhD by the University of Warwick in 2010 and held fellowships at the Huntington Library; the Lewis Walpole Library, Yale University; and the European University Institute. Her research focuses on the relationship between science, society, and culture and on how information, knowledge, and cultural influences moved (or failed to move) between nations and across social groups. In 2017 she published *Cultivating Commerce: Cultures of Botany in Britain and France, 1760–1815*.

MARGOT FINN is president of the Royal Historical Society and chair in modern British history at University College London. She is a historian of Britain and the British colonial world in the long nineteenth century. Margot was recently principal investigator on the major Leverhulme Trust–funded project 'East India Company at Home, 1757–1857.' Her publications include *After Chartism: Class and Nation in English Radical Politics 1848–1874* (2004) and *The Character of Credit: Personal Debt in English Culture, 1740–1914* (2003). Her current monograph project is entitled 'Imperial Family Formations: Domestic Strategies and Colonial Power in British India, c. 1757–1857.'

LILIANE HILAIRE-PÉREZ is professor of early modern history and director of studies at Université de Paris. She is a specialist in the history of innovation, and the history of technical culture and exchange. Among her publications are *L'invention technique au siècle des Lumières* (2000) and *La pièce et le geste. Artisans, marchands et savoirs techniques à Londres au XVIIIe siècle* (2013). She has published numerous articles and edited works including *Le livre technique avant le XXe siècle. À l'échelle du monde* (2017). She is the editor of the journal *Artefact: Techniques, histoire et sciences humaines*.

ANNE GERRITSEN is professor of history at the University of Warwick and chair of Asian art at the University of Leiden. She was educated at the University of Leiden and holds a PhD from Harvard University. She has published in a number of different areas, including Chinese history (the religious cultures of the Song-Yuan-Ming period, friendship, gender and literature, and the history of Jingdezhen), material culture (including three co-edited books with Giorgio Riello: *Writing Material Culture History* [2014; 2nd ed. 2020]; *The Global Lives of Things* [2015]; and *Global Gifts* [2018]), global design history, and the global history of porcelain trade. Her book *The City of Blue and White: Chinese Porcelain and the Early Modern World* is coming out with Cambridge University Press in 2020.

PAT HUDSON is an emeritus professor of history at Cardiff University and taught economic history previously at the University of Liverpool. She is a vice president of the Economic History Society and is an economic historian of the British Industrial Revolution whose research has focused on the wider economic, social, and cultural aspects of industrialisation. Among her publications are *The Contradictions of Capital in the Twenty-First Century* (2016) (edited with Keith Tribe); *The Routledge Handbook of Global Economic History* (2015) (edited with Francesco Boldizzoni); *History by Numbers: An Introduction to Quantitative Approaches* (2016) (2nd ed., with Mina Ishizu); *The Industrial Revolution* (1992 and 2014); and *The Genesis of Industrial Capital: A Study of the West Riding Wool Textile Industry, c. 1750–1850* (1986).

MORGAN KELLY is professor of economics at University College Dublin and completed his PhD at Yale University. From 1990 to 1995 he was an assistant professor at Cornell University. His research ranges widely over the field of economic history from analysis of the Irish economic crisis to the mainsprings of British industrialisation and critique of statistical method employed in historical work. Recent publications include 'Speed under Sail in the British Industrial Revolution (c. 1750–1830)', *Economic History Review* 72 (2019): 459–80; 'Adam Smith, Watch Prices and the Industrial Revolution', *Quarterly Journal of Economics* 131 (2016): 1727–52 (both with Cormac Ó Gráda); 'Precocious Albion: A New Interpretation of the British Industrial Revolution', *Annual Review of Economics* 6 (2014), 363–89; 'The Standard Errors of Persistence', 2019 (with Joel Mokyr and Cormac Ó Gráda).

BEVERLY LEMIRE is professor and Henry Marshall Tory Chair in the Department of History and Classics, University of Alberta. Elected a fellow of the Royal Society of Canada, Academy I in 2003, her books include *Fashion's Favourite: The Cotton Trade and the Consumer in Britain, 1660–1800* (1991); *Dress, Culture and Commerce: The English Clothing Trade before the Factory, 1660–1800* (1997); *The Business of Everyday Life: Gender, Practice and Social Politics in England, c. 1600–1900* (2005); and *Global Trade and the Transformation of Consumer Cultures: The Material World Remade, c. 1500–1820* (2018). Her publications address the history of fashion, early modern global trade, gender and economic development, and material culture studies in Britain, Europe, and comparative global locales. She has held visiting fellowships at Australian National University, All Souls College University of Oxford, and the Victoria and Albert Museum, among others.

JOEL MOKYR is professor of economics and history at Northwestern University, where he has taught since 1974. He has worked on the history of technology and knowledge and their contribution to economic growth. Among his publications are *The Lever of Riches: Technological Creativity and Economic Progress* (1992); *The Gifts of Athena: Historical Origins of the Knowledge Economy* (2002); *The Enlightened Economy: An Economic History of Britain 1700–1850* (2009); and *A Culture of Growth: The Origins of the Modern Economy* (2016). In 2006, he was awarded the biennial Heineken Award for History by the Royal Dutch Academy of Sciences and in 2015 the Balzan International Prize for economic history.

PATRICK O'BRIEN is professor of global economic history at the London School of Economics. He was the director of the Institute of Historical Research, University of London and in 1999 was appointed centennial professor of economic history by the London School of Economics where he convened the Leverhulme-funded Global Economic History Network (GEHN). He has been visiting professor at Harvard, UC Berkeley, Yale, Princeton, the European University Institute, UC San Diego, Columbia University, Carlos III University in Madrid, and Munich, Tsinghua, and Fudan Universities.

CORMAC Ó GRÁDA is professor emeritus of economics at University College Dublin. His research has focused on the economic history of Ireland, Irish demographic changes, and the Great Irish Famine. Among his books are *Ireland: A New Economic History, 1780–1939* (1994); *Famine Demography: Evidence from the Past and the Present* (2002); *Jewish Ireland in the Age of Joyce: A Socioeconomic History* (2006); *Famine: A Short History* (2009); and *Eating People Is Wrong, and Other Essays on Famine, Its Past, and Its Future* (2015).

JOHAN POUKENS currently works for the EU Horizon2020 EURHISFRIM project (https://eurhisfirm.eu) at the Accounting and Finance Department of the Faculty of Business and Economics at the University of Antwerp. He studied history at the Katholieke Universiteit Leuven and archival science at the Vrije Universiteit Brussel. His master's theses concerned the history of inns, innkeepers, and their clients in eighteenth-century Hasselt (a small town in the prince bishopric of Liège) and an archival inventory of the church and state collection in the archiepiscopal archives in Mechelen. In 2017 he completed his PhD (supervised by professor Erik Aerts) on material culture, consumption, and the industrious revolution in the Duchy of Brabant (c. 1680–1800).

GIORGIO RIELLO is chair of early modern global history at the European University Institute in Florence and professor of global history and culture at the University of Warwick. He is the author of *A Foot in the*

Past (2006), *Cotton: The Fabric That Made the Modern World* (2013), *Luxury: A Rich History* (2016), and *Back in Fashion: Western Fashion since the Middle Ages* (2020). He has published extensively on the history of textiles and fashion in early modern Europe and Asia. He is the co-editor of a dozen books including *The Spinning World* (2009), *Writing Material Culture History* (2014), and *Global Gifts* (2018). He has been a visiting fellow at Stanford University, the Australian National University, Columbia University, and the Max Planck Institute. In 2011 he was awarded the Philip Leverhulme Prize.

OSAMU SAITO is professor emeritus at Hitotsubashi University, Japan, where he has worked since 1982 in its Institute of Economic Research. He has worked extensively on both the economic and population history of Japan in a comparative perspective. Among his publications are 'Land, Labour and Market Forces in Tokugawa Japan', *Continuity and Change* 24 (2009), 169–96; 'The Frequency of Famines as Demographic Correctives in the Japanese Past', in *Famine Demography: Perspectives from the Past and Present*, eds. T. Dyson and C. Ó Gráda, (2002): 218–39; and 'The Labor Market in Tokugawa Japan: Wage Differentials and the Real Wage Level, 1727–1830', *Explorations in Economic History* 15 (1978): 84–100.

KATE SMITH is lecturer in eighteenth-century history at the University of Birmingham, UK. She completed her PhD at the University of Warwick in 2010. She was Charles Hummel Fellow at the Chipstone Foundation in Milwaukee (2010–11) and research fellow on the Leverhulme Trust–funded 'East India Company at Home, 1757–1857' project (2011–14). She is the author of *Material Goods, Moving Hands: Perceiving Production in England, 1700–1830* (2014) and has co-edited three other books among which *The East India Company at Home, 1757–1857* (2018) (with Margot Finn).

KEITH SMITH worked in the Innovation and Entrepreneurship Group and Imperial College, London (2008–17), where he remains a visiting fellow. He has worked and published extensively on the economics of innovation. From 1990 to 2000 he was director of the STEP Group in Oslo, Norway. He was then professorial fellow at the United Nations University in Maastricht. This was followed by work for the European Commission, at the Joint Research Centre in Seville. He was then professor of innovation at the University of Tasmania. In 2009–12 he was seconded to the UK government's Department of Business, Innovation and Skills, where he was head of the policy analysis team and a member of the senior team responsible for strategic management of the UK science budget and UK innovation policy instruments. He was additionally head of the UK delegation to the OECD on science and technology issues

HERMAN VAN DER WEE is professor emeritus at the University of Leuven, Belgium, where he was appointed lecturer in 1955 and promoted to full professor in 1969. He has produced seminal work on monetary and financial history and quantitative social history and has worked extensively on famine, employment, food, living standards, and poverty. He is a member of many national and international organisations, including the Royal Academy of Science, Arts and Fine Arts of Belgium, the Royal Netherlands Academy of Arts and Sciences, and the British Academy. In 1986 he was elected president of the International Economic History Association. He was knighted with the title of baron by the Belgian king in 1994.

JAN DE VRIES is Sidney Hellman Ehrman Professor Emeritus of History and professor emeritus of economics at the University of California at Berkeley. He is the recipient of the Woodrow Wilson and Guggenheim fellowships and has held grants from the National Science Foundation and National Institute of Health. Between 1991 and 1993 he was president of the Economic History Association. Among his publications are *European Urbanization, 1500–1800* (1984); *The First Modern Economy: Success, Failure, and Perseverance of the Dutch Economy from 1500 to 1815* (1997) (with A.M. van der Woude), and *The Industrious Revolution: Consumer Demand and the Household Economy, 1650 to the Present* (2008). In 2013 he was awarded an honorary degree of letters from the University of Warwick.

DAVID WASHBROOK is a fellow of Trinity College, University of Cambridge and a fellow emeritus of St Antony's College, University of Oxford. In a long career, he has taught at Harvard University and the universities of Warwick and Pennsylvania as well as Oxford and Cambridge. His specialist field is the history of south India from late mediaeval times to the present day, on which he has published extensively. He has written on a variety of themes connected to South Asian society and culture. His most recent publication is *The Routledge Handbook of the South Asian Diaspora* (with Joya Chatterji) (2013).

NATALIE ZEMON DAVIS is adjunct professor of history and anthropology and professor of medieval studies at the University of Toronto in Canada. She has taught at Brown University, the University of Toronto, Berkeley, and Princeton University. Among her well-known publications are

Society and Culture in Early Modern France (1975); *The Return of Martin Guerre* (1983); *Fiction in the Archives: Pardon Tales and Their Tellers in Sixteenth-Century France* (1987); *The Gift in Sixteenth-Century France* (2000); *Women on the Margins: Three Seventeenth-Century Lives* (1995), and *Trickster Travels: A Sixteenth-Century Muslim between Worlds* (2006).

Index

industrious revolution, 12, 116, 214, 263

industry: brewing, 214–15; cottage, 122n1; employment in, 132–3; England's growth of, 109–10; enlightenment of, 126n36, 250; espionage in, 65, 67; linen, 133; processing, 137; regional, 25; in rural areas, 107–8; skill-intensive, 134–6; systems of, 241; technology of, 35; tourism, 66; in urban areas, 143

Ingold, Tim, 60

inherited goods, 297

innovations: by artisans, 120; in cotton textile industry, 142–3; in Europe, 264–5; in fashions, 230–7; of forks, 220; human capital influenced by, 118–21; in technology, 75, 139

'In Pursuit of Luxury' (Berg), 13

institutional mechanisms, 290

intellectual mercantilism, 280–1, 285

inter-disciplinarity skills, 51

invention advertisements, 50

inventories: amenities index of, 225n16; assessment of, 215; mean and rural index of, 217–19; median index scores of, 226n19; probate, 215–16, 216; urban, 227n27

Ireland, 149–50

Ireland, William Henry, 210n2

Italy, 131, 135

Japan, 131, 134, 135

Jardin du Roi (royal botanical garden), 281–3

jardins chinois, 284

Jasper ware, 61, 66

jenny, 130, 146, 154, 173n3

Jews, 187

Jingdezhen, China, 252, 257

Jingdezhen taolu (records of Jingdezhen ceramics), 251–2

Jones, Anna M., 92

Jones, copper plate maker, 205

Jones, Eric, 28

Jones, Richard, 206

Jones & Pontifex, trade cards of, 206

Jonsson, Fredrik Albritton, 279

Julien, Stanislav, 251

Kanchipuram silk marriage sari, 77–8

Kay, John, 26, 142, 145, 155

Kelly, Morgan, 8, 125n33

kempy wool, 93, 102n29

Kermess (annual fair), 222

Kidney, William, 202

kinship system, 78, 82–3

Kirk, J., 205, 211n32

al-kisa (woollen garment), 184

Kiyokawa, Y., 139n19

Klep, Paul M.M., 111

Knapp, Friedrich Ludwig, 45

knowledge: codified, 250; complex, 67; embodied, 59–61, 63–8; in small workshops, 60; tacit, 65, 68, 277; science-based, 38–9; transfer of, 60; useful, 276–8, 282

Labor and Monopoly Capital (Braverman), 10

labour costs, 165–6

labour force: cloth weaving by, 152; countries supply to, 135; engineering, 139n20; England and Wales with, 131, 132; by gender, 76; gender bias in, 132–6; machinery saving on, 145–6; men in, 134; production management